THE CAMP WOMEN

THE CAMP WOMEN

*The Female Auxiliaries
Who Assisted the SS in Running
the Nazi Concentration Camp System*

Daniel Patrick Brown

Schiffer Military History
Atglen, PA

Acknowledgments

Over the course of the past year and a half that it has taken to assemble the materials for this resource edition, I have had to rely on the assistance of many people with many different skills to complete my work. I am pleased to acknowledge French MacLean's original idea, which has served as the model for this work. I am also grateful to John K. Roth for his willingness to write a short preface for *The Camp Women* and for Professor Roth's reading of the original version of the introduction and chapter one. In addition, I am indebted to Klaus P. Fischer for his numerous insights and helpful suggestions in both the text itself as well as the organization of the maps, photographs, and so forth. I also wish to express my sincere thanks to two Moorpark College English professors, Bruce Garber and David Birchman, for their assistance in cleansing the text of awkward phrases and convoluted sentences.

On the administrative and technical side, I appreciate the help of Shannon Myren, Kelly Kaastad, Rex Edwards, and Margaret A. R. Richards in transferring my text to 3.5" floppy disks and employing various computer functions to sort, tabulate, and, assimilate lists and directories. Karin Foreman has helped me translate German documents, and two young Berliners, Benjamin Morris and Simon Weber, have been tireless and astute researchers in tracking down innumerable files and documents on *SS-Aufseherinnen*, the subjects of my book. Certainly, without their unflagging devotion to the task, this work would not have been completed on schedule, and for that, I am most grateful. Also, I am indebted to and thank Chris Sims of the U.S. Holocaust Memorial Museum in Washington, D.C., Berit Pistora of the *Bundesarchiv* in Koblenz, Edmund L. Blanford, the author of *Under Hitler's Banner*, Ian Carter of the Imperial War Museum in London, Jerzy Wróblewski of the *Panstwowe Muzeum* in *Oswiecim,* Poland, Christa Schulz of the *Mahn-und Gedenkstätte-Ravensbrück*, and Lutz Moeser of the *Bundesdarchiv* in Berlin for helping me to procure the photographs that are found in the photograph section. The maps were created by Moorpark College geography and G.I.S. professor Andrea Ehrgott. I appreciate her important contribution to *The Camp Women*. Lastly, I wish to thank all the people at Schiffer Publishing involved in this publication, particularly my editor, Bob Biondi.

Finally I apologize to those whom I may have inadvertently omitted in my thanks. The shortcomings or errors of this work are the responsibility of the author alone.

D.P.B.

For the Victims

Book Design by Robert Biondi.

Printed in China.
ISBN: 0-7643-1444-0

We are interested in hearing from authors with book ideas on military topics.

Published by Schiffer Publishing Ltd.
4880 Lower Valley Road
Atglen, PA 19310
Phone: (610) 593-1777
FAX: (610) 593-2002
E-mail: Schifferbk@aol.com.
Visit our web site at: www.schifferbooks.com
Please write for a free catalog.
This book may be purchased from the publisher.
Please include $3.95 postage.
Try your bookstore first.

In Europe, Schiffer books are distributed by:
Bushwood Books
6 Marksbury Ave.
Kew Gardens
Surrey TW9 4JF
England
Phone: 44 (0)208 392-8585
FAX: 44 (0)208 392-9876
E-mail: Bushwd@aol.com.
Free postage in the UK. Europe: air mail at cost.
Try your bookstore first.

CONTENTS

Foreword 6

Introduction 8

Chapter 1 From Process to *Prozeß*: Recruitment, Training, Duty, and Judgment 14
Chapter 2 The SS Overseers (*Aufseherinnen*): The Camp Women - Personal Files 25
Chapter 3 The Camp Women: Assignments, Ranks, and Assorted Pertinent Data 235

Sources 249
Maps 252
Photograph Section 257
Photograph Credits 282
Index 283

FOREWORD: Ordinary Women
John K. Roth

... She was born on October 21, 1922 ...

- Bernhard Schlink, *The Reader*

Set in postwar Germany, *The Reader*, Bernard Schlink's controversial novel, achieved best seller status in the late 1990s. Through the perspective of its narrator, Michael Berg, readers encountered Hanna Schmitz, a woman in her late thirties. Michael knew little about her when she seduced him at the age of fifteen and made him her lover, but as the story unfolds, the revelations mount. Michael discovers that Hanna can neither read nor write, a fact that helps the novel to explain why she is put on trial, convicted, and sent to prison.

In many ways, Hanna was no ordinary woman. A fictional example of the real "camp women" who stand at the center of Daniel Patrick Brown's thought-provoking book, she had voluntarily served the Nazi SS as a guard, not only at Auschwitz but also on the notorious death marches that ensued when that camp's forlorn prisoners were evacuated in January 1945.

As Schlink probes the complex life of the "camp woman" he created, his fiction invites an encounter with history. Were there any "camp women" – even one – whose stories were similar to Hanna's? If there were such women, who were they, what are their stories, and where could one find them? On the other hand, if Hanna's story is entirely – or even primarily – fiction, the same questions follow: Who were the camp women, what are their stories, where could one find them?

The Camp Women provides insight about those questions and more. Thus, it is worth noting that Hanna Schmitz, as Michael Berg discovers, was born on October 21, 1922. Every "camp woman" had a birth date. That fact is as significant as it

is ordinary, because so much follows from it. A birth date entails a birth place. Since neither the date nor the place of a person's birth exists in a vacuum, those particularities entail other realities. They include the family and culture into which one is born, the language one speaks, the education one receives, the friends and enemies one makes, the politics of one's time, the economics of one's place, and much more. Such elements, along with opportunities and responsibilities that come one's way, plus the decisions that a person makes about them, create an identity and define a life. In those ways, even if people do extraordinary things, all human lives are ordinary.

But how ordinary were "the camp women?" That question parallels one that intrigued the Holocaust historian Christopher Browning when he wrote *Ordinary Men: Reserve Police Battalion 101 and the Final Solution in Poland*. Browning determined that this German battalion was responsible for the deaths of some 83,000 Jews who were murdered in Poland during the Holocaust. Nevertheless, he decided that these Germans were sufficiently unexceptional that it was appropriate to end the book with a question: "If the men of Reserve Police Battalion 101 could become killers under such circumstances," he asked," what group of men cannot?"

The question bears repeating: What about "the camp women?" How ordinary were they? Arguably, that question haunts Daniel Brown's book more than any other. That question is about us as well as them. It makes us – women and men alike – wonder what could happen if things went badly wrong in our times and places. It challenges us – men and women – to see that things do not go badly wrong. Browning's study of Police Battalion 101 provoked debate and research that continues and rightly so. Brown's study of "the camp women" should do no less. For one reason, while study about women and the Holocaust is no longer in its infancy, there is still much work to do on that topic. *The Camp Women* makes important contributions to that effort, but, as Brown himself points out, even his painstaking accomplishments often leave many questions unanswered.

Launched by Adolf Hitler and by men such as Heinrich Himmler, Reinhard Heydrich, and Adolf Eichmann, the Holocaust was male-instigated and male-dominated. The same can be said of virtually all modern genocides. German women were not the primary perpetrators of the Holocaust. Many of them, including "camp women" such as the fictional Hanna Schmitz and most of her real SS-related sisters, occupied a position between that of "perpetrator" and "bystander" – two of the categories that are often used to classify the various parts that

people played during the Holocaust. *The Camp Women* suggests, I believe, that we might speak of them as "partners," for in multiple ways that is what they were in relationship to the German men who carried out the Holocaust until military force from the outside brought Nazi Germany to its knees. That judgment should be tentative, however, for there is much more that we need to know.

All good research reveals the need for further study and reflection. A book's worth depends on its ability to inspire readers in that direction. *The Camp Women* fits that description. By focusing attention on grim details, it makes us want not only to discover more about their causes and effects but also to ponder issues that should be of even greater concern: What must we do to ensure that there are no more "camp women" or "camp men?" What should women and men be instead? What are our responsibilities if those questions are to be answered well?

Daniel Brown's work reminds its readers that we all have a birth date. We are human. We are ordinary, but what we do can make all the difference in the world.

INTRODUCTION

In my experience the matrons or guards were cruel, more vicious (sadistically vicious [survivor's parenthetical]) than any SS man. These women who, I read later, ranged from baronesses and countesses to prostitutes, were the most vicious. You rarely found SS men who play games with their dogs in which the point was for the dogs to get the prisoners' derrieres, but the matrons did.

- Susan Cernyak-Spatz

The 1996 publication of Daniel Jonah Goldhagen's *Hitler's Willing Executioners: Ordinary Germans and the Holocaust*, a blanket indictment of all Germans for the Holocaust, set off a whirlwind of debate and controversy. While Goldhagen's thesis of German "eliminationist antisemitism" was widely dissected and frequently refuted,[1] I was struck by a statement he made in the section pertaining to the mindless death marches at the end of the war. On page 338, Goldhagen notes that a head woman guard referred to her female subordinates as "SS."[2] The author theorizes that the quotation marks are used because the woman in charge recognized that these female guards were not true *SS-Aufseherinnen*,[3] since they were simply called into service late in the war without the usual training. This may very well be true; however, I believe that there is an entirely different possibility as to why the quotation marks were used: Goldhagen, like many Holocaust specialists, may not know that, technically at least, there were no "SS women." The female guards or matrons were classified as *weibliche SS-Gefolge* (female SS followers) and were thereby an auxiliary group by definition. As *Reichsangestellte* ("employees of the Reich"), they were compensated for their service via a governmental wage agreement. I think that the head woman referred to her charges as "SS" women because she had to acknowledge the limited role such employees had within the crumbling Nazi system. As we shall see later, the matrons' training was largely on-the-job training and critique, even if they were processed through the system and given alleged guard instruction.

One might logically wonder why Holocaust researchers, individuals who have devoted their scholarly lives to examining the Nazi assault on human dignity, lack such basic understanding on the participation of women in the killing machine. Certainly, the source material appears to be exhaustive. There have been more than 60,000 histories, diaries, survivor memoirs, monographs, and other works (some of dubious distinction and/or value) written about the Third Reich, the Nazi Party, and the Holocaust. Indeed, with over eighty biographies written about Adolf Hitler alone, the Nazi leader has had more studies documented about him than any other person in history – including Abraham, Confucius, Buddha, Jesus of Nazareth, and Mohammed. Despite this, relatively little attention has been afforded to the crimes of women perpetrators.[4]

One factor that might help us to illuminate why the female guards have been given little print is the fact that women in the Third Reich were never intended to play a direct role in any aspect of administration. In January 1921, the General Assembly of the National Socialist German Workers' Party (NSDAP) decreed that women could never play a leading role in the Party,[5] and Hitler himself stated fourteen years later that the woman's battlefield station would reside with every child given to the nation and that while the man stood up for his country, the woman did the same for her family.[6] Beyond that, the SS did not train the female auxiliaries to become administrators of the camps; in fact, even KFL[7]-Ravensbrück, the only major women's camp in the Nazi empire, was managed by males. To help confirm the pervasiveness of this aspect of women's subservience to men, one only has to note that British Major L.S.W. Cranfield, defense counsel for an infamous SS woman in a postwar trial, argued that one witness had to be discredited because she alleged that the SS woman had been in command of a particular *Kommando* (detail) at Birkenau with an SS man in it. The major argued that this could have never have happened, as SS regulations specifically prohibited an SS woman from ever ranking above an SS man![8] In all cases, the women merely served within the SS ranks at the behest of their male superiors. Consequently, given these factors as well as the fact that so little has been documented about these women, we can excuse specialists in this massive subject area who do not fully understand or appreciate the significance of the female guards' role in the murder of millions of innocent human beings.

I have assembled this book in an attempt to provide a source edition devoted to exposing the role of the female guards in the Holocaust (although I have previously chronicled the life of a particularly beautiful, but rapacious SS woman, it only peripherally dealt with the collective world of the so-called *SS-Aufseherinnen*[9]). While there were only 3,508 "official" matrons involved in camp duty, amid the frenzied death marches following the evacuations of the camps, a number of housewives and single women were also recruited to drive the exhausted and starving survivors away from advancing Soviet forces.[10] Also, it has no doubt been assumed that the *Einsatzgruppen* (the so-called "mobile killing units" – a euphemism for large-scale extermination detachments) that fanned out in the eastern-occupied territories to liquidate Jews, Bolsheviks, partisans, and other "subhuman" groups, were composed of only males. However, female accessories in the form of thirteen secretaries accompanied the most murderous of the killing units – *Einsatzgruppe A*.[11] Obviously, these women did not participate directly in the mass exterminations, but their presence and assistance at the sites made them valued accomplices in the wholesale slaughter.

One might suggest that only thirteen secretaries and only 3,508 female guards constitute a miniscule, perhaps even inconsequential, contingent given that there were 977 males in *Einsatzgruppe A* and that over 51,500 SS men served in the camp system between 1933 and 1945.[12] Moreover, even at FKL-Ravensbrück, the camp designated for female guard training, less than ten percent of the SS contingent were women. In addition, Konnilyn Feig has noted the irony that the Nazi system so debased the German woman that she could not exert any natural leadership without being considered anti-Nazi – except in her limited role as a concentration camp matron. Feig

goes on to note that it was *Reichsführer-SS* Heinrich Himmler himself who gave the German woman her one genuine opportunity to be a leader – the profession of an SS woman or, for the truly talented administrator, SS senior overseer.[13] In the final analysis, of course, all perpetrators are liable for their actions and "the system" cannot be glibly blamed for malicious acts of frustrated Nazis, regardless of gender.

Those who survived the brutal treatment meted out by the *SS-Aufseherinnen* wanted to alert the world to such inhumane behavior in order to prevent it from happening again. Jolana Roth had seen few SS women at Auschwitz, but remembers that "the ones you did see – they were worse than the men."[14] Susan Cernyak-Spatz echoed this sentiment when she noted that in her experience "the matrons or guards were cruel, more vicious (sadistically vicious) than any SS man."[15] Margarete Armbruster recalled that Ravensbrück had "2,000 women assistants" who made the inmates' lives wretched. Armbruster stated that "only one NS sister treated me decently. And she was transferred for punishment."[16] These sentiments have been substantiated by other women who were somehow fortunate enough to make it through the hell of the Nazi camps.

Clearly, if these female employees of the Reich are worthy of careful examination and analysis, some important questions need to be answered. First, where did these women come from? Were only German women recruited/selected to serve in the camps? How did the SS entice women to come and serve in demonstrably subordinate roles? Were any married? Did the majority of the women join? What sorts of jobs did they have prior to the war? If the Nazi regime did not believe that they were equal to men in ability, did the regime ever recognize any matrons for meritorious duty? Did they serve only in one camp or were they assigned to other sites? Were any of the women themselves directly involved in the slaughter of the camp victims or were they merely guard bystanders? Were the female guards treated any differently than their male counterparts? If so, how and in what ways? Following the war, were any ever tried for war crimes? If so, were any found guilty and what, if any, punishment(s) did they receive?

My quest to assemble the records of the overseers has been much more challenging than I had originally suspected. Despite the German predilection for accurate and complete record-keeping, there are more than a few gaps in the bank records organized and maintained by the administration at FKL-Ravensbrück (which today are the domain of the *Mahn- und Gedenkstätte-Ravensbrück*). Thanks to Frau Monika Herzog, Frau Christa Schulz, and their staffs at the Ravensbrück Commemorative Site, the initial payment records allowed Benjamin Morris, Jonas Wolf, Kevin Lidz and I to begin to assemble a database on the *SS-Aufseherinnen*, and, with this initial list, we have been able to cull additional names from the *Zentralestelle der Landesjustizverwaltungen* (Central Office of the Justice Ministry for Nazi War Crimes) in Ludwigsburg, the *Bundesarchiv* in Berlin, and other sites. Mr. Simon Weber was largely responsible for the data gleaned from the *Zentralestelle* with the assistance of Herr Uwe Schröder and Dr. Heinz-Ludger Borgert of that agency. In addition, there are occasional omissions in entries of the permanent record file of an individual matron, and the records tended to get progressively less detailed as the war drew to a close, which, of course, is understandable. In an attempt to make as comprehensive of an analysis as possible, I have also examined the micro-film records at the National Archives II in College Park, Maryland, the limited collection of documents at *Yad Vashem* (Holocaust Authority) in Jerusalem, and the card catalog section (Block 24) at the *Pánstwowe Muzeum Oswiecimiu* (the State Museum) in Auschwitz. Some of this merely replicated previous research, but the goal was to try to track down every matron's permanent record card. French MacLean has noted in *The Camp Men: The SS Officers Who Ran the Nazi Concentration Camp System* that the officers' records are, for the most part, complete, but those of the enlisted men are not.[17] And, as one might imagine, the women's files, by-and-large, rank far below the enlisted men's cards with regard to completeness and accuracy. All this notwithstanding, my task was and continues to be focused on unearthing all that I possibly can about these women and, to the best of my ability, I have retrieved all that I could.

In creating a companion work to *The Camp Men*, I have elected to follow essentially the same layout and format of the MacLean book. Consequently, in Chapter 1 we will examine the camps where the overseers served. Central to the womens' study, of course, is Ravensbrück, and this training facility for the matrons will be afforded more attention than other sites. Also, the manner in which the auxiliaries became part of the murderous makeup of the SS will be detailed. I feel that this is one of the crucial aspects of the development of Nazi mass murder, because there is a huge gap between what the Nazis envisioned for women and what ultimately occurred.

The bulk of the book will be found in Chapter 2: the biographical data on the female guards whose permanent service records remain. Since the women came later to the camps, we can find names on guards rosters or work details (*Arbeitskommandos*) that do not appear on service cards, much less within the lengthy dossiers that French MacLean had the opportunity to peruse. Naturally, the background data became less significant to SS bureaucrats as the military situation deteriorated, and the great concern was simply to put bodies "out

there" to stem the Allied onslaught. Regrettably, this also aided the matrons after the war since any sort of paper trail simply did not exist, and, unlike their male counterparts, the women were not mandated to have their blood types tattooed on their arm or upper chest (generally near the left armpit).[18] In addition, those women guards apprehended and tried by the British tended to be treated more leniently than were those apprehended by the other victorious allies, especially the Soviet forces.[19]

Chapter 3 will correlate data culled from the previously mentioned archival centers. Cross-referencing various facets of the women's backgrounds will provide us with a clearer picture of who these matrons were. This segment will also feature some documents, including a copy of the general knowledge quiz given to female candidates, a Ravensbrück guard roster, and a medical record. Regrettably, we will never be able to get the most important question answered: what really motivated them?

The fourth element of this work is comprised of numerous photographs, some never before shown in the United States – some, in fact, never revealed to the general public anywhere in the world. Since the Nazi mass murder campaign was intended to be as clandestine an operation as possible,[20] photographing "actions," "selections," "parades," etc., was strictly forbidden. True, some unauthorized snapshots were smuggled out of camps or taken during *Einsatzgruppen* "cleansings," but these were rare occasions and the ones that do exist have been frequently used in Holocaust publications. The documents are naturally significant in that they place particular SS women at particular camps at particular times. In addition, they occasionally tell us something about the individual herself.[21] Not all the photos show the sinister side of the "NS sisters"; indeed, some show the women during their free time, while they are casually conversing in military attire or leisurely relaxing in civilian dress. According to social psychologist Roy F. Baumeister, such activities are exactly what we should expect, as humans can frequently distance themselves from even their own atrocious acts.[22]

While I have attempted to make as exhaustive of a search for the records of the female perpetrators as I could, there may very well be some data that have eluded me. If anyone should come across such data, I would not be averse to include it in subsequent editions of *The Camp Women*. Upon verification and proper use authorization of such material, later printings would be augmented with the new information. However, a caveat is in order: because of the possibly lurid connections between female guards and inmates, I would advise readers to exercise caution about the accounts they have heard or read about the SS women. In popular fiction there have been frequent tendencies to generate sensationalized, licentious, and lascivious accounts about beautiful, but sadistic, blonde, blue-eyed women guards. Naturally, this sort of sensationalism finds itself to so-called "men's (adult) magazines." However, while there were clearly some SS auxiliaries who were attractive, cruel, and perverse, the vast majority were colorless, unimaginative, plain, or wretched in their physical appearance. At the end of the war, the women, like the men, claimed that they were simply caught up in the totalitarian machine and merely wanted to do their jobs, so as to survive themselves. Of course, the claim that they were merely "doing their jobs" was their own colorless and blatantly transparent rationalization for some of the most heinous acts ever committed by organized officials on helpless captives.

The reader should be aware and concerned about a critical feature of any study of this organized evil we refer to as the Holocaust. There is an inherent danger in getting too involved in the examination and analysis of Nazi genocide. Just as one can get used to inflicting pain and committing murder, so can students of atrocities become more inclined to accept such inhuman and inhumane actions as simply a part of the human condition. As the philosopher Friedrich Nietzsche warned over a half century prior to the rise of the Nazis:

> Whoever fights monsters should see to it that in the process he does not become a monster. And when you look into an abyss, the abyss will look back at you.[23]

We must always be aware that the pain and suffering inflicted on innocent people began and ended with the Nazis and that regardless of what the circumstances were that brought the murderers to their positions, the individuals involved have to accept responsibility for their actions. After observing the Majdanek Guards Trial in Düsseldorf and hearing Hildegard Lächert claim that she had only followed orders, a German reporter commented that, "after all, no one ever ordered her to turn her dog loose on pregnant women or to drown babies in latrines." Ultimately, the perpetrators, male and female, are accountable for the harm that they caused.

Daniel Patrick Brown
Moorpark California

Notes:

[1] The debate and criticism of *Willing Executioners* has been intense and, at times, furious. The author's argument that it was a disservice to Jewish victims to refer to their killers as "Nazis" or the "SS," because the entire matter was a "national project" that all Germans were a party to the genocide has been a major point of contention. As might be expected, such a bold, generalized condemnation of Germans as a whole conjured up a torrent of criticisms from a multitude of perspectives. Clive James's assessment for *The New Yorker* (April 22, 1996) attacked *Willing Executioners* for its dangerous quantum leap from chronicling the crimes to indicting every German, regardless of age, maturity, or ability. Franklin Littel edited a collection of refutations and some supporting essays (especially Yehuda Bauer's) entitled *Hyping the Holocaust: Scholars Answer Goldhagen* (New York: Marion Westfield, 1997) and an ongoing exchange between Goldhagen and *New York Review of Books* critic Josef Joffe appeared in the *Review* (February 6, 1997) following Joffe's condemnation of the Goldhagen thesis. A stinging indictment of Goldhagen's work can be found in Christopher Browning's essay review *History & Memory* (Indiana University Press, Volume 8, No. 1, Spring/Summer 1996). Other recent books devoted to the continuing assault on Goldhagen's book can be found in Peter Fritsche's *Germans into Nazis* (Cambridge, MA: Harvard University Press, 1998), Norman Finkelstein and Ruth Birn's *A Nation on Trial: The Goldhagen Thesis and Historical Truth* (New York: Owl Books, 1998), and the longest, most balanced, and most meticulously researched examination of the lot: Klaus Fischer's *The History of an Obsession: German Judeophobia and the Holocaust* (New York: Continuum, 1998). Perhaps these are only the opening salvos of a long term controversy.

[2] Daniel Jonah Goldhagen, *Hitler's Willing Executioners: Ordinary Germans and the Holocaust* (New York: Knopf, 1996), p. 338. Goldhagen continues to assert that "the sense of belonging to an elite order, and the military and intensive ideological training characterizing the SS, was not part of their makeup." While this may have contributed to the problem, these women could never be used in combat like the *Waffen-SS*, could never feel all that "elite" when they knew that the lowest-ranking SS man would never have to take orders from them, and even the women who received the full and detailed ideological training at Ravensbrück did not learn that much new about the so-called "sub-humans" that the average civilian woman wouldn't have known.

[3] Literally, "female SS-overseers" (sing. *SS-Aufseherin*), but also variously translated as "supervisors," "wardresses," and/or "matrons." The highest women's rank as an SS helper was *Chef Aufseherin* ("chief senior overseer") and there were intermediate designations known as *Erstaufseherin* ("first guard") and *Oberaufseherin* ("senior overseer"). There were only two SS women who ever attained the rank of *Chef Oberaufseherin*: Anne Klein-Plaubel and, later, Luise Brunner. Cf. Konnilyn Feig, *Hitler's Death Camps: The Sanity of Madness* (New York: Holmes & Meier, 1982), p. 138 and Irmtraud Heike, „. . . *da es sich ja lediglich um die Bewachung der Häftlinge handelt* . . ." in Claus Füllberg-Stolberg et al. (eds.), *Frauen in Konzentrationslagern: Bergen-Belsen und Ravensbrück* (Bremen: Edition Temmen, 1994), p. 225.

[4] Feig, *Hitler's Death Camps*, p. 188, Sybil Milton, "The Victims of Violence: German and German-Jewish Women," *Different Voices: Women and the Holocaust*, (eds.) Carol Rittner and John Roth (New York: Paragon, 1991), p. 224, and Claudia Koonz, *Mothers in the Fatherland: Women, the Family, and Nazi Politics* (New York: St. Martin's, 1987), pp. 3-5.

[5] Georg Franz-Willing, *Der Hitlerbewegung: Der Ursprung* (Berlin-Hamburg: Preussich Oldendorf, 1962), p. 82.

[6] *Frankfurter Zeitung*, September 15, 1935, p. 1.

[7] "FKL" was the abbreviation for *Frauenkonzentrationslager* ("womens' concentration camp"). Generally, "KL" or "KZ" were used to designate regular *Konzentrationslager* ("concentration camps").

[8] Raymond Phillips (ed.), *Trial of Josef Kramer and Forty-four Others (The Belsen Trial)* (London: William Hodge, 1949), p. 533.

[9] Daniel Patrick Brown, *The Beautiful Beast: The Life & Crimes of SS-Aufseherin Irma Grese* (Ventura, CA: Golden West Historical Publications, 1996).

[10] Goldhagen, "The Deadly Way" (Chapter 13), pp. 327-372 and Yehuda Bauer, "The Death Marches, January-May, 1945" *Modern Judaism*, Volume 3, No. 1, pp. 1-21. Also, Professor Bauer, in a personal correspondence (June 3, 1986), encouraged me to consult local Austrian newspapers from early 1945 to the end of the war to find ads for enlisting women into the SS. Unfortunately, I was unsuccessful in my examination of various Austrian and German newspapers (including the official Nazi organ, *Völkischer Beobachter* [The People's Observer]). However, I am grateful to Hans Safrian of the *Dokumentationsarchiv des Österreichischen Widerstandes* (Documentation Archives of the Austrian Resistance) for his efforts to find such advertisements. He did find an ad on page two of the January 20, 1945 edition of *Kleine Wiener Kriegszeitung* (Abbreviated Vienna War Newspaper), which initiated operation in mid-1944 to replace daily papers due to the wartime need to econo-

mize. The plea for female help reads: "The enemy is storming against our lines with the greatest vehemence. German women and girls! Clear the front for our soldiers. Join the *Wehrmachtshelferinnenkorps* (Corps of Female Helpers for the Armed Forces). Applications available at the county administration office of the NS-Women's Organization. Open all day."

[11] Helmut Krausnick and Hans-Heinrich Wilhelm, *Die Truppen des Weltanschauungskrieges: Die Einsatzgruppen der Sicherheitspolizei und des SD 1938-1942* (Stuttgart: Deutsche Verlags-Anstalt, 1981), p. 287 and Raul Hilberg, *The Destruction of the European Jews* (Chicago: Quadrangle, 1967), p. 189.

[12] The 51,500 figure was calculated by deducting the 3,500 SS women that FKL-Ravensbrück Commandant *Hauptsturmführer* Fritz Suhren cites as having been trained in the facility between November 1942 and May 1945 from the 55,000 SS personnel that Wolfgang Sofsky claims to have served in the camp system from 1933 to 1945. Cf. Affidavit of Fritz Suhren, *Trials of the Major War Criminals Before the International Military Tribunals* (42 Vols.; Nuremberg, 1945-1949), Document No. D-746a (dated March 8, 1946) and Document No. D-746b (dated March 19, 1946), and for the Wolfgang Sofsky citation, cf. French L. MacLean, *The Camp Men: The SS Officers Who Ran the Nazi Concentration Camp System* (Atglen, PA: Schiffer, 1999), p. 9.

[13] Feig, *Hitler's Death Camps*, p. 163.

[14] Koonz, *Mothers in the Fatherland,* pp. 404-405. Also, Claudia Taake has rightfully noted that "the *SS-Aufseherinnen* were often as brutal as their male counterparts in the concentration camps even though they were at the bottom of the hierarchy within the SS." Claudia Taake, *Angeklagt: SS-Frauen vor Gericht* (Oldenburg: Universität Oldenburg, 2000), p. 11.

[15] Ibid., p. 404.

[16] Ibid.

[17] MacLean, *The Camp Men,* p. 9.

[18] It was standard practice for a newly inducted SS man to have his blood type tattooed on his arm or chest. While this would obviously have a practical application for those serving in the *Waffen-SS* (Armed-SS, or actual combat units of the SS), Wehrmacht troops were not required to do the same. Of course, Hitler himself had commented that the SS, more than anyone else, "would have to pay the butcher's bill." Actually, one of the reasons that the notorious "Angel of Death" – Dr. Josef Mengele – was able to avoid postwar arrest was due to the fact that he had managed to convince his SS superiors that he did not need the tattoo, as his blood type would be cross-matched by a competent surgeon, if-and-when a requisite transfusion was required. See Gerald Posner and John Ware, *Mengele: The Complete Story* (New York: McGraw-Hill, 1986), p. 63 and Gerald Astor, *The 'Last' Nazi: The Life & Times of Dr. Joseph* [sic] *Mengele* (Toronto: Paper-Jacks, 1985), p. 150.

[19] The lenient attitude of the British tribunals is baffling. The sentences meted out were frequently downright asinine. It often appeared that an SS woman had to be in charge of large-scale "selections," sending masses of helpless people to their deaths to merit the death penalty themselves. The letters sent to the British government protesting the unjust verdicts are filled with contempt for such ridiculously lenient punishments. A certain A.D.W. Duxbury fired off a letter on November 19, 1945, lambasting a court that could allow "seven murderers to have their lives spared when they have committed their crimes in such a brutal manner." E.M.K. Green, a British woman, noted that "a woman warder kicks a defenceless prisoner to death and is given one years [sic] imprisonment" and then goes on to write that "it is appalling to think that some of those women when they come out of prison will be able to bring more

of their loathsome breed into the world." Another letter, signed by M. Barker, stated that "it is greatly to be deplored that the Belsen Trial was not conducted by a United Nations – or better still a Russian Tribunal, which would have been realistic to have given short shrift to these 'Supermen' and would have already rid the world of their vile presence." Even with the light sentences, many of these murderers were given early releases; indeed, on December 22, 1951, five of the SS women and Kapos, convicted of beating and murdering inmates, were granted their freedom. FO 371/50997, Nos. 5, 6, and 7 – T. No. 15172 (Public Record Office, Kew Gardens, London) and Feig, *Hitler's Death Camps*, p. 382.

[20] While a thick veil of secrecy was mandated in these matters, it is amazing how many visuals were able to survive. Perhaps we should look back to the meticulously detailed record-keeping that was concurrently mandated with a proclivity of the Germans to keep matters in their proper order. Even photographs taken of public hangings of alleged partisans, used as an obvious warning to would-be civilian saboteurs, had notices in German declaring that photographing was strictly forbidden (and occasionally added with the threat of death for those caught breaking this prohibition). Obviously, there will always be some things that will get smuggled out and the quick demise of the Third Reich helped matters as well. In the beginning, the Führer put matters in perspective when he stated, "While German goals and methods must be concealed from the world at large, all the necessary measures—shooting, exiling, etc. – we shall take and we can take away. The order of the day is first: conquer, second: rule, third: exploit." Quoted in Nora Levin, *The Holocaust: The Destruction of European Jewry, 1933-1945* (New York: Crowell, 1968), p. 284.

[21] A case in point is illustrated by an Auschwitz medical log and examination record card for *SS-Aufseherin* Irma Grese. The *SS-Lager-Lazarett* (the medical clinic for SS personnel) lists appointments for Grese on January 22, 23, and 24, 1944. The examination record card that survived shows that the SS woman had a Wasserman test (for syphilis) that was returned negative. Clearly, this demonstrates that the promiscuous SS woman, notorious for her late night affairs with female inmates (whom she later dispatched to the gas chambers), was worried about the consequences of such sexual liaisons. Ultimately, she had to have an abortion as a result of one of her affairs with one of the men. We have survivors Gisella Perl and Olga Lengyel to confirm these matters. See *SS-Hyg. Inst/5 segr. 3,* p. 33 (No. 10690) and *Log, SS-Lager-Lazarett* (Auschwitz), Gisella Perl, *I Was a Doctor in Auschwitz* (New York: International Universities Press, 1948), p. 52, and Olga Lengyel, *Five Chimneys: The Story of Auschwitz*, Trans. Paul B. Weiss (Chicago: Ziff-Davis, 1947), p. 186.

[22] Baumeister notes that if we can rationalize matters somehow in our minds, ultimately we can come to some sort of self-justified sense of what we are doing: in effect, we can divorce ourselves from the immorality of our deeds. The key is "crossing the line" that initially precludes us from doing what we would usually consider ethically, morally, and/or legally wrong. See especially his section entitled "Blurring the Line: Ambiguity, Uncertainty, Misinformation" and "Once You've Accepted the Premise . ." Roy Baumeister, *Evil: Inside Human Violence and Cruelty* (New York: Freeman, 1997) as well as Anthony Storr, *Human Aggression* (London: Penguin, 1968), "Aggression in Social Structure."

[23] Friedrich Nietzsche, *Jenseits von Gut und Böse: Vorspiel einer Philosophie der Zukunft* (Stuttgart: Philip Reclam, 1993 [1886]), No. 146, p. 83.

THE CAMP WOMEN

1

FROM PROCESS TO *PROZEß*:
Recruitment, Training, Duty and Judgment

Throughout the entire training process, the conditioning of the guards was made to be as perverse as possible; indeed, in the eyes of the SS, the outstanding characteristics of any good guard were his [or her] hardness and fanatical devotion to Nazi ideals.

- Helmut Krausnick et al., *Anatomy of the SS-State*

Since the end of World War II, historians have debated the issue of when Adolf Hitler decided to exterminate the Jews. In 1977, Viking Press, a mainstream, respected publisher, released David Irving's *Hitler's War*. Irving, now widely acknowledged to be a pseudo-historian of the school of Holocaust denial, claimed that since no documentary evidence can be generated that Hitler himself was ever aware of the elimination of the Jews, the Nazi Führer has to be considered free from complicity in the annihilation of the Jews. Following the inevitable challenges to his asinine assertion (to think that Hitler didn't even know about the implementation of a plan this massive and monumentally important is truly absurd), the Holocaust distorter announced that he would personally pay any historian $1,000.00 who could produce a written order from Hitler directing the implementation of the Holocaust.[1]

One might logically ask what the preceding data has to do with the development of the female guards in the concentration camps? Although Irving is clearly wrong when he claims that Hitler did not know about the Holocaust, many aspects of the Holocaust's implementation were developed and carried out by subordinates, and one such area was the decision to use women as guards in the camps. Originally, Hitler had emphasized the long-standing German tradition that women were to be limited to subordinate roles in the national fabric. Indeed, while Adolf Hitler could be accused of vacillating on virtually every political issue at one time or another, he was adamant on two points: the Nordic race would have to defeat the Jewish

menace, and males were the dominant of the sexes.[2] Beyond this, the Nazi Führer asserted that "there will never be in National Socialist Germany women's battalions as there have been in Marxist countries."[3] A more frightening threat to Nazism was the potential for professionally oriented women going into business; in fact, the idea then of a professional woman in Germany was no more acceptable than having a professional black man in Germany.[4] The initiative to create some sort of support group of women for the SS came from the *Reichsführer-SS* himself, Heinrich Himmler. That Himmler took the initiative on his own to do this is not unusual. The belief that Adolf Hitler micro-managed the Nazi regime is a myth. Numerous examples exist of Nazi luminaries initiating lower-level institutional programs/innovations without Hitler's direct consent. This "wiggle-room" for individual initiative was referred to as "Working toward the Führer," and as the war turned against Germany, more and more such strategies occurred. For example, the massive death marches at the end were instigated by camp commanders. Himmler's desire to create a female corps of SS supporters was fashioned on the Finnish organization of the *Lottas-Svard*, the "brain child" of Mrs. Fanny Luukkonen. Mrs. Luukkonen wanted to generate an organization that would "discharge Finnish militia and soldiers from all tasks not directly concerned with combat." Himmler, in turn, set up the SS-*Helferinnen* (SS auxiliaries) and directed that the women selected for the program would have to meet the same racial criteria as the men. The Reichsführer further stated that SS men were to regard the auxiliaries as equals and comrades.[5] Although most historians have presumed that the Nazi *Weltanschauung* was limited to viewing their women as relegated to the traditional four K's (*Küche, Kleider, Kinder, and Kirche* – kitchen, clothes, children, and church), a more proactive role was described in the pages of Nazi textbooks. Therein, the ideal Nazi woman shared with the women of ancient Sparta the requisite stamina and fortitude to withstand the rigors of a potentially harsh existence. In fact, the German mother would be expected to endure the loss with stoic courage if one of her sons (especially an SS offspring!) should make the ultimate sacrifice for Führer and Fatherland.[6] While the Third Reich was in its infancy, the rigid separation of males and females was emphasized, but the preparatory signals existed that allowed for the changes that would eventually cast women into more active participation when circumstances necessitated female involvement in the war effort.

An early proving ground for future female involvement in the New Order was the *Bund deutscher Mädel* (League of German Girls – abbreviated as the BdM), the female counterpart of the *Hitler Jugend* (Hitler Youth). According to Trude Burkner, one of the organizers, the goal of the group was to "emulate their brothers."[7] The Nazi movement was indeed a youth movement, and Hitler declared that the young were, "the foundation stone of our Reich."[8] As a consequence, all the recreational youth groups in existence prior to the Nazi ascent to power – scouting organizations, hiking clubs, and so forth – were incorporated into purely National Socialistic youth groups. The new organizations were no longer assembled simply for pleasure and comradeship – now all youth groups were redirected and reorganized, or *"gleichschaltet,"* into highly politicized groups in the service of Nazi objectives. Of course, membership in these organizations became restricted exclusively to "qualified" German youth – the so-called Aryan youth. These Nazi youth organizations were exploited to carry out the greater task of preparing the young to serve in the vanguard of the National Socialist movement.

The goal of the League of German Girls was two-fold: first and foremost, to prepare the girls to be National Socialist mothers and, second, to provide them with the opportunity to be nurses in the field or to be "defenders of the homeland" (*"Verteidigerinnen der Heimat"*).[9] To this end, the BdM provided rigorous physical training so as to toughen the body. In addition, a rigorous academic training was to be implemented to insure that the maidens knew that they would be expected to die for the Third Reich. The girls, in fact, were instructed to follow the ancient Roman example of committing suicide if the men failed and they were about to be taken by the enemy.[10]

Appeals were made particularly to rural BdM, those Aryan females who could lay claim to ancestry in the *"Völkischer Bauerschaft"* ("Germanic workers of the soil"). Those who worked with the soil held a sacred place in the Nazi scheme of things. While the Nazi leader held the young in very high esteem, his racist program exalted farmers. It is interesting to note that the praise for rural youth bore dividends for the Nazi propaganda machine: the farming communities reciprocated by ultimately providing the majority of the rank-and-file *Totenkopfverbände* ("Death's Head units" – the SS concentration camp guards).[11] Many of the young adherents to the "New Order" joined for more than mere defense of *Blut und Boden;*[12] indeed, some joined simply because they saw no future in the hard manual labor of the farm and sought instead the potential for adventure and glory in the dynamic Nazi movement.

While propaganda and the system of *Gleichschaltung* played major roles in preparing German youth for the challenging future to come, the war itself had more to do with the growth and development of the concept of the female concentration camp guards. Despite all their previous statements regarding "male supremacist pride" and various antifeminist slogans (including the Nazi Führer's own remark that, "a woman must be a cute, cuddly, naïve little thing – tender, sweet, and stupid"),[13] the German rulers had to reconsider women's roles in light of their labor needs. Armaments Minister Albert Speer would still consistently fight with his Nazi colleagues over their reluctance to recruit German women to the war effort.[14] Nevertheless, critical shortages and increasing losses eventually forced the Reich to employ Aryan women.

Prior to the war, the first female *Staatsfeinde* ("enemies of the state") were confined at Moringen bei Göttingen. This workhouse, which could only house approximately 104 women, was converted into a detention center in April 1933. The facility wasn't run by the terror organizations (the SA or SS), and apparently no cases of guard brutality or cruelty were documented by the inmates after the war. Because the Nazi regime was tightening its grip on the nation, a new facility for female nonconformists had to be found. Thus, in November 1938 Lichtenburg (near Torgau) became the first officially designated women's concentration camp, but it soon was incapable of accommodating the growing list of undesirables. To fill the growing need for matrons, the Nazis drew from members of the *National Socialist Frauenschaft* (the Nazi Women's Group), but with the corresponding need for additional camps, the Nazis found themselves chronically short of guards. In fact, the Nazi system of terror relied on the use of so-called *"Häftlingsselbstverwaltung"* (self-government of prisoners). Without employing these *"Funktionshäftlinge"* (prisoner functionaries called "Kapos" by fellow inmates), maintaining internal camp order would have been difficult, perhaps even untenable. In reality, they served as extensions of the guard force.

To meet the need for more room and more guards, the SS administration opened Ravensbrück on May 15, 1939 and began to recruit and train SS-Aufseherinnen. To lure women into the profession, the Nazi regime launched a clever campaign in which prospective candidates were told that " . . . one only would have to watch over prisoners" with the assurance that it would be "physically effortless work."[15] To make matters seem more benign, the prisoners were characterized as women who "had committed some violations against the *Volksgemeinschaft* (racial community) and now, to prevent further harm, had to be isolated."[16] In order to attract young women who had only dim financial prospects for the future, they offered them accommodations and clothing in addition to higher wages than they could earn in German industry.[17] In the early recruitment period (prior to 1944), candidates had to be physically fit (they had to undergo a medical examination performed by a garrison physician prior to acceptance) and have no criminal convictions.

Despite such an aggressive recruitment campaign, women did not flock to serve as guards. Once service as an Aufseherin became a wartime occupation, the supervisors were assigned as "employees of the *Waffen-SS*." One should remember that suddenly to be encouraged to join the ranks of camp guard units was a major departure from what had been viewed as normal for German women[18] and the regime had gone to great lengths to insure all German citizens knew that camp incarceration was not something one would want to experience. The magnitude of this problem can be seen from the fact that the SS administration itself stated on January 15, 1945 that it had 37,674 male SS guards coupled with the 3,508 female SS guards overseeing 714,674 enemies of the state.[19]

Since few women wanted to volunteer for concentration camp service, the SS used compulsory measures to fill the shortage. Heinrich Himmler himself visited Ravensbrück in January 1940 and, along with *SS-Wirtschafts und Verwaltungshauptamt* (WVHA) chief Oswald Pohl, ordered that henceforth the overseers were to be treated with the utmost consideration. In addition, the *Reichsarbeitsdienst* (the German Labor Service, a supernational clearing house for securing workers during the war) stepped up its efforts to fill the shortages. By 1943, this agency was empowered to force women between seventeen and forty-five into service, and while upper and middle class women could frequently evade the authorities, women at the lower strata could not.[20] Downright coercion was frequently employed and the threat of actually becoming one of the guarded as opposed to a guard is illustrated by the "proposition" given to a former Aufseherin:

> Today we have a job for you, where you don't have to physically work and if you don't take this job, then you will end up as one who refuses to work and you, yourself, will be in the camp together with the work shy riff-raffs (*arbeitscheuen Gesindel*).[21]

It appears that the Nazi authorities felt one of their best selling points was that the pay would be better and the work would be easier than in factory jobs. This sort of "pitch" was made to Anna David, a young woman who had been working at the Heinkel assembly plant and who was recruited into the guard force by an SS official.[22] As the need became even more critical late in the war, out-and-out kidnapping may have been employed. A witness during a postwar court hearing related that in September 1944, one of the *SS*-Aufseherinnen complained that she was literally snatched from her work and forced to Ravensbrück without even being able to say farewell to her parents.[23]

Another method to increase the number of female guards was an SS swindle of German business. Because the slave labor market was so lucrative for the large German concerns such as Siemens, Bayer, and I.G. Farben, these firms set up factories within the confines of concentration camps. Since the SS required certain "regulatory controls," these large German businesses had to hire, train, and compensate guards to supervise their slave laborers. As German losses mounted, the SS was then able to commandeer these female overseers for "the greater benefit of the Reich."[24] In addition, each armaments industry to which female prisoners had been allotted for work in exchange had to surrender a certain percentage of their other female employees (like Anna David of the Heinkel firm) to act as guards.

As noted previously, the majority of the women who enlisted were not the most sophisticated; indeed, a former overseer described new recruits as a "few stupid ones who lived in the back of the Black Forest [meaning inexperienced and naïve],"[25] and the inmates, who were frequently better educated and culturally more refined, almost invariably viewed their masters as "stupid types whose only claim to superiority was their uniform."[26] Although a survivor of Ravensbrück who had access to the camp's personnel files has noted that the supervisors came from all walks of life – including aristocratic families – the vast majority were unskilled, undereducated, and decidedly limited in job prospects. All this notwithstanding, by 1943, the vast majority of the supervisors were conscripts.[27]

That the overwhelming majority of female guards were drafted is an important point. There was a distinction between those women who volunteered for SS "support" employment and those who were conscripted into service. In general, women drafted during the war were classified as *SS-Kriegshelferinnen* (war auxiliaries) and they were not incorporated into the *SS-Helferinnenkorps* (the corps of SS assistants). This was an added incentive to join the camp guard force, as there was a clear delineation between those women required to serve the Fatherland and those who were considered more worthy by virtue of their own initiative and commitment. Finally, one other incentive informally existed for the female volunteers: the potential for procuring goods from the hapless prisoners. The lure of confiscating extra items from the prisoners was a direct result of ongoing Nazi propaganda that during the dark days of Weimar oppression rich Jews had lived easy, lazy lives while the rank-and-file German citizens had to struggle. Consequently, it was inevitable that Nazi guards – both male and female – would look upon such a potential benefit as an incentive. Himmler was well aware of the problem and in his infamous Posen address to the Higher SS and Police Officials on October 4, 1943, the *Reichsführer-SS* stated that, " . . . we have not the right to enrich ourselves with so much as a fur, a watch, a mark, or a cigarette or anything else."[28] Despite Himmler's warning that those "who fall short . . . will die without mercy," theft of the material wealth of prisoners was pervasive; in fact, even when *Oberaufseherin* Maria Mand[e]l, the Austrian-born chief supervisor at Auschwitz, ordered the Aufseherinnen to stop their illegal procurement of precious turpentine for personal use, women like Grese simply found "other means" (illegal) to secure the substance.[29]

Once the women were inducted into the guard force, they were assigned to a training facility. Although one might suppose that being an SS woman would be synonymous with working in the concentration camps, this wasn't necessarily the case. Women were also employed as matrons in the juvenile offenders camps (the so-called *Jugendschutzlager*) as well as the Police Protective Service (*Polizeigefängnisaufsichtsdienst*). These women were subordinated to the jurisdiction of the Security Police and Security Service (the *Sicherheitsdienst*, or SD, served to some degree as the "internal affairs department" of the SS).[30]

Once the candidate reported for training, the length and extent of that training varied. Obviously, procedures were much more systematic and thorough early on, but, as the war turned against the Nazis and conditions became more hectic, confused and chaotic, training, if given at all, was exceedingly limited. Ideally, the candidate would go through a short introductory

course on the ideological *Weltanschauung* of Nazism, a discussion of her "personal attitude," her knowledge in the subject area of service (*Dienstkunde*), followed by an on-the-job performance rating designed for, "proving herself during active service." If her evaluator(s) deemed her "suitable to be an Aufseherin," the woman would be assigned to one of the *Außenlager* (subcamp) or *Nebenlager* (adjacent camp) of the *Hauptlager* (main camp).[31] The young women quickly were taught to take a callous, unrelentingly harsh attitude toward their charges, and, for many, this led them to inflict whatever pain or punishment they felt appropriate on the inmates. Typical of such brutality is an anecdote that one survivor recounted: an inmate made an offhand statement to SS-Aufseherin Johanna Brach, and, in turn, the overseer told the inmate to remove her glasses. Then the enraged overseer beat the prisoner with her riding whip over the face that ultimately produced bruising and swelling. The inmate received permanent scarring and the overseer simply walked away, feeling she was perfectly within her rights to inflict whatever she saw fit on the victim.[32] There were exceptions to this unbridled terror campaign encouraged by the SS, but based on the testimonies of both victims and perpetrators, cruel and brutal overseers were the norm in the camps.

By almost any standard, the "conditioning" process that the female guards underwent was grueling and demanding. Herta Ehlert, one of the accused SS-women tried by the British at the so-called "Belsen Trial" (September-November 1945 in Lüneburg), claimed that she was sent through the Ravensbrück training program strictly as punishment for being too lenient towards prisoners at a Polish labor camp where she was employed.[33] Another defendant, Anna Hempel, stated that as she was entering the SS in May 1944, she too had to endure the psychologically demanding and physically challenging three week course at Ravensbrück.[34] Throughout the entire conditioning process, the candidates were subjected to as severe and harsh disciplining as the SS administrators could muster. In this perverted world, the outstanding characteristic of a good camp guard was her hardness – an absence of any tenderness or sympathy/empathy for the "subhumans" (*Tiermenschen*) she supervised.[35] In addition, fanatical devotion to National Socialist ideals was an indication of the greater potential of a candidate. A young French political prisoner witnessed first hand what the Ravensbrück guard training was like:

The beginners usually appeared frightened upon first contact with the camp, and it took some time to attain the level of cruelty and debauchery of their seniors. Some of us made a rather grim little game of measuring the time it took for a new Aufseherin to win her stripes. One little Aufseherin, twenty years old, who was at first so ignorant of proper camp "manners" that she said "excuse me" when walking in front of a prisoner, needed exactly four days to adopt her requisite manner, although it was totally new for her.

It would be a reasonable estimate that about half of the guards took visible pleasure in striking and terrorizing their prisoners, especially the weak, ill, and frightened. Others dealt their blows with the coarseness and simplicity of a peasant whipping her donkey, some simply acted for the sake of conformity particularly in front of their colleagues or the SS men. In any case, even the best of them showed no adverse reaction when a prisoner was beaten in their presence.[36]

It should be noted that there were a few honorable and strong women who ultimately stood up against the rapacious atmosphere of the guard training. Johanna Langefeld, one of the true heroines of the overseers, rose to the highest level of the female guard force at Auschwitz, and was hailed after the war by inmates for her humanitarian attitude. She had become a war widow, and because she had a child, she had to find work and decided to enlist as an Aufseherin. She claimed that she, "wanted to become a prisoner official in order to do good for the poorest of the poor."[37] In her position as *Oberaufseherin* (senior supervisor) at Ravensbrück, Mrs. Langefeld succeeded in preventing the execution of a Polish woman sentenced to death.[38] Another example of a humane overseer is recorded in an incident in which a Bavarian guard named Brigitte was assigned to a lumber detail and, as usually was the case, the inmates initially feared her; however, in short order the guard reassured the prisoners that she was not the typical cruel female overseer. Brigitte told them: "I am really proud to have so many well-educated women in my crew." The prisoners reported that they saw a real human being who was not a Nazi functionary, but, rather, a woman like them who had been taken from normal life and simply wanted to get through this terrible time and get back to regular life.[39] Again, matrons like Langefeld and Brigitte were exceptions, but at least there were some guards who stood up for decency at considerable risk (an SS-Aufseherin at the Auschwitz-Birkenau complex was given twenty-five lashes by her fellow guards for being too lenient on prisoners[40]).

In addition to being taught the finer points of inflicting pain and suffering on the inmates, the female guards were provided with instruction in the *Lagerordnung*, the basic regulations that pertained to all the camps.[41] These included punish-

ments that the guards could mete out, tips on how to detect prisoner sabotage and/or work slowdowns, and warnings to be ever suspicious of and alert to prisoner plots to escape were emphasized. Above everything else, the candidates were warned not to develop any kind of relationship – not even so much as a casual conversation – with the prisoners. Upon completion of this initial phase of the training, the candidates were promoted to the status of "overseer helpers" (*Hilfsaufseherinnen*), and their on-the-job training in collusion with Aufseherinnen now began.[42] It was during this time that an experienced overseer could be tested for both her reliability and suitability, and, upon successful completion of this segment – the final component in her training – she was promoted to overseer.

It is important to note that this was generally not the sort of mundane, tedious training that one in contemporary society would think of. The young French political prisoner Germaine Tillon observed that there was a bizarre and often times downright perverse element added to the training:

> …it seemed that liaisons between SS of opposite sexes were encouraged, and they lived in a kind of promiscuity some might call "primitive," although their situation was anything but primitive. It appeared that all the Aufseherinnen, married or unmarried, had one or more constant SS lovers . . .In addition to the lovers and shop talk, their diversions (especially around solstices and equinoxes) were monstrous eating and drinking bouts, after which they were so far gone that they were unable to recall with whom they had spent the rest of the night.[43]

There was a close relationship between debauchery and cruelty among both male and female guards, but particularly among the women. Furthermore, the prisoners began to understand that the guards could not have administered such enraged beatings of the prisoners "without feeling some degree of anguish and that the debauchery was simply an expression of this anguish, or perhaps a palliative for it."[44] What is significant here is that in such a bankrupt and despicable system that the Nazis had created, all traces of tenderness and civility were discarded. Indeed, SS trainers went to great lengths to instill in guards the idea that every prisoner should be dehumanized, employing the maximum severity, but always in such a manner that the pain was inflicted dispassionately and with the utmost discipline. While such regulations were originally drawn up for the men at KL-Dachau (the male training facility and the so-called "model camp"),[45] the women received the same instruction at FKL-Ravensbrück.[46] To understand just how severe and abrasive the training was, the recollections of

Auschwitz Commandant Rudolf Höß, awaiting execution for his participation in the wholesale murder, are pertinent here:

> Any trace of pity revealed to enemies of the state was unworthy of an SS-man. There was no place in the ranks of the SS for soft hearts and any such [man] would do well to retire quickly to a monastery. He [KL-Dachau Commandant Theodor Eicke] could only use hard, determined men who ruthlessly obeyed every order. It was not for nothing that their emblem was the Death's Head and that they carried a loaded gun. They were the soldiers who even in peace time face the enemy day and night, the enemy behind the wire . . .[47]

Theodor Eicke developed the challenging training of SS male candidates at KL-Dachau, but the chief trainers at FKL-Ravensbrück incorporated the same standards for the female guards as well. From the camp's opening in May 1939 until a dispute with the then-commandant Max Kögel, (April 1942) caused her to be transferred to Auschwitz-Birkenau, Johanna Langefeld was the chief supervisor. Dorothera ("Thea") Binz, one of the more depraved and cruel creatures to serve in the camps, was head supervisor from February 1943 until the end of the war (May 1945).[48] Even by SS standards, Binz's behavior was atrocious. During *Frühappell*,[49] Binz would "*Sport machen*"[50] with those unfortunate enough to be in her presence. Concurrently, *Oberaufseherin* Binz would instruct her trainees in the finer points of *Schadenfreude* (malicious pleasure).[51] The former maid would beat, kick, slap, and whip the prisoners ruthlessly. She appeared to take great pride in the fact that her mere presence caused the prisoners to tremble with fear. She gleefully followed the policy of "controlled and disciplined terror" laid down by Eicke in the early days of SS guard training.[52] Like all overseers, this barbarous woman was fully authorized to conduct her beatings with a nonchalant and cavalier attitude. While there were technically limits set on maltreatment of prisoners in certain situations, such acts – even those resulting in death – were punished lightly in comparison to offenses against property. Indeed, only those women who could conduct themselves in a ruthless manner could expect promotion. As a chronicler of the SS auxiliaries has noted, "one can see how 'worthless' ["*wertlos*" – author's quotations] the life of a prisoner was for the SS in the concentration camps."[53]

Following their training, the SS overseers were either assigned within the Ravensbrück system (the main facility or one of the many subcamps), to other camps, or to the juvenile prisons and/or security service facilities. The majority of the Aufseherinnen remained at a particular duty station for the duration of the war (once in, it was very difficult to get out). Also, the overwhelming majority remained ordinary overseers.[54] The possibilities of making this work into an actual career were exceedingly limited. After moving from an overseer helper during the on-the-job training probationary period, a woman was inducted as a full-fledged overseer. If a woman caught the attention of her superiors and had leadership potential, she could become a "*Erstaufseherin*" or "first guard." The "first guards" were generally assigned as the female leader of a minor camp or a very large *Arbeitskommando* ("work detail"). The next rank was that of *Oberaufseherin* and she was technically equal to that of an officer in the male military. The senior overseer was a member of the command staff and had a tremendous advantage over her subordinates: she assigned the overseers to their guard stations on a daily basis.[55] Just as the inmates knew it was absolutely critical where they were assigned to work, the overseers from day one also understood the importance of trying to get the better assignments. Some guards had to go out in foul weather with their prisoners on long marches with high stress levels. Other guards got the relatively posh jobs of working indoors with the so-called privileged inmates who had special skills and/or abilities that the Nazis needed, and, as a result, the tension levels were low or nonexistent. If a particular overseer was a favorite of the chief overseer, she could realistically expect to be assigned to the easier duty for months, sometimes even years![56] Also, overseers could occasionally be assigned to both day and night duty. Herta Ehlert worked on an *Außenkommando* (external work detail) during the day and then assumed duties as a *Blockleiterin* (female block leader) at night. Another overseer, Jane Bernigau, had daytime duties and then was responsible for a *Häftlingsblock* (prisoners' block) upon return to the compound.[57] Finally, if an overseer herself was to be punished, frequently the penalty would be assignment to a *Strafkommando* (punishment detail). The notorious Irma Grese breached some Auschwitz-Birkenau regulation shortly after her arrival in March 1943 and was put in command of a punishment detail that was charged with carrying stones from an area outside Birkenau into the camp. Although it was difficult for starving women to survive the rigors of an *Arbeitskommando*, one can only imagine what the mortality rate would be for those sentenced to a *Strafkommando*, especially when one considers that the SS leading the punishment detail would themselves be enraged that they had to supervise such hard work in the mud and muck of the Silesian plain.[58]

As the women were assigned throughout the approximately 10,000 camps, subcamps, juvenile protective custody camps, and so forth, throughout the Reich,[59] friction periodically arose between camp commandants and the female auxiliaries.

Auschwitz Commandant Höß detested the women and argued that they had been spoiled in Ravensbrück. The commandant complained that "from the very beginning most of them just wanted to run away and return to the quiet comforts and the easy life of Ravensbrück."[60] Part of the male SS resentment might have been due to the fact that the overseers had much more latitude to shrink from a duty that they found wasn't compatible with their consciences, although, of course, such decisions could put them in potential trouble.[61]

While the women guards were not issued side arms, some did obtain, carry, and use such weapons against the inmates. Many carried "accessories" in the form of whips and/or rubber truncheons to maintain their brand of camp discipline. Indeed, when the then-Birkenau Commandant Josef Kramer ordered the elimination of the use of whips by the overseers, particularly vicious guards like Irma Grese disobeyed the direct order and continued to employ them. Indeed, in her final arrest deposition following capture at Bergen-Belsen, Grese admitted that she always had a whip and that she used it, along with an unauthorized whipping stick, "consistently" whenever necessary.[62] Some women were assigned to be *Hundeführerinnen* (female dog leaders). These overseers took care of and trained the camps' own police dogs, which were taken with them on *Außenkommandos* (external work details). While these animals were intended to prevent inmates from even considering escape, ample evidence has been produced at postwar trials that the dogs were frequently turned on prisoners without justification.[63] Himmler believed that women were more likely to respond to the threat of dog attacks than men, and the *Reichsführer-SS* calculated that employing a guard with a dog could eliminate two posts.[64] For the prisoners this usually meant increased terror and intimidation. The postwar testimonies of prisoners attest to the reckless and frequently fatal use of dogs by the overseers.

As it became increasingly clear that the war would be lost, one would think that the female guards would have become more inclined to treat prisoners with dignity and respect, as postwar retribution would become a concern for the overseers. In many cases there were crude attempts to rectify old wrongs, but the overseers had to remember that their superiors wanted to intensify the mission. In fact, the more fanatical elements of the SS hierarchy were even more dedicated near the end to acts of cruelty and even outright murder, particularly against their racial enemies – the Jews. The overseers had a couple of advantages over their male counterparts in the camps. First, unlike their male counterparts, they were not "tagged" with their blood types tattooed on their arms or chest, which, naturally, would make it easier for them simply to walk away from the camps after the war. Second, the prisoners had to address the overseer with the simple "*Frau Aufseherin,*" thereby preventing the majority of the inmates from ever knowing the true identity of the woman guarding them.[65] Many of the more notorious overseers, Irma Grese, Margot Drechsel, et al., were well-known simply because they were ubiquitous and ostensibly more cruel. In fact, survivor Helen Tichauer has noted that since prisoners didn't generally know the names of SS women, these unfortunates simply projected the "ugly and nasty Aufseherin Drechsel's name on every Aufseherin and called each of them a '*Drechselke*'."[66] Because Aufseherin sounded so similar to "officer" to the French and English inmates, an SS woman was simply referred to in the phonetic equivalent. As in most prison situations, the prisoners gave derogatory nicknames to the more brutal and cruel guards (e.g., "The Mare," "The Beautiful Beast," "The Viper," "The Grey Mouse," "The Bitch of Buchenwald," and so forth). For all those involved directly in the terror of the camps (as opposed to those who merely signed orders and didn't actually come into direct contact with the inmates), there was one other potential opportunity to avoid postwar conviction for war crimes: despite the fact that the camps were literally covered with dead corpses as western Allied troops came in, and that the prisoners were eyewitnesses who were willing to identify individual guards with atrocities, their recollections were frequently challenged by defense attorneys during cross-examination. Even today, Holocaust deniers/distorters contend that hysterical, vengeful inmates could not be trusted. The perpetrators of the crimes wore uniforms that were difficult to distinguish at a distance. The prisoners, it was frequently argued, were coached, directed, and led in their testimony by prosecution lawyers. Beyond these problems, even though a witness might have seen an overseer shoot an inmate at point blank range and then have seen a body that seemed entirely lifeless, no one would dare go and physically see that murdered prisoner was indeed deceased. In effect, since no *corpus delicti* existed and the case against the guard hinged largely on eye-witness testimony, defense counsel could try to discredit and impugn the testimony and ultimately get his client off.[67] Clearly, these were problems for the western Allies, and the Nazis clearly preferred to be taken by the British, American, and French, if they were to be captured at all. Although no reliable data is available as of yet from the legal proceedings instituted by the courts of the USSR and its satellites (although the former Soviet archives are being actively examined now), it is highly likely that the number of those convicted by the Soviets was many times higher than the aggregate number of persons sentenced by all the tribunals of the western occupying forces combined.[68] When one considers the *Krieg der Vernichtung* (war of annihilation) that Hitler had decreed his forces wage against the Bolsheviks, it is easy to understand the harsh treatment that was returned in kind to those guards apprehended in the east.

As the liberators entered the camps, the women were frequently still at their posts. Regardless of how fanatical the guards were, one might question why at this point they didn't attempt to avoid the inevitable wrath of liberators and liberated alike. Two important reasons need to be examined. First, Nazism's credo of *"Weltmacht oder Niedergang"* (world domination or ruin) was deeply imbedded in the mindset of the SS, by far the most fanatical of all the Nazi organizations. As early as Christmas 1941, the Nazi cause was lost, but there could never be any consideration of surrender in the twisted minds of Hitler and his minions; indeed, just as Nazism was capable of annihilation on a massive scale, it also proved itself capable of self-destruction on an equally large scale.[69] Ironically, in this orgy of death and destruction it seems almost apropos for the true believers to stay right there with the fruits of their labors. A second reason that many were apprehended while standing amid their horrific crimes has to do with terror being turned inward on the faithful themselves. Following the attempt to assassinate Hitler on July 20, 1944, the Nazi propaganda machine invoked the notion that henceforth the Third Reich was locked in a death struggle. There could be no shameful surrender as in World War I, in which the Jews survived and prospered. From this point on, anyone who voiced defeatist rhetoric or who tried to surrender to the western allies would be tracked by a *"Fliegendes Standgericht"* (flying court martial), summarily strung up to the nearest tree, lamppost, or trestle, and a placard would be placed on the traitor's corpse to identify such a terrible betrayal of the German *Volk*. Although by this time, few had any real illusions that somehow Goebbels's "wonder weapons" and sheer Teutonic will would turn the tide against the advancing Soviets in the east and the Anglo-American forces in the west, the elimination of the Jews had not been completed, and it was felt that this task could still be accomplished if concerted efforts were made. Nevertheless, despite the merciless death marches and the gruesome spectacles of mounds of dead in the liberated camps as the war ended, the goal was not met and the SS failed in their "sacred mission" to make Europe *"Judenrein"* (clean of Jews).

The first trial of SS killers was held in the city of Krasnodar, USSR from July 14-17, 1943 and resulted in the first death convictions and lengthy prison sentences. Following the liberation of Majdanek, the first formal concentration camp trial took place in Lublin, Poland from November 27 - December 2, 1944. All six SS men were convicted and hanged. No over-

seers were apprehended until 1945, and the majority were taken in the west. As the death camps, concentration camps, and subcamps were evacuated in the east, the auxiliaries were frequently assigned to the numerous death marches and transports heading west. The first women to be tried were from Bergen-Belsen where a British tribunal was convened to judge the accused war criminals. The trial lasted from September 17 - November 17, 1945 and nineteen women were in the dock with thirty-one men. The entire proceeding appeared to be somewhat of a "cattle show" because the forty-five defendants had to sit in three tiers, each wearing tie-on, cloth numerals for efficient identification. Owing to the striking beauty and stylish dress of Defendant No.9, Irma Grese, the press initially became "taken" by the twenty-one year old's appearance. Only as the trial progressed and the atrocious acts of this overseer were revealed by numerous inmate witnesses did the focus shift more to her crimes than to her appearance. In addition, at the beginning of her trial, Irma Grese, ostensibly in a carefully orchestrated plan, maintained a contemptuous, antagonistic look. When a prosecution witness and survivor named Ada Bimko walked by the dock to identify guards who had specifically maltreated prisoners, Bimko stopped in front of Grese and momentarily the two women glared at each other. This "stare down," which was definitely a tense moment in the court proceedings, finally ended when "Fräulein Grese lowered her defiant eyes."[70] At the trial's conclusion, three women – including Grese, were sentenced to death, and most of the other overseers received prison sentences.

Unlike Grese, the majority of the accused women were far more concerned about saving their necks as public indignation turned to outrage for their hideous crimes. These women didn't wear sharply tailored uniforms, accentuate their looks with ringlets in their hair, or have the stunningly good looks of an Irma Grese. Indeed, as one courtroom observer noted, frequently their appearances, " . . . traversed the range from ugly to repellent."[71]

It is true that at the initial Ravensbrück trial one Kapo, a former prisoner turned *Blockälteste* (chief functionary), had the audacity to wear confiscated furs in the prisoner's dock, but little that is noteworthy has been recorded of the female guards' demeanor during their cases. The infamous wife of the commandant of Buchenwald, Ilse Koch, who never completed the overseer training at Ravensbrück, appeared to be anything but the rapacious female tormentor when the Americans tried her in the Buchenwald proceeding (of the thirty-one defendants, she would be the only female charged). Koch received a life sentence, but then saw it downgraded to four years imprisonment by a U.S. military court of appeals.[72]

No women sat in the prisoners' dock at the trial of the major Nazi war criminals in Nuremberg (November 1945 - October 1946). However, women were tried by French, Dutch, Norwegian, Polish, Soviet, and German courts. While there were female perpetrators executed by the Polish, Soviet, and British courts, American and French courts did not execute women (while female murderers of downed American airmen were originally sentenced to death in Case No.12-1497, a U.S. military court of appeals reduced Käthe Reinhardt and Margarete Witzler's death sentences to thirty years imprisonment).[73] However, the overseers were right to fear capture by the Soviet forces: SS-Aufseherinnen Christa Hempel (who had served in Floßenbürg), Elisabeth Höhn (who had served in Ravensbrück), Ruth Schubert (who had served in Groß-Rosen), and a certain women named Sorge (first name unknown and not listed on the original Ravensbrück bank list) were summarily convicted and presumably deported to Soviet *gulags*. No data is available on the "presumably substantial number of Germans sentenced in Yugoslavia."[74]

Very few female guards were brought to trial compared to SS men. Of course, there were many more men than women who served as guards in the camps, but even despite this fact, for reasons previously noted, it was much easier for female guards to simply walk away after the war. However, even those women who were able to escape initial apprehension and judgment were often identified under the *Entnazifierung* (denazification) program set up by the Allied Control Council after the fall of the Third Reich as either Category Two Nazis (activists, militarists, or profiteers) or Category Three Nazis (lesser offenders, such as young offenders who deserved leniency due to the corrupting influences of Nazi education and training). While the denazification process was implemented primarily as a means of keeping genuine adherents of the Nazi regime out of postwar governmental positions, the large-scale program had the effect of forcing many individuals, both male and female, out of the protective cover of the postwar chaos. It should be remembered that these were very bleak times and economic necessity forced many Germans to seek work with the occupying powers and, in turn, this led to background checks and periodic exposure of lower-level participants in the Holocaust. Owing to greater tensions between the west and east, there was a tendency to speed up German rearmament and, so, the denazification process lost most of its strength. By the time the Federal Republic of Germany was established in 1950, the Allies lifted their restrictions on the prosecutions of Nazi war criminals and German courts were finally given the authority to investigate and prosecute those of their own who had been involved in war crimes. To streamline and expedite a systematic approach to the massive number of crimes, the justice ministers of the *Länder* (states) of the Federal Republic established the *Ludwigsburger Zentralestelle* (formally referred to as "The Central Office for the Judicial Administrations of the *Länder* for Investigation of Nazi War Crimes in Ludwigsburg"). This clearing house for German prosecutions quickly assembled a large staff of attorneys, secretaries, and clerks to begin their tasks, and within the first year initiated approximately four hundred investigations.[75] Some women were tracked down in the German-instituted dragnet, and many claimed that while they had been trained as SS-Aufseherinnen, they had not committed war crimes and/or could not be held responsible because they had been conscripted against their will. Occasionally, overseers who had been convicted and sentenced by foreign courts returned to the Federal Republic and were charged by German courts for separate crimes committed in Germany. Naturally, as time went on, even those hunted down were often able to avoid prosecution owing to ill health as a result of advanced age; indeed, those prosecuted had an average age of 52.7 years in 1957, but by 1978, the average was up to 66.0.[76] Nevertheless, Luise Danz, an overseer who had served at Plaszów and Auschwitz-Birkenau, returned to the Federal Republic in 1957 following her release from a ten year prison term in Poland (she had been sentenced to life). In 1996, she was charged with the murder of a young girl at the end of the war at Malchow, a subcamp of Ravensbrück.[77] As I write, the Central Office is being dismantled as a prosecutorial agency and, despite periodic deportations by foreign countries, the days of active, full-scale Nazi hunts are coming to a close. Perhaps the last major prosecution by the German authorities occurred in the longest criminal proceeding in Federal Republic history – the Majdanek Trial of fourteen camp guards and administrators (including a woman extradited from the United States, Hermine [Braunsteiner] Ryan as well as another former overseer, Hildegard Lächert) in Düsseldorf. The trial began in November 1975 and was finally concluded in June 1981.[78]

In spite of this monumentally long proceeding, and in spite of the convictions and imprisonments of Ryan and Lächert for their crimes, as the world enters the twenty-first century, the overwhelming majority of the overseers have left the living as inconspicuously as they walked away from their duty stations at the end of the Second World War.

Notes:

[1] The current consensus among Holocaust historians is that Hitler never signed any such order. He had signed an authorization to initiate the euthanasia program that was back-dated to coincide with the Nazi invasion of Poland (September 1, 1939) and, due to the eventual outcry from religious leaders in Germany when the program was exposed, it appears that the Nazi leader decided that henceforth all the murderous orders would be passed on verbally (no written order exists for the invasion of Poland either!). While no so-called "smoking gun" exists in the form of a written order, innumerable sources, including the minutes of the Wannsee Conference that initially worked out the logistics of the organized killing, put Hitler's desire to eliminate the Jews once and for all directly into this ghastly plan. For a detailed examination of this matter, see Michael Shermer and Alex Grobman, *Denying History: Who Say the Holocaust Never Happened and Why Do They Say It?* (Berkeley, CA: University of California Press, 2000), pp. 200-228 as well as less detailed references in Deborah Lipstadt, *Denying the Holocaust: The Growing Assault on Truth and Memory* (New York: Free Press, 1993), p. 111 and 162.

[2] Koonz, *Mothers in the Fatherland*, p. 53.

[3] Norman H. Baynes (ed.), *The Speeches of Adolf Hitler: April 1922 - August 1939* (London: Oxford University Press, 1942), I, 531.

[4] David Schoenbaum, *Hitler's Social Revolution: Class and Status in Nazi Germany, 1933-39* (New York: W.W. Norton, 1980), pp. 178-179).

[5] Frederic Reider, *The Order of the SS* (London: W. Foulsham, 1981), p. 148.

[6] Gilmer W. Blackburn, *Education in the Third Reich: Race and History in Nazi Textbooks* (Albany, NY: State University of New York, 1985), pp. 106-107.

[7] Ibid., p. 107.

[8] *Völkischer Beobachter,* May 2, 1938, p. 2.

[9] Erika Mann, *Zehn Millionen Kinder: Die Erziehung der Jugend in Dritten Reich* (Amsterdam: Uerido Verlag, 1938), p. 177.

[10] Blackburn, *Education,* p. 109. Also, note that the call to German girls was to, "train your bodies, grow healthy, and fortify your powers of resistance and so grow up to be healthy women, conscious of yourselves, ready to stake your lives with strong powers of resistance." Mann, *Zehn Millionen Kinder,* p. 177.

[11] See H.W. Koch, *The Hitler Youth: Origins and Development 1922-45* (New York: Stein and Day, 1975), pp. 111-112 and Heinz Höhne, *The Order of the Death's Head: The Story of Hitler's SS*, trans. by Richard Barry (New York: Coward-McCann, 1969), p. 136. Also, it is interesting to note that a number of the more notorious SS-supervisors came from the agricultural areas surrounding FKL-Ravensbrück: Irma Grese, Dorothea Binz, Margarete Mewes (born in Fürstenberg bei Ravensbrück itself) and as well as one of the many forgotten female guards, Käthe Rupp, all were from the surrounding area. Irmtraud Heike, "*... da es sich ja lediglich um die Bewachung der Häftlinge handelt ...*" in *Frauen in Konszentrationslagern: Bergen-Belsen [und] Ravensbrück, (eds.)* Claus Füllberg-Stolberg et al. (Bremen: Edition Temmen, 1994), p. 224.

[12] This term has strong Teutonic overtones and was used as the title of a book by Nazi Agricultural Minister Walter Darré. The expression was romantically and reverently employed by Nazi leaders, including of course the former agriculturist Heinrich Himmler, to convey the sacredness of German "blood and soil," neither of which, according to Nazi racial doctrine, should be polluted by inferior stock. For additional insight into Himmler's mystic fascination with the, "holy bond between the peasant *Volk* and the German land," see Bradley F. Smith, *Heinrich Himmler: A Nazi in the Making, 1900-1926* (Palo Alto, CA: Hoover Institution Press/Stanford University Press, 1971), pp. 158-161 and George H. Stein, *The Waffen-SS: Hitler's Elite Guard at War, 1939-1945* (Ithaca, NY: Cornell University Press, 1966), pp. 122-123.

[13] See Jacques Pauwels, *Women, Nazis, and Universities: Female University Students in the Third Reich, 1933-1945* (Westport, CT: Greenwood Press, 1984), pp. 136-137.

[14] Dan van der Vat, *The Good Nazi: The Life & Lies of Albert Speer* (New York: Houghton Mifflin, 1997), p.130.

[15] Heike, "*... da es sich ja lediglich um die Bewachung der Häflinge handelt ...*" in *Frauen in Konzentationslagern,* p. 232.

[16] Ibid.

[17] Ibid., p. 224.

[18] Koonz, *Mothers in the Fatherland*, p. 404.

[19] Quoted in Heike, "*... da es sich ja lediglich um die Bewachung der Häftlinge handelt ...*" in *Frauen in Konzenzentrationslagern*, p. 222.

[20] Jack Morrison, *Ravensbrück: Everyday Life in a Women's Concentration Camp 1939-45* (Princeton, NJ: Markus Wiener, 2000), p. 25.

[21] Quoted in Heike, "*... da es sich ja lediglich um die Bewachung der Häflinge handelt ...*" *Frauen in Konzentrationslagern*, p. 234.

[22] Morrison, *Everyday Life*, pp. 24-25.

[23] Heike, "*... da es sich ja lediglich um die Bewachung der Häftlinge handelt ...*" in *Frauen in Konzentrationslagern*, p. 235.

[24] See "Affidavit of Heinrich Lehmann," *Trials of the Major War Criminals Before the International Military Tribunal* [hereafter cited as *TMWC*] (42 volumes; Nuremberg, 1945-1949), Nuremberg Document NIK-7484 – The Krupp Proceedings, dated June 17, 1947.

[25] Heike, "*... da es sich ja lediglich um die Bewachung der Häftlinge handelt ...*" in *Frauen in Konzentrationslagern,* p. 234. In addition, Helen Tichauer (nee Spitzer), a survivor of Auschwitz and known there as *"Zippi aus der Schreibstube,"* became responsible for the production and distribution of badges for women inmates while working in the Women's Camp Administration Building. As a result, she encountered many of the SS-supervisors on many occasions. She described the infamous Irma Grese in this manner: "It would be like taking some 'back woods' young girl from Iowa and giving her a position of power in a system similar to the Nazis." (Apologies to Iowa.) Quoted in Daniel Patrick Brown, *The Beautiful Beast: The Life & Crimes of SS-Aufseherin Irma Grese* (Ventura, CA: Golden West Historical Publications, 1996), xviiff.

[26] Morrison, *Everyday Life*, p. 26.

[27] Michael Hepp, "*Vorhof zur Hölle: Mädchen in Jugendschutzlager Uckermark,"* in (ed.) Angelika Ebbinghaus, *Opfer und Täterinnen* (Frankfurt/Main: Fischer Taschenbuch Verlag, 1987), p. 264.

[28] Nuremberg Document PS-1918, *TMWC,* 1946. The complete speech is also printed in *Nazi Conspiracy and Aggression*, Volume IV, Office of United States Chief Counsel for Prosecution of Axis Criminality (Washington, D.C.: U.S. Government Printing Office, 1946), pp. 558-578.

[29] See Brown, *Beautiful Beast*, p. 36ff.

[30] *Befehlsblatt des Chefs der Sipo und des SD*, April 30, 1943, Nr. 4, 127.

[31] Heike, "*... da es sich ja lediglich um die Bewachung der Häftlinge handelt ...*" in *Frauen in Konzentrationslagern*, p. 232.

[32] Morrison, *Everyday Life*, p. 26.

[33] Giles Playfair and Derrick Sington, *The Offenders: Society and the Atrocious Crime (London: Secker and Warsburg, 1957), p. 173.*

[34] Ibid.

[35] Helmut Krausnick *et al., Anatomy of the SS-State*, trans. Richard Berry, Dorothy Long, and Marian Jackson (New York: Walker, 1968), pp. 339-340.

[36] Germaine Tillon, *Ravensbrück*, trans. Gerald Satterwaite (Garden City, NJ: Doubleday, 1975), pp. 69-70.

[37] Heike, "*... da es sich ja lediglich um die Bewachung der Häftlinge handelt ...*" in *Frauen in Konzentrationslagern*, p. 223.

[38] Ibid., p. 225.

[39] Morrison, *Everyday Life*, p. 27.

[40] The SS-woman received, "twenty-five strokes on the buttocks ... because she had helped prisoners" ("*25 Stockschlagen auf das Gesäß ... weil sie Häftlingen geholfen habe*"). Hermann Langbein, *Menschen in Auschwitz* (Vienna: Europaverlag, 1972), p. 449. Playfair and Sington (*Offenders*, p. 177) merely refer to the overseer as a "disobedient colleague."

[41] Morrison, *Everyday Life*, p. 25.

[42] Ibid., pp. 25-26.

[43] Tillon, *Ravensbrück*, p. 62.

[44] Ibid., p. 63.

[45] *Organisationsbuch der NSDAP* (Munich, 1943 [original publication, 1935]), p. 416 (Nuremberg Documents 1922 Series: A-PS and 2640-PS). Also, cf. Krausnick and Broszat, *Anatomy of the SS-State*, p. 433.

[46] *Reichsführer-SS Befehl von 14.8.43.*

[47] Rudolf Höß, *Kommandant in Auschwitz: Autobiographische Aufzeichnungen* (Stuttgart: Walter Verlag, 1968), Appendix Nr. 8, 263.

[48] Binz began her service in the *weibliche SS-Gefolge* (SS Women's Auxiliary) in September 1940 and impressed her superiors with her unquestioning loyalty and absolute willingness to get the job done. She served her entire time at Ravensbrück and, following the war, was apprehended, tried, and convicted of war crimes. She was hanged on May 2, 1947. Lord Russell of Liverpool (*The Scourage of the Swastika: A Short History of Nazi War Crimes* [London: Cassell, 1954], p. 207) erroneously states that "Thea" Binz had been trained by Irma Grese.

[49] *Frühappell* was the name for the daily early morning roll-call, which was used as a portion of the daily terror for prisoners as well. Any *Appell*, whether an early one or an accounting roll-call *Zahlappell*, could last for hours and was invariably accompanied with large dose of physical abuse and mental torture.

[50] The German phrase *"Sport machen"* (literally, "to make sport") had nothing to do with recreational pursuits in our frame of reference; rather, here it carried the brutal and cruel connotation, as the SS guards used it, of intentionally torturing inmates during roll-call formations for the slightest infractions of camp regulations. Frequently, the unfortunate prisoner who simply

caught the eye of a guard could be severely beaten or, in some instances, killed on the spot (the corpse would have to remain, naturally, for accounting purposes).

[51] This German term has no English equivalent. Essentially, the term means "malicious pleasure." SS personnel were encouraged to have a good time while inflicting pain and suffering on their captives.

[52] See the *Disziplinar- und Strafforderung für das Gefängenenlager, Obergruppenführer* Theodor Eicke, October 1, 1933 (*TMWC,* Volume XXVI, Nuremberg Document PS-788).

[53] Heike, *"da es sich ja lediglich um die Bewachung der Häftlinge handelt ...,"* p. 230.

[54] Ibid., p. 225.

[55] Ibid., p. 227.

[56] Ibid.

[57] Ibid.

[58] Although it would be Grese's testimony that she only served as an *SS Aufseherin* on the punishment detail for two days, a co-defendant at her trial, Helen Kopper, the Polish "Doctor of Music," would swear under oath that Grese was in charge of this atrocious detail for seven months. Phillips (ed.), *The Belsen Trial,* xliii.

[59] Obviously some of these places were quite small and comprised only a few prisoners and guards. As one might suspect, there were myriad of arrangements and occasionally some opportunity for free-lancing. We know that there were the rare situations when SS women worked too closely with the prisoners and, as Jack Morrison has pointed out in his study of Ravensbrück, those who actually treated inmates too well in reality may "have represented a more widespread phenomenon than the SS was willing to tolerate." As evidence of this problem, Morrison notes that *SS Obergruppenführer* Richard Glücks, the concentration camp inspector-general, distributed an order to all camp commanders to remind all overseers that "under no circumstances" were they to have any sort of personal relationships with prisoners. See Morrison, *Everyday Life,* p. 27.

[60] Jadwiga Bezwinska Danuta Czech, *KL Auschwitz Seen by the SS: Höß, Broad,* [and] *Kremer,* trans. by Constantine Fitzgibbon (Oswiecim: *Panstwowe Muzeum w Oswiecimiu,* 1978), p. 80.

[61] Heike, *"da es sich ja lediglich um Bewachung der Häftlinge handelt die ...,"* p. 228.

[62] Phillips (ed.), *The Belsen Trial,* p. 713.

[63] Heike, *"da es sich ja lediglich um die Bewachung der Häftlinge handelt ...,"* p. *226.*

[64] Ibid.

[65] Ibid., p. 228.

[66] Heleln Tichauer, interview with the author, July 29, 2000, New York City.

[67] Playfair and Sington, *The Offenders,* p. 162.

[68] Adalbert Rückerl, *The Investigation of Nazi Crimes, 1945-1978: A Documentation,* trans. Derek Rutter (Hamden, CT: Archon, 1980), p. 30.

[69] Ian Kershaw, *Hitler* (Essex, UK: Pearson, 1991), pp. 193-194.

[70] "Inferno on Trial," *Time,* October 8, 1945, p. 36.

[71] Edgar Lustgarten, *The Business of Murder* (New York: Scribner, 1968), p. 94.

[72] *Report of the Deputy Judge Advocate for War Crimes – European Command,* June 1944-July 1948, p. 244.

[73] Ibid. p. 213.

[74] Rückerl, *Investigation of Nazi Crimes,* pp. 30-31.

[75] Ibid., pp. 45-46.

[76] Ibid. p. 79.

[77] See *verurteilt, vergessen und wieder angeklagt – das Leben der SS-Frau D.* ("denounced, forgotten, and accused again – the life of SS Woman D."), *Frankfurter Rundschau,* March 27, 1996, p. 6.

[78] Rückerl, *Investigations of Nazi War Crimes,* pp. 143-144ff.

2

THE SS OVERSEERS (*AUFSEHERINNEN*):
The Camp Women - Personal Files

" . . .da es sich ja lediglich um die Bewachung der Häftlinge handelt."
(" . . .You only have to watch over prisoners.")

- SS recruitment advertisement for female guards

Prior to listing the files of the *Aufseherinnen,* I have decided to include a facsimile of the summary sheet of a particularly notorious overseer, Margot Drechsel (*page 26*). This woman was one of the upper echelon female guards at Auchwitz Birkenau. She was certainly an individual one would expect would merit a great deal of attention. Looking at this document, one can easily see that only the most basic data is recorded.

As previously noted in the Introduction, the genesis for this section began with the original bank record list that had been organized and maintained by the administration of the Ravensbrück during the war and which currently is the domain of the *Mahn- und Gedenkstätte-Ravensbrück*. After a massive amount of cross-referencing data with the *Bundesarchiv-Berlin*, the *Zentralestelle der Landesjustizverwaltung* (Ludwigsburg*)*, and numerous other archives, the individual women listed in these pages represent the overwhelming majority of *The Camp Women*. Naturally, any additional women who can be verified as legitimate *Reichsangestellte* ("employees of the Reich") will be included in subsequent editions. Also, because the bank records included SS men, nurses, doctors, and other support medical personnel, there may be inadvertent inclusions of individuals who were not female guards. For example, Hildegard Lohbauer was an individual who had apparently been on the SS payroll as an informant and who attempted to portray herself as an SS woman. She has been removed. Also, Elisabeth Marschall, a nurse, could be confused with the wartime cadre of *Waffen-SS* women, as she was originally "tagged" as one by a British investigating unit at Ravensbrück (the Soviets liberated the camp, but the

British had the jurisdiction for postwar prosecutions). Needless to say, despite the painstaking attempt to include only those women who truly were overseers, I would be grateful to know if any faulty entries exist.

Regrettably, files do not exist for each *Aufseherin*. Many reasons can explain why a German bureaucracy so keenly bent on meticulous record-keeping failed to include even such basic information as birthplace, date of birth, and so forth, on these files. The Third Reich was rapidly shrinking in late 1944 and early 1945. Priorities clearly required less documentation and more action. Rapid deployment of personnel was the primary issue for the Nazis and obviously clerks themselves had their pens and typewriters taken away and weapons became their replacements. Also, as old men and young boys were being pressed into service in the so-called "People's Army" (*Volksturm*), women who had been able to previously escape the draft dragnet were now enlisted into auxiliary or support status. The innumerable death marches that began to crisscross the evaporating Reich invariably included housewives and single women who were catapulted into the breech. Amid the chaos and disintegration, no doubt some women were never even registered by name.

Finally, the frequently used abbreviations "AL" and "NL" need to be explained once again. These designations are used to note *Außenlager* (subcamp) and *Nebenlager* (adjacent camp). When one considers that there were thousands of small camps, outside work details, armaments factories of various sizes in addition to the familiar full-scale concentration and death camps, it is easy to understand why so many varieties of these subcamps and adjacent camps exist.

Name:	**Drechsel**	**Margot**		Wohnung:**R.**		**Gau: Mark Brandenburg**

Aufseherin

Geb.-Datum: **17.5.08** Geb.-Ort: **Neugersdorf**

Mitgl.-Nr.: **8920949** Aufn.: **1. April 1941**

Aufnahme beantragt am: **31.1.41**

Wiederaufn. beantragt am: .... genehm.: ....

Austritt: ....

Gelöscht: ....

Ausschluß: ....

Aufgehoben: ....

Gestrichen wegen: ....

Zurückgenommen: ....

Abgang zur Wehrmacht
Zugang von: ....

Gestorben: ....

Bemerkungen: ....

Ortsgr.: **Ravensbrück**

Ks. **Templin** *Brk. Brandbg.* Mt. ...... Bl. **73**
Monatsmeldg. Gau.

Lt. RL./ .... vom ....

Wohnung: *u. T. K. L.*

Ortsgr.: *Auschwitz* Gau: *Ob. Schles.*

Monatsmeldg. Gau: .... Mt. ...... Bl. ......

Lt. RL./ .... vom ....

Wohnung: ....

Ortsgr.: .... Gau: ....

Monatsmeldg Gau .... Mt. ...... Bl. ......

Lt. RL./ .... vom ....

Wohnung: ....

Ortsgr.: .... Gau: ....

Monatsmeldg. Gau: .... Mt. ...... Bl. ......

Lt. RL./ .... vom ....

Wohnung: ....

Ortsgr.: *Ob. Schlesien an* Gau:

Personnel File Card-Margot Drechsel (BDC-National Archives II)

Abel

First Name: Olga
Birthdate:
Birthplace:
Position: Aufseherin
File Number:
Employment Date:
Camp Service: Ravensbrück
Notes:

Achtenberg

First Name: Erna
Birthdate:
Birthplace: Berlin
Position: Aufseherin
File Number: 10 AR 1750/61
Employment Date:
Camp Service: Kommando Helmbrechts
Notes: Service as a Waffen SS auxiliary began on July 10, 1944.

Achterberg

First Name: Erna
Birthdate: October 19, 1910
Birthplace: Neugedang
Position: Aufseherin
File Number: IV 410(F) AR 2629/67
Employment Date:
Camp Service: Floßenbürg; Kommando Helmbrechts
Notes: Service as a Waffen SS auxiliary began on July 10, 1944.

Ackermann

First Name: Gertrud
Birthdate: October 10, 1918
Birthplace: Dresden
Position: Aufseherin
File Number: IV 410(F) AR 2629/67
Employment Date:
Camp Service: Floßenbürg; AL Dresden-Reick
Notes:

Ackermann

First Name: Luise
Birthdate: November 3, 1921
Birthplace:
Position: Aufseherin
File Number: IV 410(F) AR 2629/67
Employment Date: September 27, 1944
Camp Service: Floßenbürg
Notes:

Adam

First Name: Emma
Birthdate: May 16, 1922
Birthplace: Ottendorf
Position: Aufseherin
File Number:
Employment Date: September 13, 1944
Camp Service: Groß-Rosen
Notes:

Adam

First Name: Emma
Birthdate:

Birthplace:
Position: Aufseherin
File Number:
Employment Date:
Camp Service:
Notes:

Adametz (or Atametz)

First Name: Marianne
Birthdate: October 22, 1926
Birthplace:
Position: Aufseherin
File Number: IV 410(F) AR 2629/67
Employment Date:
Camp Service: Floßenbürg; AL Venusberg
Notes:

Adamski

First Name: Luise
Birthdate: February 19, 1920
Birthplace: Grünberg
Position: Aufseherin
File Number:
Employment Date: August 19, 1944
Camp Service: Groß-Rosen
Notes:

Aderhold (born Steinfeld)

First Name: Rosa
Birthdate:
Birthplace:
Position: Aufseherin
File Number:
Employment Date:
Camp Service:
Notes:

Adermann (born Machnik)

First Name: Ingeborg
Birthdate:
Birthplace:
Position: Aufseherin
File Number:
Employment Date:
Camp Service: Floßenbürg
Notes:

Adler

First Name: Else
Birthdate: May 7, 1909
Birthplace: Wüstgiersdorf
Position: Aufseherin
File Number:
Employment Date: July 29, 1944
Camp Service: Groß-Rosen
Notes:

Adler

First Name: Ingeborg
Birthdate: September 9, 1921
Birthplace: Leipzig
Position: Aufseherin
File Number:
Employment Date: September 2, 1944
Camp Service: Ravensbrück
Notes:

Admiral
First Name: Adriene-Margaretha
Birthdate:
Birthplace:
Position: Aufseherin
File Number:
Employment Date:
Camp Service:
Notes:

Adolph
First Name: Maria
Birthdate: August 5, 1902
Birthplace: Voigtdorf
Position: Aufseherin
File Number:
Employment Date: August 18, 1944
Camp Service: Groß-Rosen
Notes:

Affolter
First Name: Margarete
Birthdate: December 17, 1922
Birthplace: Berlin-Neukölln
Position: Aufseherin
File Number: IV 410(F) AR 2629/67
Employment Date: August 19, 1944
Camp Service: Floßenbürg; AL Plauen
Notes:

Ahlert
First Name: Hedwig
Birthdate:
Birthplace:
Position: Aufseherin
File Number:
Employment Date:
Camp Service:
Notes:

Ahrens
First Name: Elfriede
Birthdate: February 12, 1921
Birthplace: Warmkow
Position: Aufseherin
File Number:
Employment Date: November 16, 1944
Camp Service: Ravensbrück
Notes: Ethnic German; born and raised in Poland.

Ahrens
First Name: Elvira
Birthdate: October 10, 1920
Birthplace: Burgdorf
Position: Aufseherin
File Number:
Employment Date: September 1, 1944
Camp Service: Neuengamme
Notes:

Aichele (born Schweizer)
First Name: Maria
Birthdate: September 19, 1915
Birthplace: Geislingen

Position: Aufseherin
File Number: 419 AR 1267/67
Employment Date:
Camp Service: Natzweiler; NL Geislingen
Notes:

Albers
First Name: Lieselotte
Birthdate:
Birthplace:
Position: Aufseherin
File Number:
Employment Date:
Camp Service: Neuengamme
Notes:

Albert
First Name: Annemarie
Birthdate:
Birthplace:
Position: Aufseherin
File Number:
Employment Date:
Camp Service:
Notes:

Albert
First Name: Irene
Birthdate:
Birthplace:
Position: Aufseherin
File Number:
Employment Date:
Camp Service:
Notes:

Albrecht
First Name: Gertrud
Birthdate: October 24, 1919
Birthplace: Berlin
Position: Aufseherin
File Number: IV 410(F) AR 2629/67
Employment Date: 1945
Camp Service: Floßenbürg; AL Wolkenburg
Notes:

Albrecht
First Name: Hertha
Birthdate: August 9, 1913
Birthplace: Bromberg
Position: Aufseherin
File Number:
Employment Date: August 14, 1944
Camp Service: Groß-Rosen
Notes:

Albrecht
First Name: Wally
Birthdate: September 2, 1923
Birthplace: Robnitz, Kr. Trautenau
Position: Aufseherin
File Number:
Employment Date: March 1, 1944
Camp Service: Groß-Rosen
Notes:

Alfering (born Voorkmann)

First Name: Helene (Hillena)
Birthdate: January 20, 1914
Birthplace: Diepenveen
Position: Aufseherin
File Number:
Employment Date: September 21, 1944
Camp Service: Ravensbrück
Notes: Dutch national; born and raised in Holland; special permission granted to serve as an "employee of the Reich."

Alt

First Name: Elfriede
Birthdate: May 30, 1914
Birthplace: Merzdorf
Position: Aufseherin
File Number:
Employment Date: July 27, 1944
Camp Service: Groß-Rosen
Notes:

Altenberger

First Name: Gertrud
Birthdate: August 12, 1923
Birthplace: Qualisch
Position: Aufseherin
File Number:
Employment Date: September 19, 1944
Camp Service: Groß-Rosen
Notes:

Altermann

First Name: Frida (Frieda)
Birthdate: June 22, 1902
Birthplace: Dresden
Position: Aufseherin
File Number: IV 410(F) AR 2629/67
Employment Date:
Camp Service: Floßenbürg; AL Astrawerke Chemnitz
Notes:

Althaus

First Name: Marie
Birthdate:
Birthplace:
Position: Aufseherin
File Number:
Employment Date:
Camp Service: Ravensbrück
Notes:

Altkrüger (born Hettmann)

First Name: Charlotte
Birthdate:
Birthplace:
Position: Aufseherin
File Number:
Employment Date:
Camp Service:
Notes:

Amler

First Name: Margarete
Birthdate: August 21, 1922

Birthplace: Friesehof
Position: Aufseherin
File Number:
Employment Date: August 31, 1944
Camp Service: Groß-Rosen
Notes:

Amme

First Name: Lona
Birthdate: December 7, 1922
Birthplace: Hettstedt
Position: Aufseherin
File Number: IV 406 AR-Z 21/71
Employment Date:
Camp Service: Genshagen
Notes:

Amrhein

First Name: Margarete (Gretl)
Birthdate: July 18, 1917
Birthplace: Nuremberg
Position: Aufseherin
File Number:
Employment Date: July 11, 1944
Camp Service: Ravensbrück
Notes:

Anchrich (born Kärmer)

First Name: Ilse
Birthdate:
Birthplace:
Position: Aufseherin
File Number:
Employment Date:
Camp Service:
Notes:

Anders

First Name: Edith Johanna
Birthdate: June 21, 1923
Birthplace: Limbach
Position: Aufseherin
File Number: 404 AR 1545/67
Employment Date:
Camp Service: Neuengamme
Notes:

Anders

First Name: Elfriede
Birthdate:
Birthplace:
Position: Aufseherin
File Number:
Employment Date:
Camp Service:
Notes:

Anders

First Name: Olga
Birthdate: December 18, 1919
Birthplace: Kiel
Position: Aufseherin
File Number:
Employment Date: August 23, 1944
Camp Service: Floßenbürg; Groß-Rosen
Notes:

Andreas

First Name: Hildegard
Birthdate: August 21, 1922
Birthplace: Grünberg
Position: Aufseherin
File Number:
Employment Date: August 19, 1944
Camp Service: Groß-Rosen
Notes:

Anfang (married Karius)

First Name: Rosa
Birthdate: May 29, 1916
Birthplace: Niederklein
Position: Aufseherin
File Number: IV 406 AR 2467/66, IV 406 AR-Z 21/71
Employment Date:
Camp Service: Ravensbrück; AL Genshagen
Notes:

Antesberger

First Name: Karolina
Birthdate:
Birthplace:
Position: Aufseherin
File Number:
Employment Date:
Camp Service:
Notes:

Apel

First Name: Helene
Birthdate: September 20, 1923
Birthplace: Wittenberg
Position: Aufseherin
File Number:
Employment Date: September 8, 1944
Camp Service: Ravensbrück
Notes:

Appelt

First Name: Käthe
Birthdate:
Birthplace:
Position: Aufseherin
File Number:
Employment Date:
Camp Service: Ravensbrück
Notes:

Arbeiter (born Sander)

First Name: Hildegard
Birthdate:
Birthplace:
Position: Aufseherin
File Number:
Employment Date:
Camp Service: Groß-Rosen
Notes:

Archner

First Name: Liesbeth
Birthdate: July 12, 1920
Birthplace: Trockenau
Position: Aufseherin

File Number:
Employment Date: October 11, 1944
Camp Service: Groß-Rosen
Notes:

Arndt

First Name: Berta
Birthdate: April 9, 1911
Birthplace: Lanken (Pomerania)
Position: Kommandoführerin
File Number:
Employment Date:
Camp Service: Floßenbürg; Kommando Helmbrechts
Notes: Service as Waffen SS auxiliary began on September 6, 1944.

Arndt

First Name: Wally
Birthdate: November 31, 1920
Birthplace: Mulllwitz
Position: Aufseherin
File Number: IV 410 (F) AR 2629/67
Employment Date: November 16, 1943
Camp Service: Floßenbürg; AL Neu Rohlau
Notes:

Arneth

First Name: Elisabeth
Birthdate:
Birthplace:
Position: Aufseherin
File Number: IV 402 AR-Z 37/58
Employment Date:
Camp Service: Ravensbrück; Auschwitz
Notes:

Arnholz

First Name: Elli
Birthdate: December 12, 1912
Birthplace: Berlin-Spandau
Position: Aufseherin
File Number:
Employment Date: October 4, 1944
Camp Service: Ravensbrück
Notes:

Arlt

First Name: Margarethe
Birthdate: August 25, 1912
Birthplace: Friedsberg
Position: Aufseherin
File Number:
Employment Date: August 16, 1944
Camp Service: Groß-Rosen
Notes:

Arps

First Name: Charlotte
Birthdate: March 23, 1919
Birthplace:
Position: Aufseherin
File Number:
Employment Date:
Camp Service: Ravensbrück
Notes: Sentenced to one to three years imprisonment by an East German court.

Arscholl
First Name: Betti
Birthdate: May 19, 1921
Birthplace: Höhenschwerfs or Rostock
Position: Aufseherin
File Number: IV 410(F) AR 2629/67
Employment Date: November 1, 1943
Camp Service: Floßenbürg; AL Chemnitz
Notes:

Artmann
First Name: Dora
Birthdate:
Birthplace:
Position: Aufseherin
File Number:
Employment Date:
Camp Service: Ravensbrück
Notes:

Asselborn
First Name: Rosa
Birthdate:
Birthplace:
Position: Aufseherin
File Number:
Employment Date:
Camp Service:
Notes:

Augustin
First Name: Anna
Birthdate:
Birthplace:
Position: Aufseherin
File Number:
Employment Date:
Camp Service: Ravensbrück
Notes:

Aurich
First Name: Ilse
Birthdate: January 17, 1914
Birthplace: Eimsiedel
Position: Aufseherin
File Number:
Employment Date: August 26, 1944
Camp Service: Ravensbrück
Notes:

Ayasse
First Name: Meta
Birthdate: June 8, 1922
Birthplace: Neuhengstadt
Position: Aufseherin
File Number:
Employment Date: December 15, 1944
Camp Service: Ravensbrück
Notes:

Babiel (born Hakkert)
First Name: Charlotte
Birthdate: December 23, 1920
Birthplace:
Position: Aufseherin

File Number: IV 410(F) AR 2629/67
Employment Date: November 29, 1944
Camp Service: Floßenbürg; Ravensbrück
Notes:

Bachofner
First Name: Anna (Anni)
Birthdate: May 11, 1923
Birthplace: Hermannshütte
Position: Aufseherin
File Number: IV 410(F) AR 2629/67
Employment Date: April 30, 1944
Camp Service: Ravensbrück; Floßenbürg; AL Zwodau
Notes:

Bachmann (divorced Liberra; born Rudolf)
First Name: Anna
Birthdate: October 31, 1904
Birthplace:
Position: Aufseherin
File Number: IV 406 AR 2476/66
Employment Date:
Camp Service: Ravensbrück; AL Genshagen
Notes:

Bachmann
First Name: Annemarie
Birthdate:
Birthplace:
Position: Aufseherin
File Number:
Employment Date:
Camp Service:
Notes:

Bachmann
First Name: Milda
Birthdate: January 8, 1903
Birthplace:
Position: Aufseherin
File Number: IV 410(F) AR 2629/67
Employment Date:
Camp Service: Floßenbürg; AL Oederan
Notes:

Backhaus
First Name: Elisabeth
Birthdate:
Birthplace:
Position: Aufseherin
File Number:
Employment Date:
Camp Service:
Notes:

Backhaus
First Name: Ursula
Birthdate: July 15, 1920
Birthplace: Osterwald
Position: Aufseherin
File Number:
Employment Date: October 23, 1944
Camp Service: Neuengamme
Notes:

Bade (born Rygus)
First Name: Gertrud
Birthdate: May 3, 1913
Birthplace: Gladbeck
Position: Aufseherin
File Number:
Employment Date: August 23, 1944
Camp Service: Ravensbrück
Notes:

Bade (born Wagner)
First Name: Käthe
Birthdate:
Birthplace:
Position: Aufseherin
File Number:
Employment Date:
Camp Service: Ravensbrück
Notes:

Bärtl
First Name: Therese
Birthdate: April 2, 1920
Birthplace:
Position: Aufseherin
File Number: IV 410(F) AR 2629/67
Employment Date:
Camp Service: AL Hertine
Notes:

Bäschnitt
First Name: Charlotte
Birthdate:
Birthplace:
Position: Aufseherin
File Number:
Employment Date:
Camp Service: Groß-Rosen
Notes:

Bäßler (born Wenderoth)
First Name: Anna
Birthdate:
Birthplace:
Position: Aufseherin
File Number:
Employment Date:
Camp Service:
Notes:

Bässler (or Bäsler)
First Name: Elisabeth (Else)
Birthdate: February 7, 1923
Birthplace: Essen
Position: Aufseherin
File Number: IV 429 AR-Z 51/71 (B)
Employment Date:
Camp Service: Buchenwald
Notes: Served as an SS member after July 10, 1944.

Bahn
First Name: Erika
Birthdate: June 17 [?], 1922
Birthplace:
Position: Aufseherin

File Number:
Employment Date:
Camp Service:
Notes:

Bahnsen
First Name: Martha
Birthdate:
Birthplace:
Position: Aufseherin
File Number:
Employment Date:
Camp Service: Neuengamme
Notes:

Baier
First Name: Anna
Birthdate:
Birthplace:
Position: Aufseherin
File Number:
Employment Date:
Camp Service:
Notes:

Baier
First Name: Käthe
Birthdate:
Birthplace:
Position: Aufseherin
File Number:
Employment Date:
Camp Service:
Notes:

Baierl
First Name: Klara
Birthdate: February 13, 1923
Birthplace: Waldsaßen
Position: Aufseherin
File Number:
Employment Date: November 7, 1944
Camp Service: Ravensbrück
Notes:

Balkenhol
First Name: Maria (Marta)
Birthdate: March 1, 1918
Birthplace: Mühlheim-Ruhr
Position: Aufseherin
File Number: IV 429 AR-Z 51/1 (B)
Employment Date:
Camp Service: Buchenwald
Notes: Designated as an SS member in her file.

Balleis
First Name: Rosa
Birthdate: November 12, 1922 (no month or day noted in her file)
Birthplace: Augsburg
Position: Aufseherin
File Number:
Employment Date: August 21, 1944
Camp Service: Ravensbrück
Notes:

Balowski

First Name: Maria (Marta)
Birthdate: September 3, 1921
Birthplace:
Position: Aufseherin
File Number: IV 429 AR 1959/66
Employment Date:
Camp Service: NL Essen
Notes:

Bals

First Name: Margot
Birthdate: May 16, 1923
Birthplace: Kastrop
Position: Aufseherin
File Number:
Employment Date: November 7, 1944
Camp Service: Ravensbrück
Notes:

Balthasar

First Name: Olga
Birthdate: July 7, 1913
Birthplace: Petershof
Position: Aufseherin
File Number:
Employment Date: July 3, 1944
Camp Service: Ravensbrück
Notes:

Bambink

First Name: Frieda
Birthdate:
Birthplace:
Position: Aufseherin
File Number:
Employment Date:
Camp Service: Neuengamme
Notes:

Bambyneck

First Name: Maria
Birthdate:
Birthplace:
Position: Aufseherin
File Number: IV 409 AR-Z 39/59
Employment Date:
Camp Service: Ravensbrück
Notes:

Bandisch

First Name: Margarethe
Birthdate:
Birthplace:
Position: Aufseherin
File Number:
Employment Date:
Camp Service: Groß-Rosen
Notes:

Bandmann (born Schmidmaier)

First Name: Margarete
Birthdate:
Birthplace:
Position: Aufseherin

File Number:
Employment Date:
Camp Service:
Notes:

Bandomir

First Name: Inge
Birthdate:
Birthplace:
Position: Aufseherin
File Number:
Employment Date:
Camp Service: Neuengamme
Notes:

Baraneck

First Name: Margot
Birthdate:
Birthplace:
Position: Aufseherin
File Number:
Employment Date:
Camp Service:
Notes:

Barke (born Kolle)

First Name: Elsa
Birthdate:
Birthplace:
Position: Aufseherin
File Number:
Employment Date:
Camp Service:
Notes:

Barnbaum

First Name: Elfriede
Birthdate:
Birthplace:
Position: Aufseherin
File Number:
Employment Date:
Camp Service:
Notes:

Barnisch

First Name: Helene
Birthdate: May 25, 1923
Birthplace: Berlin
Position: Aufseherin
File Number:
Employment Date: September 5, 1944
Camp Service: Ravensbrück
Notes:

Baron

First Name: Caecilie
Birthdate:
Birthplace:
Position: Aufseherin
File Number:
Employment Date:
Camp Service: Groß-Rosen
Notes:

Barsch (born Rück)
First Name: Lina
Birthdate:
Birthplace:
Position: Aufseherin
File Number:
Employment Date:
Camp Service:
Notes:

Barschties
First Name: Herta
Birthdate:
Birthplace:
Position: Aufseherin
File Number:
Employment Date:
Camp Service: Neuengamme
Notes:

Bartel
First Name: Meta
Birthdate:
Birthplace:
Position: Aufseherin
File Number:
Employment Date:
Camp Service:
Notes:

Bartels
First Name: Sophie
Birthdate:
Birthplace:
Position: Aufseherin
File Number:
Employment Date:
Camp Service:
Notes:

Barten
First Name: Elfriede
Birthdate: February 27, 1924
Birthplace: Kühlungsborn
Position: Aufseherin
File Number:
Employment Date: November 8, 1944
Camp Service: Ravensbrück
Notes:

Barth
First Name: Elsa
Birthdate:
Birthplace:
Position: Aufseherin
File Number:
Employment Date:
Camp Service: Neuengamme
Notes:

Barth
First Name: Lena
Birthdate: November 27, 1922
Birthplace: Roßbach
Position: Aufseherin

File Number:
Employment Date: August 16, 1944
Camp Service: Ravensbrück
Notes:

Barth
First Name: Liesbeth
Birthdate:
Birthplace:
Position: Aufseherin
File Number:
Employment Date:
Camp Service:
Notes:

Barth
First Name: Lina
Birthdate: January 29, 1921
Birthplace: Schönbach
Position: Aufseherin
File Number: IV 410(F) Ar 2629/67
Employment Date: August 17, 1944
Camp Service: Floßenbürg; Hainichen
Notes:

Barth
First Name: (Gretel) Margarete
Birthdate:
Birthplace:
Position: Aufseherin
File Number: 419 AR-Z 172/69
Employment Date:
Camp Service: Geisenheim
Notes:

Barthel
First Name: Margret
Birthdate: October 25, 1922
Birthplace: Walsum
Position: Aufseherin
File Number:
Employment Date: August 14, 1944
Camp Service: Ravensbrück
Notes: Ethnic German; born and raised in Poland.

Bartke
First Name: Lotte
Birthdate: March 8, 1920
Birthplace: Königsberg
Position: Aufseherin
File Number:
Employment Date: December 20, 1944
Camp Service: Ravensbrück
Notes:

Bartl (or Bartel; born Mehlen)
First Name: Herta
Birthdate:
Birthplace:
Position: Aufseherin
File Number:
Employment Date:
Camp Service:
Notes:

Bartodziey

First Name: Lucie
Birthdate:
Birthplace:
Position: Aufseherin
File Number:
Employment Date:
Camp Service: Neuengamme
Notes:

Bartram

First Name: Edith
Birthdate:
Birthplace:
Position: Aufseherin
File Number:
Employment Date:
Camp Service: Neuengamme
Notes:

Bartsch (born Groß)

First Name: Elli
Birthdate: October 2, 1918
Birthplace: Breslau
Position: Aufseherin
File Number:
Employment Date: April 1, 1944
Camp Service: Ravensbrück
Notes:

Bartsch

First Name: Emma
Birthdate:
Birthplace:
Position: Aufseherin
File Number:
Employment Date:
Camp Service: Groß-Rosen
Notes:

Bartz

First Name: Lieselotte
Birthdate:
Birthplace:
Position: Aufseherin
File Number:
Employment Date:
Camp Service:
Notes:

Basalla

First Name: Anneliese
Birthdate:
Birthplace:
Position: Aufseherin
File Number:
Employment Date:
Camp Service:
Notes:

Baschab

First Name: Elisabeth
Birthdate: October 7, 1923
Birthplace:
Position: Aufseherin

File Number: IV 429 AR 1941/66
Employment Date:
Camp Service: Penig
Notes:

Basner

First Name: Rosa
Birthdate:
Birthplace:
Position: Aufseherin
File Number:
Employment Date:
Camp Service: Ravensbrück
Notes:

Bassmann

First Name: Ursula
Birthdate:
Birthplace:
Position: Aufseherin
File Number:
Employment Date:
Camp Service:
Notes:

Batz

First Name: Rosa
Birthdate:
Birthplace:
Position: Aufseherin
File Number:
Employment Date:
Camp Service:
Notes:

Bauch

First Name: Olga
Birthdate:
Birthplace:
Position: Aufseherin
File Number:
Employment Date:
Camp Service: Ravensbrück
Notes:

Bauer

First Name: Babette
Birthdate: February 29, 1912
Birthplace: Röthenbach
Position: Aufseherin
File Number:
Employment Date:
Camp Service: Floßenbürg
Notes:

Bauer

First Name: Else
Birthdate:
Birthplace:
Position: Aufseherin
File Number:
Employment Date:
Camp Service:
Notes:

Bauer (born Strutz)
First Name: Eva-Maria
Birthdate:
Birthplace:
Position: Aufseherin
File Number:
Employment Date:
Camp Service:
Notes:

Bauer
First Name: Luise
Birthdate: June 18, 1921
Birthplace: Böberach
Position: Aufseherin
File Number: IV 410(F) AR 2629/67
Employment Date: September 30, 1944
Camp Service: Floßenbürg; Holleischen; AL Graslitz
Notes:

Bauer
First Name: Lydia
Birthdate: July 31, 1922
Birthplace: Marktredwitz
Position: Aufseherin
File Number: IV 410(F) AR 2629/67
Employment Date: September 30, 1944
Camp Service: Floßenbürg, Holleischen
Notes:

Bauernfeind (born Arnold)
First Name: Anna
Birthdate:
Birthplace:
Position: Aufseherin
File Number:
Employment Date:
Camp Service:
Notes:

Baumann
First Name: Herta
Birthdate: December 29, 1903
Birthplace: Berlin
Position: Aufseherin
File Number:
Employment Date: July 26, 1944
Camp Service: Ravensbrück
Notes:

Baumann (born Forthofer)
First Name: Johanna
Birthdate: May 14, 1905
Birthplace: Lechhausen
Position: Unclear: some sources say she was a prisoner, some say she was an Aufseherin; possibly recruited from the Kapo ranks?
File Number: IV 409 AR-Z 39/59
Employment Date:
Camp Service: Floßenbürg; Ravensbrück; AL Zwodau
Notes:

Baumeister
First Name: Rosa
Birthdate:

Birthplace:
Position: Aufseherin
File Number:
Employment Date:
Camp Service:
Notes:

Baur (possibly Bauer)
First Name: Fanny
Birthdate: October 25, 1922
Birthplace: Augsburg
Position: Aufseherin
File Number:
Employment Date: September 1, 1944
Camp Service: Dachau
Notes:

Bayer (born Ziegler)
First Name: Rosalina
Birthdate:
Birthplace:
Position: Aufseherin
File Number:
Employment Date:
Camp Service:
Notes:

Bayer
First Name: Sydonia
Birthdate:
Birthplace:
Position: Aufseherin
File Number: V 203 AR-Z 182/69
Employment Date:
Camp Service: Litzmannstadt (Lodz Ghetto)
Notes: Executed by the Poles; date and exact circumstances unknown.

Bayer
First Name: Waltraud
Birthdate: June 2, 1913
Birthplace: Braunschweig
Position: Aufseherin
File Number: IV 410(F) AR 2629/67
Employment Date:
Camp Service: Floßenbürg; AL Freiberg
Notes:

Bayrle (or Bayerle)
First Name: Maria
Birthdate:
Birthplace:
Position: Aufseherin
File Number:
Employment Date:
Camp Service:
Notes:

Beck (born Seipt or Seibt)
First Name: Hildegard
Birthdate:
Birthplace:
Position: Aufseherin
File Number: IV 409 AR-Z 39/59
Employment Date:

Camp Service: Ravensbrück
Notes:

Beck (born Link)

First Name: Maria
Birthdate:
Birthplace:
Position: Aufseherin
File Number:
Employment Date:
Camp Service:
Notes:

Becker (married Brandt)

First Name: Anni
Birthdate:
Birthplace:
Position: Aufseherin
File Number:
Employment Date:
Camp Service: Ravensbrück
Notes:

Becker

First Name: Elfriede
Birthdate:
Birthplace:
Position: Aufseherin
File Number:
Employment Date:
Camp Service: Ravensbrück
Notes:

Becker

First Name: Elisabeth
Birthdate: July 20, 1923
Birthplace: Neuteich
Position: Aufseherin
File Number:
Employment Date: September 11, 1944
Camp Service: Stutthof
Notes:

Becker

First Name: Erika Ruth
Birthdate: March 22, 1920
Birthplace: Frankfurt/Main
Position: Aufseherin
File Number: 429 AR-Z 117/70
Employment Date: August 1944 (no day noted in her file)
Camp Service: Ravensbrück
Notes: Service as an SS member began on September 14, 1944.

Becker

First Name: Felixa
Birthdate:
Birthplace:
Position: Aufseherin
File Number:
Employment Date:
Camp Service: Neuengamme
Notes:

Becker (born Stark)

First Name: Gertrud
Birthdate: May 26, 1909
Birthplace: Bojanowo
Position: Oberaufseherin
File Number: IV 410 AR-Z 54/70, 100 AR-Z 84/88
Employment Date: October 1944
Camp Service: Floßenbürg
Notes: Prosecuted for murdering several prisoners on the Hainichen Death March, but died in 1990 before her trial concluded.

Becker

First Name: Käthe
Birthdate: May 25, 1923
Birthplace: Herrensohr or Saarbrücken
Position: Aufseherin
File Number: IV 410(F) AR 2629/67
Employment Date: August 9, 1944
Camp Service: Floßenbürg; AL Bändorf, Neuengamme, AL Zwodau, Holleischen
Notes:

Beckmann

First Name: Anni Brigitte
Birthdate: December 27, 1917
Birthplace: Seeburg
Position: Aufseherin
File Number: IV 409 AR-Z 39/59
Employment Date:
Camp Service: Ravensbrück
Notes:

Bednorz (born Tyalik)

First Name: Anna
Birthdate:
Birthplace:
Position: Aufseherin
File Number:
Employment Date:
Camp Service:
Notes: Croat national; special permission granted for service as "an employee of the Reich."

Beer

First Name: Anneliese
Birthdate:
Birthplace:
Position: Aufseherin
File Number:
Employment Date:
Camp Service:
Notes:

Beermann

First Name: Agnes
Birthdate: March 19, 1921
Birthplace: Rumbeck
Position: Aufseherin
File Number:
Employment Date:
Camp Service: Ravensbrück
Notes:

Beger
First Name: Käte
Birthdate:
Birthplace:
Position: Aufseherin
File Number:
Employment Date:
Camp Service: Ravensbrück
Notes:

Behmer
First Name: Charlotte
Birthdate:
Birthplace:
Position: Aufseherin
File Number:
Employment Date:
Camp Service:
Notes:

Behn
First Name: Lieselotte
Birthdate:
Birthplace:
Position: Aufseherin
File Number:
Employment Date:
Camp Service: Ravensbrück
Notes:

Behnke (married Semrau)
First Name: Christel
Birthdate: December 12, 1920
Birthplace:
Position: Aufseherin
File Number: IV 429 AR-Z 51/70
Employment Date:
Camp Service: AL Allendorf
Notes:

Behnstedt (born Gehrecke)
First Name: Ida
Birthdate: June 17, 1898
Birthplace:
Position: Aufseherin
File Number: IV 410(F) AR 2629/67
Employment Date: October 9, 1944
Camp Service: Floßenbürg; AL Holleischen
Notes:

Behrens
First Name: Johanna
Birthdate:
Birthplace:
Position: Aufseherin
File Number:
Employment Date:
Camp Service:
Notes:

Beilhardt
First Name: Erna
Birthdate: February 7, 1907
Birthplace: Neuteich (near Danzig)
Position: Aufseherin
File Number:

Employment Date: September 18, 1944
Camp Service: Stutthof
Notes:

Beinlich
First Name: Ilse
Birthdate:
Birthplace:
Position: Aufseherin
File Number:
Employment Date:
Camp Service: Ravensbrück
Notes:

Beitler
First Name: Johanna
Birthdate: March 9, 1913
Birthplace: Munich
Position: Aufseherin
File Number:
Employment Date:
Camp Service: Ravensbrück
Notes: Was dismissed from service for medical reasons.

Bellach
First Name: Ida
Birthdate: February 10, 1910
Birthplace: Sternberg
Position: Aufseherin
File Number:
Employment Date: April 1, 1944
Camp Service: Ravensbrück
Notes:

Belze
First Name: Irmgard
Birthdate:
Birthplace:
Position: Aufseherin
File Number:
Employment Date:
Camp Service:
Notes:

Belza
First Name: Stanislawa
Birthdate: October 24, 1918
Birthplace: Lublin
Position: Kommandoführerin
File Number: IV 410(F) AR 2629/67
Employment Date:
Camp Service: Floßenbürg
Notes: Polish national; born and raised in Poland; special permission granted for service as an "employee of the Reich."

Bendfeld
First Name: Anita
Birthdate:
Birthplace:
Position: Aufseherin
File Number:
Employment Date:
Camp Service:
Notes:

Bengartz
First Name: Luise
Birthdate:
Birthplace:
Position: Aufseherin
File Number:
Employment Date:
Camp Service: Neuengamme
Notes:

Bengert (born Himpel)
First Name: Anna
Birthdate: January 17, 1903
Birthplace: Unterliederbach
Position: Aufseherin
File Number: IV 429 AR-Z 51/70
Employment Date:
Camp Service: AL Allendorf; AL Geislingen
Notes:

Benzin
First Name: Hanna
Birthdate:
Birthplace:
Position: Aufseherin
File Number:
Employment Date:
Camp Service:
Notes:

Berger
First Name: Margot
Birthdate:
Birthplace:
Position: Aufseherin
File Number:
Employment Date:
Camp Service:
Notes:

Bergholz (born Brandes)
First Name: Anneliese
Birthdate: June 26, 1922
Birthplace: Magdeburg
Position: Aufseherin
File Number:
Employment Date: June 28, 1944
Camp Service: Ravensbrück
Notes:

Bergmann
First Name: Edith
Birthdate:
Birthplace:
Position: Aufseherin
File Number:
Employment Date:
Camp Service:
Notes:

Bergmann
First Name: Ella
Birthdate: April 17, 1923
Birthplace:
Position: Aufseherin

File Number:
Employment Date: September 11, 1944
Camp Service: Stutthof
Notes:

Bergmann
First Name: Erika
Birthdate: January 3, 1915
Birthplace:
Position: Aufseherin
File Number:
Employment Date:
Camp Service: Ravensbrück
Notes: Sentenced to life imprisonment by the East Germans for murder (no other explanation in her file).

Berkert
First Name: Hildegard
Birthdate: December 12, 1920
Birthplace: Tzschacha
Position: Aufseherin
File Number:
Employment Date: October 4, 1944
Camp Service: Groß-Rosen
Notes: Ethnic German; born and raised in the Sudetenland.

Berksen
First Name: Katharina
Birthdate:
Birthplace:
Position: Aufseherin
File Number:
Employment Date:
Camp Service:
Notes:

Berlin
First Name: Gertrud
Birthdate: May 4, 1922
Birthplace: Münster
Position: Aufseherin
File Number: IV 410(F) AR 2629/67
Employment Date: September 25, 1944
Camp Service: Floßenbürg; AL Graslitz; AL Plauen
Notes:

Berner
First Name: Ursula
Birthdate: October 31, 1921
Birthplace: Magdeburg
Position: Aufseherin
File Number:
Employment Date: July 25, 1944
Camp Service: Ravensbrück
Notes:

Bernigau
First Name: Jane (Gerda)
Birthdate: October 5, 1908
Birthplace: Sagan
Position: Oberaufseherin
File Number: 405 AR 1651/64
Employment Date:

Camp Service: Ravensbrück; Groß-Rosen; Mauthausen; Lichtenburg

Notes: Received the *Kriegsverdienstkreuz II. Klasse ohne Schwerter* (War Service Cross – 2nd Class without swords).

Bernstein

First Name: Käthe
Birthdate:
Birthplace:
Position: Aufseherin
File Number:
Employment Date:
Camp Service:
Notes:

Bernstein

First Name: Liesbeth
Birthdate:
Birthplace:
Position: Aufseherin
File Number:
Employment Date:
Camp Service:
Notes:

Berthold

First Name: Meta
Birthdate:
Birthplace:
Position: Aufseherin
File Number:
Employment Date:
Camp Service:
Notes:

Berthold

First Name: Ruth
Birthdate:
Birthplace:
Position: Aufseherin
File Number:
Employment Date:
Camp Service:
Notes:

Beßerdich

First Name: Lieselotte
Birthdate: December 22, 1918
Birthplace: Staffenhagen
Position: Aufseherin
File Number:
Employment Date: November 7, 1944
Camp Service: Ravensbrück
Notes:

Best

First Name: Elisabeth (Elisbeth, Liesbeth)
Birthdate: March 23, 1922
Birthplace: Schwelm
Position: Aufseherin
File Number: IV 410(F) AR 2629/67
Employment Date:
Camp Service: Floßenbürg; AL Zwodau; Neuengamme
Notes:

Bethe

First Name: Waltraud
Birthdate: June 25, 1922
Birthplace:
Position: Aufseherin
File Number: IV 429 AR 1941/66 (B)
Employment Date:
Camp Service: AL Torgau; Ravensbrück
Notes:

Betsch

First Name: Katharina
Birthdate: August 14, 1922
Birthplace: Peschlze
Position: Aufseherin
File Number:
Employment Date: August 19, 1944
Camp Service: Ravensbrück
Notes:

Bettler

First Name: Ella
Birthdate:
Birthplace:
Position: Aufseherin
File Number:
Employment Date:
Camp Service: Groß-Rosen
Notes:

Betzien (born Briesemeister)

First Name: Hildegard
Birthdate:
Birthplace:
Position: Aufseherin
File Number:
Employment Date:
Camp Service:
Notes:

Betzold

First Name: Johanna
Birthdate: January 8, 1912
Birthplace:
Position: Aufseherin
File Number: IV 410(F) AR 2629/67
Employment Date:
Camp Service: Floßenbürg; AL Hertine
Notes:

Beyer

First Name: Annemarie
Birthdate:
Birthplace:
Position: Aufseherin
File Number:
Employment Date:
Camp Service: Ravensbrück
Notes:

Beyer

First Name: Hildegard
Birthdate:
Birthplace:
Position: Aufseherin

File Number:
Employment Date:
Camp Service:
Notes:

Beyer
First Name: Isolde
Birthdate: May 10, 1925
Birthplace:
Position: Aufseherin
File Number: IV 410(F) AR 2629/67
Employment Date:
Camp Service:
Notes:

Beyer
First Name: Käthe
Birthdate:
Birthplace:
Position: Aufseherin
File Number:
Employment Date:
Camp Service:
Notes:

Beyer
First Name: Waltraut
Birthdate:
Birthplace:
Position: Aufseherin
File Number:
Employment Date:
Camp Service: Floßenbürg
Notes:

Biedermann
First Name: Margot
Birthdate: August 3, 1921
Birthplace: Freiberg
Position: Aufseherin
File Number: IV 410(F) AR 2629/67
Employment Date:
Camp Service: Floßenbürg; AL Chemnitz; Ravensbrück
Notes:

Biehl
First Name: Klara
Birthdate: April 16, 1920
Birthplace: Dortmund
Position: Aufseherin
File Number:
Employment Date: September 18, 1944
Camp Service: Ravensbrück
Notes:

Biehlig (married Lippmann)
First Name: Hildegard
Birthdate: August 7, 1923
Birthplace: Hainichen
Position: Aufseherin
File Number: II 410(F) AR 2629/67
Employment Date:
Camp Service: Floßenbürg; AL Hainichen
Notes:

Bielesch
First Name: Elisabeth
Birthdate:
Birthplace:
Position: Aufseherin
File Number:
Employment Date:
Camp Service:
Notes:

Bieneck (married Pakozdi)
First Name: Herta
Birthdate: June 20, 1921
Birthplace: Greppin
Position: Aufseherin
File Number: 409 AR-Z 39/59
Employment Date: June 1, 1943
Camp Service: Lublin-Majdanek
Notes:

Bier
First Name: Charlotte
Birthdate: August 14, 1919
Birthplace: Hehendorf
Position: Aufseherin
File Number:
Employment Date: August 31, 1944
Camp Service: Groß-Rosen
Notes:

Biermann
First Name: Liesbeth
Birthdate: February 26, 1923
Birthplace: Thiene
Position: Aufseherin
File Number: IV 410(F) AR 2629/67
Employment Date:
Camp Service: Floßenbürg; AL Chemnitz
Notes:

Bienert
First Name: Erna
Birthdate: June 26, 1921
Birthplace:
Position: Aufseherin
File Number:
Employment Date:
Camp Service: Ravensbrück
Notes:

Bilek
First Name: Erika
Birthdate:
Birthplace:
Position: Aufseherin
File Number:
Employment Date:
Camp Service:
Notes:

Billmeier
First Name: Maria (Marie)
Birthdate: January 1, 1900
Birthplace: Nuremberg
Position: Aufseherin

File Number: IV 410(F) AR 2629/67
Employment Date:
Camp Service: Floßenbürg; AL Holleischen; AL Mehltheuer
Notes:

Binz

First Name: Dorothea (Thea)
Birthdate: March 16, 1920
Birthplace: Dusterlake
Position: Aufseherin, *Stellvertretende Oberaufseherin* (Replacement Oberaufseherin)
File Number:
Employment Date: September 1, 1939
Camp Service: Ravensbrück
Notes: Executed for war crimes by the British on May 2, 1947.

Bindzeil

First Name: Hildegard
Birthdate:
Birthplace:
Position: Aufseherin
File Number:
Employment Date:
Camp Service: Neuengamme
Notes:

Binnefeld (born Köhler)

First Name: Gertrude
Birthdate:
Birthplace:
Position: Aufseherin
File Number:
Employment Date:
Camp Service: Neuengamme
Notes:

Binnenböse

First Name: Adelheid
Birthdate:
Birthplace:
Position: Aufseherin
File Number:
Employment Date:
Camp Service: Ravensbrück
Notes:

Birker

First Name: Eva
Birthdate:
Birthplace:
Position: Aufseherin
File Number:
Employment Date:
Camp Service:
Notes:

Birkholz (born Franz)

First Name: Margarete
Birthdate: June 17, 1918
Birthplace:
Position: Aufseherin
File Number: IV 406 AR-Z 21/71
Employment Date:
Camp Service: AL Genshagen
Notes:

Bisäke (or Biesäcke)

First Name: Margarete
Birthdate: August 27, 1922
Birthplace:
Position: Aufseherin (originally SS Helferin)
File Number:
Employment Date:
Camp Service: Ravensbrück; Magdeburg
Notes: Sentenced to one year imprisonment for maltreatment of prisoners (only details in her file).

Bischof

First Name: Selma
Birthdate:
Birthplace:
Position: Aufseherin
File Number:
Employment Date:
Camp Service:
Notes:

Biskup

First Name: Helene
Birthdate: April 29, 1921
Birthplace:
Position: Aufseherin
File Number: IV 429 AR 1959/66
Employment Date:
Camp Service: NL Essen
Notes:

Bitinsky (born Schlote)

First Name: Else
Birthdate: June 16, 1908
Birthplace: Gladbeck
Position: Aufseherin
File Number:
Employment Date: August 6, 1944
Camp Service: Ravensbrück
Notes:

Bitterlich

First Name: Anneliese
Birthdate: July 17, 1922
Birthplace: Chemnitz
Position: Aufseherin
File Number: IV 410(F) AR 2629/67
Employment Date:
Camp Service: Floßenbürg; AL Astrawerke Chemnitz
Notes:

Bitterling

First Name: Ursula
Birthdate:
Birthplace:
Position: Aufseherin
File Number:
Employment Date:
Camp Service:
Notes:

Bittermann

First Name: Leopoldine
Birthdate:

Birthplace:
Position: Aufseherin
File Number:
Employment Date:
Camp Service: Dachau
Notes:

Bittner

First Name: Edith
Birthdate: 1912
Birthplace:
Position: Aufseherin
File Number: 3-6/313
Employment Date:
Camp Service:
Notes:

Bittner

First Name: Elisabeth
Birthdate:
Birthplace:
Position: Aufseherin
File Number:
Employment Date:
Camp Service: Groß-Rosen
Notes:

Bittner

First Name: Emma
Birthdate:
Birthplace:
Position: Aufseherin
File Number:
Employment Date:
Camp Service: Groß-Rosen
Notes:

Bittner

First Name: Gertrud
Birthdate: December 1, 1909
Birthplace: Waldenburg
Position: Aufseherin
File Number: IV 410(F) AR 2629/67
Employment Date:
Camp Service: Floßenbürg; AL Plauen
Notes:

Bittner

First Name: Hildegard
Birthdate: December 6, 1922
Birthplace: Hermsdorf
Position: Aufseherin
File Number:
Employment Date: July 26, 1944
Camp Service: Groß-Rosen
Notes:

Bittner (born Ludewig)

First Name: Margarete
Birthdate: October 30, 1922
Birthplace: Mügwitz
Position: Aufseherin
File Number:
Employment Date: August 14, 1944
Camp Service: Groß-Rosen
Notes:

Bitton

First Name: Lieselotte
Birthdate:
Birthplace:
Position: Aufseherin
File Number:
Employment Date:
Camp Service:
Notes:

Bitz

First Name: Liesl
Birthdate: January 24, 1915
Birthplace: Mainz
Position: Aufseherin
File Number:
Employment Date: July 15, 1944
Camp Service: Groß-Rosen
Notes:

Blaha (or Blacha)

First Name: Frieda
Birthdate: May 6, 1922
Birthplace: Oberleutensdorf
Position: Aufseherin
File Number: IV 410 AR 3039/66(B)
Employment Date:
Camp Service: Floßenbürg; AL Venuswerke Venusberg; AL Zwodau
Notes:

Blank

First Name: Elfriede
Birthdate: April 18, 1923
Birthplace: Tiegenhof
Position:
File Number:
Employment Date: September 11, 1944
Camp Service: Stutthof
Notes:

Blaschka

First Name: Ida
Birthdate: January 16, 1921
Birthplace: Oels Doeberney
Position: Aufseherin
File Number:
Employment Date: September 28, 1944
Camp Service: Groß-Rosen
Notes: Slavic ethnicity; special permission granted to serve as an "employee of the Reich."

Blaschke

First Name: Hermine
Birthdate: July 5, 1905
Birthplace: Ober-Wernersdorf
Position: Aufseherin
File Number:
Employment Date: October 11, 1944
Camp Service: Groß-Rosen
Notes:

Blaszok (born Schneider)

First Name: Irmgard
Birthdate: January 9, 1918

Birthplace: Berlin
Position: Aufseherin
File Number:
Employment Date: August 23, 1944
Camp Service: Ravensbrück; Waldbau
Notes:

Blüml

First Name: Anna
Birthdate: July 19, 1918
Birthplace: Saack
Position: Aufseherin
File Number:
Employment Date: September 1, 1943
Camp Service: Ravensbrück
Notes:

Bluhm

First Name: Else
Birthdate:
Birthplace:
Position: Aufseherin
File Number:
Employment Date:
Camp Service:
Notes:

Blume

First Name: Erna
Birthdate:
Birthplace:
Position: Aufseherin
File Number:
Employment Date:
Camp Service:
Notes:

Blume

First Name: Irene
Birthdate:
Birthplace:
Position: Aufseherin
File Number:
Employment Date:
Camp Service:
Notes:

Blume (born Lellinger)

First Name: Maria
Birthdate:
Birthplace:
Position: Aufseherin
File Number:
Employment Date:
Camp Service:
Notes:

Boche (born Kloy)

First Name: Käte
Birthdate:
Birthplace:
Position: Aufseherin
File Number:
Employment Date:
Camp Service:
Notes:

Bock (born Kutscher)

First Name: Anna
Birthdate:
Birthplace:
Position: Aufseherin
File Number:
Employment Date:
Camp Service: Ravensbrück
Notes:

Bockelmann

First Name: Elfriede
Birthdate:
Birthplace:
Position: Aufseherin
File Number:
Employment Date:
Camp Service: Ravensbrück
Notes:

Bodem

First Name: Erna Katharina
Birthdate: October 10, 1919
Birthplace: Zwodau
Position: Aufseherin
File Number: IV 409 AR-Z 39/59
Employment Date:
Camp Service: Ravensbrück; Auschwitz; Birkenau; Lublin-Maidanek
Notes: Extradited to Poland by the American authorities after the war (no record of her fate).

Boden

First Name: Hildegard
Birthdate:
Birthplace:
Position: Aufseherin
File Number:
Employment Date:
Camp Service:
Notes:

Bodi (born Ficker)

First Name: Hermine
Birthdate:
Birthplace:
Position: Aufseherin
File Number:
Employment Date:
Camp Service:
Notes:

Boeddeker

First Name: Erika
Birthdate: July 1, 1917
Birthplace: Finkenwalde
Position:
File Number:
Employment Date: October 1, 1940
Camp Service: Ravensbrück
Notes:

Böhm (born Beckert)

First Name: Anneliese
Birthdate: October 26, 1916

Birthplace: Chemnitz
Position: Aufseherin
File Number: IV 410(F) AR 2629/67
Employment Date:
Camp Service: Floßenbürg; AL Astrawerke Chemnitz.
Notes:

Böhm (born Vent)

First Name: Gertrud
Birthdate:
Birthplace:
Position: Aufseherin
File Number:
Employment Date:
Camp Service:
Notes:

Böhme

First Name: Charlotte
Birthdate:
Birthplace:
Position: Aufseherin
File Number:
Employment Date:
Camp Service: Ravensbrück
Notes:

Böhme (born Zitzmann)

First Name: Hedwig
Birthdate: March 20, 1900
Birthplace: Erfurt
Position: Aufseherin
File Number:
Employment Date: September 19, 1944
Camp Service: Sachsenhausen
Notes:

Böhme

First Name: Käthe
Birthdate:
Birthplace:
Position: Aufseherin
File Number:
Employment Date:
Camp Service: Ravensbrück
Notes:

Böhme

First Name: Margarete
Birthdate: September 22, 1922
Birthplace: Schoßdorf
Position: Aufseherin
File Number:
Employment Date: August 25, 1944
Camp Service: Groß-Rosen
Notes:

Böhmert

First Name: Lina
Birthdate:
Birthplace:
Position: Aufseherin
File Number:
Employment Date:
Camp Service:
Notes:

Böhn

First Name: Erna
Birthdate:
Birthplace:
Position: Aufseherin
File Number:
Employment Date:
Camp Service:
Notes:

Böhnisch

First Name: Elisabeth
Birthdate: May 11, 1920
Birthplace: Wildschuetz.
Position: Aufseherin
File Number:
Employment Date: March 1, 1944
Camp Service: Groß-Rosen
Notes:

Bönisch

First Name: Hedwig
Birthdate: March 30, 1922
Birthplace: Schwarzenthal
Position: Aufseherin
File Number:
Employment Date: August 21, 1944
Camp Service: Groß-Rosen
Notes:

Börck

First Name: Anneliese
Birthdate:
Birthplace:
Position: Aufseherin
File Number:
Employment Date:
Camp Service:
Notes:

Börstler

First Name: Frieda
Birthdate: September 3, 1914
Birthplace:
Position: Aufseherin
File Number: DP3/56
Employment Date:
Camp Service: Arado Werke Wittenberg
Notes: Service as Waffen SS auxiliary granted on October 12, 1943.

Börwall

First Name: Christine
Birthdate:
Birthplace:
Position: Aufseherin
File Number:
Employment Date:
Camp Service:
Notes:

Böse

First Name: Gertrud
Birthdate: May 1, 1918
Birthplace: Breslau

Position:
File Number:
Employment Date: September 20, 1944
Camp Service: Groß-Rosen
Notes:

Bösel

First Name: Charlotte
Birthdate:
Birthplace:
Position: Aufseherin
File Number:
Employment Date:
Camp Service:
Notes:

Bösel (born Müller)

First Name: Greta
Birthdate: May 9, 1908
Birthplace: Wuppertal-Elberfeld
Position: Arbeitseinsatzfüherin
File Number:
Employment Date:
Camp Service: Ravensbrück
Notes: Helped carry out selections at Ravensbrück. Tried and sentenced to death by a British court and executed on May 2, 1947.

Böttcher

First Name: Erna
Birthdate:
Birthplace:
Position: Aufseherin
File Number:
Employment Date:
Camp Service: Bergen-Belsen
Notes:

Boge

First Name: Martha
Birthdate: February 14, 1914
Birthplace: Hamburg
Position: Aufseherin
File Number:
Employment Date: September 12, 1944
Camp Service: Groß-Rosen
Notes:

Bohl (born Hauck)

First Name: Martha
Birthdate:
Birthplace:
Position: Aufseherin
File Number:
Employment Date:
Camp Service:
Notes:

Bohm

First Name: Annemarie
Birthdate:
Birthplace:
Position: Aufseherin
File Number:
Employment Date:

Camp Service:
Notes:

Bohnat

First Name: Gerda
Birthdate: September 26, 1923
Birthplace: Magdeburg
Position: Aufseherin
File Number:
Employment Date: June 30, 1944
Camp Service: Ravensbrück
Notes:

Bohne

First Name: Gertrud
Birthdate: March 3, 1911
Birthplace: Magdeburg
Position: Aufseherin
File Number:
Employment Date: May 10, 1944
Camp Service: Ravensbrück
Notes:

Bohrer

First Name: Irma
Birthdate:
Birthplace:
Position: Aufseherin
File Number:
Employment Date:
Camp Service:
Notes:

Bolle (born Klöbel)

First Name: Gerda
Birthdate:
Birthplace:
Position: Aufseherin
File Number:
Employment Date:
Camp Service: Ravensbrück
Notes:

Bollmann (born Doritz)

First Name: Auguste
Birthdate:
Birthplace:
Position: Aufseherin
File Number:
Employment Date:
Camp Service:
Notes:

Bonath

First Name: Gerda
Birthdate:
Birthplace:
Position: Aufseherin
File Number:
Employment Date:
Camp Service:
Notes:

Bonk

First Name: Gertrud
Birthdate:

Birthplace:
Position: Aufseherin
File Number:
Employment Date:
Camp Service:
Notes:

Bommer
First Name: Berta
Birthdate: September 15, 1903
Birthplace: Kirchheim
Position: Aufseherin
File Number:
Employment Date:
Camp Service: Natzweiler
Notes:

Bonia (born Schneider)
First Name: Emmi
Birthdate: September 16, 1920
Birthplace: Zschoelkau
Position: Aufseherin
File Number: IV 406 AR 645/69
Employment Date:
Camp Service: Berlin-Neukölln
Notes:

Bork
First Name: Gerda
Birthdate: April 25, 1922
Birthplace: Danzig-Ohra
Position: Aufseherin
File Number:
Employment Date: September 11, 1944
Camp Service: Stutthof
Notes:

Borkowski (born Hoppe)
First Name: Helene
Birthdate:
Birthplace:
Position: Aufseherin
File Number:
Employment Date:
Camp Service:
Notes:

Bormann
First Name: Anneliese
Birthdate: March 20, 1922
Birthplace:
Position: Aufseherin
File Number: IV 410(F) 2629/67
Employment Date:
Camp Service: Floßenbürg; AL Freiberg
Notes:

Bormann
First Name: Juana
Birthdate: September 10, 1893
Birthplace: Birkenfelde
Position: Aufseherin
File Number:
Employment Date:
Camp Service: Ravensbrück; Auschwitz Birkenau;

Hindenburg; Bergen-Belsen
Notes: Executed by the British for war crimes on December 13, 1945.

Born (born Weisheit)
First Name: Irma
Birthdate:
Birthplace:
Position: Aufseherin
File Number:
Employment Date:
Camp Service:
Notes:

Bornberg
First Name: Elisabeth
Birthdate:
Birthplace:
Position: Aufseherin
File Number:
Employment Date:
Camp Service: Ravensbrück
Notes:

Bornschein
First Name: Lieselotte
Birthdate:
Birthplace:
Position: Aufseherin
File Number:
Employment Date:
Camp Service:
Notes:

Borrmann
First Name: Hanna
Birthdate:
Birthplace:
Position: Aufseherin
File Number:
Employment Date:
Camp Service: Auschwitz
Notes:

Bos (born van Burg)
First Name: Neeltje
Birthdate:
Birthplace:
Position: Aufseherin
File Number:
Employment Date:
Camp Service: Sachsenhausen
Notes:

Bothe
First Name: Herta
Birthdate: January 8, 1921
Birthplace: Teterow
Position: Aufseherin
File Number: 40-2/3
Employment Date:
Camp Service: Ravensbrück; Stutthof; Bergen-Belsen
Notes: Sentenced to ten years imprisonment by British, but released on December 22, 1951.

Böttcher (born Brückner)
First Name: Hermine
Birthdate: April 26, 1918
Birthplace: Wustung
Position: Aufseherin
File Number: IV 407 AR-Z 297/60
Employment Date:
Camp Service: Lublin-Majdanek; NL Neurohlau; Stutthof
Notes:

Bouillon (born Braun)
First Name: Getrud
Birthdate:
Birthplace:
Position: Aufseherin
File Number:
Employment Date:
Camp Service:
Notes:

Bouvain (born Kowalewski)
First Name: Frieda
Birthdate:
Birthplace:
Position: Aufseherin
File Number:
Employment Date:
Camp Service:
Notes:

Brach
First Name: Johanna
Birthdate:
Birthplace:
Position: Aufseherin
File Number:
Employment Date:
Camp Service:
Notes: After the war, Ravensbrück prisoners recounted Brach's vicious beatings of inmates.

Brachmann
First Name: Lieselotte
Birthdate:
Birthplace:
Position: Aufseherin
File Number:
Employment Date:
Camp Service:
Notes:

Bräsick (or Bralsick)
First Name: Anni, Emma, Erna
Birthdate: March 1, 1921
Birthplace: Münsterberg
Position: Aufseherin
File Number: IV 410(F) AR 2629/67
Employment Date: August 15, 1944
Camp Service: Floßenbürg; AL Holleischen; AL Zwodau
Notes: Arrested by Polish partisans. Fate unknown.

Bräuer
First Name: Irene
Birthdate:
Birthplace:

Position: Aufseherin
File Number:
Employment Date:
Camp Service: Ravensbrück
Notes:

Bramburger
First Name: Helga
Birthdate:
Birthplace:
Position: Aufseherin
File Number:
Employment Date:
Camp Service:
Notes:

Braml (or Bramel)
First Name: Luise
Birthdate:
Birthplace:
Position: Aufseherin
File Number:
Employment Date:
Camp Service:
Notes:

Brand
First Name: Marianne
Birthdate:
Birthplace:
Position: Aufseherin
File Number:
Employment Date:
Camp Service: Helmbrechts, Ravensbrück
Notes:

Brandel
First Name: Kläre
Birthdate:
Birthplace:
Position: Aufseherin
File Number: 410 AR 2350/65
Employment Date:
Camp Service: Floßenbürg, AL Zwodau
Notes:

Brandenburg
First Name: Gertrud
Birthdate:
Birthplace:
Position: Aufseherin
File Number:
Employment Date:
Camp Service:
Notes:

Brandenburger
First Name: Käthe
Birthdate: October 21, 1920
Birthplace: Wiesenburg
Position: Aufseherin
File Number: IV 409 AR-Z 39/59
Employment Date:
Camp Service: Ravensbrück; NL Belzig
Notes:

Brandinger

First Name: Berta
Birthdate:
Birthplace:
Position: Aufseherin
File Number:
Employment Date:
Camp Service:
Notes:

Brandl (or Brandel)

First Name: Therese ("Rosi")
Birthdate: February 1, 1909
Birthplace: Staudach (Austria)
Position: Aufseherin, Rapportführerin (Auschwitz Birkenau); *Totenkopf Sturmbann* member
File Number: IV 409 AR-Z 39/59; 9-1/704
Employment Date: September 15, 1940
Camp Service: Ravensbrück (September 1940-March 1942), Auschwitz (April 1942-December 1944), Mühlbach (December 1944-April 1945)
Notes: Extradited to Poland on February 25, 1947 and executed on December 2, 1947 for war crimes.

Brandt

First Name: Anna ("Rossa")
Birthdate: March 12, 1922
Birthplace: Wiernsheim
Position: Aufseherin
File Number: IV 429 AR-Z 130/70(B)
Employment Date:
Camp Service: Sömmerda; Ravensbrück
Notes:

Braue

First Name: Dora
Birthdate:
Birthplace:
Position: Aufseherin
File Number:
Employment Date:
Camp Service:
Notes:

Brauer

First Name: Erika
Birthdate:
Birthplace:
Position: Aufseherin
File Number:
Employment Date:
Camp Service:
Notes:

Braun

First Name: Magdalene
Birthdate: July 22, 1922
Birthplace: Neusaltz
Position: Aufseherin
File Number:
Employment Date: August 19, 1944
Camp Service: Groß-Rosen
Notes:

Braune (born Bormann)

First Name: Cäcilie
Birthdate:
Birthplace:
Position: Aufseherin
File Number:
Employment Date:
Camp Service: Ravensbrück
Notes:

Braune

First Name: Dora
Birthdate: March 6, 1913
Birthplace: Chemnitz
Position: Aufseherin
File Number: IV 410(F) AR 2629/67
Employment Date:
Camp Service: Floßenbürg; AL Chemnitz
Notes:

Braune (born Wolf)

First Name: Frieda
Birthdate:
Birthplace:
Position: Aufseherin
File Number:
Employment Date:
Camp Service: Floßenbürg
Notes:

Brechthold

First Name: Josefa
Birthdate:
Birthplace:
Position: Aufseherin
File Number:
Employment Date:
Camp Service:
Notes:

Breck

First Name: Helga
Birthdate:
Birthplace:
Position: Aufseherin
File Number:
Employment Date:
Camp Service:
Notes:

Breidenberger (born Schwemmlein)

First Name: Elisabeth
Birthdate:
Birthplace:
Position: Aufseherin
File Number:
Employment Date:
Camp Service: Ravensbrück
Notes:

Brenner

First Name: Ernestine
Birthdate: May 26, 1923
Birthplace: Augsburg
Position: Aufseherin

File Number:
Employment Date: August 15, 1944
Camp Service: Dachau
Notes:

Breuer
First Name: Auguste
Birthdate: November 3, 1903
Birthplace:
Position: Erstaufseherin
File Number: IV 410(F) AR 2629/67
Employment Date:
Camp Service: Floßenbürg; AL Mehltheuer;
AL Dresden-Reick
Notes:

Breuer
First Name: Gertrud
Birthdate:
Birthplace:
Position: Aufseherin
File Number:
Employment Date:
Camp Service:
Notes:

Breuer
First Name: Hildegard
Birthdate: November 11, 1911
Birthplace: Langenbielau
Position: Aufseherin
File Number:
Employment Date: August 1, 1944
Camp Service: Groß-Rosen
Notes:

Brillowski
First Name: Steffi
Birthdate: April 23, 1916
Birthplace: Klosterwalde
Position: Aufseherin
File Number:
Employment Date: September 11, 1944
Camp Service: Stutthof
Notes:

Brings
First Name: Luzie
Birthdate: November 22, 1905
Birthplace:
Position: Aufseherin
File Number: IV 429 AR-Z 89/71
Employment Date:
Camp Service: Ravensbrück; AL Markkleeberg
Notes:

Brinkmann (born Schüpfel or Schöpfel)
First Name: Emmi (Else Matha)
Birthdate: March 22, 1921
Birthplace: Dortmund-Brechten or Ellenbruch
Position: Aufseherin
File Number: IV 410 AR-Z 60/67
Employment Date:
Camp Service: Floßenbürg; Zwodau; AL Dresden
Notes:

Brinkmann
First Name: Ilse
Birthdate: November 4, 1923
Birthplace:
Position: Aufseherin
File Number: IV 410(F) AR 2629/67
Employment Date:
Camp Service: Floßenbürg; AL Holleischen
Notes:

Britzkow
First Name: Irma
Birthdate: June 17, 1914
Birthplace:
Position: Aufseherin
File Number: IV 410(F) AR 2629/67
Employment Date:
Camp Service: Floßenbürg; AL Chemnitz
Notes:

Brix
First Name: Adelheid
Birthdate: February 20, 1922
Birthplace: Drusens
Position: Aufseherin
File Number: IV 410(F) AR 2629/67
Employment Date:
Camp Service: Floßenbürg; AL Holleischen
Notes:

Brockmüller (born Gas)
First Name: Anneliese
Birthdate:
Birthplace:
Position: Aufseherin
File Number:
Employment Date:
Camp Service:
Notes:

Brödner (born Müller)
First Name: Wally
Birthdate:
Birthplace:
Position: Aufseherin
File Number:
Employment Date:
Camp Service: Floßenbürg
Notes:

Brosch
First Name: Else
Birthdate: December 12, 1903
Birthplace: Groß-Röhrsdorf
Position: Aufseherin
File Number:
Employment Date: August 10, 1944
Camp Service: Groß-Rosen
Notes:

Brosch
First Name: Else
Birthdate: August 5, 1920
Birthplace: Berlin
Position: Aufseherin

File Number:
Employment Date: September 1, 1944
Camp Service: Groß-Rosen
Notes:

Bruchhart
First Name: Johanna
Birthdate:
Birthplace:
Position: Aufseherin
File Number:
Employment Date:
Camp Service:
Notes:

Brückner
First Name: Else
Birthdate:
Birthplace:
Position: Aufseherin
File Number:
Employment Date:
Camp Service:
Notes:

Brückner (born Bohm)
First Name: Emma
Birthdate:
Birthplace:
Position: Aufseherin
File Number:
Employment Date:
Camp Service:
Notes:

Brückner
First Name: Hermine
Birthdate: April 26, 1918
Birthplace: Wustung (Friedland)
Position: Aufseherin
File Number:
Employment Date: October 26, 1942
Camp Service: Sachsenhausen
Notes:

Brüggemann
First Name: Margarete
Birthdate:
Birthplace:
Position: Aufseherin
File Number:
Employment Date:
Camp Service:
Notes:

Bruhn (born Heitmann)
First Name: Liselotte
Birthdate:
Birthplace:
Position: Aufseherin
File Number:
Employment Date:
Camp Service: Neuengamme
Notes:

Brummeiol
First Name: Valeria
Birthdate:
Birthplace:
Position: Aufseherin
File Number:
Employment Date:
Camp Service: Ravensbrück
Notes:

Brunke
First Name: Elfriede
Birthdate:
Birthplace:
Position: Aufseherin
File Number:
Employment Date:
Camp Service: Neuengamme
Notes:

Brunner (born Käb)
First Name: Luise
Birthdate: August 25, 1908
Birthplace: Aidhausen
Position: Aufseherin; Chef Oberaufseherin
File Number:
Employment Date: June 15, 1942
Camp Service: Auschwitz
Notes: One of only two women to ever attain the rank of *Chef Oberaufseherin* (Chief Senior Overseer).

Bruns
First Name: Franziska
Birthdate:
Birthplace:
Position: Aufseherin
File Number:
Employment Date:
Camp Service: Ravensbrück
Notes:

Brusdau (born Tietböhl)
First Name: Elfriede
Birthdate:
Birthplace:
Position: Aufseherin
File Number:
Employment Date:
Camp Service:
Notes:

Buch (born Nitker)
First Name: Luise
Birthdate:
Birthplace:
Position: Aufseherin
File Number:
Employment Date:
Camp Service:
Notes:

Buchen
First Name: Helena
Birthdate:

Birthplace:
Position: Aufseherin
File Number:
Employment Date:
Camp Service:
Notes:

Bucher

First Name: Franziska
Birthdate:
Birthplace:
Position: Aufseherin
File Number:
Employment Date:
Camp Service:
Notes:

Buchinger

First Name: Anna
Birthdate:
Birthplace:
Position: Aufseherin
File Number:
Employment Date:
Camp Service:
Notes:

Buck

First Name: Anna
Birthdate: December 11, 1920
Birthplace: Augsburg
Position: Aufseherin
File Number:
Employment Date: August 20, 1944
Camp Service: Dachau
Notes:

Buckl (or Buckel)

First Name: Martha
Birthdate:
Birthplace:
Position: Aufseherin
File Number:
Employment Date:
Camp Service:
Notes:

Buder

First Name: Ilse (Lise)
Birthdate: November 16, 1921
Birthplace: Silchow
Position: Aufseherin
File Number: IV 410 (F) AR 2629/67
Employment Date:
Camp Service: Floßenbürg; AL Hertine
Notes:

Büchtemann

First Name: Lieselotte
Birthdate:
Birthplace:
Position: Aufseherin
File Number:
Employment Date:
Camp Service:
Notes:

Bünning

First Name: Magdalene
Birthdate: January 30, 1923
Birthplace: Siedenbollentin or Demmin
Position: Aufseherin
File Number:
Employment Date: May 16, 1944
Camp Service: Sachsenhausen
Notes:

Bürkner

First Name: Eleonore
Birthdate: November 2, 1918
Birthplace: Sonnenbaum or Mohringen
Position: Aufseherin
File Number:
Employment Date: November 14, 1944
Camp Service: Sachsenhausen
Notes:

Buest

First Name: Eva
Birthdate:
Birthplace:
Position: Aufseherin
File Number:
Employment Date:
Camp Service:
Notes:

Büttner

First Name: Johanna
Birthdate: March 3, 1922
Birthplace: Leipzig
Position: Aufseherin
File Number:
Employment Date: July 1, 1944
Camp Service: Sachsenhausen
Notes:

Bugge

First Name: Anneliese
Birthdate:
Birthplace:
Position: Aufseherin
File Number:
Employment Date:
Camp Service: Groß-Rosen
Notes:

Buhrke

First Name: Irene
Birthdate:
Birthplace:
Position: Aufseherin
File Number:
Employment Date:
Camp Service: Neuengamme
Notes:

Bukowski

First Name: Charlotte
Birthdate:
Birthplace:
Position: Aufseherin
File Number:

Employment Date:
Camp Service: Ravensbrück
Notes:

Bukowski
First Name: Rosemarie
Birthdate:
Birthplace:
Position: Aufseherin
File Number:
Employment Date:
Camp Service: Stutthof
Notes:

Bunsel
First Name: Erna
Birthdate: February 13, 1922
Birthplace: Landeshut
Position: Aufseherin
File Number:
Employment Date: October 4, 1944
Camp Service: Gross-Rosen
Notes:

Burdack
First Name: Gertraud
Birthdate:
Birthplace:
Position: Aufseherin
File Number:
Employment Date:
Camp Service:
Notes:

Burg
First Name: Helene
Birthdate:
Birthplace:
Position: Aufseherin
File Number:
Employment Date:
Camp Service:
Notes:

Burghard
First Name: Elisabeth
Birthdate:
Birthplace:
Position: Aufseherin
File Number:
Employment Date:
Camp Service: Groß-Rosen
Notes:

Burkert
First Name: Hildegard
Birthdate:
Birthplace:
Position: Aufseherin
File Number:
Employment Date:
Camp Service: Gross-Rosen
Notes:

Burkl (or Burkel)
First Name: Hedwig
Birthdate: August 11, 1919
Birthplace: Fischern
Position: Aufseherin
File Number: IV 410(F) AR 2629/67
Employment Date:
Camp Service: Floßenbürg; NL Mehltheuer; AL Venusberg;
AL Zwodau
Notes:

Burkhardt
First Name: Dorothea
Birthdate:
Birthplace:
Position: Aufseherin
File Number:
Employment Date:
Camp Service:
Notes:

Burkhardt
First Name: Elfriede
Birthdate: 1921
Birthplace:
Position: Aufseherin
File Number:
Employment Date:
Camp Service: Wittenberg
Notes: Designated an SS member in her file.

Burkhardt
First Name: Lieselotte
Birthdate: November 9, 1922
Birthplace: Hamburg
Position: Aufseherin
File Number:
Employment Date: August 19, 1944
Camp Service: Groß-Rosen
Notes:

Burmeister
First Name: Juliane
Birthdate: April 23, 1920
Birthplace: Hamburg
Position: Aufseherin
File Number: IV 410(F) AR 2629/67
Employment Date:
Camp Service: Floßenbürg, AL Neu Rohlau
Notes:

Burzynski
First Name: Sophie
Birthdate:
Birthplace:
Position: Aufseherin
File Number:
Employment Date:
Camp Service:
Notes:

Busalla (or Busalle)
First Name: Marianne
Birthdate: October 13, 1919
Birthplace: Leipzig

Position: Aufseherin
File Number: IV 410(F) AR 2629/67
Employment Date:
Camp Service: Floßenbürg; AL Plauen
Notes:

Buschmann

First Name: Anni
Birthdate:
Birthplace:
Position: Aufseherin
File Number:
Employment Date:
Camp Service: Ravensbrück
Notes:

Buss

First Name: Anna
Birthdate:
Birthplace:
Position: Aufseherin
File Number:
Employment Date:
Camp Service:
Notes:

Busse

First Name: Gertrud
Birthdate: November 18, 1919
Birthplace:
Position: Aufseherin
File Number: IV 429 AR 1941/66(B)
Employment Date:
Camp Service: NL Torgau; Ravensbrück
Notes:

Busse

First Name: Ida
Birthdate:
Birthplace:
Position: Aufseherin
File Number:
Employment Date:
Camp Service:
Notes:

Busskamp

First Name: Johanna
Birthdate:
Birthplace:
Position: Aufseherin
File Number:
Employment Date:
Camp Service: Groß-Rosen
Notes:

Butzko

First Name: Else
Birthdate:
Birthplace:
Position: Aufseherin
File Number:
Employment Date:
Camp Service:
Notes:

Carls (born Kubaile)

First Name: Frieda
Birthdate: November 28, 19??
Birthplace: Grünberg
Position: Aufseherin
File Number:
Employment Date: June 1, 1944
Camp Service: Groß-Rosen
Notes:

Carus

First Name: Agathe
Birthdate:
Birthplace:
Position: Aufseherin
File Number:
Employment Date:
Camp Service: Ravensbrück
Notes:

Cerny

First Name: Barbara
Birthdate:
Birthplace:
Position: Aufseherin
File Number:
Employment Date:
Camp Service: Ravensbrück
Notes:

Cersowski

First Name: Helene
Birthdate: October 29, 1921
Birthplace: Proschwitz
Position: Aufseherin
File Number:
Employment Date: August 21, 1944
Camp Service: Groß-Rosen
Notes:

Cheuner

First Name: Hildegard
Birthdate:
Birthplace:
Position: Aufseherin
File Number:
Employment Date:
Camp Service: Groß-Rosen
Notes:

Christen

First Name: Anna
Birthdate: August 17, 1903
Birthplace: Bretgrund
Position: Aufseherin
File Number:
Employment Date: March 1, 1944
Camp Service: Groß-Rosen
Notes:

Closius

First Name: Ruth
Birthdate: July 5, 1920
Birthplace: Breslau
Position: Oberaufseherin

File Number:
Employment Date:
Camp Service: Youth Protective Custody Camp Neudeck
Notes: Executed by the British on July 29, 1948 for maltreating inmates and selecting them to be gassed. She admitted to most of the accusations in her deposition.

Ciarzinski

First Name: Apolinia
Birthdate: November 30, 1925
Birthplace: Radom
Position: Aufseherin
File Number:
Employment Date: November 3, 1944
Camp Service: Ravensbrück
Notes: Polish national; special permission granted for service as an "employee of the Reich."

Cichon

First Name: Florentine (Flora)
Birthdate: May 3, 1921
Birthplace:
Position: Erstaufseherin
File Number: IV 410(F) AR 2629/67
Employment Date:
Camp Service: Floßenbürg; Auschwitz; NL Rajsko; AL Venusberg
Notes:

Classen

First Name: Alma
Birthdate:
Birthplace:
Position: Aufseherin
File Number:
Employment Date:
Camp Service:
Notes:

Claus

First Name: Irmgard
Birthdate:
Birthplace:
Position: Aufseherin
File Number: 410 AR 3217/66
Employment Date:
Camp Service: NL Plauen
Notes:

Clausen

First Name: Beate
Birthdate:
Birthplace:
Position: Aufseherin
File Number:
Employment Date:
Camp Service: Stutthof/Danzig
Notes:

Code

First Name: Sophie
Birthdate: March 25, 1907
Birthplace: Bremen
Position: Aufseherin

File Number: 110 AR 551/97
Employment Date:
Camp Service: Ravensbrück
Notes:

Cojocar

First Name: Sieglinde
Birthdate:
Birthplace:
Position: Aufseherin
File Number:
Employment Date:
Camp Service:
Notes:

Conrad

First Name: Margarete
Birthdate:
Birthplace:
Position: Aufseherin
File Number: IV 40(F) AR 2629/67
Employment Date:
Camp Service: Floßenbürg; AL Holleischen
Notes:

Constabel

First Name: Klara
Birthdate: October 26, 1922
Birthplace: Duisburg
Position: Aufseherin
File Number:
Employment Date: August 3, 1944
Camp Service: Sachsenhausen
Notes:

Corda (born Kuchartz)

First Name: Thea
Birthdate:
Birthplace:
Position: Aufseherin
File Number:
Employment Date:
Camp Service: Floßenbürg
Notes:

Cuchardt

First Name: Gerda
Birthdate:
Birthplace:
Position: Aufseherin
File Number:
Employment Date:
Camp Service: Ravensbrück
Notes:

Cyralla

First Name: Gerda
Birthdate:
Birthplace:
Position: Aufseherin
File Number:
Employment Date:
Camp Service: Groß-Rosen
Notes:

Czeplak

First Name: Hildegard
Birthdate:
Birthplace:
Position: Aufseherin
File Number:
Employment Date:
Camp Service: Ravensbrück
Notes:

Czerwenka (born Müller)

First Name: Johanna (Hanne)
Birthdate: May 14, 1922
Birthplace:
Position: Aufseherin
File Number: IV 410(F) AR 2629/67
Employment Date:
Camp Service: Floßenbürg; AL Hertine
Notes:

Czyzewski

First Name: Elsa
Birthdate: July 2, 1922
Birthplace: Grünberg
Position: Aufseherin
File Number:
Employment Date: June 1, 1944
Camp Service: Groß-Rosen
Notes:

Dahl

First Name: Hildegard
Birthdate:
Birthplace:
Position: Aufseherin
File Number:
Employment Date:
Camp Service: Ravensbrück
Notes:

Dähn

First Name: Herta
Birthdate:
Birthplace:
Position: Aufseherin
File Number:
Employment Date:
Camp Service:
Notes:

Dännhardt

First Name: Elsa
Birthdate: Unclear: May 17, 1923, March 17, 1923, or May 11, 1923.
Birthplace: Leipzig
Position: Aufseherin
File Number: IV 410((F) AR 2629/67
Employment Date: August 15, 1944
Camp Service: Floßenbürg; AL Rochlitz; AL Wolkenburg
Notes:

Dalchow

First Name: Irmgard
Birthdate:
Birthplace:

Position: Aufseherin
File Number:
Employment Date:
Camp Service:
Notes:

Dalbors

First Name: Henriette
Birthdate: February 12, 1922
Birthplace:
Position: Aufseherin
File Number: IV 410(F) AR 2629/67
Employment Date:
Camp Service: Floßenbürg; AL Zwodau
Notes:

Damel

First Name: Elisabeth
Birthdate:
Birthplace:
Position: Aufseherin
File Number:
Employment Date:
Camp Service:
Notes:

Damgriess

First Name: Hilde
Birthdate: May 2, 1921
Birthplace: Mittweida
Position: Aufseherin
File Number: IV 410(F) AR 2629/67
Employment Date:
Camp Service: Floßenbürg; AL Graslitz
Notes:

Damm

First Name: Martha
Birthdate: April 23, 1908
Birthplace: Mühltroff or Plauen
Position: Aufseherin
File Number:
Employment Date: September 6, 1944
Camp Service: Ravensbrück, Floßenbürg, AL Chemnitz
Notes:

Dammann (born Albers)

First Name: Irmgard
Birthdate:
Birthplace:
Position: Aufseherin
File Number:
Employment Date:
Camp Service: Neuengamme
Notes:

Dammer

First Name: Maria
Birthdate:
Birthplace:
Position: Aufseherin
File Number:
Employment Date:
Camp Service:
Notes:

Dangrieß (or Danngries)

First Name: Hilde
Birthdate: July 2, 1921
Birthplace: Wolkenburg
Position: Aufseherin
File Number: IV 410(F) AR 2629/67
Employment Date: August 21, 1944
Camp Service: Floßenbürg, AL Rochlitz
Notes:

Daniszewski

First Name: Sophie
Birthdate:
Birthplace:
Position: Aufseherin
File Number:
Employment Date:
Camp Service:
Notes:

Dann

First Name: Irmgard
Birthdate: November 26, 1919
Birthplace: Crimmitsghau
Position: Aufseherin
File Number:
Employment Date: August 26, 1944
Camp Service:
Notes:

Danneboom

First Name: Christa
Birthdate:
Birthplace:
Position: Aufseherin
File Number: Order 99 B. 144
Employment Date:
Camp Service: Altendorf
Notes: Dutch national; special permission granted to serve as an "employee of the Reich."

Dannehl (born Koch)

First Name: Hertha
Birthdate: April 11, 1916
Birthplace: Berlin
Position: Aufseherin
File Number: IV 410(F) AR 2629/67
Employment Date:
Camp Service: Floßenbürg; AL Neu Rohlau
Notes:

Danz

First Name: Luise
Birthdate: December 11, 1917
Birthplace: Walldorf (Meiningen)
Position: Aufseherin
File Number:
Employment Date: January 24, 1943
Camp Service: Plazsów; Majdanek; Auschwitz Birkenau; AL Malchow
Notes: Tried by Poles after the war and sentenced to life imprisonment. Released in 1957, but tried by a German court in 1996 for an AL Malchow murder. Result of that case unknown.

Darnstädt

First Name: Liselotte
Birthdate: 1908
Birthplace:
Position: Aufseherin
File Number:
Employment Date:
Camp Service: Ravensbrück; Salzwedel
Notes:

Darnstedt

First Name: Elisabeth
Birthdate:
Birthplace:
Position: Aufseherin
File Number:
Employment Date:
Camp Service: Neuengamme
Notes:

Dauer (born Fiebig)

First Name: Hildegard
Birthdate:
Birthplace:
Position: Aufseherin
File Number:
Employment Date:
Camp Service:
Notes:

Daunhauer

First Name: Hildegard
Birthdate:
Birthplace:
Position: Aufseherin
File Number:
Employment Date:
Camp Service:
Notes:

Davam

First Name: Martha
Birthdate:
Birthplace:
Position: Aufseherin
File Number:
Employment Date:
Camp Service:
Notes:

David

First Name: Anna
Birthdate:
Birthplace:
Position: Aufseherin
File Number:
Employment Date:
Camp Service: Ravensbrück
Notes: Claimed after the war that while working at a Heinkel assembly plant she was lured into the auxiliary service with the promise of better working conditions.

de Hüber

First Name: Margarethe
Birthdate: May 12, 1910
Birthplace: Vienna
Position: Oberaufseherin
File Number: IV 410(F) AR 2629/67
Employment Date: April 15, 1939
Camp Service: Floßenbürg; AL Neu-Rohlau
Notes:

Debel

First Name: Anni
Birthdate:
Birthplace:
Position: Aufseherin
File Number:
Employment Date:
Camp Service:
Notes:

Deffner

First Name: Lieselotte
Birthdate:
Birthplace:
Position: Aufseherin
File Number:
Employment Date:
Camp Service: Ravensbrück
Notes:

Degel

First Name: Martha
Birthdate:
Birthplace:
Position: Aufseherin
File Number:
Employment Date:
Camp Service:
Notes:

Degen

First Name: Elfriede
Birthdate:
Birthplace:
Position: Aufseherin
File Number:
Employment Date:
Camp Service:
Notes:

Dehn

First Name: Eva
Birthdate:
Birthplace:
Position: Aufseherin
File Number:
Employment Date:
Camp Service:
Notes:

Dehne

First Name: Ilse
Birthdate:
Birthplace:
Position: Aufseherin

File Number:
Employment Date:
Camp Service: Ravensbrück
Notes:

Deiners

First Name: Lotte
Birthdate:
Birthplace:
Position: Aufseherin
File Number:
Employment Date:
Camp Service: Ravensbrück
Notes:

Deinert

First Name: Gertrud
Birthdate:
Birthplace:
Position: Aufseherin
File Number:
Employment Date:
Camp Service: Groß-Rosen
Notes:

Deinert

First Name: Hertha
Birthdate: October 6, 1910
Birthplace:
Position: Aufseherin
File Number: IV 410(F) AR 2629
Employment Date: September 27, 1944
Camp Service: Floßenbürg; AL Dresden Universelle
Notes:

Deliga

First Name: Edith
Birthdate:
Birthplace:
Position: Aufseherin
File Number:
Employment Date:
Camp Service:
Notes:

Deliga

First Name: Margarete (Mathilde)
Birthdate: April 13, 1922
Birthplace: Leipzig
Position: Aufseherin
File Number: 409 AR-Z 39/59
Employment Date:
Camp Service: Ravensbrück; Hassag Werke Leipzig;
Markkleeberg
Notes:

Dell'Antonia

First Name: Martha
Birthdate: September 21, 1911
Birthplace: Hartmannsdorf
Position: Aufseherin; Oberaufseherin, Kommando
Helmbrechts:
File Number: IV 410(F) AR 2629/67
Employment Date: August 25, 1944
Camp Service: Ravensbrück; Helmbrechts

Notes: Still sought by German authorities for war crimes; Waffen SS auxiliary since August 25, 1944.

Demmler

First Name: Ruth
Birthdate: September 30, 1912
Birthplace: Dresden
Position: Aufseherin
File Number: IV 410(F) 2629/67
Employment Date:
Camp Service: Floßenbürg; AL Goehle Werk Dresden
Notes:

Deneke

First Name: Marta
Birthdate:
Birthplace:
Position: Aufseherin
File Number:
Employment Date:
Camp Service:
Notes:

Dettmann (born Wiedenhöft)

First Name: Johanna
Birthdate:
Birthplace:
Position: Aufseherin
File Number:
Employment Date:
Camp Service:
Notes:

Dettmer (born Jung)

First Name: Amalie
Birthdate:
Birthplace:
Position: Aufseherin
File Number:
Employment Date:
Camp Service:
Notes:

Deubner

First Name: Ruth
Birthdate:
Birthplace:
Position: Aufseherin
File Number:
Employment Date:
Camp Service:
Notes:

Deutsch

First Name: Gertrud
Birthdate:
Birthplace:
Position: Aufseherin
File Number:
Employment Date:
Camp Service: Ravensbrück
Notes:

Deutschmann (born Lindner or Linder)

First Name: Ilse
Birthdate: April 3, 1920
Birthplace: Naundorf
Position: Aufseherin
File Number: IV 410(F) AR 2620/67
Employment Date: October 13, 1944
Camp Service: Floßenbürg; AL Freiberg
Notes:

Dickert

First Name: Anna
Birthdate: October 13, 1920
Birthplace: Flöha
Position: Aufseherin
File Number: IV 410(F) AR 2629/67
Employment Date:
Camp Service: Floßenbürg; AL Oederan
Notes:

Dickmann (or Dieckmann) (born Sowinski)

First Name: Erna
Birthdate: August 16, 1912
Birthplace: Dortmund
Position: Aufseherin
File Number: IV 410(F) AR 2629/67
Employment Date:
Camp Service: Floßenbürg; AL Zwodau; AL Holleischen; Neuengamme; AL Bändorf
Notes:

Diegruber

First Name: Josephine
Birthdate:
Birthplace:
Position: Aufseherin
File Number:
Employment Date:
Camp Service:
Notes:

Diekow (born Stökkel)

First Name: Luise
Birthdate:
Birthplace:
Position: Aufseherin
File Number:
Employment Date:
Camp Service: Ravensbrück
Notes:

Dienstbach

First Name: Annemarie
Birthdate:
Birthplace:
Position: Aufseherin
File Number:
Employment Date:
Camp Service:
Notes:

Dienwiebel

First Name: Hedwig
Birthdate: May 22, 1920
Birthplace:

Position: Aufseherin
File Number: IV 410(F) AR 2629/67
Employment Date:
Camp Service: Floßenbürg; AL Zwodau; AL Mittweida
Notes:

Dietz
First Name: Hert
Birthdate:
Birthplace:
Position: Aufseherin
File Number:
Employment Date:
Camp Service: Floßenbürg
Notes:

Dietze
First Name: Irene
Birthdate: November 3, 1923
Birthplace:
Position: Aufseherin
File Number: IV 409 AR-Z 39/59
Employment Date:
Camp Service: Ravensbrück
Notes:

Diez (or Diek)
First Name: Elly (Elli)
Birthdate: March 2, 1917
Birthplace: Kattowitz
Position: Aufseherin
File Number: IV 410(F) AR 2629/67
Employment Date: September 30, 1944
Camp Service: Floßenbürg; AL Siemens
Notes: Ethnic German; born and raised in Poland.

Dittmann
First Name: Elisabeth
Birthdate:
Birthplace:
Position: Aufseherin
File Number:
Employment Date:
Camp Service:
Notes:

Dittmer
First Name: Elsa
Birthdate:
Birthplace:
Position: Aufseherin
File Number:
Employment Date:
Camp Service: Ravensbrück
Notes:

Dittrich
First Name: Gerda
Birthdate:
Birthplace:
Position: Aufseherin
File Number:
Employment Date:
Camp Service:
Notes:

Dittrich
First Name: Marie
Birthdate:
Birthplace:
Position: Aufseherin
File Number:
Employment Date:
Camp Service: Groß-Rosen
Notes:

Dlugosch (born Herrmann)
First Name: Else
Birthdate:
Birthplace:
Position: Aufseherin
File Number:
Employment Date:
Camp Service:
Notes:

Dobler
First Name: Aloisia
Birthdate:
Birthplace:
Position: Aufseherin
File Number:
Employment Date:
Camp Service: Ravensbrück
Notes:

Dobner
First Name: Maria
Birthdate: February 1, 1920
Birthplace: Schlowitz
Position: Aufseherin
File Number: IV 410(F) 2629/67
Employment Date:
Camp Service: Floßenbürg; AL Holleischen
Notes:

Dobry
First Name: Maria
Birthdate: January 22, 1919
Birthplace:
Position: Aufseherin
File Number: IV 410(F) 2629/67
Employment Date:
Camp Service: Floßenbürg; AL Neurohlau
Notes:

Dockhorn
First Name: Gertrud
Birthdate:
Birthplace:
Position: Aufseherin
File Number:
Employment Date:
Camp Service:
Notes:

Dödler
First Name: Hanni
Birthdate:
Birthplace:
Position: Aufseherin

File Number:
Employment Date:
Camp Service:
Notes:

Döllmann
First Name: Katharina
Birthdate: October 7, 1917
Birthplace:
Position: Aufseherin
File Number: IV 409 AR-Z 39/59
Employment Date:
Camp Service: Ravensbrück; NL Markkleeburg
Notes:

Döppert (born Brähmle)
First Name: Klothilde
Birthdate:
Birthplace:
Position: Aufseherin
File Number:
Employment Date:
Camp Service: Ravensbrück
Notes:

Döring
First Name: Anneliese
Birthdate:
Birthplace:
Position: Aufseherin
File Number:
Employment Date:
Camp Service:
Notes:

Döring (born Bednarsch)
First Name: Irma
Birthdate:
Birthplace:
Position: Aufseherin
File Number:
Employment Date:
Camp Service:
Notes:

Dörnbrack
First Name: Helene
Birthdate:
Birthplace:
Position: Aufseherin
File Number:
Employment Date:
Camp Service:
Notes:

Doetsch
First Name: Mathilde
Birthdate: December 31, 1920
Birthplace:
Position: Aufseherin
File Number: IV 410(F) AR 2629/67
Employment Date:
Camp Service: Floßenbürg; AL Holleischen
Notes:

Dohlus
First Name: Elise
Birthdate: September 27, 1917
Birthplace: Neundorf
Position: Aufseherin
File Number: IV 410(F) 2629/67
Employment Date:
Camp Service: Floßenbürg, AL Plauen
Notes:

Dolaschko (or Dolatschko)
First Name: Rosa
Birthdate: July 8, 1922
Birthplace: Munich
Position: SS Helferin
File Number: 409 AR-Z 39/59
Employment Date: August 28, 1944
Camp Service: Dachau; Ravensbrück; Agfa-Camera-Werk Munich
Notes:

Dolatschko (born Mistler)
First Name: Loni
Birthdate:
Birthplace:
Position: Aufseherin
File Number:
Employment Date:
Camp Service:
Notes:

Dolp
First Name: Anna
Birthdate:
Birthplace:
Position: Aufseherin
File Number:
Employment Date:
Camp Service:
Notes:

Dominik (born Labjon)
First Name: Henriette
Birthdate: August 7, 1922
Birthplace:
Position: Aufseherin
File Number:
Employment Date:
Camp Service: Kruppwerke; Allendorf
Notes: French national; granted special permission to serve as an "employee of the Reich."

Donat (born Schmids-berger)
First Name: Johanna
Birthdate:
Birthplace:
Position: Aufseherin
File Number:
Employment Date:
Camp Service: Ravensbrück
Notes:

Dors
First Name: Margarete
Birthdate:

Birthplace:
Position: Aufseherin
File Number:
Employment Date:
Camp Service: Neue
Notes:

Dorschner
First Name: Hildegard
Birthdate:
Birthplace:
Position: Aufseherin
File Number:
Employment Date:
Camp Service:
Notes:

Dorst (or Drost) (born Wagner)
First Name: Marie
Birthdate: August 7, 1914
Birthplace: Dröschkau (Torgau)
Position: Aufseherin
File Number: IV 429 AR 1941/66(B)
Employment Date: 1940 (no day or month noted)
Camp Service: NL Torgau
Notes:

Dossler
First Name: Hilde
Birthdate: October 29, 1919
Birthplace:
Position: Aufseherin
File Number: IV 410(F) AR 2629/67
Employment Date:
Camp Service: Floßenbürg; AL Holleischen
Notes:

Drazak (born Hoffmann)
First Name: Eleonora
Birthdate:
Birthplace:
Position: Aufseherin
File Number:
Employment Date:
Camp Service: Groß-Rosen
Notes:

Drechsel
First Name: Margot
Birthdate: May 17, 1908
Birthplace: Neugersdorf
Position: Rapportaufseherin
File Number: 108 AR-Z 550/88
Employment Date: January 31, 1941
Camp Service: Ravensbrück; Auschwitz Birkenau
Notes: Was able to avoid capture after the war.

Drechsler
First Name: Ruth
Birthdate: August 3, 1920
Birthplace: Zwickau
Position: Aufseherin
File Number:
Employment Date: September 5, 1944
Camp Service: Floßenbürg
Notes: Designated an SS member in her file.

Drescher
First Name: Ruth
Birthdate:
Birthplace:
Position: Aufseherin
File Number:
Employment Date:
Camp Service: Groß-Rosen
Notes:

Drescher
First Name: Ruth
Birthdate: January 14, 1923
Birthplace: Halle
Position: Aufseherin
File Number: 3-6/313
Employment Date:
Camp Service: Wittenberg; AL Schönau, AL Leipzig
Notes: Acknowledged for distinguished service to the SS.

Dress (born Simon)
First Name: Ilse
Birthdate:
Birthplace:
Position: Aufseherin
File Number:
Employment Date:
Camp Service:
Notes:

Dressler
First Name: Käthe
Birthdate: January 1, 1902
Birthplace: Dresden
Position: Aufseherin
File Number: IV 410(F) AR 2629/67
Employment Date: August 16, 1944
Camp Service: Floßenbürg; AL Goehle-Werk Dresden
Notes:

Dreyer (born Siller)
First Name: Hedwig
Birthdate:
Birthplace:
Position: Aufseherin
File Number:
Employment Date:
Camp Service:
Notes:

Drittler
First Name: Elisabeth
Birthdate: October 17, 1899
Birthplace: Halle a.d. Saale
Position: Aufseherin
File Number: IV 410(F) AR 2629/67
Employment Date: September 30, 1944
Camp Service: Floßenbürg
Notes:

Dröst (born Martin)
First Name: Rosa
Birthdate:
Birthplace:
Position: Aufseherin

File Number:
Employment Date:
Camp Service:
Notes:

Drogge

First Name: Lucie
Birthdate:
Birthplace:
Position: Aufseherin
File Number:
Employment Date:
Camp Service: Groß-Rosen
Notes:

Droßmann

First Name: Charlotte
Birthdate:
Birthplace:
Position: Aufseherin
File Number:
Employment Date:
Camp Service: Ravensbrück
Notes:

Druselmann (born Stang)

First Name: Johanna
Birthdate:
Birthplace:
Position: Aufseherin
File Number:
Employment Date:
Camp Service:
Notes:

Dück

First Name: Margarete
Birthdate: October 13, 1922
Birthplace: Alexandrowka
Position: Aufseherin
File Number: IV 410(F) AR 2629/67
Employment Date: August 19, 1944
Camp Service: Floßenbürg; AL Zwodau; AL Graslitz
Notes: Ethnic German; born and raised in Poland.

Dürkop

First Name: Elisabeth
Birthdate:
Birthplace:
Position: Aufseherin
File Number:
Employment Date:
Camp Service:
Notes:

Durzcak

First Name: Ida
Birthdate:
Birthplace:
Position: Aufseherin
File Number:
Employment Date:
Camp Service: Groß-Rosen
Notes:

Dutz (born Schlicht)

First Name: Auguste
Birthdate:
Birthplace:
Position: Aufseherin
File Number:
Employment Date:
Camp Service:
Notes:

Duwe

First Name: Irmgard
Birthdate:
Birthplace:
Position: Aufseherin
File Number:
Employment Date:
Camp Service: Neuengamme
Notes:

Dykala (born Seyfarth)

First Name: Irmgard
Birthdate:
Birthplace:
Position: Aufseherin
File Number:
Employment Date:
Camp Service:
Notes:

Eberhardt

First Name: Else
Birthdate: September 24, 1919
Birthplace: Weissbach
Position: Aufseherin
File Number: IV 410(F) AR 2629/67
Employment Date: September 30, 1944
Camp Service: Floßenbürg, AL Holleischen
Notes:

Eberhardt

First Name: Martha
Birthdate: January 12, 1902
Birthplace: Nuremberg
Position: Aufseherin
File Number:
Employment Date: September 30, 1944
Camp Service: Floßenbürg
Notes:

Eberstein

First Name: Ursula
Birthdate: November 22, 1922
Birthplace:
Position: Aufseherin
File Number: IV 404 AR 605/67
Employment Date:
Camp Service: NL Hamburg-Sasel
Notes:

Ebert

First Name: Charlotte
Birthdate:
Birthplace:
Position: Aufseherin

File Number: IV 402 AR-Z 37/58
Employment Date:
Camp Service: Auschwitz Birkenau
Notes: Supposedly tried in Poland, but her fate is not certain.

Ebert
First Name: Elli
Birthdate:
Birthplace:
Position: Aufseherin
File Number: IV 429 AR 1981/66
Employment Date:
Camp Service: Buchenwald; Ravensbrück
Notes:

Ebert
First Name: Marie
Birthdate:
Birthplace:
Position: Aufseherin
File Number:
Employment Date:
Camp Service:
Notes:

Echtermeyer
First Name: Vera
Birthdate:
Birthplace:
Position: Aufseherin
File Number:
Employment Date:
Camp Service: Sachsenhausen
Notes:

Eckert
First Name: Anni
Birthdate: August 29, 1914
Birthplace: Nuremberg
Position: Aufseherin
File Number: IV 410(F) AR 2629/67
Employment Date: September 30, 1944
Camp Service: Floßenbürg; AL Graslitz; AL Holleischen; Nuremberg
Notes:

Eckert
First Name: Elisabeth
Birthdate:
Birthplace:
Position: Aufseherin
File Number:
Employment Date:
Camp Service:
Notes:

Eckert
First Name: Helene
Birthdate:
Birthplace:
Position: Aufseherin
File Number:
Employment Date:
Camp Service: Ravensbrück
Notes:

Eckl
First Name: Therese
Birthdate:
Birthplace:
Position: Aufseherin
File Number:
Employment Date:
Camp Service:
Notes:

Eckle
First Name: Marianne
Birthdate:
Birthplace:
Position: Aufseherin
File Number:
Employment Date:
Camp Service:
Notes:

Eckold
First Name: Else
Birthdate:
Birthplace:
Position: Aufseherin
File Number:
Employment Date:
Camp Service:
Notes:

Edel
First Name: Margarete
Birthdate:
Birthplace:
Position: Aufseherin
File Number:
Employment Date:
Camp Service:
Notes:

Eder
First Name: Maria
Birthdate: February 24, 1915
Birthplace: Straubing
Position: Aufseherin
File Number: 409 AR-Z 39/59
Employment Date:
Camp Service: Ravensbrück; Agfa Camera-Werke Munich; Dachau
Notes: Appears in the files from Ravensbrück, but denied being trained there.

Edler
First Name: Gertrude
Birthdate:
Birthplace:
Position: Aufseherin
File Number:
Employment Date:
Camp Service:
Notes:

Egemann
First Name: Johanna
Birthdate:
Birthplace:

Position: Aufseherin
File Number:
Employment Date:
Camp Service:
Notes:

Eggerdinger
First Name: Martha
Birthdate:
Birthplace:
Position: Aufseherin
File Number:
Employment Date:
Camp Service:
Notes:

Eggers
First Name: Helga
Birthdate:
Birthplace:
Position: Aufseherin
File Number:
Employment Date:
Camp Service:
Notes:

Eggerstedt (born Pawelzick)
First Name: Herta
Birthdate:
Birthplace:
Position: Aufseherin
File Number: IV 429 AR 1959/66
Employment Date:
Camp Service: NL Essen
Notes:

Ehlert
First Name: Herta
Birthdate: March 26, 1905
Birthplace: Berlin
Position: Aufseherin
File Number:
Employment Date: November 15, 1939
Camp Service: Bergen-Belsen
Notes: Tried for war crimes by the British, claimed that she was forced to undergo Ravensbrück training as a punishment for being too lenient to Polish inmates at *Arbeitslager* ("work camp").

Ehrenberg
First Name: Anna-Luise
Birthdate:
Birthplace:
Position: Aufseherin
File Number:
Employment Date:
Camp Service:
Notes:

Eichwalder
First Name: Elsa
Birthdate:
Birthplace:
Position: Aufseherin

File Number:
Employment Date:
Camp Service:
Notes:

Eickhoff
First Name: Elisabeth
Birthdate:
Birthplace:
Position: Aufseherin
File Number:
Employment Date:
Camp Service: Groß-Rosen
Notes:

Eidam
First Name: Gerda
Birthdate:
Birthplace:
Position: Aufseherin
File Number:
Employment Date:
Camp Service: Neuengamme
Notes:

Eifert
First Name: Anna
Birthdate:
Birthplace:
Position: Aufseherin
File Number:
Employment Date:
Camp Service: Neuengamme
Notes:

Eifler
First Name: Elisabeth (Lisbeth)
Birthdate: November 2, 1910
Birthplace: Dresden
Position: Aufseherin
File Number: IV 410(F) AR 2629/67
Employment Date: August 16, 1944
Camp Service: Floßenbürg; AL Goehle-Werke Dresden
Notes:

Eilenberger
First Name: Bringfriede
Birthdate:
Birthplace:
Position: Aufseherin
File Number:
Employment Date:
Camp Service:
Notes:

Eimert
First Name: Martha
Birthdate:
Birthplace:
Position: Aufseherin
File Number:
Employment Date:
Camp Service:
Notes:

Eisenhut (born Fikkert)

First Name: Elfriede
Birthdate: June 24, 1920
Birthplace: Chemnitz
Position: Aufseherin
File Number: IV 410(F) AR 2629/67
Employment Date: August 16, 1944
Camp Service: Floßenbürg; AL Astrawerke Chemnitz
Notes:

Eiser

First Name: Irene
Birthdate:
Birthplace:
Position: Aufseherin
File Number:
Employment Date:
Camp Service: Floßenbürg
Notes:

Ekhardt

First Name: Anneliese
Birthdate:
Birthplace:
Position: Aufseherin
File Number:
Employment Date:
Camp Service: Ravensbrück
Notes:

Ellermann (born Harant)

First Name: Adolfine
Birthdate:
Birthplace:
Position: Aufseherin
File Number:
Employment Date:
Camp Service:
Notes:

Ellerwald

First Name: Elisabeth
Birthdate:
Birthplace:
Position: Aufseherin
File Number:
Employment Date:
Camp Service:
Notes:

Elm

First Name: Erna
Birthdate: August 8, 1922
Birthplace:
Position: Aufseherin
File Number: IV 409 AR-Z 39/59
Employment Date:
Camp Service: Ravensbrück; Meuselwitz
Notes:

Elsebith

First Name: Frieda
Birthdate:
Birthplace:
Position: Aufseherin

File Number:
Employment Date:
Camp Service: Groß-Rosen
Notes:

Elsen

First Name: Josefine
Birthdate:
Birthplace:
Position: Aufseherin
File Number:
Employment Date:
Camp Service:
Notes:

Elssner

First Name: Else
Birthdate: October 8, 1922
Birthplace: Reinsdorf
Position: Aufseherin
File Number:
Employment Date: August 25, 1944
Camp Service: Floßenbürg
Notes:

Elste

First Name: Ingeborg
Birthdate:
Birthplace:
Position: Aufseherin
File Number:
Employment Date:
Camp Service:
Notes:

Ende

First Name: Gerda
Birthdate: October 15, 1919
Birthplace: Thomasdorf
Position: Aufseherin
File Number:
Employment Date: October 4, 1944
Camp Service: Groß-Rosen
Notes:

Ende

First Name: Selma
Birthdate:
Birthplace:
Position: Aufseherin
File Number:
Employment Date:
Camp Service: Groß-Rosen
Notes:

Enders (born Meixner)

First Name: Annemarie
Birthdate: March 17, 1914
Birthplace:
Position: Aufseherin
File Number: IV 409 AR-Z 39/59
Employment Date:
Camp Service: Ravensbrück; Meuselwitz
Notes:

Endres
First Name: Lotte
Birthdate: August 21, 1920
Birthplace: Behringersdorf
Position: Aufseherin
File Number: IV 410(F) AR 2629/67
Employment Date:
Camp Service: Floßenbürg; AL Holleischen; AL Graslitz
Notes:

Engel
First Name: Hedwig
Birthdate:
Birthplace:
Position: Aufseherin
File Number:
Employment Date:
Camp Service:
Notes:

Engel
First Name: Helene
Birthdate:
Birthplace:
Position: Aufseherin
File Number:
Employment Date:
Camp Service:
Notes:

Engel
First Name: Hertha
Birthdate:
Birthplace:
Position: Aufseherin
File Number:
Employment Date:
Camp Service: Groß-Rosen
Notes:

Engel
First Name: Martha
Birthdate: February 13, 1921
Birthplace: Berlin
Position: Aufseherin
File Number:
Employment Date: October 13, 1944
Camp Service: Groß-Rosen
Notes:

Engel (born Schulze)
First Name: Käthe
Birthdate:
Birthplace:
Position: Aufseherin
File Number:
Employment Date:
Camp Service: Ravensbrück
Notes:

Engeleit
First Name: Frieda
Birthdate:
Birthplace:
Position: Aufseherin

File Number:
Employment Date:
Camp Service: Ravensbrück
Notes:

Engelmann
First Name: Anna
Birthdate: January 20, 1910
Birthplace: Neusals
Position: Aufseherin
File Number:
Employment Date: October 11, 1944
Camp Service: Groß-Rosen
Notes:

Engelmann (born Mylius)
First Name: Charlotte
Birthdate:
Birthplace:
Position: Aufseherin
File Number:
Employment Date:
Camp Service: Neuengamme
Notes:

Engels (born Pilz)
First Name: Wilhelmine
Birthdate:
Birthplace:
Position: Aufseherin
File Number:
Employment Date:
Camp Service:
Notes:

Enke
First Name: Edith
Birthdate:
Birthplace:
Position: Aufseherin
File Number:
Employment Date:
Camp Service:
Notes:

Enke
First Name: Lotte
Birthdate: October 24, 1921
Birthplace: Haan or Berlin
Position: Aufseherin
File Number: IV 410 (F) AR 2629/67
Employment Date: September 8, 1944
Camp Service: Floßenbürg; Groß-Rosen; AL Graslitz
Notes:

Enneberg
First Name: Helga
Birthdate: May 20, 1923
Birthplace:
Position: Aufseherin
File Number: IV 429 AR 1959/66
Employment Date:
Camp Service: NL Essen
Notes:

Enschel

First Name: Ingeborg
Birthdate: November 4, 1922
Birthplace: Welbsleben
Position: Aufseherin
File Number:
Employment Date: December 19, 1944
Camp Service: Ravensbrück
Notes:

Erben

First Name: Elfriede
Birthdate: July 19, 1923
Birthplace: Niederaltstadt
Position: Aufseherin
File Number:
Employment Date: March 1, 1944
Camp Service: Groß-Rosen
Notes:

Erben

First Name: Erna
Birthdate: June 5, 1923
Birthplace: Hackelsdorf
Position: Aufseherin
File Number:
Employment Date: October 24, 1944
Camp Service: Groß-Rosen
Notes:

Erben

First Name: Margarethe
Birthdate: March 2, 1924
Birthplace: Vordermastig
Position: Aufseherin
File Number:
Employment Date: March 1, 1944
Camp Service: Groß-Rosen
Notes:

Erdmann

First Name: Helma
Birthdate:
Birthplace:
Position: Aufseherin
File Number:
Employment Date:
Camp Service: Ravensbrück
Notes:

Erkens (born Kretschmer)

First Name: Ursula
Birthdate:
Birthplace:
Position: Aufseherin
File Number:
Employment Date:
Camp Service:
Notes:

Erler

First Name: Elfriede
Birthdate:
Birthplace:
Position: Aufseherin
File Number:
Employment Date:
Camp Service:
Notes:

Erler

First Name: Irmtraud
Birthdate: April 12, 1923
Birthplace:
Position: Aufseherin
File Number: IV 409 AR-Z 39/59
Employment Date:
Camp Service: Ravensbrück; Meuselwitz
Notes:

Erler

First Name: Marianne
Birthdate: October 27, 1918
Birthplace: Groß Stepnitz
Position: Aufseherin
File Number:
Employment Date: August 16, 1944
Camp Service: Ravensbrück
Notes:

Ermuth

First Name: Annemarie
Birthdate: July 21, 1922
Birthplace: Stolbergsdorf
Position: Aufseherin
File Number:
Employment Date: March 1, 1944
Camp Service: Groß-Rosen
Notes:

Ernst

First Name: Elsbeth
Birthdate: November 13, 1920
Birthplace: Stieten
Position: Aufseherin
File Number:
Employment Date: November 7, 1944
Camp Service: Ravensbrück
Notes:

Ernst

First Name: Gerda
Birthdate: August 30, 1923
Birthplace: Haynau
Position: SS Helferin; Aufseherin
File Number: IV 402 AR-Z 37/58
Employment Date:
Camp Service: Auschwitz
Notes:

Ertel

First Name: Dorothea
Birthdate: December 23, 1907
Birthplace: Breslau
Position: Aufseherin
File Number:
Employment Date: October 5, 1944
Camp Service: Groß-Rosen
Notes:

Ertelt

First Name: Selma
Birthdate:
Birthplace:
Position: Aufseherin
File Number:
Employment Date:
Camp Service:
Notes:

Ertlmeier (or Ertelmeyer)

First Name: Elisabeth
Birthdate: October 14, 1917
Birthplace: Freising
Position: Aufseherin
File Number:
Employment Date: September 10, 1944
Camp Service: Ravensbrück
Notes:

Eschwalder

First Name: Elsa
Birthdate:
Birthplace:
Position: Aufseherin
File Number:
Employment Date:
Camp Service: Sachsenhausen
Notes:

Esper

First Name: Charlotte
Birthdate:
Birthplace:
Position: Aufseherin
File Number:
Employment Date:
Camp Service: Groß-Rosen
Notes:

Essmann

First Name: Marianne
Birthdate: September 30, 1921
Birthplace: Köln
Position: Oberaufseherin
File Number: IV 410(F) AR 2629/67
Employment Date:
Camp Service: Floßenbürg; AL Rochlitz; AL Graslitz
Notes:

Essmann

First Name: Maud
Birthdate:
Birthplace:
Position: Aufseherin
File Number:
Employment Date:
Camp Service: Neuengamme
Notes:

Euchner

First Name: Emma
Birthdate: June 19, 1916
Birthplace:
Position: Aufseherin

File Number:
Employment Date: September 13, 1944
Camp Service: Groß-Rosen
Notes:

Eulink

First Name: Klara
Birthdate: December 4, 1907
Birthplace: Mirordorf
Position: Aufseherin
File Number:
Employment Date: October 30, 1943
Camp Service: Ravensbrück
Notes:

Exner

First Name: Erna
Birthdate: February 17, 1905
Birthplace: Görlitz
Position: Aufseherin
File Number:
Employment Date: September 23, 1944
Camp Service: Groß-Rosen
Notes:

Fabritzek

First Name: Agnes
Birthdate: 1908
Birthplace:
Position: Aufseherin
File Number:
Employment Date:
Camp Service: Ravensbrück; Polte
Notes: Sentenced to five years imprisonment by the East Germans for maltreatment of prisoners.

Fabritzel (born Römer)

First Name: Agnes
Birthdate:
Birthplace:
Position: Aufseherin
File Number:
Employment Date:
Camp Service:
Notes:

Färber

First Name: Agnes
Birthdate: February 20, 1916
Birthplace: Lauterbach
Position: Aufseherin
File Number:
Employment Date: August 1, 1944
Camp Service: Groß-Rosen
Notes:

Fäskorn (born Ohde)

First Name: Ella
Birthdate: May 7, 1905
Birthplace: Feterow
Position: Aufseherin
File Number:
Employment Date: September 13, 1944
Camp Service: Ravensbrück
Notes:

Fahle

First Name: Magda
Birthdate: November 26, 1910
Birthplace: Bregeholz
Position: Aufseherin
File Number:
Employment Date: October 30, 1944
Camp Service: Groß-Rosen
Notes:

Falke

First Name: Erika
Birthdate:
Birthplace:
Position: Aufseherin
File Number:
Employment Date:
Camp Service:
Notes:

Falke

First Name: Luise
Birthdate:
Birthplace:
Position: Aufseherin
File Number:
Employment Date:
Camp Service: Neuengamme
Notes:

Farchy

First Name: Vera
Birthdate: October 19, 1921
Birthplace: Vienna
Position: Aufseherin
File Number:
Employment Date: September 11, 1944
Camp Service: Ravensbrück
Notes:

Farke

First Name: Ilse
Birthdate:
Birthplace:
Position: Aufseherin
File Number:
Employment Date:
Camp Service: Neuengamme
Notes:

Fath

First Name: Wilma
Birthdate: October 8, 1913
Birthplace: Bad Ragaz
Position: Aufseherin
File Number: IV 409 AR-Z 39/59
Employment Date: September 19, 1944
Camp Service: Ravensbrück (three week training course);
NL Allendorf
Notes: Denied participation in maltreatment of prisoners before denazification hearing.

Faust

First Name: Käthe
Birthdate: February 25 (no year noted in her file).

Birthplace: Löden
Position: Aufseherin
File Number:
Employment Date: November 25, 1944
Camp Service: Ravensbrück
Notes:

Febel

First Name: Viktoria
Birthdate:
Birthplace:
Position: Aufseherin
File Number:
Employment Date:
Camp Service:
Notes:

Fechner

First Name: Klara
Birthdate: June 25, 1915
Birthplace:
Position: Aufseherin
File Number: IV 410(F) AR 2629/67
Employment Date:
Camp Service: Floßenbürg; AL Dresden-Reick
Notes:

Fechner (born Bredlow)

First Name: Klara
Birthdate: June 25, 1910
Birthplace: Friedrichsort
Position: Aufseherin
File Number:
Employment Date: June 1, 1944
Camp Service: Groß-Rosen
Notes:

Feege

First Name: Gertrud
Birthdate:
Birthplace:
Position: Aufseherin
File Number:
Employment Date:
Camp Service:
Notes:

Fehlings

First Name: Else-Maria
Birthdate:
Birthplace:
Position: Aufseherin
File Number:
Employment Date:
Camp Service:
Notes:

Fehlner

First Name: Margarete
Birthdate: February 14, 1922
Birthplace: Hirschau
Position: Aufseherin
File Number:
Employment Date: September 26, 1944
Camp Service: Groß-Rosen
Notes:

Fehmer
First Name: Lisa
Birthdate: September 1921 (no day noted in her file).
Birthplace: Dömitz
Position: Auseherin
File Number:
Employment Date: November 7, 1944
Camp Service: Ravensbrück
Notes:

Feige
First Name: Johanna
Birthdate: January 9, 1944
Birthplace: Groß-Rosen
Position: Aufseherin
File Number:
Employment Date: October 3, 1944
Camp Service: Groß-Rosen
Notes:

Feinbube
First Name: Selma
Birthdate: April 8, 1910
Birthplace: Neusaltz
Position: Aufseherin
File Number:
Employment Date: June 1, 1944
Camp Service: Groß-Rosen
Notes:

Feind
First Name: Charlotte
Birthdate: January 1, 1922
Birthplace: Berlin
Position: Aufseherin
File Number:
Employment Date: October 30, 1944
Camp Service: Ravensbrück
Notes:

Feind
First Name: Erna
Birthdate: March 12, 1918
Birthplace: Berlin
Position: Aufseherin
File Number:
Employment Date: August 31, 1944
Camp Service: Ravensbrück
Notes:

Feinhube (born Wandrey)
First Name: Anna
Birthdate:
Birthplace:
Position: Aufseherin
File Number:
Employment Date:
Camp Service:
Notes:

Feist
First Name: Emma
Birthdate: April 3, 1905
Birthplace: Trautenau
Position: Aufseherin

File Number:
Employment Date: September 28, 1944
Camp Service: Groß-Rosen
Notes:

Feist
First Name: Gertrud
Birthdate: May 31, 1918
Birthplace: Neu-Gebhardsdorf
Position: Aufseherin
File Number:
Employment Date: August 16, 1944
Camp Service: Groß-Rosen
Notes:

Felchner
First Name: Dora or (Dorle)
Birthdate:
Birthplace:
Position: Aufseherin
File Number: IV 429 AR-Z 89/71
Employment Date:
Camp Service: NL Markkleeberg; Hasag-Werke Leipzig
Notes:

Feldtner
First Name: Ursula
Birthdate: September 16, 1923
Birthplace: Dortmund
Position: Aufseherin
File Number:
Employment Date: September 18, 1944
Camp Service: Ravensbrück
Notes:

Fellmann
First Name: Else
Birthdate:
Birthplace:
Position: Aufseherin
File Number:
Employment Date:
Camp Service:
Notes:

Felsmann
First Name: Marta
Birthdate:
Birthplace:
Position: Aufseherin
File Number:
Employment Date:
Camp Service: Groß-Rosen
Notes:

Felsmann
First Name: Wally
Birthdate:
Birthplace:
Position: Aufseherin
File Number:
Employment Date:
Camp Service: Groß-Rosen
Notes:

Fest
First Name: Anna
Birthdate: 1920 (month and day unlisted)
Birthplace: Sonnenfeld
Position: Aufseherin
File Number:
Employment Date:
Camp Service: Ravensbrück; Allendorf; Sömmerda
Notes: Tried in 1947 by the Americans for war crimes and acquitted. Her story is documented in *Frauen: German Women Recall the Third Reich.*

Festbaum (born Kriehebauer)
First Name: Maria
Birthdate:
Birthplace:
Position: Aufseherin
File Number:
Employment Date:
Camp Service: Ravensbrück
Notes:

Fetters (born Zschunke)
First Name: Ilse
Birthdate:
Birthplace:
Position: Aufseherin
File Number:
Employment Date:
Camp Service:
Notes:

Fey
First Name: Georgine
Birthdate:
Birthplace:
Position: Aufseherin
File Number:
Employment Date:
Camp Service:
Notes:

Fichtner
First Name: Anna
Birthdate: July 9, 1924
Birthplace: Parschnitz
Position: Aufseherin
File Number:
Employment Date: April 15, 1944
Camp Service: Groß-Rosen
Notes:

Fiebig
First Name: Anna
Birthdate: July 11, 1920
Birthplace: Grünberg
Position: Aufseherin
File Number:
Employment Date: June 1, 1944
Camp Service: Groß-Rosen
Notes:

Fickert
First Name: Helene

Birthdate: August 26, 1904
Birthplace: Plauen
Position: Aufseherin
File Number: IV 410 AR-Z 94/70(B)
Employment Date:
Camp Service: NL Nuremberg
Notes:

Fiedler
First Name: Erika
Birthdate: September 4, 1923
Birthplace: Grünberg
Position: Aufseherin
File Number:
Employment Date: June 1, 1944
Camp Service: Groß-Rosen
Notes:

Fiedler
First Name: Hildegard
Birthdate: September 26, 1922
Birthplace: Jibka
Position: Aufseherin
File Number:
Employment Date: September 13, 1944
Camp Service: Groß-Rosen
Notes: Ethnic German; born and raised in Croatia.

Fiedler
First Name: Luise
Birthdate: March 29, 1909
Birthplace: Mügeln near Dresden
Position: Aufseherin
File Number: IV 410(F) AR 2629/67
Employment Date:
Camp Service: Floßenbürg; AL Goehle-Werk Dresden
Notes:

Fiedler (born Rudolf)
First Name: Maria
Birthdate:
Birthplace:
Position: Aufseherin
File Number:
Employment Date:
Camp Service:
Notes:

Finck
First Name: Gertrud
Birthdate: November 16, 1922
Birthplace: Hamburg
Position: Aufseherin
File Number:
Employment Date: April 1, 1944
Camp Service: Ravensbrück
Notes:

Fincke (born Blank)
First Name: Helene
Birthdate:
Birthplace:
Position: Aufseherin
File Number:
Employment Date:

Camp Service:
Notes:

Findeigen
First Name: Margarete
Birthdate: July 9, 1908
Birthplace: Berlin
Position: Aufseherin
File Number:
Employment Date: August 12, 1944
Camp Service: Groß-Rosen
Notes:

Finger
First Name: Anneliese
Birthdate:
Birthplace:
Position: Aufseherin
File Number:
Employment Date:
Camp Service: Ravensbrück
Notes:

Finger
First Name: Elfriede
Birthdate: August 27, 1923
Birthplace: Frankenberg
Position: Aufseherin
File Number:
Employment Date: September 8, 1944
Camp Service: Ravensbrück
Notes:

Finger
First Name: Hildegard
Birthdate: September 1, 1921
Birthplace: Thotenburg
Position: Aufseherin
File Number:
Employment Date: September 1, 1944
Camp Service: Groß-Rosen
Notes:

Fink
First Name: Marie
Birthdate:
Birthplace:
Position: Aufseherin
File Number:
Employment Date:
Camp Service:
Notes:

Finnern (born Wermann)
First Name: Hildegard
Birthdate:
Birthplace:
Position: Aufseherin
File Number:
Employment Date:
Camp Service: Neuengamme
Notes:

Finster (born Schulz)
First Name: Emmi

Birthdate: December 13, 1909
Birthplace: Liedemaiden
Position: Aufseherin
File Number:
Employment Date: September 12, 1944
Camp Service: Ravensbrück
Notes:

Fischbach
First Name: Elfriede
Birthdate: February 25, 1916
Birthplace: Dresden
Position: Aufseherin
File Number: IV 410(F) AR 2629/67
Employment Date:
Camp Service: Floßenbürg; AL Goehle-Werk Dresden
Notes:

Fischer
First Name: Elfriede
Birthdate: March 16, 1923
Birthplace: Neu-Weistritz
Position: Aufseherin
File Number:
Employment Date: September 1, 1944
Camp Service: Groß-Rosen
Notes:

Fischer
First Name: Else
Birthdate: September 11, 1907
Birthplace: Berlin
Position: Aufseherin
File Number: IV 410(F) AR 2629/67
Employment Date: September 8, 1944
Camp Service: Floßenbürg; Groß-Rosen; AL Graslitz
Notes:

Fischer
First Name: Emma
Birthdate:
Birthplace:
Position: Aufseherin
File Number:
Employment Date:
Camp Service:
Notes:

Fischer
First Name: Ernestine
Birthdate: March 12, 1922
Birthplace: Schneidemühl
Position: Aufseherin
File Number: IV 410(F) AR 2629/67
Employment Date:
Camp Service: Floßenbürg; AL Neu Rohlau, AL Dresden-Goehle-Werk, AL Hertine
Notes:

Fischer
First Name: Irene
Birthdate: February 12, 1923
Birthplace: Neue Welt
Position: Aufseherin
File Number:

Employment Date: August 8, 1944
Camp Service: Groß-Rosen
Notes: *Neue Welt* may be the name of a small town or village, but in all likelihood she was born in a country of the *"New World."*

Fischer

First Name: Lina
Birthdate:
Birthplace:
Position: Aufseherin
File Number:
Employment Date:
Camp Service:
Notes:

Fischer

First Name: Martha
Birthdate: December 11, 1910
Birthplace: Harnsdorf
Position: Aufseherin
File Number:
Employment Date: August 24, 1944
Camp Service: Groß-Rosen
Notes:

Fischer

First Name: Martha
Birthdate: June 29, 1922
Birthplace: Münchberg
Position: Aufseherin
File Number:
Employment Date: August 17, 1944
Camp Service: Ravensbrück
Notes:

Fischer

First Name: Pauline
Birthdate: November 10, 1908
Birthplace:
Position: Aufseherin
File Number: IV 410(F) AR 2629/67
Employment Date:
Camp Service: Floßenbürg, AL Hertine
Notes:

Fischer

First Name: Waltraut
Birthdate:
Birthplace:
Position: Aufseherin
File Number:
Employment Date:
Camp Service:
Notes:

Fischer (born Krisbel)

First Name: Charlotte
Birthdate:
Birthplace:
Position: Aufseherin
File Number:
Employment Date:
Camp Service:
Notes:

Fischkert

First Name: Helene
Birthdate:
Birthplace:
Position: Aufseherin
File Number:
Employment Date:
Camp Service: Ravensbrück
Notes:

Fittkow

First Name: Luise
Birthdate: November 12, 1922
Birthplace: Posen
Position: Aufseherin
File Number:
Employment Date: August 16, 1944
Camp Service: Ravensbrück
Notes:

Fitzner

First Name: Lisbeth
Birthdate:
Birthplace:
Position: Aufseherin
File Number:
Employment Date:
Camp Service: Groß-Rosen
Notes:

Flechtner

First Name: Elfriede
Birthdate: October 25, 1911
Birthplace: Harthau
Position: Aufseherin
File Number:
Employment Date: August 1, 1944
Camp Service: Groß-Rosen
Notes:

Fleischer

First Name: Hertha
Birthdate: October 11, 1920
Birthplace:
Position: Aufseherin
File Number: IV 410(F) AR 2629/67
Employment Date:
Camp Service: Floßenbürg; NL Holleischen; AL Freiberg
Notes:

Flige

First Name: Johanna
Birthdate:
Birthplace:
Position: Aufseherin
File Number:
Employment Date:
Camp Service:
Notes:

Florianschütz (or Florianschitz?)

First Name: Käthe (or Katharina)
Birthdate: July 22, 1916
Birthplace: Villach
Position: Aufseherin

File Number: IV 410(F) AR 2629/67
Employment Date: September 20, 1943
Camp Service: Floßenbürg; AL Neu Rohlau
Notes:

Flott (born Leupold)

First Name: Martha
Birthdate: March 26, 1905
Birthplace: Peterswaldau
Position: Aufseherin
File Number:
Employment Date: April 15, 1944
Camp Service: Groß-Rosen
Notes:

Focht

First Name: Mathilde
Birthdate:
Birthplace:
Position: Aufseherin
File Number:
Employment Date:
Camp Service:
Notes:

Fochtmann

First Name: Isolde
Birthdate: May 1, 1921
Birthplace:
Position: Aufseherin
File Number: IV 410(F) Ar 2628/67
Employment Date:
Camp Service: Floßenbürg; AL Holleischen
Notes:

Fock

First Name: Wilhelmine
Birthdate: January 25, 1918
Birthplace: Oberglinde
Position: Aufseherin
File Number:
Employment Date: August 18, 1944
Camp Service: Floßenbürg
Notes:

Förster

First Name: Anna
Birthdate: December 1, 1913
Birthplace: Parschnitz
Position: Aufseherin
File Number:
Employment Date: September 13, 1944
Camp Service: Groß-Rosen
Notes:

Förster

First Name: Elfriede
Birthdate:
Birthplace:
Position: Aufseherin
File Number:
Employment Date:
Camp Service: Floßenbürg
Notes:

Förster

First Name: Ida
Birthdate: May 15, 1902
Birthplace: Blumendorf
Position: Aufseherin
File Number:
Employment Date: August 16, 1944
Camp Service: Groß-Rosen; Bergen-Belsen
Notes:

Förster

First Name: Ilse
Birthdate: September 2, 1922
Birthplace: Neusalz
Position: Aufseherin
File Number:
Employment Date: August 18, 1944
Camp Service: Groß-Rosen; Bergen–Belsen
Notes: Sentenced to 10 years imprisonment by the British in November 1945 for war crimes

Fohlert

First Name: Antonie
Birthdate: November 25, 1920
Birthplace: Bausnitz
Position: Aufseherin
File Number:
Employment Date: September 28, 1944
Camp Service: Groß-Rosen
Notes:

Forstenberg

First Name: Charlotte
Birthdate:
Birthplace:
Position: Aufseherin
File Number:
Employment Date:
Camp Service:
Notes:

Foxius

First Name: Luise
Birthdate:
Birthplace:
Position: Aufseherin
File Number:
Employment Date:
Camp Service:
Notes:

Fräde

First Name: Edith
Birthdate: December 6, 1915
Birthplace: Berlin
Position: Aufseherin
File Number:
Employment Date: September 1, 1940
Camp Service: Ravensbrück
Notes:

Frahm

First Name: Henny
Birthdate: March 24, 1918
Birthplace: Tresteierhagen/Kiel

Position: Aufseherin
File Number:
Employment Date: December 15, 1943
Camp Service: Sachsenhausen
Notes:

Frank

First Name: Berta
Birthdate: April 9, 1900
Birthplace: Hamburg-Altona
Position: Aufseherin
File Number:
Employment Date: December 15, 1944
Camp Service: Groß-Rosen
Notes:

Frank

First Name: Henriette
Birthdate:
Birthplace:
Position: Aufseherin
File Number:
Employment Date:
Camp Service:
Notes:

Franke

First Name: Erna
Birthdate: July 4, 1923
Birthplace: Hallgrund
Position: Aufseherin
File Number:
Employment Date: August 1, 1944
Camp Service: Groß-Rosen
Notes:

Franke

First Name: Gerda
Birthdate:
Birthplace:
Position: Aufseherin
File Number:
Employment Date:
Camp Service: Ravensbrück
Notes:

Franke

First Name: Helma
Birthdate:
Birthplace:
Position: Aufseherin
File Number:
Employment Date:
Camp Service: Ravensbrück
Notes:

Franke

First Name: Ilse
Birthdate:
Birthplace:
Position: Aufseherin
File Number:
Employment Date:
Camp Service:
Notes:

Franke

First Name: Waltraud
Birthdate: February 18, 1921
Birthplace: Adelabsen
Position: Aufseherin
File Number:
Employment Date: November 7, 1944
Camp Service: Ravensbrück
Notes:

Franz

First Name: Charlotte
Birthdate: December 23, 1919
Birthplace: Schwarzbach
Position: Aufseherin
File Number:
Employment Date: September 20, 1944
Camp Service: Groß-Rosen
Notes:

Franz

First Name: Charlotte
Birthdate: April 12, 1922
Birthplace: Ladowitz/Sudetengau
Position: Aufseherin
File Number: IV 410(F) AR 2629/67
Employment Date: September 20, 1944
Camp Service: Floßenbürg; AL Hertine
Notes: Permission for employment not granted *(Einstellung nicht genehmigt: Verfg.SS-WVHA-GO-Dr.Sch./Kl./To.v.31.10.1944)* but, due to the desperate situation of the Third Reich, employed anyway.

Franz

First Name: Dora
Birthdate: May 7, 1923
Birthplace:
Position: Aufseherin
File Number: IV 410(F) AR 2629/67
Employment Date:
Camp Service: Floßenbürg; Holleischen
Notes:

Franz

First Name: Erna
Birthdate: January 9, 1921
Birthplace: Oberquell
Position: Aufseherin
File Number:
Employment Date: June 1, 1944
Camp Service: Groß-Rosen
Notes:

Franz

First Name: Helene
Birthdate: July 2, 1923
Birthplace: Suchental (White Russia)
Position: Aufseherin
File Number: IV 410 AR 3039/66(B)
Employment Date:
Camp Service: Ravensbrück, Holleischen; Dresden; Mehlteuer, Floßenbürg
Notes: Ethnic German; born and raised in White Russia.

Franz

First Name: Hertha
Birthdate:
Birthplace:
Position: Aufseherin
File Number:
Employment Date:
Camp Service:
Notes:

Franz

First Name: Johanna
Birthdate:
Birthplace:
Position: Aufseherin
File Number:
Employment Date:
Camp Service:
Notes:

Franzen (married Wilbert)

First Name: Margarete
Birthdate: January 13, 1921
Birthplace: Trier
Position: Aufseherin
File Number: IV 429 AR-Z 130/70
Employment Date:
Camp Service: Sömmerda
Notes:

Franzkowiak

First Name: Rosa
Birthdate:
Birthplace:
Position: Aufseherin
File Number:
Employment Date:
Camp Service:
Notes: Czech national; permission to join auxiliaries granted.

Franzisky

First Name: Lieselotte
Birthdate: February 1, 1915
Birthplace: Potsdam-Bornstedt
Position: Aufseherin
File Number:
Employment Date: October 31, 1944
Camp Service: Groß-Rosen
Notes:

Fras (born Tauchmann)

First Name: Ella
Birthdate: March 9, 1914
Birthplace: Duisburg
Position: Aufseherin
File Number:
Employment Date: July 21, 1944
Camp Service: Ravensbrück
Notes:

Frater (born Loof)

First Name: Leni
Birthdate: March 5, 1920
Birthplace: Braunschweig

Position: Aufseherin
File Number:
Employment Date: July 1, 1944
Camp Service: Ravensbrück
Notes:

Frauenhofer

First Name: Rosa
Birthdate: July 3, 1920
Birthplace: Nuremberg
Position: Aufseherin
File Number: IV 410(F) AR 2629/67
Employment Date:
Camp Service: Floßenbürg; AL Nuremberg; AL Graslitz
Notes:

Frauke

First Name: Elsa, Gertrud
Birthdate:
Birthplace:
Position: Aufseherin
File Number:
Employment Date:
Camp Service:
Notes:

Freiberg

First Name: Frieda
Birthdate:
Birthplace:
Position: Aufseherin
File Number:
Employment Date:
Camp Service:
Notes:

Freienstein

First Name: Ingeborg
Birthdate: July 23, 1915
Birthplace: Berlin-Neukölln
Position: Aufseherin
File Number: IV 410(F) AR 2629/67
Employment Date:
Camp Service: Floßenbürg; AL Wolkenburg
Notes:

Freinberger

First Name: Margarete
Birthdate: June 11, 1919
Birthplace: Grieskirchen
Position: Oberaufseherin
File Number: IV 419 AR 1292/69
Employment Date:
Camp Service: Mauthausen; Lenzing
Notes:

Freinberger

First Name: Margarethe
Birthdate:
Birthplace:
Position: Aufseherin
File Number:
Employment Date:
Camp Service: Ravensbrück
Notes:

Freinstein (born Hoffmann)
First Name: Ingeborg
Birthdate:
Birthplace:
Position: Aufseherin
File Number:
Employment Date:
Camp Service:
Notes:

Freitag
First Name: Magdalene
Birthdate:
Birthplace:
Position: Aufseherin
File Number:
Employment Date:
Camp Service:
Notes:

Frenzel
First Name: Anni
Birthdate: February 23, 1923
Birthplace: Forst-Lausitz
Position: Aufseherin
File Number:
Employment Date: June 26, 1944
Camp Service: Groß-Rosen
Notes:

Fretscher
First Name: Anna-Dora
Birthdate: August 24, 1902
Birthplace: Dresden
Position: Aufseherin
File Number:
Employment Date: October 24, 1944
Camp Service: Floßenbürg
Notes:

Freudenhammer (married Meuer)
First Name: Emmi (Emma)
Birthdate: October 16, 1919
Birthplace: Gladbeck
Position: Aufseherin
File Number: IV 409 AR-Z 78/72
Employment Date: August 30, 1944
Camp Service: Ravensbrück; NL Geisenheim
Notes:

Freund
First Name: Johanna
Birthdate: February 23, 1924
Birthplace:
Position: SS Helferin, later Aufseherin
File Number: 404 AR-Z 45/81
Employment Date:
Camp Service: NL Hamburg-Sasel; Neuengamme
Notes: Tried for maltreatment of prisoners in Hamburg-Sasel by American Judge Advocate Corps (April 23 – June 10, 1946).

Frick (born Huber)
First Name: Maria
Birthdate:

Birthplace:
Position: Aufseherin
File Number:
Employment Date:
Camp Service:
Notes:

Fricke
First Name: Ella
Birthdate:
Birthplace:
Position: Aufseherin
File Number:
Employment Date:
Camp Service: Ravensbrück
Notes:

Fricke
First Name: Elfriede
Birthdate: February 13, 1920
Birthplace: Zollenstedt
Position: Aufseherin
File Number:
Employment Date: August 3, 1944
Camp Service: Ravensbrück
Notes:

Friedlein
First Name: Elisabeth
Birthdate:
Birthplace:
Position: Aufseherin
File Number:
Employment Date:
Camp Service: Ravensbrück
Notes:

Friedrich
First Name: Erna
Birthdate: December 31, 1921
Birthplace: Rudelstadt
Position: Aufseherin
File Number:
Employment Date: September 29, 19??
Camp Service: Groß-Rosen
Notes:

Friedrich
First Name: Johanna
Birthdate: November 5, 1911
Birthplace: Friedeberg
Position: Aufseherin
File Number:
Employment Date: August 16, 1944
Camp Service: Groß-Rosen
Notes:

Friedrich
First Name: Margarete
Birthdate:
Birthplace:
Position: Aufseherin
File Number:
Employment Date:
Camp Service:
Notes:

Friedrich
First Name: Susanne
Birthdate: September 30, 1921
Birthplace: Lunzenau
Position: Aufseherin
File Number: IV 410(F) AR 2629/67
Employment Date:
Camp Service: Floßenbürg; AL Rochlitz
Notes:

Friedrichs
First Name: Frieda
Birthdate:
Birthplace:
Position: Aufseherin
File Number: IV 409 AR 1491/66
Employment Date:
Camp Service: Buchenwald; NL Magdeburg; NL Comthurey
Notes:

Friemelt
First Name: Gertrud
Birthdate: January 2, 1903
Birthplace: Petersdorf
Position: Aufseherin
File Number:
Employment Date: July 27, 1944
Camp Service: Groß-Rosen
Notes:

Frisch
First Name: Ernestine
Birthdate: March 4, 1920
Birthplace: Cottbus
Position: Aufseherin
File Number: IV 410(F) AR 2629/67
Employment Date:
Camp Service: Floßenbürg; AL Holleischen
Notes:

Frister
First Name: Erika
Birthdate: January 19, 1923
Birthplace: Wurzen
Position: Aufseherin
File Number:
Employment Date: August 28, 1944
Camp Service: Ravensbrück
Notes:

Fritsch
First Name: Erna
Birthdate:
Birthplace:
Position: Aufseherin
File Number:
Employment Date:
Camp Service: Floßenbürg
Notes:

Fritsche
First Name: Margarete
Birthdate: July 29, 1923
Birthplace: Daubern
Position: Aufseherin
File Number: IV 410(F) AR 2629/67

Employment Date:
Camp Service: Floßenbürg; AL Neu Rohlau
Notes:

Fritsche
First Name: Maria
Birthdate: March 30, 1907
Birthplace: Weisskirchen
Position: Aufseherin
File Number:
Employment Date: September 5, 1944
Camp Service: Groß-Rosen
Notes:

Fritz
First Name: Lilly
Birthdate:
Birthplace:
Position: Aufseherin
File Number:
Employment Date:
Camp Service: Ravensbrück
Notes:

Fritzler
First Name: Anna
Birthdate:
Birthplace:
Position: Aufseherin
File Number:
Employment Date:
Camp Service: Floßenbürg
Notes:

Fritzsche
First Name: Elfriede
Birthdate: April 19, 1922
Birthplace: Ronneburg
Position: Aufseherin
File Number:
Employment Date: August 21, 1944
Camp Service: Ravensbrück
Notes:

Fröbrich
First Name: Emilie
Birthdate: June 27, 1923
Birthplace: Bernsdorf
Position: Aufseherin
File Number:
Employment Date: March 1, 1944
Camp Service: Groß-Rosen
Notes: Official permission for employment as an "employee of the Reich" granted on December 11, 1944.

Fröde
First Name: Nora
Birthdate:
Birthplace:
Position: Aufseherin
File Number:
Employment Date:
Camp Service: Ravensbrück
Notes:

Fröhlich
First Name: Margarete
Birthdate:
Birthplace:
Position: Aufseherin
File Number:
Employment Date:
Camp Service: Neuengamme
Notes:

Frömel
First Name: Johanna
Birthdate: January 15, 1921
Birthplace: Landeshut
Position: Aufseherin
File Number:
Employment Date: October 4, 1944
Camp Service: Groß-Rosen
Notes:

Frommholz (born Golz)
First Name: Ursula
Birthdate: April 18, 1923
Birthplace: Berlin
Position: Aufseherin
File Number:
Employment Date: August 15, 1944
Camp Service: Sachsenhausen
Notes:

Frühauf
First Name: Lilly
Birthdate:
Birthplace:
Position: Aufseherin
File Number:
Employment Date:
Camp Service:
Notes:

Fründt
First Name: Lotte
Birthdate: December 8, 1923
Birthplace: Waren/Müritz
Position: Aufseherin
File Number:
Employment Date: November 7, 1944
Camp Service: Ravensbrück
Notes:

Fuchs
First Name: Paula
Birthdate:
Birthplace:
Position: Aufseherin
File Number:
Employment Date:
Camp Service:
Notes:

Fuchs (born Bredi)
First Name: Gertraud
Birthdate:
Birthplace:
Position: Aufseherin

File Number:
Employment Date:
Camp Service: Ravensbrück
Notes:

Fuchs (born Storchmaier)
First Name: Philipine
Birthdate:
Birthplace:
Position: Aufseherin
File Number:
Employment Date:
Camp Service:
Notes:

Führer
First Name: Käthe
Birthdate:
Birthplace:
Position: Aufseherin
File Number:
Employment Date:
Camp Service:
Notes:

Fülle
First Name: Erna
Birthdate:
Birthplace:
Position: Aufseherin
File Number:
Employment Date:
Camp Service:
Notes:

Füller
First Name: Maria
Birthdate: April 25, 1923
Birthplace: Augsburg
Position: Aufseherin
File Number:
Employment Date: August 21, 1944
Camp Service: Sachsenhausen
Notes:

Fürstenberg
First Name: Charlotte
Birthdate: October 16, 1923
Birthplace: Leipzig
Position: Aufseherin
File Number:
Employment Date: August 1, 1944
Camp Service: Ravensbrück
Notes:

Fuhrmeister
First Name: Margot
Birthdate: August 22, 1920
Birthplace:
Position: Aufseherin
File Number: IV 429 AR-Z 89/71
Employment Date:
Camp Service: NL Markkleeberg
Notes:

Fulde

First Name: Helene
Birthdate: February 11, 1917
Birthplace: Langenbielau
Position: Aufseherin
File Number:
Employment Date: August 23, 1944
Camp Service: Groß-Rosen
Notes:

Funk

First Name: Helene
Birthdate:
Birthplace:
Position: Aufseherin
File Number:
Employment Date:
Camp Service:
Notes:

Funk

First Name: Margaret (or Margarete)
Birthdate: December 31, 1922
Birthplace: Stettin
Position: Aufseherin
File Number: IV 410(F) AR 2629/67
Employment Date:
Camp Service: Floßenbürg; AL Holleischen
Notes:

Funke

First Name: Elfriede
Birthdate:
Birthplace:
Position: Aufseherin
File Number:
Employment Date:
Camp Service:
Notes:

Gabloner

First Name: Mathilde
Birthdate: June 10, 1922
Birthplace: Bozen
Position: Aufseherin
File Number:
Employment Date: March 16, 1943
Camp Service: Ravensbrück
Notes:

Gabrisch

First Name: Marie
Birthdate: December 9, 1923
Birthplace: Eindenburg
Position: Aufseherin
File Number:
Employment Date: June 1, 1944
Camp Service: Floßenbürg
Notes:

Gäbeler

First Name: Therese
Birthdate: November 9, 1901
Birthplace: Berlin
Position: Aufseherin

File Number:
Employment Date: May 1, 1943
Camp Service: Ravensbrück
Notes:

Gäbler

First Name: Gertrud
Birthdate:
Birthplace:
Position: Aufseherin
File Number:
Employment Date:
Camp Service: Ravensbrück
Notes:

Gäbler

First Name: Hertha
Birthdate:
Birthplace:
Position: Aufseherin
File Number:
Employment Date:
Camp Service: Groß-Rosen
Notes:

Gädcke

First Name: Herta
Birthdate: January 15, 1920
Birthplace: Röbel
Position: Aufseherin
File Number:
Employment Date: November 8, 1944
Camp Service: Ravensbrück
Notes:

Gärke

First Name: Agathe
Birthdate: October 14, 1911
Birthplace: Berlin
Position: Aufseherin
File Number:
Employment Date: September 1, 1944
Camp Service: Ravensbrück
Notes:

Gärtner

First Name: Elisabeth
Birthdate: January 1, 1920
Birthplace: "India" (city in Croatia)
Position: Aufseherin
File Number:
Employment Date: August 19, 1944
Camp Service: Sachsenhausen
Notes:

Gärtner

First Name: Maria
Birthdate: May 19, 1921
Birthplace: Hottendorf
Position: Aufseherin
File Number:
Employment Date: September 13, 1944
Camp Service: Groß-Rosen
Notes:

Galach
First Name: Marianne
Birthdate: December 17, 1917
Birthplace: Bilin
Position: Aufseherin
File Number: IV 410(F) AR 2629/67
Employment Date: September 8, 1944
Camp Service: Floßenbürg; AL Hertine
Notes:

Galfe (or Calfe; married Hain)
First Name: Franziska
Birthdate: December 9, 1922
Birthplace: Hertine, Krs. Teplitz
Position: Aufseherin
File Number: IV 410(F) AR 2629/67
Employment Date: September 8, 1944
Camp Service: Floßenbürg; AL Hertine
Notes:

Gall
First Name: Ida
Birthdate:
Birthplace:
Position: Aufseherin
File Number:
Employment Date:
Camp Service:
Notes: Ethnic German; born and raised in Croatia.

Gall (born Theuß)
First Name: Gertrud
Birthdate:
Birthplace:
Position: Aufseherin
File Number:
Employment Date:
Camp Service: Ravensbrück
Notes:

Gallinat
First Name: Margarete
Birthdate:
Birthplace:
Position: Aufseherin
File Number:
Employment Date:
Camp Service:
Notes:

Gallitzdorfer
First Name: Margot
Birthdate: February 18, 1923
Birthplace: Lunzenau
Position: Aufseherin
File Number: IV 410(F) AR 2629/67
Employment Date:
Camp Service: Floßenbürg; AL Rochlitz
Notes:

Galkowski
First Name: Ilse
Birthdate: June 10, 1920
Birthplace: Landsberg Warthe
Position: Aufseherin

File Number:
Employment Date: September 1, 1944
Camp Service: Sachsenhausen
Notes:

Galsterer
First Name: Elise (Elisa)
Birthdate: September 26, 1903
Birthplace:
Position: Aufseherin
File Number: IV 410(F) AR 2629/67
Employment Date:
Camp Service: Floßenbürg; AL Nuremberg; AL Holleischen
Notes:

Gangel (born Lehm)
First Name: Martha
Birthdate:
Birthplace:
Position: Aufseherin
File Number:
Employment Date:
Camp Service:
Notes:

Garbisch
First Name: Maria
Birthdate: December 9, 1923
Birthplace: Hindenburg
Position: Aufseherin
File Number:
Employment Date: Service as a Waffen SS auxiliary began on June 15, 1944.
Camp Service: Kommando Helmbrechts
Notes:

Garschig
First Name: Gertrud
Birthdate:
Birthplace:
Position: Aufseherin
File Number:
Employment Date:
Camp Service: Groß-Rosen
Notes:

Garske
First Name: Brunhilde
Birthdate: May 23, 1921
Birthplace: Berlin-Wilmersdorf
Position: Aufseherin
File Number:
Employment Date: September 16, 1944
Camp Service: Ravensbrück; Sachsenhausen
Notes:

Gaßner
First Name: Maria
Birthdate:
Birthplace:
Position: Aufseherin
File Number:
Employment Date:
Camp Service: Ravensbrück
Notes:

Gatter
First Name: Ella
Birthdate:
Birthplace:
Position: Aufseherin
File Number:
Employment Date:
Camp Service: Groß-Rosen
Notes:

Gaugg
First Name: Emma
Birthdate:
Birthplace:
Position: Aufseherin
File Number:
Employment Date:
Camp Service:
Notes:

Gaugg
First Name: Irma
Birthdate: August 15, 1922
Birthplace: Trugel
Position: Aufseherin
File Number:
Employment Date: April 23, 1944
Camp Service: Ravensbrück
Notes:

Gawlek
First Name: Ursula
Birthdate:
Birthplace:
Position: Aufseherin
File Number:
Employment Date:
Camp Service:
Notes:

Gazza
First Name: Anna
Birthdate:
Birthplace:
Position: Aufseherin
File Number:
Employment Date:
Camp Service: Stutthof/Danzig
Notes:

Gebauer
First Name: Lieselotte
Birthdate:
Birthplace:
Position: Aufseherin
File Number:
Employment Date:
Camp Service:
Notes:

Gebauer
First Name: Ursula
Birthdate: October 12, 1921
Birthplace: Berlin

Position: Aufseherin
File Number: IV 429 AR 1941/66 (B)
Employment Date:
Camp Service: NL Torgau; NL Elsnig; Kommando Kassel; Ravensbrück
Notes:

Gebhardt
First Name: Karoline (or Karola)
Birthdate: June 11, 1921
Birthplace: Nuremberg
Position: Aufseherin
File Number: IV 410(F) AR 2629/67
Employment Date: September 30, 1944
Camp Service: Floßenbürg; AL Siemens Nuremberg; AL Holleischen
Notes: Official permission for employment as an "employee of the Reich" granted on November 22, 1944.

Gebhardt
First Name: Luise
Birthdate: February 8, 1919
Birthplace: Strassburg
Position: Aufseherin
File Number: IV 409 AR-Z 39/59
Employment Date:
Camp Service: Ravensbrück
Notes:

Gebhardt (born Boin)
First Name: Luise
Birthdate: 1919
Birthplace:
Position: Aufseherin
File Number:
Employment Date:
Camp Service: Ravensbrück
Notes: Sentenced to five years imprisonment for war crimes by an East German court.

Gehrke (now Weiss)
First Name: Ernestine
Birthdate: August 28, 1922 or August 29, 1922
Birthplace: Neusattl
Position: Aufseherin
File Number: IV 410(F) AR 2629/67
Employment Date: April 1, 1944
Camp Service: Floßenbürg; Holleischen
Notes:

Geiger
First Name: Cäcilie
Birthdate:
Birthplace:
Position: Aufseherin
File Number:
Employment Date:
Camp Service:
Notes:

Geiger
First Name: Martha
Birthdate: February 13, 1921
Birthplace: Schnehenlohe (Kronach)

Position: Aufseherin
File Number:
Employment Date: August 17, 1944
Camp Service: Sachsenhausen
Notes:

Geil
First Name: Klara
Birthdate:
Birthplace:
Position: Aufseherin
File Number:
Employment Date:
Camp Service:
Notes:

Geis (born Neumann)
First Name: Margarete
Birthdate:
Birthplace:
Position: Aufseherin
File Number:
Employment Date:
Camp Service:
Notes:

Geiser
First Name: Babette
Birthdate:
Birthplace:
Position: Aufseherin
File Number:
Employment Date:
Camp Service:
Notes:

Geisler
First Name: Margot
Birthdate:
Birthplace:
Position: Aufseherin
File Number:
Employment Date:
Camp Service:
Notes:

Geißler
First Name: Gertrud
Birthdate:
Birthplace:
Position: Aufseherin
File Number:
Employment Date:
Camp Service:
Notes:

Geißler
First Name: Martha
Birthdate:
Birthplace:
Position: Aufseherin
File Number:
Employment Date:
Camp Service: Groß-Rosen
Notes:

Geißler
First Name: Rosa
Birthdate:
Birthplace:
Position: Aufseherin
File Number:
Employment Date:
Camp Service:
Notes:

Gelbhaar
First Name: Irmgard
Birthdate:
Birthplace:
Position: Aufseherin
File Number:
Employment Date:
Camp Service: Ravensbrück
Notes:

Gellhorn
First Name: Betty
Birthdate:
Birthplace:
Position: Aufseherin
File Number:
Employment Date:
Camp Service:
Notes:

Gellner
First Name: Ursula
Birthdate:
Birthplace:
Position: Aufseherin
File Number:
Employment Date:
Camp Service:
Notes:

Genschmer
First Name: Erika
Birthdate: Decmber 6, 1923
Birthplace:
Position: Aufseherin
File Number: IV 410(F) AR 2629/67
Employment Date:
Camp Service: Floßenbürg; AL Osram (Berlin)
Notes:

Gentek
First Name: Martha
Birthdate:
Birthplace:
Position: Aufseherin
File Number:
Employment Date:
Camp Service:
Notes:

Genz
First Name: Irmgard
Birthdate:
Birthplace:
Position: Aufseherin

File Number:
Employment Date:
Camp Service:
Notes:

George

First Name: Hedwig
Birthdate:
Birthplace:
Position: Aufseherin
File Number:
Employment Date:
Camp Service:
Notes:

George

First Name: Käte (or Käthe)
Birthdate: December 12, 1921
Birthplace:
Position: Aufseherin
File Number: IV 429 AR 1941/66(B)
Employment Date:
Camp Service: NL Torgau; Ravensbrück
Notes:

Georgi

First Name: Helga
Birthdate:
Birthplace:
Position: Aufseherin
File Number:
Employment Date:
Camp Service:
Notes:

Geppert

First Name: Dorothea
Birthdate:
Birthplace:
Position: Aufseherin
File Number:
Employment Date:
Camp Service: Ravensbrück
Notes:

Geppert

First Name: Elfriede
Birthdate:
Birthplace:
Position: Aufseherin
File Number:
Employment Date:
Camp Service: Groß-Rosen
Notes:

Geppert (born Dell)

First Name: Lucie
Birthdate:
Birthplace:
Position: Aufseherin
File Number:
Employment Date:
Camp Service: Ravensbrück
Notes:

Geretschläger

First Name: Rosa
Birthdate:
Birthplace:
Position: Aufseherin
File Number:
Employment Date:
Camp Service: Ravensbrück
Notes:

Gerhardt

First Name: Ursula
Birthdate:
Birthplace:
Position: Aufseherin
File Number:
Employment Date:
Camp Service: Ravensbrück
Notes:

Gerl

First Name: Erna
Birthdate: July 27, 1902
Birthplace:
Position: Aufseherin
File Number: IV 410(F) AR 2629/67
Employment Date:
Camp Service: Floßenbürg; AL Plauen
Notes:

Gerlach

First Name: Elfriede
Birthdate: November 7, 1923
Birthplace: Chemnitz
Position: Aufseherin
File Number: IV 410(F) AR 2629/67
Employment Date: August 25, 1944
Camp Service: AL Astrawerke Chemnitz
Notes:

Gerlach (born Strowig)

First Name: Lucie
Birthdate:
Birthplace:
Position: Aufseherin
File Number:
Employment Date:
Camp Service:
Notes:

Gerlich

First Name: Ruth
Birthdate:
Birthplace:
Position: Aufseherin
File Number:
Employment Date:
Camp Service:
Notes:

Gerloff

First Name: Charlotte
Birthdate:
Birthplace:
Position: Aufseherin

File Number:
Employment Date:
Camp Service:
Notes:

Gersch (born Pawlinka)
First Name: Elisabeth
Birthdate:
Birthplace:
Position: Aufseherin
File Number:
Employment Date:
Camp Service:
Notes:

Gerth
First Name: Olga
Birthdate: June 29, 1913
Birthplace:
Position: Aufseherin
File Number: IV 410(F) AR 2629/67
Employment Date:
Camp Service: Floßenbürg; Al Hertine
Notes:

Gerwing
First Name: Anna
Birthdate: August 5, 1921
Birthplace: Hanau
Position: Rapportführerin
File Number: IV 410(F) AR 2629/67
Employment Date: October 28, 1942
Camp Service: Plaszów; AL Zittau
Notes:

Gethlich
First Name: Ruth
Birthdate:
Birthplace:
Position: Aufseherin
File Number:
Employment Date:
Camp Service:
Notes:

Geulen
First Name: Karoline
Birthdate: April 3, 1922
Birthplace:
Position: *Strafkommando-führerin* (punishment detail leader): SS Member
File Number: IV 429 AR-Z 51/71 (B)
Employment Date:
Camp Service: Buchenwald; NL Essen
Notes:

Geupel
First Name: Charlotte
Birthdate: July 21 1909
Birthplace: Plauen
Position: Aufseherin
File Number: IV 410(F) AR 2629/67
Employment Date: November 11, 1944
Camp Service: Floßenbürg; AL Chemnitz; Ravensbrück
Notes:

Geyer
First Name: Anna
Birthdate:
Birthplace:
Position: Aufseherin
File Number:
Employment Date:
Camp Service:
Notes:

Geyer
First Name: Hanna
Birthdate:
Birthplace:
Position: Aufseherin
File Number:
Employment Date:
Camp Service:
Notes:

Geyer
First Name: Irene
Birthdate:
Birthplace:
Position: Aufseherin
File Number:
Employment Date:
Camp Service:
Notes:

Giasdowski
First Name: Anna
Birthdate:
Birthplace:
Position: Aufseherin
File Number:
Employment Date:
Camp Service:
Notes:

Gierck
First Name: Lisa
Birthdate:
Birthplace:
Position: Aufseherin
File Number:
Employment Date:
Camp Service:
Notes:

Giese
First Name: Anneliese
Birthdate:
Birthplace:
Position: Aufseherin
File Number:
Employment Date:
Camp Service:
Notes:

Giese (born Voigt)
First Name: Emmy
Birthdate:
Birthplace:
Position: Aufseherin

File Number:
Employment Date:
Camp Service:
Notes:

Giesin

First Name: Irma
Birthdate:
Birthplace:
Position: Aufseherin
File Number:
Employment Date:
Camp Service: Ravensbrück
Notes:

Gießmann

First Name: Elfriede
Birthdate:
Birthplace:
Position: Aufseherin
File Number:
Employment Date:
Camp Service: Groß-Rosen
Notes:

Girgdies

First Name: Herta
Birthdate: July 14, 1922
Birthplace: Templin
Position: Aufseherin
File Number:
Employment Date: June 1, 1944
Camp Service: Ravensbrück
Notes:

Gisher (born Becker)

First Name: Sibylle
Birthdate:
Birthplace:
Position: Aufseherin
File Number:
Employment Date:
Camp Service:
Notes:

Giskes

First Name: Renate
Birthdate:
Birthplace:
Position: Aufseherin
File Number:
Employment Date:
Camp Service: Ravensbrück
Notes:

Giskes (born Becker)

First Name: Sybille
Birthdate: August 22, 1921
Birthplace: Wervelinghofen
Position: Aufseherin
File Number: IV 410(F) AR 2629/67
Employment Date:
Camp Service: Floßenbürg; AL Hainichhen
Notes:

Gitzel

First Name: Adina
Birthdate:
Birthplace:
Position: Aufseherin
File Number:
Employment Date:
Camp Service: Neuengamme
Notes:

Gläser

First Name: Elfriede
Birthdate:
Birthplace:
Position: Aufseherin
File Number:
Employment Date:
Camp Service: Groß-Rosen
Notes:

Gläser

First Name: Helga
Birthdate:
Birthplace:
Position: Aufseherin
File Number:
Employment Date:
Camp Service:
Notes:

Gläser

First Name: Ilse
Birthdate:
Birthplace:
Position: Aufseherin
File Number:
Employment Date:
Camp Service: Ravensbrück
Notes:

Glässer

First Name: Ilse
Birthdate: May 15, 1922
Birthplace: Großrückerswalde
Position: Aufseherin
File Number: IV 410(F) AR 2629/67
Employment Date:
Camp Service: Floßenbürg; AL Chemnitz
Notes:

Glas (born Meisburger)

First Name: Maria
Birthdate:
Birthplace:
Position: Aufseherin
File Number:
Employment Date:
Camp Service:
Notes:

Glaser

First Name: Hildegard
Birthdate:
Birthplace:
Position: Aufseherin

File Number:
Employment Date:
Camp Service:
Notes:

Glaser

First Name: Maria
Birthdate:
Birthplace:
Position: Aufseherin
File Number:
Employment Date:
Camp Service:
Notes:

Glass (or Class)

First Name: Ruth
Birthdate: September 29, 1921
Birthplace: Herne
Position: Aufseherin
File Number:
Employment Date: August 30, 1944
Camp Service: Ravensbrück; Floßenbürg; AL Plauen
Notes:

Gleich

First Name: Elfriede
Birthdate: March 23, 1921
Birthplace: Hainichen
Position: Aufseherin
File Number: IV 410(F) AR 2629/67
Employment Date: November 2, 1944
Camp Service: Floßenbürg; AL Hainichen
Notes:

Gleitsmann

First Name: Wally
Birthdate:
Birthplace:
Position: Aufseherin
File Number:
Employment Date:
Camp Service:
Notes:

Glitza

First Name: Berta
Birthdate: January 13, 1912
Birthplace: Verhalten (East Prussia)
Position: Aufseherin
File Number: IV 410(F) AR 2629/67
Employment Date:
Camp Service: Floßenbürg; AL Wolkenburg; AL Holleischen
Notes:

Globisch

First Name: Agathe
Birthdate:
Birthplace:
Position: Aufseherin
File Number:
Employment Date:
Camp Service: Neuengamme
Notes:

Glöckner

First Name: Gisela
Birthdate: January 21, 1923
Birthplace:
Position: Aufseherin
File Number: IV 410(F) AR 2629/67
Employment Date:
Camp Service: Floßenbürg; AL Neu Rohlau
Notes:

Glöß (or Gläss; born Heimann)

First Name: Anna
Birthdate: August 23, 1916
Birthplace: Kirschlau
Position: Aufseherin
File Number: IV 410(F) AR 2629/67
Employment Date:
Camp Service: Floßenbürg; AL Hainichen; Ravensbrück
Notes:

Glowacki

First Name: Gerda
Birthdate:
Birthplace:
Position: Aufseherin
File Number:
Employment Date:
Camp Service:
Notes:

Glowake

First Name: Anna
Birthdate:
Birthplace:
Position: Aufseherin
File Number:
Employment Date:
Camp Service: Sachsenhausen
Notes:

Glunz

First Name: Margarete
Birthdate:
Birthplace:
Position: Aufseherin
File Number:
Employment Date:
Camp Service:
Notes:

Gobernatz

First Name: Gertrud
Birthdate: November 14, 1921
Birthplace: Schießelitz
Position: Aufseherin
File Number: IV 410(F) AR 2629/67
Employment Date: September 8, 1944
Camp Service: Floßenbürg; AL Neu Rohlau
Notes:

Gockel (born Wessel)

First Name: Anna
Birthdate:
Birthplace:
Position: Aufseherin

File Number:
Employment Date:
Camp Service:
Notes:

Gode
First Name: Sophie
Birthdate: March 25, 1907
Birthplace: Bremen
Position:
File Number:
Employment Date: October 1, 1940
Camp Service: Ravensbrück
Notes:

Göcke
First Name: Ruth
Birthdate:
Birthplace:
Position: Aufseherin
File Number:
Employment Date:
Camp Service:
Notes:

Göckler (born Göken)
First Name: Henriette
Birthdate: April 1, 1923
Birthplace: Essen
Position: Wächterin
File Number: IV 429 AR-Z 51/71
Employment Date: September 1944
Camp Service: NL Essen
Notes:

Gödke
First Name: Gerda
Birthdate: October 6, 1923
Birthplace: Godenswege
Position: Aufseherin
File Number: IV 410(F) AR 2629/67
Employment Date: November 1, 1944
Camp Service: Ravensbrück; Floßenbürg; AL Dresden
Notes:

Göhre (or Göre)
First Name: Herta
Birthdate: November 3, 1919
Birthplace:
Position: Aufseherin
File Number: IV 410(F) AR 2629/67
Employment Date:
Camp Service: Floßenbürg; AL Mittweida
Notes:

Göhrs
First Name: Hertha
Birthdate:
Birthplace:
Position: Aufseherin
File Number:
Employment Date:
Camp Service:
Notes:

Göldner
First Name: Margarete
Birthdate:
Birthplace:
Position: Aufseherin
File Number:
Employment Date:
Camp Service:
Notes:

Göpel
First Name: Christl (or Christa)
Birthdate:
Birthplace:
Position: Aufseherin
File Number: IV 409 AR-Z 39/59
Employment Date:
Camp Service: Ravensbrück; Meuselwitz
Notes:

Göpel (born Wiesen)
First Name: Christa
Birthdate:
Birthplace:
Position: Aufseherin
File Number:
Employment Date:
Camp Service:
Notes:

Görgs
First Name: Elisabeth
Birthdate:
Birthplace:
Position: Aufseherin
File Number:
Employment Date:
Camp Service:
Notes:

Göritz
First Name: Ilse
Birthdate: 1922 (no month or day noted in her file)
Birthplace:
Position: Designated *Kommandoführerin*
File Number:
Employment Date:
Camp Service: Ravensbrück; Neubrandenburg; Barth
Notes: Sentenced to life imprisonment by an East German court for maltreatment of prisoners and murder between 1943 and 1945.

Görke
First Name: Agathe
Birthdate:
Birthplace:
Position: Aufseherin
File Number: IV 409 AR-Z 39/59
Employment Date: March 22, 1944
Camp Service: Ravensbrück
Notes:

Görlach (born Fischer)
First Name: Berta
Birthdate:

Birthplace:
Position: Aufseherin
File Number:
Employment Date:
Camp Service: Groß-Rosen
Notes:

Göthling

First Name: Frieda
Birthdate:
Birthplace:
Position: Aufseherin
File Number:
Employment Date:
Camp Service:
Notes:

Götsch (born Gienke)

First Name: Margarete
Birthdate: June 14, 1909
Birthplace: Hamburg
Position: Aufseherin
File Number:
Employment Date: July 8, 1944
Camp Service: Ravensbrück
Notes:

Götze

First Name: Charlotte
Birthdate:
Birthplace:
Position: Aufseherin
File Number: IV 410 AR 2960/66
Employment Date:
Camp Service: Floßenbürg; NL Holleischen
Notes:

Götze

First Name: Else
Birthdate:
Birthplace:
Position: Aufseherin
File Number:
Employment Date:
Camp Service:
Notes:

Götzel

First Name: Marianne
Birthdate:
Birthplace:
Position: Aufseherin
File Number:
Employment Date:
Camp Service:
Notes:

Golchert

First Name: Helene
Birthdate:
Birthplace:
Position: Aufseherin
File Number:
Employment Date:
Camp Service:
Notes:

Goldschmidt

First Name: Dorothea
Birthdate:
Birthplace:
Position: Aufseherin
File Number:
Employment Date:
Camp Service: Neuengamme
Notes:

Gollasch

First Name: Hildegard
Birthdate:
Birthplace: Kotbus
Position: Aufseherin; Rapportführerin
File Number:
Employment Date:
Camp Service: Bergen-Belsen
Notes: Avoided postwar apprehension
and prosecution

Golz (born Wurst)

First Name: Frieda
Birthdate: July 29, 1901
Birthplace: Köslin
Position: Aufseherin
File Number:
Employment Date: August 18, 1944
Camp Service: Sachsenhausen
Notes:

Gombert

First Name: Marcella
Birthdate: March 23, 1921
Birthplace: Pope
Position: Aufseherin
File Number:
Employment Date: September 22, 1944
Camp Service: Ravensbrück
Notes: Italian national; born and raised in Italy;
special permission for service as an "employee
of the Reich" granted.

Gomringer

First Name: Hildegard
Birthdate: May 21, 1921
Birthplace: Hainichs
Position: Aufseherin
File Number:
Employment Date: August 18, 1944
Camp Service: Ravensbrück
Notes:

Goretzki

First Name: Frieda
Birthdate: January 20, 1905
Birthplace: Rosental
Position: Aufseherin
File Number:
Employment Date: November 20, 1944
Camp Service: Ravensbrück
Notes:

Goretzki

First Name: Gertrud
Birthdate:

Birthplace:
Position: Aufseherin
File Number:
Employment Date:
Camp Service:
Notes:

Gorny (born Bartz)

First Name: Christine
Birthdate:
Birthplace:
Position: Aufseherin
File Number:
Employment Date:
Camp Service:
Notes:

Gottschalk

First Name: Ruth
Birthdate: November 20, 1919
Birthplace: Breslau
Position: Aufseherin
File Number:
Employment Date: July 1, 1944
Camp Service: Groß-Rosen
Notes:

Gottschalk

First Name: Margarete
Birthdate:
Birthplace:
Position: Aufseherin
File Number:
Employment Date:
Camp Service:
Notes:

Gottwald

First Name: Gertrud
Birthdate: December 15, 1923
Birthplace: Reichenbach
Position: Aufseherin
File Number:
Employment Date: March 1, 1944
Camp Service: Groß-Rosen
Notes:

Gotzes

First Name: Therese
Birthdate: December 23, 1922
Birthplace:
Position: Aufseherin
File Number: IV 429 AR 1821/66 (B)
Employment Date:
Camp Service: Mühlhausen; Allendorf; NL Essen
Notes:

Grabber

First Name: Maria
Birthdate:
Birthplace:
Position: Aufseherin
File Number:
Employment Date:
Camp Service:
Notes:

Grabein

First Name: Veneta
Birthdate: April 22, 1921
Birthplace: Loz (Bulgaria)
Position: Aufseherin
File Number:
Employment Date: September 28, 1944
Camp Service: Groß-Rosen
Notes:

Grabiger (born Kinzel)

First Name: Berta
Birthdate:
Birthplace:
Position: Aufseherin
File Number:
Employment Date:
Camp Service:
Notes:

Grabner

First Name: Anna (Anni)
Birthdate:
Birthplace:
Position: Aufseherin
File Number:
Employment Date:
Camp Service:
Notes:

Grabner

First Name: Else
Birthdate: March 10, 1908
Birthplace: Strehla
Position: Lagerleiterin; Oberaufseherin
File Number: 108 AR-Z 225/88
Employment Date:
Camp Service: Ravensbrück
Notes:

Grabowski

First Name: Magda
Birthdate:
Birthplace:
Position: Aufseherin
File Number:
Employment Date:
Camp Service: Ravensbrück
Notes:

Grabowski

First Name: Martha
Birthdate: March 23, 1921
Birthplace: Labant/Gleiwitz
Position: Aufseherin
File Number:
Employment Date: September 2, 1944
Camp Service: Sachsenhausen
Notes: Polish national; special persmission granted for admission to the Helferinnen Korps; later transferred to Aufseherin training at Ravensbrück.

Grabs

First Name: Frieda
Birthdate: July 12, 1923

Birthplace: Marklissa
Position: Aufseherin
File Number:
Employment Date: June 26, 1944
Camp Service: Groß-Rosen
Notes:

Grabscheid
First Name: Erna
Birthdate: June 4, 1921
Birthplace: Grünberg
Position: Aufseherin
File Number:
Employment Date: August 19, 1944
Camp Service: Groß-Rosen
Notes:

Gräfe
First Name: Martha
Birthdate:
Birthplace:
Position: Aufseherin
File Number:
Employment Date:
Camp Service:
Notes:

Graehl
First Name: Marta
Birthdate: December 15, 1913
Birthplace: Wülfelsdorf
Position: Aufseherin
File Number:
Employment Date: August 10, 1944
Camp Service: Groß-Rosen
Notes:

Grätz
First Name: Erika
Birthdate:
Birthplace:
Position: Aufseherin
File Number:
Employment Date:
Camp Service:
Notes:

Gräupner
First Name: Elsa
Birthdate: November 26, 1920
Birthplace:
Position: Aufseherin
File Number: IV 410(F) AR 2629/67
Employment Date:
Camp Service: Floßenbürg; AL Holleischen
Notes:

Graf
First Name: Anna (Anni)
Birthdate: May 19, 1923
Birthplace: Pernatitz
Position: Aufseherin
File Number: IV 410 AR 2960/66

Employment Date: August 14, 1944
Camp Service: Ravensbrück; Floßenbürg; NL Holleischen
Notes:

Graf
First Name: Gerda
Birthdate:
Birthplace:
Position: Aufseherin
File Number:
Employment Date:
Camp Service:
Notes:

Graf
First Name: Klara
Birthdate:
Birthplace:
Position: Aufseherin
File Number:
Employment Date:
Camp Service: Neuengamme
Notes:

Graf
First Name: Maria
Birthdate: November 5, 1923
Birthplace: Burglengenfeld
Position: Aufseherin
File Number: IV 409 AR 1482/66
Employment Date:
Camp Service: Oranienburg
Notes:

Gramer
First Name: Elfriede
Birthdate: September 17, 1921
Birthplace: Freudenthal (Schweidnitz)
Position: Aufseherin
File Number:
Employment Date: April 15, 1944
Camp Service: Sachsenhausen
Notes:

Grande
First Name: Margarethe
Birthdate: December 28, 1921
Birthplace: Markersdorf
Position: Aufseherin
File Number:
Employment Date: August 16, 1944
Camp Service: Floßenbürg
Notes:

Gransow
First Name: Lotte
Birthdate:
Birthplace:
Position: Aufseherin
File Number:
Employment Date:
Camp Service: Ravensbrück
Notes:

Grasmann
First Name: Rosa
Birthdate: January 7, 1923
Birthplace: Augsburg
Position: Aufseherin
File Number:
Employment Date: August 13, 1944
Camp Service: Dachau
Notes:

Graß (or Gras)
First Name: Angelika
Birthdate: February 10, 1922
Birthplace: Berlin
Position: Aufseherin
File Number: IV 410(F) AR 2629/67
Employment Date:
Camp Service: Floßenbürg; AL Beendorf; Neuengamme
Notes:

Graße
First Name: Martha
Birthdate: February 20, 1920
Birthplace:
Position: Aufseherin
File Number:
Employment Date:
Camp Service: Ravensbrück; Auschwitz Birkenau
Notes:

Graße (born Liebig)
First Name: Maria
Birthdate:
Birthplace:
Position: Aufseherin
File Number:
Employment Date:
Camp Service:
Notes:

Graze (born Bülow)
First Name: Käte
Birthdate:
Birthplace:
Position: Aufseherin
File Number:
Employment Date:
Camp Service:
Notes:

Grebe
First Name: Emma
Birthdate:
Birthplace:
Position: Aufseherin
File Number:
Employment Date:
Camp Service:
Notes:

Grebs
First Name: Herta
Birthdate: February 3, 1918
Birthplace: Schnepffurth
Position: Aufseherin: Waffen SS

File Number: IV 410(F) AR 2629/67
Employment Date:
Camp Service: Kommando Helmbrechts
Notes: Service as a Waffen SS auxiliary began on July 1, 1944.

Greger
First Name: Anna
Birthdate: January 19, 1921
Birthplace:
Position: Aufseherin
File Number: IV 410(F) AR 2629/67
Employment Date:
Camp Service: Floßenbürg
Notes:

Gregor
First Name: Charlotte
Birthdate:
Birthplace:
Position: Aufseherin
File Number:
Employment Date:
Camp Service:
Notes:

Grehn (born Leder)
First Name: Ruth
Birthdate:
Birthplace:
Position: Aufseherin
File Number:
Employment Date:
Camp Service:
Notes:

Grein
First Name: Hedwig
Birthdate:
Birthplace:
Position: Aufseherin
File Number:
Employment Date:
Camp Service:
Notes:

Greiter
First Name: Kandida
Birthdate: January 19, 1922
Birthplace: Thalkirchdorf
Position: Aufseherin
File Number: IV 410(F) AR 2629/67
Employment Date:
Camp Service: Floßenbürg; AL Holleischen
Notes:

Grese
First Name: Irma
Birthdate: October 7, 1923
Birthplace: Wrechen (bei Neubrandenburg)
Position: Aufseherin; Rapportführerin; Oberaufseherin
File Number:
Employment Date: January 7, 1942
Camp Service: Ravensbrück; Auschwitz Birkenau; Bergen-Belsen

Notes: Tried by the British for war crimes (September 17-November 17, 1945), convicted and executed December 13, 1945.

Grewe
First Name: Renate
Birthdate:
Birthplace:
Position: Aufseherin
File Number:
Employment Date:
Camp Service: Groß-Rosen
Notes:

Grieger (or Griger; born Pfüller)
First Name: Herta
Birthdate: June 29, 1914
Birthplace: Reichebrand or Chemnitz
Position: Aufseherin
File Number: IV 410(F) AR 2629/67
Employment Date: August 16, 1944
Camp Service: Floßenbürg; AL Chemnitz
Notes:

Griepentrog
First Name: Gisela
Birthdate:
Birthplace:
Position: Aufseherin
File Number:
Employment Date:
Camp Service:
Notes:

Griesbeck
First Name: Johanna
Birthdate:
Birthplace:
Position: Aufseherin
File Number:
Employment Date:
Camp Service:
Notes:

Grim
First Name: Luzie
Birthdate:
Birthplace:
Position: Aufseherin
File Number:
Employment Date:
Camp Service: Groß-Rosen
Notes:

Grime
First Name: Erika
Birthdate:
Birthplace:
Position: Aufseherin
File Number:
Employment Date:
Camp Service: Neuengamme
Notes:

Grimm
First Name: Elfriede
Birthdate: March 15, 1921
Birthplace: Scheibenberg
Position: Aufseherin
File Number: IV 410 (F) AR 2629/67
Employment Date: October 5, 1944
Camp Service: Floßenbürg; AL Zwodau; Kommando Auer; Sachsenhausen
Notes:

Grimm
First Name: Margarete
Birthdate:
Birthplace:
Position: Aufseherin
File Number:
Employment Date:
Camp Service:
Notes:

Grobe
First Name: Hildegard
Birthdate:
Birthplace:
Position: Aufseherin
File Number:
Employment Date:
Camp Service: Neuengamme
Notes:

Gröger
First Name: Marie
Birthdate:
Birthplace:
Position: Aufseherin
File Number:
Employment Date:
Camp Service:
Notes:

Grünert (or Könert; born Hänsel)
First Name: Elisabeth
Birthdate: December 25, 1919
Birthplace:
Position: Aufseherin
File Number: IV 410(F) AR 2629/67
Employment Date:
Camp Service: Floßenbürg; AL Freiberg
Notes:

Gröschel
First Name: Anastasia
Birthdate:
Birthplace:
Position: Aufseherin
File Number:
Employment Date:
Camp Service: Ravensbrück
Notes:

Grohmann
First Name: Edeltraud
Birthdate: December 12, 1922
Birthplace:

Position: Aufseherin
File Number: IV 410(F) AR 2629/67
Employment Date:
Camp Service: Floßenbürg; AL Hertine
Notes:

Gronwaldt (born Gloy)
First Name: Agnes
Birthdate:
Birthplace:
Position: Aufseherin
File Number:
Employment Date:
Camp Service: Neuengamme
Notes:

Große
First Name: Cäcilie
Birthdate:
Birthplace:
Position: Aufseherin
File Number:
Employment Date:
Camp Service:
Notes:

Große
First Name: Frieda
Birthdate:
Birthplace:
Position: Aufseherin
File Number:
Employment Date:
Camp Service:
Notes:

Grosser
First Name: Else
Birthdate:
Birthplace:
Position: Aufseherin
File Number:
Employment Date:
Camp Service:
Notes:

Großkopf
First Name: Hildegard
Birthdate:
Birthplace:
Position: Aufseherin
File Number:
Employment Date:
Camp Service:
Notes:

Großmann
First Name: Charlotte
Birthdate: July 24, 1911
Birthplace: Marienfeld
Position: Aufseherin
File Number:
Employment Date: August 31, 1944
Camp Service: Groß-Rosen
Notes:

Großmann
First Name: Olga
Birthdate: January 13, 1907
Birthplace: Ledachow
Position: Aufseherin
File Number:
Employment Date: August 23, 1944
Camp Service: Groß-Rosen
Notes:

Groth
First Name: Hildegard
Birthdate:
Birthplace:
Position: Aufseherin
File Number:
Employment Date:
Camp Service: Ravensbrück
Notes:

Grothe
First Name: Martha
Birthdate:
Birthplace:
Position: Aufseherin
File Number:
Employment Date:
Camp Service:
Notes:

Grün
First Name: Lusi (Luzi)
Birthdate: March 4, 1913
Birthplace: Berlin
Position: Aufseherin
File Number:
Employment Date: October 13, 1944
Camp Service: Groß-Rosen
Notes:

Grünberg
First Name: Irene
Birthdate:
Birthplace:
Position: Aufseherin
File Number:
Employment Date:
Camp Service:
Notes:

Grünberg (born Grikowski)
First Name: Bettina
Birthdate:
Birthplace:
Position: Aufseherin
File Number:
Employment Date:
Camp Service:
Notes:

Gründel
First Name: Rosa
Birthdate: November 4, 1910
Birthplace: Mittelsteine
Position: Aufseherin

File Number:
Employment Date: August 23, 1944
Camp Service: Groß-Rosen
Notes:

Grünert
First Name: Melanie
Birthdate: February 6, 1916
Birthplace:
Position: Aufseherin
File Number: IV 429 AR 1248/68
Employment Date:
Camp Service: Markkleeberg
Notes:

Grünewald (married Schagerl)
First Name: Lieselotte
Birthdate: November 4, 1921
Birthplace: Oberhausen
Position: Aufseherin
File Number: IV 409 AR 14448/66
Employment Date: August 1944
Camp Service: Ravensbrück; NL Königsberg (Neumarkt)
Notes:

Grüßhaber
First Name: Eugenie
Birthdate:
Birthplace:
Position: Aufseherin
File Number:
Employment Date:
Camp Service:
Notes:

Grumow
First Name: Anna
Birthdate:
Birthplace:
Position: Aufseherin
File Number:
Employment Date:
Camp Service:
Notes:

Grund
First Name: Maria
Birthdate:
Birthplace:
Position: Aufseherin
File Number:
Employment Date:
Camp Service: Ravensbrück
Notes:

Grundmann
First Name: Elsbeth
Birthdate:
Birthplace:
Position: Aufseherin
File Number:
Employment Date:
Camp Service:
Notes:

Grundmann
First Name: Margarete
Birthdate:
Birthplace:
Position: Aufseherin
File Number:
Employment Date:
Camp Service: Ravensbrück
Notes:

Grundwald
First Name: Elisabeth
Birthdate:
Birthplace:
Position: Aufseherin
File Number:
Employment Date:
Camp Service:
Notes:

Grunert
First Name: Hildegard
Birthdate:
Birthplace:
Position: Aufseherin
File Number:
Employment Date:
Camp Service: Ravensbrück
Notes:

Grunert
First Name: Margarete
Birthdate:
Birthplace:
Position: Aufseherin
File Number:
Employment Date:
Camp Service: Ravensbrück
Notes:

Grunow
First Name: Ina
Birthdate:
Birthplace:
Position: Aufseherin
File Number:
Employment Date:
Camp Service: Groß-Rosen
Notes:

Grunwald
First Name: Elisabeth
Birthdate: April 24, 1923
Birthplace: Grünberg
Position: Aufseherin
File Number:
Employment Date: June 1, 1944
Camp Service: Groß-Rosen
Notes:

Grunwald
First Name: Margarete
Birthdate: June 15, 1918
Birthplace: Reichenbach
Position: Aufseherin

File Number:
Employment Date: August 1, 1944
Camp Service: Groß-Rosen
Notes:

Grunwald
First Name: Martha
Birthdate: February 21, 1909
Birthplace: Samter
Position: Aufseherin
File Number:
Employment Date: June 1, 1944
Camp Service: Groß-Rosen
Notes:

Gruschwitz
First Name: Martha
Birthdate: April 21, 1904
Birthplace:
Position: Aufseherin
File Number: IV 410(F) AR 2629/67
Employment Date:
Camp Service: Floßenbürg; AL Plauen
Notes:

Grusenick
First Name: Hildegard
Birthdate: July 19, 1914
Birthplace: Luebs (Upper Pomerania)
Position: Aufseherin
File Number:
Employment Date: August 18, 1944
Camp Service: Groß-Rosen
Notes:

Gruß
First Name: Johanna
Birthdate:
Birthplace:
Position: Aufseherin
File Number:
Employment Date:
Camp Service:
Notes:

Gryska
First Name: Elfriede
Birthdate: October 3, 1900
Birthplace: Reichenbach
Position: Aufseherin
File Number:
Employment Date: April 15, 1944
Camp Service: Groß-Rosen
Notes: Czech national; official permission for employment granted on December 11, 1944.

Gschwender
First Name: Frieda
Birthdate:
Birthplace:
Position: Aufseherin
File Number:
Employment Date:
Camp Service:
Notes:

Gstrein
First Name: Agnes
Birthdate: October 30, 1922
Birthplace: Müsiders
Position: Aufseherin
File Number: IV 410(F) AR 2629/67
Employment Date: July 1, 1943
Camp Service: Floßenbürg
Notes:

Gülland
First Name: Erna
Birthdate:
Birthplace:
Position: Aufseherin
File Number:
Employment Date:
Camp Service:
Notes:

Günther
First Name: Annemarie
Birthdate: March 8, 1920
Birthplace:
Position: Aufseherin
File Number: IV 429 AR 1973/66(B)
Employment Date:
Camp Service: Ravensbrück
Notes:

Günther (born Bernert)
First Name: Helene
Birthdate: September 19, 1923
Birthplace: Kühnau/Niemsch
Position: Aufseherin
File Number:
Employment Date: July 1, 1944
Camp Service: Groß-Rosen
Notes:

Günther
First Name: Rosa (Rosel)
Birthdate: July 31, 1922
Birthplace: Kosten/Teplitz
Position: Aufseherin
File Number: IV 410(F) AR 2629/67
Employment Date: September 8, 1944
Camp Service: Floßenbürg; AL Neu Rohlau
Notes: Official permission for employment as "employee of the Reich" granted on November 20, 1944.

Günther
First Name: Susanne
Birthdate: December 18, 1921
Birthplace:
Position: Auseherin
File Number: IV 410(F) AR 2629/67
Employment Date:
Camp Service: Floßenbürg; AL Mittweida
Notes:

Günther
First Name: Thea
Birthdate:

Birthplace:
Position: Aufseherin
File Number:
Employment Date:
Camp Service:
Notes:

Gürrmann
First Name: Lieselotte
Birthdate:
Birthplace:
Position: Aufseherin
File Number:
Employment Date:
Camp Service: Ravensbrück
Notes:

Güthlein
First Name: Erika
Birthdate:
Birthplace:
Position: Aufseherin
File Number:
Employment Date:
Camp Service:
Notes:

Guhl
First Name: Erna
Birthdate: May 31, 1921
Birthplace: Grossaupa
Position: Aufseherin
File Number:
Employment Date: August 21, 1944
Camp Service: Groß-Rosen
Notes:

Guhl
First Name: Ida
Birthdate: March 7, 1903
Birthplace: Dresden
Position: Aufseherin
File Number: IV 410(F) AR 2629/67
Employment Date: August 16, 1944
Camp Service: Floßenbürg; Ravensbrück; AL Dresden-Reick
Notes:

Gullasch (born Krüger)
First Name: Irma
Birthdate:
Birthplace:
Position: Aufseherin
File Number:
Employment Date:
Camp Service:
Notes:

Gunkler
First Name: Auguste
Birthdate:
Birthplace:
Position: Aufseherin
File Number:
Employment Date:
Camp Service:
Notes:

Gunsch
First Name: Berta
Birthdate:
Birthplace:
Position: Aufseherin
File Number:
Employment Date:
Camp Service: Ravensbrück
Notes:

Gurnig
First Name: Ilse
Birthdate: May 26, 1921
Birthplace: Wüstewaldersdorf
Position: Aufseherin
File Number:
Employment Date: July 29, 1944
Camp Service: Groß-Rosen
Notes: Official permission for employment as "employee of the Reich" granted on November 25, 1944.

Guschelbauer
First Name: Christine
Birthdate:
Birthplace:
Position: Aufseherin
File Number:
Employment Date:
Camp Service:
Notes:

Guth
First Name: Erna
Birthdate: November 24, 1923
Birthplace: Breitenbach
Position: Aufseherin
File Number:
Employment Date: December 11, 1944
Camp Service: Ravensbrück
Notes:

Gutsche
First Name: Erna
Birthdate:
Birthplace:
Position: Aufseherin
File Number:
Employment Date:
Camp Service:
Notes:

Gutschera
First Name: Ursula
Birthdate:
Birthplace:
Position: Aufseherin
File Number:
Employment Date:
Camp Service:
Notes:

Guttenberger
First Name: Marga
Birthdate: April 21, 1922

Birthplace: Nuremberg
Position: Aufseherin
File Number: IV 410(F) AR 2629/67
Employment Date: October 24, 1944
Camp Service: Floßenbürg; AL Graslitz
Notes:

Gutzeit (born Kütterer)
First Name: Loni
Birthdate:
Birthplace:
Position: Kommandoführerin: SS Member
File Number: IV 404(F) AR 2629/67
Employment Date:
Camp Service: Neuengamme; NL Hamburg-Wandsbeck
Notes: Inmates nicknamed her: *"Der Drache Wandsbeck"* ("The Dragon Wandsbeck").

Gwiadowski (or Gwiazdowski)
First Name: Erika
Birthdate: June 12, 1922
Birthplace: Berlin
Position: Aufseherin
File Number: IV 410(F) AR 2629/67
Employment Date:
Camp Service: Floßenbürg; AL Graslitz
Notes:

Gwozdz (born Tkotz)
First Name: Helene
Birthdate:
Birthplace:
Position: Aufseherin
File Number:
Employment Date:
Camp Service:
Notes:

Haas
First Name: Dora
Birthdate: April 23, 1913
Birthplace:
Position: Aufseherin
File Number: IV 410(F) AR 2629/67
Employment Date:
Camp Service: Floßenbürg; AL Dresden
Notes:

Haas (born Fielenbach)
First Name: Maria
Birthdate:
Birthplace:
Position: Aufseherin
File Number:
Employment Date:
Camp Service:
Notes:

Haase
First Name: Charlotte
Birthdate: December 7, 1922
Birthplace:
Position: Aufseherin
File Number: IV 429 AR 1941/66(B)
Employment Date:

Camp Service: NL Torgau
Notes:

Haase
First Name: Christa
Birthdate:
Birthplace:
Position: Aufseherin
File Number:
Employment Date:
Camp Service:
Notes:

Haase
First Name: Elisabeth
Birthdate:
Birthplace:
Position: Aufseherin
File Number:
Employment Date:
Camp Service: Groß-Rosen
Notes:

Haase (born Thrum)
First Name: Erna
Birthdate:
Birthplace:
Position: Aufseherin
File Number:
Employment Date:
Camp Service: Ravensbrück
Notes:

Haase (born Schmidt)
First Name: Herta
Birthdate: May 18, 1918
Birthplace: Chemnitz
Position: Kommandoleiterin: Waffen SS
File Number: IV 410(F) AR 2629/67
Employment Date: August 26, 1944
Camp Service: Floßenbürg; Kommando Helmbrechts
Notes: Initial entry date: August 2, 1944.

Haase
First Name: Louise
Birthdate: February 18, 1915
Birthplace:
Position: Aufseherin
File Number: IV 410(F) AR 2629/67
Employment Date:
Camp Service: Floßenbürg; AL Willischtal
Notes:

Habenicht
First Name: Frieda
Birthdate: September 5, 1912
Birthplace: Braunschweig
Position: Aufseherin
File Number:
Employment Date: October 24, 1944
Camp Service: Floßenbürg
Notes: Official permission for employment as an "employee of the Reich" granted on December 12, 1944.

Haberkorn (born Berner)
First Name: Elisabeth
Birthdate:
Birthplace:
Position: Aufseherin
File Number:
Employment Date:
Camp Service: Ravensbrück
Notes:

Haberl (born Dorbrietz)
First Name: Margarete
Birthdate:
Birthplace:
Position: Aufseherin
File Number:
Employment Date:
Camp Service:
Notes:

Haberland (born Bayer)
First Name: Gertrud
Birthdate:
Birthplace:
Position: Aufseherin
File Number:
Employment Date:
Camp Service:
Notes:

Habermann
First Name: Helma
Birthdate:
Birthplace:
Position: Aufseherin
File Number:
Employment Date:
Camp Service:
Notes:

Hackebeil
First Name: Herta
Birthdate:
Birthplace:
Position: Aufseherin
File Number:
Employment Date:
Camp Service: Ravensbrück
Notes:

Hackler (married Brendel)
First Name: Helene
Birthdate: September 3, 1913
Birthplace: Laasphe
Position: Aufseherin
File Number: IV 406 AR-Z 21/71
Employment Date:
Camp Service: NL Genshagen; Ravensbrück
Notes:

Häder
First Name: Katharina
Birthdate: January 25, 1899
Birthplace:
Position: Aufseherin

File Number: IV 410(F) AR 2629/67
Employment Date:
Camp Service: Floßenbürg; AL Dresden-Universelle
Notes:

Häneke
First Name: Margot
Birthdate:
Birthplace:
Position: Aufseherin
File Number:
Employment Date:
Camp Service: Ravensbrück
Notes:

Hänel
First Name: Käte
Birthdate:
Birthplace:
Position: Aufseherin
File Number:
Employment Date:
Camp Service:
Notes:

Haenel
First Name: Martha
Birthdate: March 17, 1917
Birthplace: Krumhermersdorf
Position: Aufseherin
File Number: IV 410(F) AR 2629/67
Employment Date:
Camp Service: Floßenbürg; AL Holleischen
Notes:

Haenisch
First Name: Charlotte
Birthdate:
Birthplace:
Position: Aufseherin
File Number:
Employment Date:
Camp Service: Groß-Rosen
Notes:

Haering
First Name: Elfriede
Birthdate:
Birthplace:
Position: Aufseherin
File Number:
Employment Date:
Camp Service:
Notes:

Härtel
First Name: Charlotte
Birthdate: July 13, 1910
Birthplace: Dresden
Position: Erstaufseherin; *Strafkommandoführerin* (punishment detail leader)
File Number: IV 410(F) AR 2629/67
Employment Date: August 16, 1944
Camp Service: Floßenbürg; AL Goehle-Werk Dresden
Notes:

Hässler

First Name: Anna
Birthdate: July 15, 1920
Birthplace: Plan/Marienbad
Position: Aufseherin
File Number: IV 410(F) AR 2629/67
Employment Date: October 9, 1944
Camp Service: Floßenbürg; AL Holleischen
Notes:

Häßler

First Name: Elli (or Else)
Birthdate: October 4, 1916
Birthplace: Plauen
Position: Aufseherin
File Number: IV 410 AR-Z 94/70 (B)
Employment Date:
Camp Service: Ravensbrück; Floßenbürg; NL Plauen
Notes:

Hafermann

First Name: Elfriede
Birthdate:
Birthplace:
Position: Aufseherin
File Number:
Employment Date:
Camp Service:
Notes:

Hage

First Name: Hendrike
Birthdate:
Birthplace:
Position: Aufseherin
File Number:
Employment Date:
Camp Service: Ravensbrück
Notes:

Hahn

First Name: Berta
Birthdate:
Birthplace:
Position: Aufseherin
File Number:
Employment Date:
Camp Service:
Notes:

Hahn

First Name: Gertrud
Birthdate:
Birthplace:
Position: Aufseherin
File Number:
Employment Date:
Camp Service:
Notes:

Hahn

First Name: Ilse
Birthdate:
Birthplace:
Position: Aufseherin

File Number:
Employment Date:
Camp Service: Ravensbrück
Notes:

Hahn (born Warming)

First Name: Irmgard
Birthdate:
Birthplace:
Position: Aufseherin
File Number:
Employment Date:
Camp Service:
Notes:

Hahn (born Wergin)

First Name: Ursula
Birthdate:
Birthplace:
Position: Aufseherin
File Number:
Employment Date:
Camp Service:
Notes:

Hailer

First Name: Ilse
Birthdate:
Birthplace:
Position: Aufseherin
File Number:
Employment Date:
Camp Service: Ravensbrück
Notes:

Haim

First Name: Elsa
Birthdate:
Birthplace:
Position: Aufseherin
File Number:
Employment Date:
Camp Service:
Notes:

Hakenberg

First Name: Anna
Birthdate:
Birthplace:
Position: Aufseherin
File Number:
Employment Date:
Camp Service:
Notes:

Hakenes (born Wermuth)

First Name: Johanna
Birthdate:
Birthplace:
Position: Aufseherin
File Number:
Employment Date:
Camp Service:
Notes:

Halata
First Name: Luzie
Birthdate:
Birthplace:
Position: Aufseherin
File Number:
Employment Date:
Camp Service:
Notes:

Hallasch
First Name: Ilse
Birthdate:
Birthplace:
Position: Aufseherin
File Number:
Employment Date:
Camp Service: Groß-Rosen
Notes:

Hallmann
First Name: Erna
Birthdate:
Birthplace:
Position: Aufseherin
File Number:
Employment Date:
Camp Service:
Notes:

Hallmann
First Name: Hildegard
Birthdate:
Birthplace:
Position: Aufseherin
File Number:
Employment Date:
Camp Service: Groß-Rosen
Notes:

Hamann
First Name: Lizzi
Birthdate:
Birthplace:
Position: Aufseherin
File Number:
Employment Date:
Camp Service: Ravensbrück
Notes:

Hambauer
First Name: Hildegard
Birthdate:
Birthplace:
Position: Aufseherin
File Number:
Employment Date:
Camp Service:
Notes:

Hamel (born Tonicke)
First Name: Walli
Birthdate:
Birthplace:
Position: Aufseherin

File Number:
Employment Date:
Camp Service:
Notes:

Hamm
First Name: Maria
Birthdate:
Birthplace:
Position: Aufseherin
File Number:
Employment Date:
Camp Service:
Notes:

Hammerschik
First Name: Mathilde
Birthdate:
Birthplace:
Position: Aufseherin
File Number:
Employment Date:
Camp Service:
Notes:

Hampel (born Christof)
First Name: Selma
Birthdate:
Birthplace:
Position: Aufseherin
File Number:
Employment Date:
Camp Service:
Notes:

Hampel (born John)
First Name: Georgette
Birthdate:
Birthplace:
Position: Aufseherin
File Number:
Employment Date:
Camp Service: Ravensbrück
Notes:

Hamplewski
First Name: Elisabeth
Birthdate:
Birthplace:
Position: Aufseherin
File Number:
Employment Date:
Camp Service:
Notes:

Hamzel
First Name: Irene
Birthdate:
Birthplace:
Position: Aufseherin
File Number:
Employment Date:
Camp Service: Groß-Rosen
Notes:

Hanakam

First Name:	Charlotte
Birthdate:	
Birthplace:	
Position:	Kommandoführerin
File Number:	IV 410 AR 2669/67
Employment Date:	
Camp Service:	Kommando Dresden Universelle; Floßenbürg
Notes:	

Handke

First Name:	Helene
Birthdate:	
Birthplace:	
Position:	Aufseherin
File Number:	
Employment Date:	
Camp Service:	
Notes:	

Handschuh

First Name:	Emmi
Birthdate:	
Birthplace:	
Position:	Aufseherin
File Number:	
Employment Date:	
Camp Service:	
Notes:	

Hangebrauk

First Name:	Erna
Birthdate:	
Birthplace:	
Position:	Aufseherin
File Number:	
Employment Date:	
Camp Service:	Ravensbrück
Notes:	

Hanke

First Name:	Elfriede
Birthdate:	
Birthplace:	
Position:	Aufseherin
File Number:	
Employment Date:	
Camp Service:	
Notes:	

Hanke

First Name:	Hildegard
Birthdate:	
Birthplace:	
Position:	Aufseherin
File Number:	
Employment Date:	
Camp Service:	
Notes:	

Hanke (born Köppert)

First Name:	Frieda
Birthdate:	
Birthplace:	
Position:	Aufseherin

File Number:	
Employment Date:	
Camp Service:	
Notes:	

Hanneschläger

First Name:	Betty
Birthdate:	August 2, 1916
Birthplace:	Augsburg
Position:	Aufseherin
File Number:	
Employment Date:	August 20, 1944
Camp Service:	Ravensbrück; Dachau
Notes:	

Hannsch

First Name:	Angela
Birthdate:	
Birthplace:	
Position:	Aufseherin
File Number:	
Employment Date:	
Camp Service:	
Notes:	

Hansen

First Name:	Dorothea (Thea)
Birthdate:	
Birthplace:	
Position:	Aufseherin
File Number:	
Employment Date:	
Camp Service:	
Notes:	

Hansen

First Name:	Marie
Birthdate:	
Birthplace:	
Position:	Aufseherin
File Number:	
Employment Date:	
Camp Service:	Ravensbrück
Notes:	

Happ

First Name:	Herta
Birthdate:	
Birthplace:	Hamburg
Position:	Aufseherin
File Number:	IV 409 AR-Z 39/59
Employment Date:	
Camp Service:	Ravensbrück; NL Barth
Notes:	

Harke (born Schöler)

First Name:	Käthe
Birthdate:	
Birthplace:	
Position:	Aufseherin
File Number:	
Employment Date:	
Camp Service:	
Notes:	

Harneid
First Name: Frieda
Birthdate:
Birthplace:
Position: Aufseherin
File Number:
Employment Date:
Camp Service: Neuengamme
Notes:

Harnisch
First Name: Anneliese
Birthdate:
Birthplace:
Position: Aufseherin
File Number:
Employment Date:
Camp Service: Ravensbrück
Notes:

Haronska (born Buchholz)
First Name: Therese
Birthdate:
Birthplace:
Position: Aufseherin
File Number:
Employment Date:
Camp Service: Ravensbrück
Notes:

Harsching
First Name: Margit
Birthdate:
Birthplace:
Position: Aufseherin
File Number:
Employment Date:
Camp Service: Ravensbrück
Notes:

Hartel
First Name: Lydia
Birthdate:
Birthplace:
Position: Aufseherin
File Number:
Employment Date:
Camp Service: Ravensbrück
Notes:

Hartknopf
First Name: Elfriede
Birthdate:
Birthplace:
Position: Aufseherin
File Number:
Employment Date:
Camp Service:
Notes:

Hartmann (born Goldhorn)
First Name: Elly (or Elli)
Birthdate: 1920
Birthplace:
Position: Aufseherin
File Number: IV 402 AR-Z 37/58
Employment Date:
Camp Service: Auschwitz; Ravensbrück
Notes: Prosecuted for murder, but findings absent from *Zentralestelle* (Ludwigsburg) file.

Hartwig
First Name: Thea
Birthdate:
Birthplace:
Position: Aufseherin
File Number:
Employment Date:
Camp Service: Ravensbrück
Notes:

Harzberger
First Name: Liesbeth
Birthdate:
Birthplace:
Position: Aufseherin
File Number:
Employment Date:
Camp Service: Ravensbrück
Notes:

Harzer
First Name: Elfriede
Birthdate:
Birthplace:
Position: Aufseherin
File Number:
Employment Date:
Camp Service: Floßenbürg
Notes:

Haselof (born Radojewski; married Rapior)
First Name: Elisabeth (Liesel)
Birthdate: July 19, 1921
Birthplace: Greppin
Position: Aufseherin
File Number: 409 AR-Z 39/59
Employment Date: June 1, 1943
Camp Service: Auschwitz; Lublin-Majdanek
Notes:

Hasler
First Name: Magdalena
Birthdate:
Birthplace:
Position: Aufseherin
File Number:
Employment Date:
Camp Service: Groß-Rosen
Notes:

Hass
First Name: Dora
Birthdate:
Birthplace:
Position: Aufseherin
File Number: IV 410(F) AR 2629/67; 410 AR-Z 23/68
Employment Date:
Camp Service: Floßenbürg; AL Zwodau
Notes:

Hass

First Name: Margarethe
Birthdate: October 12, 1919
Birthplace: Wittenberg
Position: Aufseherin
File Number: IV 410(F) AR 2629/67
Employment Date: August 16, 1944
Camp Service: Floßenbürg; AL Zwodau; AL Dresden-Reick
Notes:

Hatlapa (born König)

First Name: Helene
Birthdate:
Birthplace:
Position: Aufseherin
File Number:
Employment Date:
Camp Service:
Notes:

Haubner

First Name: Natalie
Birthdate:
Birthplace:
Position: Aufseherin
File Number:
Employment Date:
Camp Service: Groß-Rosen
Notes:

Haubold

First Name: Elsa
Birthdate: March 22, 1909
Birthplace:
Position: Aufseherin
File Number: IV 410(F) AR 2629/67
Employment Date:
Camp Service: Floßenbürg; AL Oederan
Notes:

Haufe

First Name: Margarete
Birthdate:
Birthplace:
Position: Aufseherin
File Number:
Employment Date:
Camp Service: Neuengamme
Notes:

Haug

First Name: Anna
Birthdate:
Birthplace:
Position: Aufseherin
File Number:
Employment Date:
Camp Service:
Notes:

Hauk (born Kästner)

First Name: Irmgard
Birthdate: December 24, 1919
Birthplace: Bertelsdorf
Position: Aufseherin

File Number: IV 410(F) AR 2629/67
Employment Date: September 8, 1944
Camp Service: Ravensbrück; Floßenbürg; AL Hainichen
Notes:

Hauk (born Uhlemann)

First Name: Margarete
Birthdate: December 4, 1919
Birthplace: Bertelsdorf
Position: Aufseherin
File Number: IV 410(F) AR 2629/67
Employment Date: August 17, 1944
Camp Service: Floßenbürg; AL Hainichen
Notes:

Haupt

First Name: Dora
Birthdate: December 17, 1919
Birthplace: Hainichen
Position: Aufseherin
File Number: IV 410(F) AR 2629/67
Employment Date: August 17, 1944
Camp Service: Floßenbürg; AL Hainichen
Notes:

Haupt

First Name: Erika
Birthdate: December 14, 1921
Birthplace: Chemnitz
Position: Aufseherin: Waffen SS
File Number: IV 410(F) AR 2629/67
Employment Date: August 26, 1944
Camp Service: Floßenbürg; Kommando Helmbrechts
Notes:

Hausherr

First Name: Anni (Fanny)
Birthdate: July 18, 1921
Birthplace: Straube (or Strube)
Position: Aufseherin
File Number: IV 409 AR-Z 39/59
Employment Date: May 15, 1944
Camp Service: Auschwitz; Ravensbrück; NL Allendorf
Notes:

Hausherr

First Name: Irmgard
Birthdate: June 8, 1923
Birthplace: Berlin
Position: Aufseherin
File Number: IV 402 AR-Z 37/58
Employment Date:
Camp Service: Auschwitz
Notes: In an affidavit, denied ever having been in Auschwitz.

Hautz (born Riemann)

First Name: Ursel
Birthdate: March 2, 1922
Birthplace: Hainichen
Position: Aufseherin
File Number: IV 410(F) AR 2629/67
Employment Date: August 22, 1944
Camp Service: Floßenbürg; AL Hainichen
Notes:

Haverkamp

First Name: Irmgard
Birthdate:
Birthplace:
Position: Aufseherin
File Number:
Employment Date:
Camp Service: Neuengamme
Notes: Service as a Waffen SS auxiliary began on August 25, 1944.

Heber

First Name: Katharina
Birthdate:
Birthplace:
Position: Aufseherin
File Number:
Employment Date:
Camp Service:
Notes:

Hechler

First Name: Irmgard
Birthdate:
Birthplace:
Position: Aufseherin
File Number:
Employment Date:
Camp Service:
Notes:

Hecker

First Name: Margot
Birthdate:
Birthplace:
Position: Aufseherin
File Number:
Employment Date:
Camp Service: Groß-Rosen
Notes:

Hedwig (or Hewdig)

First Name: Walli (or Wally)
Birthdate: June 14, 1922
Birthplace: Breslau
Position: Aufseherin
File Number: IV 410(F) AR 2629/67
Employment Date: October 4, 1944
Camp Service: Floßenbürg; NL Mehltheuer; NL Venusberg; NL Graslitz; NL Zwodau; AL Dresden-Reick
Notes:

Heeren (born Koopmann)

First Name: Käthe
Birthdate:
Birthplace:
Position: Aufseherin
File Number:
Employment Date:
Camp Service:
Notes:

Heese

First Name: Elsa
Birthdate:

Birthplace:
Position: Aufseherin
File Number:
Employment Date:
Camp Service: Ravensbrück
Notes:

Heffgen (born Schwörer)

First Name: Elisabeth
Birthdate:
Birthplace:
Position: Aufseherin
File Number:
Employment Date:
Camp Service:
Notes:

Heger

First Name: Hermine
Birthdate:
Birthplace:
Position: Aufseherin
File Number:
Employment Date:
Camp Service: Ravensbrück
Notes:

Hegewald

First Name: Gertraude
Birthdate: March 12, 1923
Birthplace:
Position: Aufseherin
File Number: IV 410(F) AR 2629/67
Employment Date:
Camp Service: Floßenbürg; AL Dresden-Reick
Notes:

Heiden

First Name: Gerda
Birthdate:
Birthplace:
Position: Aufseherin
File Number:
Employment Date:
Camp Service: Ravensbrück
Notes:

Heider

First Name: Gertrud
Birthdate: August 23, 1920
Birthplace:
Position: Aufseherin
File Number: IV 410(F) AR 2629/67
Employment Date:
Camp Service: Floßenbürg; AL Oederan; AL Holleischen
Notes:

Heidler

First Name: Elsa
Birthdate:
Birthplace:
Position: Aufseherin
File Number:
Employment Date:
Camp Service:
Notes:

Heidmann

First Name: Resi
Birthdate:
Birthplace:
Position: Aufseherin
File Number:
Employment Date:
Camp Service:
Notes:

Heidrich (born Jentz)

First Name: Ida
Birthdate: April 13, 1912
Birthplace: Standorf
Position: Aufseherin
File Number: IV 405 AR 2796/67
Employment Date:
Camp Service: Groß-Rosen; NL Gräben
Notes:

Heikens

First Name: Hilliena-Grietje
Birthdate:
Birthplace:
Position: Aufseherin
File Number:
Employment Date:
Camp Service:
Notes: Dutch national; special permission for admission into service as a Waffen SS auxiliary.

Heilemann

First Name: Marta
Birthdate:
Birthplace:
Position: Aufseherin
File Number:
Employment Date:
Camp Service:
Notes:

Heim

First Name: Käthe
Birthdate:
Birthplace:
Position: Aufseherin
File Number:
Employment Date:
Camp Service: Ravensbrück
Notes:

Heimel

First Name: Maria
Birthdate:
Birthplace:
Position: Aufseherin
File Number:
Employment Date:
Camp Service:
Notes:

Hein (born Just)

First Name: Dorothea (Thea)
Birthdate: October 10, 1922

Birthplace:
Position: Aufseherin
File Number: IV 410(F) 2629/67
Employment Date: March 3, 1945
Camp Service: Floßenbürg; AL Graslitz; Mittweida; Ravensbrück
Notes:

Hein

First Name: Elfriede
Birthdate:
Birthplace:
Position: Aufseherin
File Number:
Employment Date:
Camp Service:
Notes:

Hein

First Name: Gertrud
Birthdate: February 19, 1922
Birthplace:
Position: Aufseherin
File Number: IV 409 AR-Z 39/59
Employment Date:
Camp Service: Ravensbrück
Notes:

Hein (born Fröhlich)

First Name: Gertrud
Birthdate:
Birthplace:
Position: Aufseherin
File Number:
Employment Date:
Camp Service:
Notes:

Hein

First Name: Paula
Birthdate:
Birthplace:
Position: Aufseherin
File Number:
Employment Date:
Camp Service:
Notes:

Heine

First Name: Emmi
Birthdate:
Birthplace:
Position: Aufseherin
File Number:
Employment Date:
Camp Service: Ravensbrück
Notes:

Heine

First Name: Lisbeth
Birthdate: April 15, 1922
Birthplace:
Position: Aufseherin
File Number: IV 429 AR 1941/66 (B)
Employment Date:

Camp Service: NL Torgau
Notes:

Heine

First Name: Ursula
Birthdate: April 6, 1922
Birthplace:
Position: Aufseherin
File Number: IV 410(F) AR 2629/67
Employment Date:
Camp Service: Floßenbürg, AL Rochlitz
Notes:

Heinemann (Srubek)

First Name: Maria
Birthdate: June 9, 1922
Birthplace: Eschenstroth
Position: Aufseherin
File Number: 409 AR-Z 39/59
Employment Date: July 15, 1944
Camp Service: Ravensbrück (three week training); NL Heßisch-Lichtenau
Notes:

Heinemann

First Name: Martha
Birthdate:
Birthplace:
Position: Aufseherin
File Number:
Employment Date:
Camp Service:
Notes:

Heinemann (born Hoffmann)

First Name: Lucretia
Birthdate:
Birthplace:
Position: Aufseherin
File Number:
Employment Date:
Camp Service:
Notes:

Heinen

First Name: Aracelli
Birthdate: June 1, 1920
Birthplace: St. Moritz
Position: Aufseherin
File Number:
Employment Date: December 15, 1944
Camp Service: Ravensbrück
Notes: French national; special request for service as an "employee of the Reich" granted.

Heinig

First Name: Dora
Birthdate: April 30, 1922
Birthplace: Gößnitz
Position: Aufseherin
File Number:
Employment Date: September 6, 1944
Camp Service: Ravensbrück
Notes:

Heinrich

First Name: Irmgard
Birthdate: 1916 (no month or day noted in her file)
Birthplace: Torgau
Position: Aufseherin
File Number: IV 429 AR 1941/66(B)
Employment Date:
Camp Service: NL Torgau
Notes:

Heinrich

First Name: Käthe
Birthdate: February 1, 1920
Birthplace:
Position: Aufseherin
File Number: IV 410(F) AR 2629/67
Employment Date:
Camp Service: Floßenbürg; AL Oederan
Notes:

Heinrich (born Zimmer)

First Name: Elvira
Birthdate:
Birthplace:
Position: Aufseherin
File Number:
Employment Date:
Camp Service:
Notes:

Heinrich (born Schlesinger)

First Name: Ursula
Birthdate:
Birthplace:
Position: Aufseherin
File Number:
Employment Date:
Camp Service: Ravensbrück
Notes:

Heinrich (born Kelleter)

First Name: Veronika
Birthdate:
Birthplace:
Position: Aufseherin
File Number:
Employment Date:
Camp Service:
Notes:

Heinz

First Name: Maria
Birthdate:
Birthplace:
Position: Aufseherin
File Number:
Employment Date:
Camp Service:
Notes:

Heinz

First Name: Marianne
Birthdate: October 30, 1922
Birthplace:
Position: Aufseherin

File Number: IV 410(F) AR 2629/67
Employment Date:
Camp Service: Floßenbürg; AL Hainichen;
Ravensbrück
Notes:

Heinze

First Name: Erna
Birthdate:
Birthplace:
Position: Aufseherin
File Number:
Employment Date:
Camp Service:
Notes:

Heinzel

First Name: Hildegard
Birthdate:
Birthplace:
Position: Aufseherin
File Number:
Employment Date:
Camp Service: Groß-Rosen
Notes:

Heise (married Senff)

First Name: Gertrud
Birthdate: July 23, 1921
Birthplace: Berlin
Position: Aufseherin
File Number: 40-2/3; IV 409 AR-Z 297/60;
IV 407 AR-Z 297/60
Employment Date: November 21, 1941
Camp Service: Ravensbrück; Lublin-Majdanek, Auschwitz
Birkenau; Krakow-Plaszów; Neuengamme
Notes: Sentenced to seven years imprisonment for war
crimes by a British court in Celle on May 22,
1946.

Heise

First Name: Herta
Birthdate:
Birthplace:
Position: Aufseherin
File Number:
Employment Date:
Camp Service: Ravensbrück
Notes:

Heitler

First Name: Barbara
Birthdate:
Birthplace:
Position: Aufseherin
File Number:
Employment Date:
Camp Service:
Notes:

Heitler

First Name: Margit
Birthdate: October 11, 1921
Birthplace: Drachowitz
Position: Aufseherin

File Number: IV 410(F) AR 2629/67
Employment Date: October 9, 1944
Camp Service: Floßenbürg; AL Holleischen
Notes:

Helbig

First Name: Anneliese
Birthdate:
Birthplace:
Position: Aufseherin
File Number:
Employment Date:
Camp Service:
Notes:

Helbig (born Naumann)

First Name: Hedwig
Birthdate: June 11, 1906
Birthplace: Pappendorf
Position: Aufseherin
File Number: IV 410(F) AR 2629/67
Employment Date: August 17, 1944
Camp Service: Floßenbürg; AL Hainichen
Notes:

Helbig

First Name: Hildegard
Birthdate: January 8, 1920
Birthplace: Tauscha
Position: Aufseherin
File Number: IV 410(F) AR 2629/67
Employment Date: August 21, 1944
Camp Service: Floßenbürg; AL Rochlitz
Notes:

Helbig

First Name: Olympia
Birthdate:
Birthplace:
Position: Aufseherin
File Number:
Employment Date:
Camp Service:
Notes:

Hehnal

First Name: Hildegard
Birthdate:
Birthplace:
Position: Aufseherin
File Number:
Employment Date:
Camp Service: Ravensbrück; Bergen-Belsen
Notes:

Helke

First Name: Erna
Birthdate: January 7, 1923
Birthplace: Breitenau
Position: Aufseherin
File Number: IV 410(F) AR 2629/67
Employment Date: September 8, 1944
Camp Service: Floßenbürg; Oederan
Notes:

Hellenkamp

First Name: Gertrud
Birthdate:
Birthplace:
Position: Aufseherin
File Number:
Employment Date:
Camp Service:
Notes:

Hellenschmidt

First Name: Anneliese
Birthdate: June 30, 1920
Birthplace: Nuremberg
Position: Aufseherin
File Number: IV 410(F) AR 2629/67
Employment Date: September 30, 1944
Camp Service: Floßenbürg; AL Graslitz; AL Holleischen
Notes: Permission for employment as an "employee of the Reich" granted on December 12, 1944.

Hellmeßen

First Name: Katharina
Birthdate: 1901
Birthplace:
Position: Aufseherin; Rapportführerin
File Number:
Employment Date:
Camp Service: Kleinschönau bei. Zittau
Notes: *Zentralestelle* (Ludwigsburg) file states that defendant worked at "Häftlingslager der Zitt-Werke," but the location of the crimes she was punished for was "Kleinschönau bei Zittau."

Hellner

First Name: Erna
Birthdate:
Birthplace:
Position: Aufseherin
File Number:
Employment Date:
Camp Service: Groß-Rosen
Notes:

Hellterf (born Hager)

First Name: Irmgard
Birthdate:
Birthplace:
Position: Aufseherin
File Number:
Employment Date:
Camp Service:
Notes:

Hellwich

First Name: Nelli
Birthdate: September 30, 1913
Birthplace: Köln
Position: Aufseherin
File Number:
Employment Date: July 1, 1944
Camp Service: Ravensbrück
Notes:

Hellwig

First Name: Martha
Birthdate: October 12, 1919
Birthplace: Zeldenick
Position: Aufseherin
File Number:
Employment Date: November 23, 1944
Camp Service: Ravensbrück
Notes:

Helm (born Sperling)

First Name: Hertha
Birthdate:
Birthplace:
Position: Aufseherin
File Number:
Employment Date:
Camp Service:
Notes:

Helmreich

First Name: Klara (Kläre)
Birthdate: January 4, 1908
Birthplace: Leipzig
Position: Aufseherin
File Number: IV 410(F) AR 2629/67
Employment Date: September 8, 1944
Camp Service: Floßenbürg; AL Hertine
Notes:

Helms

First Name: Alma
Birthdate:
Birthplace:
Position: Aufseherin
File Number:
Employment Date:
Camp Service:
Notes:

Hempel (born Herdlitschke)

First Name: Anna
Birthdate: June 22, 1900
Birthplace: Grünberg
Position: Aufseherin
File Number: 40-2/3, 410 AR 1750/61
Employment Date:
Camp Service: KL Grünberg
Notes: Sentenced to ten years imprisonment by a British court, but was released on December 22, 1951 after serving less than six years.

Hempel

First Name: Christa
Birthdate:
Birthplace:
Position: Aufseherin
File Number:
Employment Date:
Camp Service: Floßenbürg
Notes: Captured by the Soviet forces and ostensibly taken to a *gulag*; fate unknown.

Hempel (born Lohse)
First Name: Lieselotte
Birthdate:
Birthplace:
Position: Aufseherin
File Number:
Employment Date:
Camp Service:
Notes:

Henkel
First Name: Edeltrud
Birthdate:
Birthplace:
Position: Aufseherin
File Number:
Employment Date:
Camp Service: Sachsenhausen
Notes:

Henkemeier (born Müller)
First Name: Hildegard
Birthdate: October 20, 1912
Birthplace:
Position: Aufseherin
File Number: 10 AR 355/96
Employment Date:
Camp Service:
Notes:

Henschel
First Name: Else
Birthdate:
Birthplace:
Position: Aufseherin
File Number:
Employment Date:
Camp Service: Groß-Rosen
Notes:

Hense
First Name: Elise
Birthdate:
Birthplace:
Position: Aufseherin
File Number:
Employment Date:
Camp Service: Neuengamme
Notes:

Hensel
First Name: Elisabeth
Birthdate:
Birthplace:
Position: Aufseherin
File Number:
Employment Date:
Camp Service:
Notes:

Hentschel (born Ruske)
First Name: Margarete (or Margaretha)
Birthdate: Juuly 29, 1902
Birthplace: Bad Landeck
Position: Aufsehrin; Rapportführerin

File Number: IV 405 AR 2796/67
Employment Date: 1944 (no month or date noted in her file)
Camp Service: Groß-Rosen, NL Gräben
Notes:

Heppeler
First Name: Irma
Birthdate:
Birthplace:
Position: Aufseherin
File Number:
Employment Date:
Camp Service: Neuengamme
Notes:

Heppner
First Name: Maria
Birthdate: February 2, 1922
Birthplace: Hilgersdorf
Position: Aufseherin
File Number:
Employment Date: July 31, 1944
Camp Service: Ravensbrück
Notes:

Herbst
First Name: Helene
Birthdate: August 12, 1922
Birthplace: Reinfeld
Position: Aufseherin
File Number:
Employment Date: June 1, 1944
Camp Service: Groß-Rosen
Notes:

Hering
First Name: Elisabeth
Birthdate:
Birthplace:
Position: Aufseherin
File Number:
Employment Date:
Camp Service:
Notes:

Hering
First Name: Margot
Birthdate:
Birthplace:
Position: Aufseherin
File Number:
Employment Date:
Camp Service:
Notes:

Herklotz
First Name: Ilse
Birthdate:
Birthplace:
Position: Aufseherin
File Number:
Employment Date:
Camp Service:
Notes:

Herklotz

First Name: Ursula
Birthdate:
Birthplace:
Position: Aufseherin
File Number:
Employment Date:
Camp Service: Ravensbrück
Notes:

Herkner

First Name: Lisbeth
Birthdate: June 25, 1913
Birthplace: Friedensdorf
Position: Aufseherin
File Number:
Employment Date: September 5, 1944
Camp Service: Groß-Rosen
Notes:

Herm (born Dittmann)

First Name: Meta
Birthdate:
Birthplace:
Position: Aufseherin
File Number:
Employment Date:
Camp Service:
Notes:

Hermann

First Name: Erna
Birthdate:
Birthplace:
Position: Aufseherin
File Number:
Employment Date:
Camp Service:
Notes:

Hermann

First Name: Ilse
Birthdate: September 9, 1921
Birthplace: Markersdorf
Position: Aufseherin
File Number: IV 410(F) AR 2629/67
Employment Date: September 19, 1944
Camp Service: Floßenbürg; AL Mitweida
Notes:

Hermann

First Name: Lydia
Birthdate: April 14, 1914
Birthplace: Breslau
Position: Aufseherin
File Number:
Employment Date: August 8, 1944
Camp Service: Groß-Rosen
Notes:

Hermges

First Name: Elfriede
Birthdate:
Birthplace:
Position: Aufseherin

File Number:
Employment Date:
Camp Service:
Notes:

Herold

First Name: Marie
Birthdate: July 31, 1918
Birthplace: Zetterding
Position: Aufseherin
File Number:
Employment Date: September 15, 1944
Camp Service: Mauthausen; Ravensbrück
Notes:

Herr

First Name: Ellen
Birthdate:
Birthplace:
Position: Aufseherin
File Number:
Employment Date:
Camp Service: Floßenbürg
Notes:

Herrmann

First Name: Brigitte
Birthdate:
Birthplace:
Position: Aufseherin
File Number:
Employment Date:
Camp Service:
Notes:

Herrmann

First Name: Dorothea
Birthdate: September 21, 1900
Birthplace: Strehla a. d. Elbe
Position: Aufseherin
File Number:
Employment Date: August 16, 1944
Camp Service: Floßenbürg
Notes:

Herrmann

First Name: Ilse
Birthdate: March 12, 1922
Birthplace: Ramsin
Position: Aufseherin
File Number:
Employment Date: June 1, 1943
Camp Service: Ravensbrück
Notes:

Herrmann

First Name: Käthe
Birthdate:
Birthplace:
Position: Aufseherin
File Number:
Employment Date:
Camp Service: Groß-Rosen
Notes:

Herrmann (born Kaprolat)
First Name: Marta
Birthdate:
Birthplace:
Position: Aufseherin
File Number:
Employment Date:
Camp Service:
Notes:

Herrmanns (born Helsper)
First Name: Maria
Birthdate:
Birthplace:
Position: Aufseherin
File Number:
Employment Date:
Camp Service:
Notes:

Hertel
First Name: Irma
Birthdate:
Birthplace:
Position: Aufseherin
File Number:
Employment Date:
Camp Service:
Notes:

Hertkorn
First Name: Theresia
Birthdate: October 9, 1923
Birthplace: Reichenbach im Tale
Position: Aufseherin
File Number: IV 409 AR-Z 39/59
Employment Date:
Camp Service: Ravensbrück; Geislingen
Notes: Was extradited to Poland by American authorities; fate unknown.

Herzberger
First Name: Elisabeth
Birthdate:
Birthplace:
Position: Aufseherin
File Number:
Employment Date:
Camp Service:
Notes:

Herzig
First Name: Agnes
Birthdate: January 21, 1916
Birthplace: Neurode-Buchau
Position: Aufseherin
File Number:
Employment Date: August 1, 1944
Camp Service: Groß-Rosen
Notes:

Herzig
First Name: Erna
Birthdate:
Birthplace:

Position: Aufseherin
File Number:
Employment Date:
Camp Service:
Notes:

Herzig (born Kubaile)
First Name: Anna
Birthdate: March 16, 1919
Birthplace: Grünberg
Position: Aufseherin
File Number:
Employment Date: June 1, 1944
Camp Service: Groß-Rosen
Notes:

Herzinger
First Name: Betti
Birthdate: November 4, 1914
Birthplace: Oberneukirchen
Position: Aufseherin
File Number:
Employment Date: September 1, 1940
Camp Service: Ravensbrück
Notes:

Herzog
First Name: Anna
Birthdate: February 8, 1922
Birthplace: Hainburg
Position: Aufseherin
File Number:
Employment Date: July 1, 1943
Camp Service: Floßenbürg; AL Zwodau
Notes:

Herzog
First Name: Elfriede
Birthdate: April 6, 1914
Birthplace: Langenbielau
Position: Aufseherin
File Number:
Employment Date: October 30, 1944
Camp Service: Groß-Rosen
Notes: Official permission for employment as an "employee of the Reich" granted on December 11, 1944.

Herzog
First Name: Käte
Birthdate:
Birthplace:
Position: Aufseherin
File Number:
Employment Date:
Camp Service:
Notes:

Hesse
First Name: Charlotte
Birthdate:
Birthplace:
Position: Aufseherin
File Number:
Employment Date:

Camp Service: Ravensbrück
Notes:

Hesse (born Koch)
First Name: Johanna
Birthdate:
Birthplace:
Position: Aufseherin
File Number:
Employment Date:
Camp Service:
Notes:

Heßler
First Name: Elli
Birthdate: May 7, 1924
Birthplace: Roitsch
Position: Aufseherin
File Number: IV 410(F) AR 2629/67
Employment Date: November 15, 1943
Camp Service: Floßenbürg; AL Graslitz
Notes:

Heukemeyer
First Name: Hildegard
Birthdate:
Birthplace:
Position: Aufseherin
File Number:
Employment Date:
Camp Service: Ravensbrück
Notes:

Heydenreich
First Name: Frieda
Birthdate: January 27, 1913
Birthplace: Siegmar
Position: Aufseherin
File Number: IV 410(F) AR 2629/67
Employment Date: October 1, 1944
Camp Service: Floßenbürg; AL Holleischen
Notes:

Heyer
First Name: Frieda
Birthdate:
Birthplace:
Position: Aufseherin
File Number:
Employment Date:
Camp Service:
Notes:

Heykop
First Name: Ceuntje Jacoba
Birthdate:
Birthplace:
Position: Aufseherin
File Number:
Employment Date:
Camp Service:
Notes: Ethnic Slav; special permission to serve as an "employee of the Reich" granted.

Heyne
First Name: Annemarie
Birthdate:
Birthplace:
Position: Aufseherin
File Number:
Employment Date:
Camp Service:
Notes:

Heyne
First Name: Johanna
Birthdate:
Birthplace:
Position: Aufseherin
File Number:
Employment Date:
Camp Service: Floßenbürg
Notes:

Hickel
First Name: Leopoldine
Birthdate: November 14, 1921
Birthplace: Zachtel
Position: Aufseherin
File Number:
Employment Date: April 15, 1944
Camp Service: Ravensbrück
Notes:

Hielscher
First Name: Charlotte
Birthdate: March 22, 1913
Birthplace: Langenbielau
Position: Aufseherin
File Number:
Employment Date: April 15, 1944
Camp Service: Groß-Rosen
Notes:

Hielscher
First Name: Helene
Birthdate: November 4, 1909
Birthplace: Sackisch
Position: Aufseherin
File Number:
Employment Date: August 1, 1944
Camp Service: Groß-Rosen
Notes:

Hielscher
First Name: Martha
Birthdate: October 30, 1921
Birthplace: Forst-Lausitz
Position: Aufseherin
File Number:
Employment Date: June 15, 1944
Camp Service: Groß-Rosen
Notes:

Hierl
First Name: Franziska
Birthdate:
Birthplace:
Position: Aufseherin

File Number:
Employment Date:
Camp Service: Ravensbrück
Notes:

Hildebrand (born Greiß)

First Name: Margarete
Birthdate: Neuengamme
Birthplace:
Position: Aufseherin
File Number:
Employment Date:
Camp Service:
Notes:

Hildenbrandt (or Hildenbrand)

First Name: Lieselotte
Birthdate: November 19, 1922
Birthplace: Berlin
Position: Aufseherin
File Number: IV 410(F) AR 2629/67
Employment Date: September 11, 1944
Camp Service: Floßenbürg; AL Plauen
Notes: Permission to serve as an "employee of the Reich" granted on November 20, 1944.

Hildner

First Name: Ruth Elfriede
Birthdate: November 1, 1919
Birthplace: Nuremberg
Position: Aufseherin
File Number: IV 409 AR-Z 39/59
Employment Date: July 10, 1944
Camp Service: Ravensbrück; Dachau; NL Munich; Henningsdorf; Wittenberg; Haselhorst; Kommando Helmbrechts
Notes: Sentenced to death and executed the same day (May 2, 1947) by a military court in Prague.

Hilger

First Name: Magda
Birthdate:
Birthplace:
Position: Aufseherin
File Number:
Employment Date:
Camp Service:
Notes:

Hillar

First Name: Gertrud
Birthdate: August 15, 1920
Birthplace: Grünberg
Position: Aufseherin
File Number:
Employment Date: May 1, 1944
Camp Service: Groß-Rosen
Notes:

Hille

First Name: Anni
Birthdate:
Birthplace:
Position: Aufseherin
File Number:

Employment Date:
Camp Service: Groß-Rosen
Notes:

Hille

First Name: Susanne
Birthdate: 1923
Birthplace:
Position: Kommandoführerin
File Number: 103 AR 8289/87
Employment Date:
Camp Service: Vuterluß
Notes: Prosecuted for torturing inmates; no details provided regarding her fate. Service as an SS auxiliary according to her file.

Hillebrecht

First Name: Lina
Birthdate:
Birthplace:
Position: Aufseherin
File Number:
Employment Date:
Camp Service:
Notes:

Hiller

First Name: Elise
Birthdate:
Birthplace:
Position: Aufseherin
File Number:
Employment Date:
Camp Service:
Notes:

Hiller

First Name: Frieda
Birthdate:
Birthplace:
Position: Aufseherin
File Number:
Employment Date:
Camp Service: Sachsenhausen
Notes:

Hillmann

First Name: Gertraude
Birthdate:
Birthplace:
Position: Aufseherin
File Number:
Employment Date:
Camp Service: Ravensbrück
Notes:

Hilse

First Name: Elfriede
Birthdate:
Birthplace:
Position: Aufseherin
File Number:
Employment Date:
Camp Service: Groß-Rosen
Notes:

Hilse

First Name: Hildegard
Birthdate: October 28, 1922
Birthplace: Peterswaldau
Position: Aufseherin
File Number:
Employment Date: November 24, 1944
Camp Service: Groß-Rosen
Notes:

Hinrichs (born Wiegmann)

First Name: Jantiene
Birthdate:
Birthplace:
Position: Aufseherin
File Number:
Employment Date:
Camp Service:
Notes:

Hinsberger

First Name: Irmgard
Birthdate:
Birthplace:
Position: Aufseherin
File Number:
Employment Date:
Camp Service:
Notes:

Hinsche

First Name: Ruth
Birthdate:
Birthplace:
Position: Aufseherin
File Number:
Employment Date:
Camp Service: Ravensbrück
Notes:

Hintzmann

First Name: Ursula
Birthdate:
Birthplace:
Position: Aufseherin
File Number:
Employment Date:
Camp Service:
Notes:

Hirsemann (born Adam)

First Name: Elisabeth
Birthdate: January 3, 1920
Birthplace: Rottleben
Position: Aufseherin
File Number: IV 429 AR-Z 50/71B
Employment Date:
Camp Service: Buchenwald; NL Gelsenkirchen; Sömmerda; Ravensbrück
Notes:

Hitz

First Name: Gertrud
Birthdate:
Birthplace:

Position: Aufseherin
File Number:
Employment Date:
Camp Service:
Notes:

Hladik

First Name: Annelies
Birthdate:
Birthplace:
Position: Aufseherin
File Number:
Employment Date:
Camp Service: Groß-Rosen
Notes:

Hochhaus (born Zacharias)

First Name: Erna
Birthdate:
Birthplace:
Position: Aufseherin
File Number:
Employment Date:
Camp Service:
Notes:

Hodina

First Name: Charlotte
Birthdate: January 24, 1920
Birthplace: Breslau
Position: Aufseherin
File Number:
Employment Date: July 1, 1944
Camp Service: Groß-Rosen
Notes:

Höhn

First Name: Elisabeth
Birthdate: June 13, 1922
Birthplace: Hindenburg
Position: Aufseherin
File Number:
Employment Date: September 8, 1944
Camp Service: Ravensbrück
Notes: Captured by Soviet forces and ostensibly taken to a *gulag*; fate unknown.

Höhne

First Name: Charlotte
Birthdate:
Birthplace:
Position: Aufseherin
File Number:
Employment Date:
Camp Service:
Notes:

Höhne

First Name: Gerda
Birthdate: November 4, 1922
Birthplace: Dresden
Position: Aufseherin
File Number: IV 410(F) AR 2629/67
Employment Date: August 16, 1944
Camp Service: Floßenbürg; AL Goehle-Werk Dresden
Notes:

Höhne

First Name: Inge
Birthdate: May 23, 1922
Birthplace: Berlin
Position: Aufseherin
File Number:
Employment Date: December 15, 1944
Camp Service: Ravensbrück
Notes:

Hoeland (born Bechstelz)

First Name: Martha
Birthdate:
Birthplace:
Position: Aufseherin
File Number:
Employment Date:
Camp Service: Ravensbrück
Notes:

Hölter (born Pohl)

First Name: Marianne
Birthdate:
Birthplace:
Position: Aufseherin
File Number:
Employment Date:
Camp Service:
Notes:

Hölzel

First Name: Anny
Birthdate: May 22, 1920
Birthplace: Neustädtel
Position: Aufseherin
File Number:
Employment Date: August 16, 1944
Camp Service: Floßenbürg
Notes:

Höngesberg (born Aatforst or Autforst)

First Name: Franziska
Birthdate: February 6, 1900
Birthplace: Essen
Position: Blockführerin: SS Member
File Number: IV 429 AR-Z 51/71 (B)
Employment Date:
Camp Service: Buchenwald; NL Essen
Notes:

Hönne

First Name: Gerda
Birthdate:
Birthplace:
Position: Aufseherin
File Number:
Employment Date:
Camp Service:
Notes:

Hoepfner

First Name: Elisabeth
Birthdate:
Birthplace:
Position: Aufseherin

File Number:
Employment Date:
Camp Service: Neuengamme
Notes:

Höppner

First Name: Elfriede
Birthdate: March 27, 1921
Birthplace: Köpernitz
Position: Aufseherin
File Number:
Employment Date: November 1, 1941
Camp Service: Ravensbrück
Notes:

Höritzbauer (or Höritzauer; born Rost)

First Name: Luise
Birthdate: August 20, 1920
Birthplace: Crumbach
Position: Aufseherin
File Number: IV 410(F) AR 2629/67
Employment Date: August 17, 1944
Camp Service: Floßenbürg; AL Hainichen
Notes:

Hörn

First Name: Käthe
Birthdate:
Birthplace:
Position: Oberaufseherin
File Number:
Employment Date:
Camp Service: Ravensbrück; Allendorf
Notes: Sentenced to seven years imprisonment by an American court.

Hösel

First Name: Gertrud
Birthdate: July 25, 1920
Birthplace: Chemnitz
Position: Aufseherin
File Number: IV 410(F) AR 2629/67
Employment Date: August 16, 1944
Camp Service: Floßenbürg; AL Astrawerke Chemnitz
Notes:

Hofbauer

First Name: Margarete
Birthdate: July 15, 1908
Birthplace: Neufahren
Position: Aufseherin
File Number:
Employment Date: December 1, 1938
Camp Service: Ravensbrück
Notes:

Hoffmann

First Name: Anna
Birthdate: June 17, 1922
Birthplace: Buchwalde
Position: Aufseherin
File Number:
Employment Date: September 29, 1944
Camp Service: Groß-Rosen
Notes:

Hoffmann

First Name: Eleonore
Birthdate:
Birthplace:
Position: Aufseherin
File Number:
Employment Date:
Camp Service:
Notes:

Hoffmann

First Name: Elfriede
Birthdate: February 14, 1902
Birthplace: Rückers
Position: Aufseherin
File Number:
Employment Date: October 5, 1944
Camp Service: Groß-Rosen
Notes:

Hoffmann

First Name: Else
Birthdate: May 10, 1913
Birthplace: Hermsdorf (Waldenburg)
Position: Aufseherin
File Number:
Employment Date: April 15, 1944
Camp Service: Groß-Rosen
Notes:

Hoffmann (born Menzel)

First Name: Else
Birthdate:
Birthplace:
Position: Aufseherin
File Number:
Employment Date:
Camp Service:
Notes: Unclear if there are two "Else Hoffmans" or if there are duplicate files.

Hoffmann

First Name: Erna
Birthdate: August 20, 1921
Birthplace: Breslau
Position: Aufseherin
File Number:
Employment Date: July 1, 1944
Camp Service: Groß-Rosen
Notes:

Hoffmann

First Name: Frieda
Birthdate: December 19, 1921
Birthplace: Buschacker
Position: Aufseherin
File Number:
Employment Date: September 12, 1944
Camp Service: Groß-Rosen
Notes:

Hoffmann

First Name: Gertrud
Birthdate: December 1, 1923
Birthplace: Peterswaldau

Position: Aufseherin
File Number:
Employment Date: March 1, 1944
Camp Service: Groß-Rosen
Notes:

Hoffmann

First Name: Gertrud
Birthdate: September 22, 1922
Birthplace: Leibschuetz
Position: Aufseherin
File Number:
Employment Date: June 1, 1944
Camp Service: Groß-Rosen
Notes:

Hoffmann

First Name: Herta
Birthdate: December 23, 1920
Birthplace: Bornau-Guhren
Position: Aufseherin
File Number:
Employment Date: June 4, 1944
Camp Service: Ravensbrück; Groß-Rosen
Notes:

Hoffmann

First Name: Irmgard
Birthdate: May 25, 1903
Birthplace: Oberaltstadt
Position: Aufseherin
File Number:
Employment Date: March 1, 1944
Camp Service: Groß-Rosen
Notes:

Hoffmann

First Name: Johanna
Birthdate: August 19, 1904
Birthplace: Auerbach
Position: Kommandoführerin
File Number:
Employment Date: September 7, 1944
Camp Service: Floßenbürg
Notes:

Hoffmann

First Name: Lisa
Birthdate:
Birthplace:
Position: Aufseherin
File Number:
Employment Date:
Camp Service:
Notes:

Hoffmann (born Anders)

First Name: Luzia (Luzie)
Birthdate: September 28, 1919
Birthplace: Standorf
Position: Aufseherin
File Number:
Employment Date: June 1, 1944
Camp Service: Groß-Rosen
Notes:

Hoffmann

First Name: Magdalene
Birthdate:
Birthplace:
Position: Aufseherin
File Number:
Employment Date:
Camp Service:
Notes:

Hoffmann

First Name: Margarete
Birthdate:
Birthplace:
Position: Aufseherin
File Number:
Employment Date:
Camp Service:
Notes:

Hoffmann

First Name: Maria
Birthdate: December 7, 1917
Birthplace: Wittenberge
Position: Aufseherin
File Number:
Employment Date: November 7, 1944
Camp Service: Ravensbrück
Notes:

Hoffmann

First Name: Martha
Birthdate: October 7, 1921
Birthplace: Glatz
Position:
File Number:
Employment Date: August 16, 1944
Camp Service: Groß-Rosen
Notes:

Hofmann

First Name: Helene
Birthdate:
Birthplace:
Position: Aufseherin
File Number:
Employment Date:
Camp Service:
Notes:

Hofmann

First Name: Irmgard
Birthdate: May 27, 1903
Birthplace: Landshut (Bavaria)
Position: Lagerführerin
File Number: IV 405 AR-Z 66/71
Employment Date: 1944
Camp Service: Oberaltstadt
Notes: Is alleged to have been Aufseherin in a camp by the Company Kluge; was nominated for the *Kriegsverdienst- kruez II. Klasse ohne Schweter* (war service cross, second class without swords) medal.

Hofmann

First Name: Johanna
Birthdate:
Birthplace:
Position: Aufseherin
File Number:
Employment Date:
Camp Service: Ravensbrück
Notes:

Hofmann

First Name: Margarete
Birthdate:
Birthplace:
Position: Aufseherin
File Number:
Employment Date:
Camp Service: Ravensbrück
Notes:

Hoheisl (or Hoheißel)

First Name: Irmgard
Birthdate: October 26, 1913
Birthplace: Berlin-Lichtenberg
Position: Aufseherin
File Number: IV 410(F) AR 2629/67
Employment Date: September 8, 1944
Camp Service: Floßenbürg; Kommando Helmbrechts
Notes: Permission for service as an "employee of the Reich" granted on November 20, 1944.

Hohenberger

First Name: Herta
Birthdate:
Birthplace:
Position: Aufseherin
File Number:
Employment Date:
Camp Service:
Notes:

Hohenleitner

First Name: Rosa
Birthdate:
Birthplace:
Position: Aufseherin
File Number:
Employment Date:
Camp Service:
Notes:

Hohl

First Name: Elfriede
Birthdate: December 22, 1920
Birthplace: Meuselwitz
Position: Aufseherin
File Number:
Employment Date: November 20, 1944
Camp Service: Ravensbrück
Notes:

Hohlbein

First Name: Rosa
Birthdate: July 10, 1922
Birthplace: Heyerode

Position: Aufseherin
File Number:
Employment Date: December 19, 1944
Camp Service: Ravensbrück
Notes:

Hohmann

First Name: Elisabeth
Birthdate:
Birthplace:
Position: Aufseherin
File Number:
Employment Date:
Camp Service:
Notes:

Hollevoet (born Hörschen)

First Name: Josefine (Josephine)
Birthdate: September 2, 1902
Birthplace: Viersen
Position: Aufseherin
File Number:
Employment Date: December 7, 1944
Camp Service: Ravensbrück
Notes:

Hollmann (born Rudolph)

First Name: Luise
Birthdate: August 11, 1904
Birthplace: Buchwald
Position: Aufseherin
File Number:
Employment Date: June 29, 1944
Camp Service: Groß-Rosen
Notes:

Holm

First Name: Marie
Birthdate:
Birthplace:
Position: Aufseherin
File Number:
Employment Date:
Camp Service: Ravensbrück
Notes:

Holschke

First Name: Erna
Birthdate: February 27, 1922
Birthplace: Hermsdorf
Position: Aufseherin
File Number:
Employment Date: September 23, 1944
Camp Service: Groß-Rosen
Notes:

Holthöfer

First Name: Christine
Birthdate: February 9, 1899
Birthplace: Lengsdorf
Position: Aufseherin
File Number:
Employment Date: May 1, 1943
Camp Service: Ravensbrück
Notes:

Holtzhueter

First Name: Margarete
Birthdate: June 10, 1915
Birthplace: Brunshaupten
Position: Aufseherin
File Number:
Employment Date: March 1, 1943
Camp Service: Ravensbrück
Notes:

Holub

First Name: Josefine
Birthdate:
Birthplace:
Position: Aufseherin
File Number:
Employment Date:
Camp Service:
Notes:

Holz

First Name: Anneliese
Birthdate:
Birthplace:
Position: Aufseherin
File Number:
Employment Date:
Camp Service:
Notes:

Homilius (born Köhler)

First Name: Lina
Birthdate: March 1, 1923
Birthplace: Altenhain
Position: Aufseherin
File Number: IV 410(F) AR 2629/67
Employment Date: August 17, 1944
Camp Service: Floßenbürg; AL Hainichen
Notes:

Hoppe

First Name: Dora
Birthdate: February 27, 1920
Birthplace:
Position: Aufseherin
File Number: IV 429 AR 1941/61
Employment Date:
Camp Service: NL Torgau; Ravensbrück
Notes:

Hoppe

First Name: Eva-Maria
Birthdate:
Birthplace:
Position: Aufseherin
File Number:
Employment Date:
Camp Service: Groß-Rosen
Notes:

Hoppmann (born Katzmarek)

First Name: Margarete
Birthdate:
Birthplace:

Position: Aufseherin
File Number:
Employment Date:
Camp Service:
Notes:

Horche

First Name: Johanna
Birthdate:
Birthplace:
Position: Aufseherin
File Number:
Employment Date:
Camp Service: Groß-Rosen
Notes:

Horn

First Name: Ruth
Birthdate: July 24, 1922
Birthplace: Beinsdorf
Position: Aufseherin
File Number: IV 410(F) AR 2629/67
Employment Date: August 26, 1944
Camp Service: Ravensbrück; Floßenbürg; AL Chemnitz
Notes:

Horna

First Name: Adolfine
Birthdate:
Birthplace:
Position: Aufseherin
File Number:
Employment Date:
Camp Service:
Notes:

Horstkotte

First Name: Herma
Birthdate:
Birthplace:
Position: Aufseherin
File Number:
Employment Date:
Camp Service: Neuengamme
Notes:

Hortig

First Name: Hildegard
Birthdate:
Birthplace:
Position: Aufseherin
File Number:
Employment Date:
Camp Service:
Notes:

Hrdy

(possibly misspelled in the original file or perhaps
a Hungarian national?)
First Name: Anna
Birthdate: July 26, 1909
Birthplace: Trautenau
Position: Aufseherin
File Number:
Employment Date: March 1, 1944

Camp Service: Groß-Rosen
Notes: Permission for service as an "employee of the
                Reich" granted on December 11, 1944.

Huber

First Name: Therese
Birthdate:
Birthplace:
Position: Aufseherin
File Number:
Employment Date:
Camp Service:
Notes:

Hübel (born Leonhardt)

First Name: Irmgard
Birthdate: August 18, 1915
Birthplace:
Position: Aufseherin
File Number: IV 429 AR 1973/66(B)
Employment Date:
Camp Service: Sömmerda
Notes:

Hübner

First Name: Elisabeth
Birthdate: October 3, 1907
Birthplace:
Position: Aufseherin
File Number: IV 410(F) AR 2629/67
Employment Date:
Camp Service: Floßenburg; AL Hertine
Notes:

Hübner

First Name: Erika
Birthdate: June 27, 1921
Birthplace: Wiesau
Position: Aufseherin
File Number:
Employment Date: November 2, 1944
Camp Service: Ravensbrück; Stutthof
Notes:

Hübner

First Name: Liesbeth
Birthdate:
Birthplace:
Position: Aufseherin
File Number:
Employment Date:
Camp Service: Ravensbrück
Notes:

Hübner

First Name: Liese-Lotte
Birthdate: June 4, 1922
Birthplace: Warnsdorf
Position: Aufseherin
File Number:
Employment Date: September 23, 1944
Camp Service: Groß-Rosen
Notes:

Hübner

First Name: Martha
Birthdate: November 9, 1921
Birthplace: Neurode
Position: Aufseherin
File Number:
Employment Date: August 1, 1944
Camp Service: Groß-Rosen
Notes:

Hühnerbein

First Name: Ruth
Birthdate: 1923 (no month or day noted in her file).
Birthplace:
Position: Aufseherin; Rapportführerin
File Number:
Employment Date:
Camp Service: AL Junkerwerke Plauen
Notes: Service as an SS auxiliary noted in her file.

Hüllemann

First Name: Hildegard
Birthdate: September 20, 1919
Birthplace: Zeitz
Position: Aufseherin
File Number: IV 410 AR-Z 60/67
Employment Date: September 5, 1944
Camp Service: Ravensbrück; Floßenbürg
Notes:

Hünemörder

First Name: Ursula
Birthdate: April 18, 1920
Birthplace: Retschow
Position: Aufseherin
File Number:
Employment Date: April 1, 1944
Camp Service: Ravensbrück
Notes:

Hürth

First Name: Sybille (Sybilla)
Birthdate: February 15, 1911
Birthplace: Frechem
Position: Aufseherin
File Number:
Employment Date: October 1, 1942
Camp Service: Ravensbrück
Notes:

Hüttig

First Name: Irene
Birthdate: December 21, 1921
Birthplace: Hainichen
Position: Aufseherin
File Number:
Employment Date: September 4, 1944
Camp Service: Floßenbürg; Ravensbrück
Notes:

Hüttinger

First Name: Ruth
Birthdate: June 24, 1922
Birthplace: Rochlitz
Position: Aufseherin
File Number: IV 410(F) AR 2629/67
Employment Date: August 21, 1944
Camp Service: Floßenbürg; AL Rochlitz
Notes:

Hulan

First Name: Hilde
Birthdate: February 27, 1914
Birthplace: Schlackenwerth
Position: Aufseherin
File Number:
Employment Date: August 1, 1940
Camp Service: Ravensbrück
Notes:

Hulsch

First Name: Ilse
Birthdate:
Birthplace:
Position: Aufseherin
File Number:
Employment Date:
Camp Service: Stutthof/Danzig
Notes:

Hundelage

First Name: Edith
Birthdate:
Birthplace:
Position: Aufseherin
File Number:
Employment Date:
Camp Service: Neuengamme
Notes:

Hunger (born Krogmann)

First Name: Lotte
Birthdate:
Birthplace:
Position: Aufseherin
File Number:
Employment Date:
Camp Service:
Notes:

Hunsicker

First Name: Rösel
Birthdate:
Birthplace:
Position: Aufseherin
File Number:
Employment Date:
Camp Service:
Notes:

Hupfer

First Name: Ilse
Birthdate: May 7, 1923
Birthplace: Eppemdorf
Position: Aufseherin
File Number: IV 410(F) AR 2629/67
Employment Date: October 1, 1944
Camp Service: Floßenbürg; AL Holleischen
Notes: Permission for service as an "employee of the Reich" granted on November 22, 1944.

Hußel
First Name: Lina
Birthdate: August 2, 1920
Birthplace: Nuremberg
Position: Aufseherin
File Number: IV 410(F) AR 2629/67
Employment Date: September 30, 1944
Camp Service: Floßenbürg; AL Holleischen
Notes:

Huster (born Eßbach)
First Name: Hildegard
Birthdate: April 6, 1915
Birthplace: Brunndöbra
Position: Aufseherin
File Number:
Employment Date: September 7, 1944
Camp Service: Ravensbrück; Floßenbürg
Notes:

Hustig
First Name: Ella
Birthdate:
Birthplace:
Position: Aufseherin
File Number:
Employment Date:
Camp Service:
Notes:

Huth
First Name: Elfriede
Birthdate: July 14, 1922
Birthplace: Leipzig
Position: Aufseherin
File Number:
Employment Date: June 15, 1944
Camp Service: Ravensbrück
Notes:

Idaszewski
First Name: Veronika
Birthdate: January 12, 1916
Birthplace: Herne (Westphalia)
Position: Aufseherin
File Number:
Employment Date: September 29, 1944
Camp Service: Groß-Rosen
Notes:

Idziak
First Name: Klara
Birthdate:
Birthplace:
Position: Aufseherin
File Number:
Employment Date:
Camp Service:
Notes:

Ignatowitz (born Schrader)
First Name: Frieda or Elfriede
Birthdate: June 24, 1915

Birthplace:
Position: Aufseherin
File Number: IV 404 AR 605/67
Employment Date:
Camp Service: Hamburg-Sasel; Neuengamme
Notes: Appears on a list of people tried between (April 23-June 10, 1946) by the British for maltreatment of Allied camp inmates.

Ihle
First Name: Elfriede
Birthdate:
Birthplace:
Position: Aufseherin
File Number:
Employment Date:
Camp Service:
Notes:

Ihle (born Fleuti)
First Name: Hildegard (or Hilde)
Birthdate: February 2, 1910
Birthplace: Reinholzhain
Position: Aufseherin
File Number: IV 410(F) AR 2629/67
Employment Date: September 7, 1944
Camp Service: Ravensbrück; Floßenbürg; AL Hainichen
Notes:

Ilgner
First Name: Helene
Birthdate: September 8, 1907
Birthplace: Friedeberg
Position: Aufseherin
File Number:
Employment Date: August 16, 1944
Camp Service: Groß-Rosen
Notes:

Illich
First Name: Rosa
Birthdate:
Birthplace:
Position: Aufseherin
File Number:
Employment Date:
Camp Service:
Notes:

Im Ort (born Küpper)
First Name: Maria
Birthdate:
Birthplace:
Position: Aufseherin
File Number:
Employment Date:
Camp Service:
Notes:

Immerheise
First Name: Susanne
Birthdate:
Birthplace:
Position: Aufseherin

File Number:
Employment Date:
Camp Service:
Notes:

Immerzeder
First Name: Gunta
Birthdate:
Birthplace:
Position: Aufseherin
File Number: IV 410(F) AR 2629/67
Employment Date:
Camp Service: Floßenbürg; AL Diehl; Nuremberg
Notes:

Imort (perhaps 'Im Ort'?)
First Name: Irene
Birthdate: August 11, 1921
Birthplace: Löhne
Position: Aufseherin
File Number:
Employment Date: August 16, 1944
Camp Service: Ravensbrück
Notes:

Impelmann
First Name: Elisabeth
Birthdate:
Birthplace:
Position: Aufseherin
File Number:
Employment Date:
Camp Service:
Notes:

Ingenkamp
First Name: Maria
Birthdate:
Birthplace:
Position: Aufseherin
File Number:
Employment Date:
Camp Service:
Notes:

Inhofer (born Wagner)
First Name: Wilhelmine
Birthdate:
Birthplace:
Position: Aufseherin
File Number:
Employment Date:
Camp Service:
Notes:

Irmen (born Qual)
First Name: Frieda
Birthdate:
Birthplace:
Position: Aufseherin
File Number:
Employment Date:
Camp Service: Neuengamme
Notes:

Irmler (born Bernart)
First Name: Aloisje
Birthdate: May 7, 1919
Birthplace: Stara Voda
Position: Aufseherin
File Number: IV 402 AR 890/68
Employment Date:
Camp Service: Auschwitz; NL Lichtenwerden
Notes:

Irmsch
First Name: Martha
Birthdate: December 10, 1914
Birthplace: Peterswaldau
Position: Aufseherin
File Number:
Employment Date: August 1, 1944
Camp Service: Groß-Rosen
Notes:

Isaak
First Name: Ella
Birthdate:
Birthplace:
Position: Aufseherin
File Number:
Employment Date:
Camp Service: Stutthof/Danzig
Notes:

Iserbeck (born Hippe)
First Name: Käthe
Birthdate: August 10, 1917
Birthplace:
Position: Aufseherin
File Number: IV 429 AR 1973/66(B)
Employment Date:
Camp Service: Ravensbrück
Notes:

Isert
First Name: Maria
Birthdate: May 11, 1906
Birthplace:
Position: Aufseherin: SS Member
File Number: IV 429 AR-Z 51/71 (B)
Employment Date:
Camp Service: Buchenwald; NL Essen
Notes:

Israel
First Name: Herta
Birthdate:
Birthplace:
Position: Aufseherin
File Number:
Employment Date:
Camp Service: Ravensbrück
Notes:

Itzek
First Name: Gertrud
Birthdate:
Birthplace:
Position: Aufseherin

File Number:
Employment Date:
Camp Service:
Notes:

Jablonski

First Name: Luzia
Birthdate: March 23, 1922
Birthplace: Grünberg
Position: Aufseherin
File Number:
Employment Date: June 1, 1944
Camp Service: Groß-Rosen
Notes: Permission for service as an "employee of the Reich" granted on December 11, 1944.

Jachmann

First Name: Hildegard
Birthdate:
Birthplace:
Position: Aufseherin
File Number:
Employment Date:
Camp Service: Ravensbrück
Notes:

Jacht

First Name: Anneliese
Birthdate:
Birthplace:
Position: Aufseherin
File Number:
Employment Date:
Camp Service:
Notes:

Jacob

First Name: Anna
Birthdate:
Birthplace:
Position: Aufseherin
File Number:
Employment Date:
Camp Service: Sachsenhausen
Notes:

Jacob

First Name: Elisabeth
Birthdate:
Birthplace:
Position: Aufseherin
File Number:
Employment Date:
Camp Service:
Notes:

Jacob

First Name: Johanna
Birthdate:
Birthplace:
Position: Aufseherin
File Number:
Employment Date:
Camp Service:
Notes:

Jacob

First Name: Ursula
Birthdate:
Birthplace:
Position: Aufseherin
File Number:
Employment Date:
Camp Service: Ravensbrück
Notes:

Jäckel

First Name: Else
Birthdate: September 23, 1916
Birthplace: Weißstein
Position: Aufseherin
File Number:
Employment Date: July 27, 1944
Camp Service: Groß-Rosen
Notes: Permission for service as an "employee of the Reich" granted on November 25, 1944.

Jäckel

First Name: Erna
Birthdate: January 28, 1923
Birthplace: Weigensdorf
Position: Aufseherin
File Number:
Employment Date: July 1, 1944
Camp Service: Groß-Rosen
Notes:

Jäckel

First Name: Gertrud
Birthdate: April 14, 1920
Birthplace: Wolmsdorf
Position: Aufseherin
File Number:
Employment Date: September 13, 1944
Camp Service: Groß-Rosen
Notes:

Jäckel (or Jäkel)

First Name: Ingeborg
Birthdate: March 3, 1923
Birthplace: Plessa or Thorgau
Position: Aufseherin
File Number: IV 410(F) AR 2629/67
Employment Date: August 1, 1944
Camp Service: Flossenbürg; AL Chemnitz
Notes:

Jäcker

First Name: Margarete
Birthdate:
Birthplace:
Position: Aufseherin
File Number:
Employment Date:
Camp Service:
Notes:

Jäger

First Name: Hilde
Birthdate:
Birthplace:

Position: Aufseherin
File Number:
Employment Date:
Camp Service: Ravensbrück
Notes:

Jäger (or Liehn)
First Name: Johanna (Luise; Helene)
Birthdate: August 13, 1908
Birthplace: Halle a.d. Saale
Position: Aufseherin
File Number: IV 409 AR-Z 39/59
Employment Date: December 1941
Camp Service: Ravensbrück; Auschwitz; Berlin Kommando; Frankfurt/Oder Kommando
Notes:

Jäger
First Name: Josephine
Birthdate:
Birthplace:
Position: Aufseherin
File Number:
Employment Date:
Camp Service: Ravensbrück
Notes:

Jähnische
First Name: Agnes
Birthdate: November 11, 1915
Birthplace: Guben
Position: Aufseherin
File Number:
Employment Date: July 31, 1944
Camp Service: Groß-Rosen
Notes:

Jäkel
First Name: Gertrud
Birthdate:
Birthplace:
Position: Aufseherin
File Number:
Employment Date:
Camp Service: Groß-Rosen
Notes:

Jäntsch
First Name: Margarete
Birthdate:
Birthplace:
Position: Aufseherin
File Number:
Employment Date:
Camp Service:
Notes:

Jagla
First Name: Lieselotte
Birthdate:
Birthplace:
Position: Aufseherin
File Number:
Employment Date:
Camp Service:
Notes:

Jahn
First Name: Elisabeth
Birthdate:
Birthplace:
Position: Aufseherin
File Number:
Employment Date:
Camp Service:
Notes:

Jahn
First Name: Eva
Birthdate:
Birthplace:
Position: Aufseherin
File Number:
Employment Date:
Camp Service: Ravensbrück
Notes:

Jahn
First Name: Käthe
Birthdate:
Birthplace:
Position: Aufseherin
File Number:
Employment Date:
Camp Service:
Notes:

Jahn
First Name: Wilhelmine
Birthdate: April 8, 1913
Birthplace: Kratzau
Position: Aufseherin
File Number:
Employment Date: September 6, 1944
Camp Service: Groß-Rosen
Notes:

Jahnke
First Name: Frieda
Birthdate: July 9, 1906
Birthplace: Neubrandenburg
Position: Aufseherin
File Number: IV 429 AR 1941/66 (B)
Employment Date:
Camp Service: NL Torgau; NL Markkleeberg; Buchenwald; Ravensbrück
Notes:

Jahns
First Name: Elfriede
Birthdate:
Birthplace:
Position: Aufseherin
File Number:
Employment Date:
Camp Service: Ravensbrück
Notes:

Jainczik (born Laße)
First Name: Edith
Birthdate: July 28, 1920
Birthplace: Berlin

Position: Aufseherin
File Number: IV 406 AR-Z 200/72
Employment Date:
Camp Service: Ravensbrück; NL Auer/Oranienburg
Notes:

Jakob

First Name: Charlotte
Birthdate: October 12, 1919
Birthplace: Neusalz
Position: Aufseherin
File Number:
Employment Date: August 29, 1944
Camp Service: Groß-Rosen
Notes:

Jakob

First Name: Hedwig
Birthdate: September 28, 1902
Birthplace: Dresden
Position: Stv. (Replacement) Lagerleiterin; Aufseherin
File Number: IV 410(F) AR 2629/67
Employment Date: August 16, 1944
Camp Service: Floßenbürg; AL Goehlewerk Dresden
Notes: Permission for service as an "employee of the Reich" granted on November 20, 1944.

Jakob (or Jacob)

First Name: Olga
Birthdate: March 24, 1923
Birthplace: Cossen
Position: Aufseherin
File Number: IV 410(F) AR 2629/67
Employment Date: August 21, 1944
Camp Service: Floßenbürg; AL Rochlitz
Notes:

Janela

First Name: Lieselotte
Birthdate:
Birthplace:
Position: Aufseherin
File Number:
Employment Date:
Camp Service:
Notes:

Janke

First Name: Else (Ilse)
Birthdate: September 4, 1923
Birthplace: Grünberg
Position: Aufseherin
File Number: IV 410(F) AR 2629/67
Employment Date: June 15, 1944
Camp Service: Floßenbürg; AL Zwodau
Notes:

Janke

First Name: Grete
Birthdate: March 8, 1919
Birthplace: Weißwasser
Position: Aufseherin
File Number:
Employment Date: August 18, 1944
Camp Service: Groß-Rosen
Notes:

Jankowiak

First Name: Edith
Birthdate: June 23, 1923
Birthplace: Neusalz
Position: Aufseherin
File Number:
Employment Date: June 1, 1944
Camp Service: Groß-Rosen
Notes:

Jankowski

First Name: Christel
Birthdate: December 25, 1912
Birthplace: Rangnit
Position: Aufseherin
File Number: IV 410(F) AR 2629/67
Employment Date: June 22, 1944
Camp Service: Floßenbürg; AL Neu Rohlau
Notes:

Jankowsky

First Name: Christel
Birthdate: 1919 (no month or day noted in her file)
Birthplace:
Position: Aufseherin; SS Scharführerin
File Number:
Employment Date:
Camp Service: Ravensbrück
Notes: Sentenced to death in 1954 by the East Germans for multiple murders; ultimate fate unknown.

Janouch

First Name: Elvira
Birthdate: June 18, 1914
Birthplace: Trautenau
Position: Aufseherin
File Number:
Employment Date: March 1, 1944
Camp Service: Gross-Rosen
Notes: Permission for service as an "employee of the Reich" granted: on December 11, 1944.

Jansen

First Name: Alwine
Birthdate: April 18, 1917
Birthplace: Nordhorn
Position: Aufseherin
File Number:
Employment Date: July 15, 1944
Camp Service: Groß-Rosen
Notes:

Janssen

First Name: Vera
Birthdate: Hamburg
Birthplace: November 5, 1919
Position: Aufseherin
File Number:
Employment Date: September 26, 1944
Camp Service: Groß-Rosen
Notes:

Jantsch

First Name: Charlotte
Birthdate: April 28, 1921

Birthplace: Fratzen
Position: Aufseherin
File Number:
Employment Date: September 6, 1944
Camp Service: Groß-Rosen
Notes:

Jarolinek
First Name: Rosa
Birthdate: July 31, 1920
Birthplace: Braunau
Position: Aufseherin
File Number:
Employment Date: September 13, 1944
Camp Service: Groß-Rosen
Notes:

Jaromin
First Name: Franziska
Birthdate: December 9, 1913
Birthplace: Lemberg
Position: Aufseherin
File Number: IV 410(F) AR 2629/67
Employment Date: August 16, 1944
Camp Service: Floßenbürg; AL Zwodau
Notes:

Jaroß
First Name: Helene
Birthdate:
Birthplace:
Position: Aufseherin
File Number:
Employment Date:
Camp Service:
Notes:

Jasper
First Name: Lieselotte
Birthdate:
Birthplace:
Position: Aufseherin
File Number:
Employment Date:
Camp Service:
Notes:

Jeglorzt
First Name: Irmgard
Birthdate:
Birthplace:
Position: Aufseherin
File Number:
Employment Date:
Camp Service:
Notes:

Jennerhahn
First Name: Irmgard
Birthdate:
Birthplace:
Position: Aufseherin
File Number:
Employment Date:
Camp Service:
Notes:

Jensch
First Name: Frieda
Birthdate: February 28, 1922
Birthplace:
Position: Aufseherin
File Number: IV 429 AR 1941/66
Employment Date:
Camp Service: NL Torgau
Notes:

Jensch (born Schmidt)
First Name: Frieda
Birthdate:
Birthplace:
Position: Aufseherin
File Number:
Employment Date:
Camp Service:
Notes: Question whether Frieda Schmidt and Frieda Jensch are one in the same?

Jentsch
First Name: Else
Birthdate: August 28, 1912
Birthplace: Standorf
Position: Aufseherin
File Number:
Employment Date: June 1, 1944
Camp Service: Groß-Rosen
Notes: Permission for employment as an "employee of the Reich" granted on December 11, 1944.

Jentsch (born Berndt)
First Name: Irmgard
Birthdate: September 5, 1922
Birthplace: Roßecken
Position: Aufseherin
File Number: 409 AR-Z 55/71
Employment Date:
Camp Service: Ravensbrück
Notes:

Jeschke
First Name: Anneliese
Birthdate: March 9, 1922
Birthplace: Meuselwitz
Position: Aufseherin
File Number:
Employment Date: November 20, 1944
Camp Service: Ravensbrück
Notes:

Jochmann
First Name: Rosa
Birthdate: March 20, 1918
Birthplace: Mariaschein
Position: Aufseherin
File Number:
Employment Date: September 25, 1944
Camp Service: Floßenbürg
Notes:

John (born Senftleben)
First Name: Anna (Emma)
Birthdate: April 26, 1899
Birthplace: Hamburg-Harburg

Position: Second Lagerleiterin
File Number: 405 AR 523/63
Employment Date: 1944
Camp Service: NL Grünberg
Notes: Recommended for the *Kriegsverdienst-medalle* (war service medal).

John

First Name: Else
Birthdate: May 7, 1905
Birthplace: Nieder-Wüstegiersdorf
Position: Aufseherin
File Number:
Employment Date:
Camp Service: Groß-Rosen
Notes: Permission for service as an "employee of the Reich" granted on November 25, 1944.

John (born Müller)

First Name: Hedwig
Birthdate:
Birthplace:
Position: Aufseherin
File Number:
Employment Date:
Camp Service: Ravensbrück
Notes:

John (born Schwarz)

First Name: Hertha (Herte); Charlotte
Birthdate: June 26, 1912
Birthplace: Berlin-Lichterfelde
Position: Aufseherin
File Number: IV 409 AR-Z 39/59
Employment Date:
Camp Service: Ravensbrück; Berlin-Schönefeld
Notes:

John (born Müller)

First Name: Klara
Birthdate:
Birthplace:
Position: Aufseherin
File Number:
Employment Date:
Camp Service:
Notes:

Jonert

First Name: Klara
Birthdate: November 22, 1910
Birthplace:
Position: Aufseherin
File Number: IV 429 AR 1959/66
Employment Date:
Camp Service: NL Essen
Notes:

Jonscher

First Name: Hedwig
Birthdate:
Birthplace:
Position: Aufseherin
File Number:
Employment Date:

Camp Service:
Notes:

Joppe

First Name: Margarete
Birthdate:
Birthplace:
Position: Aufseherin
File Number:
Employment Date:
Camp Service: Groß-Rosen
Notes:

Jubelt

First Name: Elsa
Birthdate: May 5, 1908
Birthplace: Lichtentanne
Position: Aufseherin
File Number: IV 410(F) AR 2629/67
Employment Date: August 26, 1944
Camp Service: Floßenbürg; AL Chemnitz
Notes:

Jüngst

First Name: Frieda
Birthdate:
Birthplace:
Position: Aufseherin
File Number:
Employment Date:
Camp Service:
Notes:

Jürss

First Name: Ulla Erna Frieda
Birthdate: August 2, 1923
Birthplace: Rabenhorst
Position: Aufseherin; Blockführerin
File Number: 110 AR 899/94, 3-6/313
Employment Date:
Camp Service: Ravensbrück
Notes: Sentenced to life imprisonment by an East German court in 1966 for multiple murders in Ravensbrück; ultimate fate unknown.

Jung (born Prause)

First Name: Elisabeth
Birthdate:
Birthplace:
Position: Aufseherin
File Number:
Employment Date:
Camp Service:
Notes:

Jung

First Name: Erika
Birthdate: May 30, 1922
Birthplace:
Position: Aufseherin
File Number: IV 410(F) AR 2629/67
Employment Date:
Camp Service: Floßenbürg; AL Zwodau; Groß-Rosen
Notes:

Jung

First Name: Irmgard
Birthdate: January 4, 1919
Birthplace:
Position: Aufseherin
File Number: IIV 429 AR 1248/68
Employment Date:
Camp Service: Markkleeburg; Ravensbrück
Notes:

Junge

First Name: Olga
Birthdate:
Birthplace:
Position: Aufseherin
File Number:
Employment Date:
Camp Service:
Notes:

Junghans

First Name: Marianne
Birthdate:
Birthplace:
Position: Aufseherin
File Number:
Employment Date:
Camp Service:
Notes:

Junghaus (born Richter)

First Name: Hildegard
Birthdate:
Birthplace:
Position: Aufseherin
File Number:
Employment Date:
Camp Service:
Notes:

Jungholz

First Name: Irmgard
Birthdate: January 11, 1924
Birthplace: Mannheim
Position: Aufseherin
File Number:
Employment Date: November 16, 1944
Camp Service: Ravensbrück
Notes:

Jungk

First Name: Martha
Birthdate:
Birthplace:
Position: Aufseherin
File Number:
Employment Date:
Camp Service: Neuengamme
Notes:

Junke

First Name: Johanna
Birthdate: January 19, 1921
Birthplace: Tscherndorf
Position: Aufseherin

File Number:
Employment Date: June 1, 1943
Camp Service: Ravensbrück
Notes: Official permission for service as an "employee of the Reich" granted on September 4, 1943.

Jurak

First Name: Maria
Birthdate:
Birthplace:
Position: Aufseherin
File Number:
Employment Date:
Camp Service:
Notes:

Juretzek

First Name: Erna
Birthdate: December 10, 1921
Birthplace: Klein Dachowitz
Position: Aufseherin
File Number:
Employment Date: June 1, 1944
Camp Service: Groß-Rosen
Notes:

Just

First Name: Berta
Birthdate: May 2, 1922
Birthplace: Maschendorf
Position: Aufseherin
File Number:
Employment Date: April 15, 1944
Camp Service: Groß-Rosen
Notes:

Just

First Name: Rosa
Birthdate: April 20, 1924
Birthplace: Parschnitz
Position: Aufseherin
File Number:
Employment Date: March 1, 1944
Camp Service: Groß-Rosen
Notes:

Kabelitz

First Name: Charlotte
Birthdate: June 22, 1922
Birthplace: Halle a.d. Saale
Position: Aufseherin
File Number:
Employment Date: November 25, 1944
Camp Service:
Notes:

Kachau

First Name: Maria
Birthdate:
Birthplace:
Position: Aufseherin
File Number:
Employment Date:
Camp Service:
Notes:

Kaczmarik

First Name: Frieda
Birthdate: September 15, 1917
Birthplace: Cossebaude
Position: Aufseherin
File Number: IV 410(F) AR 2629/67
Employment Date: August 16, 1944
Camp Service: Floßenbürg; AL Goehle-Werk Dresden; AL Hertine
Notes: Permission for service as an "employee of the Reich" granted on November 20, 1944.

Kälber

First Name: Sofie
Birthdate: July 11, 1921
Birthplace: Eibach
Position: Aufseherin
File Number: IV 410(F) AR 2629/67
Employment Date: September 30, 1944
Camp Service: Floßenbürg; AL Holleischen
Notes: November 25, 1944

Kärger

First Name: Janina
Birthdate:
Birthplace:
Position: Aufseherin
File Number:
Employment Date:
Camp Service: Neuengamme
Notes:

Käske (divorced Binder)

First Name: Elisabeth
Birthdate: November 29, 1908
Birthplace: Berlin-Britz
Position: Aufseherin
File Number: IV 410(F) AR 2629/67
Employment Date: August 11, 1944
Camp Service: Floßenbürg; AL Wolkenburg; AL Holleischen; Sachsenhausen
Notes:

Kässner (born Wolter)

First Name: Margarete
Birthdate: 1904 (no month or day provided in her file)
Birthplace:
Position: Aufseher
File Number:
Employment Date:
Camp Service: Arado-Werke Wittenberg
Notes: Service as an SS auxiliary (file notation).

Kästner

First Name: Hildegard
Birthdate: October 21, 1914 (possibly or October 20, 1914)
Birthplace: Dresden
Position: Aufseherin
File Number: IV 410(F) AR 2629/67
Employment Date: September 8, 1944
Camp Service: Floßenbürg; AL Oederan
Notes:

Kästner

First Name: Margarete
Birthdate: September 4, 1902
Birthplace: Ebersdorf
Position: Aufseherin
File Number: IV 410(F) AR 2629/67
Employment Date: August 16, 1944
Camp Service: Floßenbürg; AL Chemnitz
Notes:

Kahl

First Name: Johanna
Birthdate: February 2, 1923
Birthplace: Neurode-Glatz
Position: Aufseherin
File Number:
Employment Date: March 1, 1944
Camp Service: Groß-Rosen
Notes: Permission for service as an "employee of the Reich" granted on December 11, 1944.

Kahl (born Zuleila)

First Name: Luise
Birthdate: September 30, 1911
Birthplace: Dortmund
Position: Aufseherin
File Number:
Employment Date: September 18, 1944
Camp Service: Ravensbrück
Notes:

Kahle (born Gruber)

First Name: Anna
Birthdate:
Birthplace:
Position: Aufseherin
File Number:
Employment Date:
Camp Service:
Notes:

Kailuweit

First Name: Lina
Birthdate: September 24, 1901
Birthplace: Popelke
Position: Aufseherin
File Number: IV 410(F) AR 2629/67
Employment Date: August 8, 1944
Camp Service: Floßenbürg; AL Wolkenburg; AL Holleischen
Notes:

Kainz

First Name: Olga
Birthdate:
Birthplace:
Position: Aufseherin
File Number:
Employment Date:
Camp Service: Ravensbrück
Notes:

Kaiser

First Name: Gertrud
Birthdate: October 17, 1916
Birthplace: Göttingen

Position: Aufseherin
File Number:
Employment Date: December 15, 1944
Camp Service: Ravensbrück
Notes:

Kaiser (born Herold)

First Name: Helene
Birthdate: April 21, 1916
Birthplace: Jakobsthal
Position: Aufseherin
File Number: IV 410(F) AR 2629/67
Employment Date: October 13, 1944
Camp Service: Floßenbürg; AL Freiberg
Notes:

Kaiser

First Name: Ottilie
Birthdate: June 7, 1913
Birthplace: Ebrach
Position: Aufseherin
File Number:
Employment Date: December 15, 1938
Camp Service: Ravensbrück
Notes:

Kaiser

First Name: Ursula
Birthdate: July 7, 1922
Birthplace:
Position: Aufseherin
File Number: IV 429 AR 1248/68
Employment Date:
Camp Service: Markkleeburg
Notes:

Kalaene

First Name: Ilse
Birthdate: October 1, 1923
Birthplace: Guben
Position: Aufseherin
File Number:
Employment Date: November 20, 1944
Camp Service: Ravensbrück
Notes:

Kalberg

First Name: Wilhelmine
Birthdate:
Birthplace:
Position: Aufseherin
File Number:
Employment Date:
Camp Service:
Notes:

Kalina

First Name: Anna
Birthdate: September 13, 1923
Birthplace: Duisburg
Position: Aufseherin
File Number:
Employment Date: August 3, 1944
Camp Service: Ravensbrück
Notes:

Kalis

First Name: Johanna
Birthdate: May 10, 1921
Birthplace: Hindenburg
Position: Aufseherin
File Number:
Employment Date: September 20, 1944
Camp Service: Groß-Rosen
Notes:

Kallisch (or Kalisch; born Eggert)

First Name: Emilie
Birthdate:
Birthplace: Berlin
Position: Aufseherin
File Number: IV 406 AR 503/60
Employment Date:
Camp Service: AL Berlin-Schönholz
Notes:

Kalms

First Name: Hedwig
Birthdate:
Birthplace:
Position: Aufseherin
File Number:
Employment Date:
Camp Service: Ravensbrück
Notes:

Kalmutzke

First Name: Hildegard
Birthdate:
Birthplace:
Position: Aufseherin
File Number:
Employment Date:
Camp Service:
Notes:

Kaltofen (born Lehmann)

First Name: Elfriede
Birthdate: March 20, 1921
Birthplace: Leipzig
Position: Aufseherin
File Number: 409 AR-Z 39/59
Employment Date: June 15, 1944
Camp Service: Ravensbrück; AL Braunschweig; Hamburg; Hasag-Werke Leipzig; NL Markkleeberg
Notes:

Kaltofen

First Name: Elfriede
Birthdate: February 24, 1920
Birthplace:
Position: Aushilfsaufseherin
File Number: IV 410(F) AR 2629/67
Employment Date:
Camp Service: Floßenbürg (trained in Holleischen)
Notes:

Kalus

First Name: Hedwig
Birthdate: September 27, 1909
Birthplace: Gleiwitz

Position: Aufseherin
File Number: IV 410(F) AR 2629/67
Employment Date: August 20, 1944
Camp Service: Floßenbürg, AL Plauen
Notes: Permission for service as an "employee of the Reich" granted on November 22, 1944.

Kalwak

First Name: Anna
Birthdate:
Birthplace:
Position: Aufseherin
File Number:
Employment Date:
Camp Service: Groß-Rosen
Notes:

Kaminski

First Name: Emma
Birthdate:
Birthplace:
Position: Aufseherin
File Number:
Employment Date:
Camp Service: Ravensbück
Notes:

Kaminski (born Eurich)

First Name: Erika
Birthdate:
Birthplace:
Position: Aufseherin
File Number:
Employment Date:
Camp Service:
Notes:

Kaminski (born Dempewolf)

First Name: Erika
Birthdate: January 22,1920
Birthplace: Braunschweig
Position: Aufseherin
File Number: IV 4007 AR 91/65
Employment Date:
Camp Service: Stutthof
Notes: Denied to *Zentralestelle (Ludwigsburg)* prosecutors that she had ever been in Stutthof, but *Kommandanturbefehl Nr. 60* (September 6, 1944) specifically places her at that camp.

Kamka

First Name: Agnes
Birthdate: March 10, 1921
Birthplace:
Position: Aufseherin
File Number: IV 410(F) AR 2629/67
Employment Date:
Camp Service: Floßenbürg; AL Hertine
Notes:

Kamm

First Name: Anna
Birthdate: November 10, 1944
Birthplace: Sundersleben
Position: Aufseherin

File Number:
Employment Date: October 24, 1944
Camp Service: Floßenbürg
Notes: Permission for service as an "employee of the Reich" granted on December 12, 1944.

Kammel

First Name: Irma
Birthdate:
Birthplace:
Position: Aufseherin
File Number:
Employment Date:
Camp Service:
Notes:

Kammer

First Name: Elisabeth
Birthdate: 1918 (no month or day provided in her file)
Birthplace:
Position: Kommandoführerin
File Number:
Employment Date:
Camp Service: Ravensbrück
Notes: Escorted prisoners from Ravensbrück to nearby companies to fulfill slave labor quotas.

Kammer

First Name: Helene
Birthdate:
Birthplace:
Position: Aufseherin
File Number:
Employment Date:
Camp Service:
Notes:

Kammerloher (born Morche; now Kulschik)

First Name: Erna Linda
Birthdate: April 4, 1921
Birthplace: Domtizsch
Position: Aufseherin; Blockleiterin
File Number: IV 409 AR 1965/66, IV 409 AR-Z 39/59
Employment Date: 1943
Camp Service: Ravensbrück; I.G.-Farben in Wolfen.
Notes:

Kampfrath

First Name: Erika
Birthdate:
Birthplace:
Position: Aufseherin
File Number:
Employment Date:
Camp Service:
Notes:

Kamradt

First Name: Meta
Birthdate: October 26, 1918
Birthplace: Schlüchow
Position: Aufseherin
File Number:
Employment Date: November 7, 1944
Camp Service: Ravensbrück
Notes:

Kandziora
First Name: Martha
Birthdate:
Birthplace:
Position: Aufseherin
File Number:
Employment Date:
Camp Service:
Notes:

Kania
First Name: Hilde
Birthdate:
Birthplace:
Position: Aufseherin
File Number:
Employment Date:
Camp Service:
Notes:

Kaniewski (born Jung)
First Name: Erna
Birthdate:
Birthplace:
Position: Aufseherin
File Number:
Employment Date:
Camp Service:
Notes:

Kanis
First Name: Johanna
Birthdate: July 13, 1920
Birthplace: Meißen
Position: Aufseherin
File Number: IV 410(F) AR 2629/67
Employment Date: August 16, 1944
Camp Service: Floßenbürg; AL Zwodau; AL Goehle-Werk Dresden
Notes:

Kaphammel (born Müller)
First Name: Rosa
Birthdate: November 15, 1901
Birthplace: Colditz
Position: Aufseherin
File Number: IV 410(F) AR 2629/67
Employment Date: August 22, 1944
Camp Service: Floßenbürg; AL Hainichen
Notes:

Kapschak
First Name: Margarete
Birthdate: March 13, 1923
Birthplace:
Position: Aufseherin
File Number:
Employment Date: November 3, 1944
Camp Service: Ravensbrück; Sachsenhausen
Notes:

Karger (married Dzwiza)
First Name: Helene
Birthdate: July 7, 1922
Birthplace: Hermsdorf

Position: Aufseherin
File Number: IV 405 AR 1651/64
Employment Date: August 1944
Camp Service: Groß-Rosen; AL Hundsfeld; Kratzan
Notes:

Karl
First Name: Gertrud
Birthdate: February 10, 1921
Birthplace:
Position: Aufseherin
File Number: IV 406 AR-Z 21/71
Employment Date:
Camp Service: NL Genshagen
Notes:

Karl
First Name: Hertha
Birthdate:
Birthplace:
Position: Aufseherin
File Number:
Employment Date:
Camp Service:
Notes:

Karl
First Name: Martha
Birthdate: April 26, 1921
Birthplace: Teplitz-Schönau
Position: Aufseherin
File Number: IV 410(F) AR 2629/67
Employment Date: September 8, 1944
Camp Service: Floßenbürg; AL Hertine
Notes: Permission for service as an "employee of the Reich" granted on November 20, 1944.

Karth
First Name: Erika
Birthdate: May 24, 1923
Birthplace: Neuenhagen
Position: Aufseherin
File Number: IV 410(F) AR 2629/67
Employment Date: August 20, 1944
Camp Service: Floßenbürg; AL Plauen
Notes: Permission for service as an "employee of the Reich" granted on November 20, 1944.

Kasella
First Name: Josepha
Birthdate: October 12, 1922
Birthplace: Börnichen
Position: Aufseherin
File Number: IV 410(F) AR 2629/67
Employment Date: October 4, 1944
Camp Service: Floßenbürg; AL Holleischenn
Notes:

Kasmierski
First Name: Martha
Birthdate:
Birthplace:
Position: Aufseherin
File Number: IV 429 AR 1923/66 (B)
Employment Date:

Camp Service: Ravensbrück; Sömmerda
Notes:

Kassen

First Name: Gartrud
Birthdate:
Birthplace:
Position: Aufseherin
File Number:
Employment Date:
Camp Service:
Notes:

Kassner

First Name: Ida
Birthdate:
Birthplace:
Position: Aufseherin
File Number:
Employment Date:
Camp Service: Groß-Rosen
Notes:

Kast (born Koniczka)

First Name: Lotte
Birthdate:
Birthplace:
Position: Aufseherin
File Number:
Employment Date:
Camp Service:
Notes:

Kastl

First Name: Margarete
Birthdate: October 14, 1920
Birthplace: Mühlhausen
Position: Aufseherin
File Number:
Employment Date: November 7, 1944
Camp Service: Ravensbrück
Notes:

Kastl

First Name: Maria (Marie)
Birthdate: July 6, 1922
Birthplace: Falkenau
Position: Aufseherin
File Number: IV 410(F) AR 2629/67
Employment Date: April 1, 1944
Camp Service: Floßenbürg; AL Zwodau; AL Dresden-Reick
Notes:

Kästner

First Name: Margarete
Birthdate:
Birthplace:
Position: Aufseherin
File Number:
Employment Date:
Camp Service:
Notes:

Kaubach

First Name: Hildegard
Birthdate:
Birthplace:
Position: Aufseherin
File Number:
Employment Date:
Camp Service: Neuengamme
Notes:

Kauder

First Name: Charlotte
Birthdate: November 8, 1915
Birthplace: Raichenbach
Position: Aufseherin
File Number:
Employment Date: August 23, 1944
Camp Service: Groß-Rosen
Notes:

Kauf

First Name: Klara
Birthdate:
Birthplace:
Position: Aufseherin
File Number:
Employment Date:
Camp Service:
Notes:

Kaufmann

First Name: Elisabeth
Birthdate:
Birthplace:
Position: Aufseherin
File Number:
Employment Date:
Camp Service: Ravensbrück
Notes:

Kaufmann (born Schreiter)

First Name: Gertrud
Birthdate:
Birthplace:
Position: Aufseherin
File Number:
Employment Date:
Camp Service:
Notes:

Kaul

First Name: Elfriede
Birthdate:
Birthplace:
Position: Aufseherin
File Number:
Employment Date:
Camp Service:
Notes:

Kaul (born Gietzelz)

First Name: Ingeburg
Birthdate:
Birthplace:
Position: Aufseherin

File Number:
Employment Date:
Camp Service: Floßenbürg
Notes:

Kausch
First Name: Elfriede
Birthdate:
Birthplace:
Position: Aufseherin
File Number:
Employment Date:
Camp Service:
Notes:

Kauschke (born Bürger)
First Name: Irmgard
Birthdate: April 22, 1921
Birthplace: Pethau
Position: Aufseherin
File Number:
Employment Date: May 15, 1944
Camp Service: Ravensbrück
Notes:

Katzwinkel (born Wiesendahl)
First Name: Paula
Birthdate: October 7, 1906
Birthplace: Holzen
Position: Aufseherin
File Number: IV 429 AR 1964/66
Employment Date:
Camp Service: Dortmund
Notes:

Kayser
First Name: Martha
Birthdate: September 5, 1907
Birthplace:
Position: Aufseherin
File Number: IV 429 AR 1973/66(B)
Employment Date:
Camp Service: Ravensbrück
Notes:

Kblitz
First Name: Elfriede
Birthdate: May 30, 1922
Birthplace: Neurode
Position: Aufseherin
File Number:
Employment Date: August 1, 1944
Camp Service: Groß-Rosen
Notes:

Kedziora
First Name: Luzia (or Lucia)
Birthdate: December 27, 1922
Birthplace:
Position: Aufseherin
File Number: 429 AR 1932/66
Employment Date:
Camp Service: Lippstädt
Notes:

Keil
First Name: Magdalene
Birthdate:
Birthplace:
Position: Aufseherin
File Number:
Employment Date:
Camp Service: Groß-Rosen
Notes:

Keller
First Name: Josefa
Birthdate: August 10, 1922
Birthplace: Augsburg
Position: Aufseherin
File Number:
Employment Date: August 20, 1944
Camp Service: Dachau
Notes:

Kelm
First Name: Herta
Birthdate:
Birthplace:
Position: Aufseherin
File Number:
Employment Date:
Camp Service:
Notes:

Kempe
First Name: Lisa
Birthdate: July 1, 1922
Birthplace: Mistroj
Position: Aufseherin
File Number: IV 410(F) AR 2629/67
Employment Date: August 17, 1944
Camp Service: Floßenbürg
Notes:

Kerfel
First Name: Luise
Birthdate:
Birthplace:
Position: Aufseherin
File Number:
Employment Date:
Camp Service:
Notes:

Kern
First Name: Anna
Birthdate: March 9, 1921
Birthplace: Gainfarm
Position: Aufseherin
File Number:
Employment Date: September 1, 1944
Camp Service: Mauthausen
Notes:

Kersting
First Name: Elisabeth
Birthdate:
Birthplace:
Position: Aufseherin

File Number:
Employment Date:
Camp Service: Ravensbrück
Notes:

Kertscher

First Name: Irene
Birthdate: June 13, 1922
Birthplace: Groß Stöbnitz
Position: Aufseherin
File Number:
Employment Date: August 2, 1944
Camp Service: Ravensbrück
Notes:

Kertscher (born Ludwig)

First Name: Johanna
Birthdate: January 11, 1922
Birthplace: Klein Heyna
Position: Aufseherin
File Number:
Employment Date: August 11, 1944
Camp Service: Ravensbrück
Notes:

Kessel

First Name: Magdalene
Birthdate:
Birthplace:
Position: Aufseherin
File Number:
Employment Date:
Camp Service: Ravensbrück; Bergen-Belsen
Notes:

Ketelhut

First Name: Maria
Birthdate:
Birthplace:
Position: Aufseherin
File Number:
Employment Date:
Camp Service:
Notes:

Kienitz

First Name: Elisabeth
Birthdate:
Birthplace:
Position: Aufseherin
File Number:
Employment Date:
Camp Service:
Notes:

Kiesewalter

First Name: Irmgard
Birthdate:
Birthplace:
Position: Aufseherin
File Number:
Employment Date:
Camp Service:
Notes:

Kiesig

First Name: Charlotte
Birthdate: November 20, 1920
Birthplace: Dresden
Position: Aufseherin
File Number: IV 410(F) AR 2629/67
Employment Date: August 10, 1944
Camp Service: Floßenbürg; AL Dresden-Reick
Notes:

Kiessling

First Name: Gertrud
Birthdate: August 13, 1919
Birthplace: Regiß-Breitg.
Position: Aufseherin
File Number:
Employment Date: December 29, 1944
Camp Service: Ravensbrück
Notes:

Kietzmann

First Name: Anneliese
Birthdate:
Birthplace:
Position: Aufseherin
File Number:
Employment Date:
Camp Service:
Notes:

Kilian (born Isaak)

First Name: Maria
Birthdate: May 26, 1913
Birthplace: Millorowo
Position: Aufseherin
File Number: IV 410(F) AR 2629/67
Employment Date:
Camp Service: Floßenbürg; AL Junkers Werke Plauen; Ravensbrück
Notes:

Kilkowski

First Name: Wally, Meta
Birthdate: September 26, 1921
Birthplace: Berlin
Position: Aufseherin
File Number: 409 AR-Z 23/70
Employment Date: 1941
Camp Service: Ravensbrück; NL Neustadt-Glewe
Notes: Sentenced to nine months imprisonment for crimes against humanity by an East German court.

Kimplinger

First Name: Berta
Birthdate: August 1, 1923
Birthplace: Augsburg
Position:
File Number:
Employment Date: August 21, 1944
Camp Service: Dachau
Notes:

Kirchhammer
First Name: Sofie
Birthdate: May 22, 1921 (or July 11, 1921)
Birthplace: Probfeld
Position: Aufseherin
File Number: IV 410(F) AR 2629/67
Employment Date: September 30, 1944
Camp Service: Floßenbürg; Hollesichen
Notes:

Kirsch (born Kriegel)
First Name: Maria
Birthdate: May 9, 1909
Birthplace: Nieder-Albersdorf
Position: Aufseherin
File Number: IV 405 AR-Z 635/67
Employment Date:
Camp Service: NL Bernsdorf
Notes:

Kirschlager (or Kirchschlager; born Potutschek)
First Name: Berta
Birthdate:
Birthplace:
Position: Aufseherin
File Number: IV 505 AR-Z 25/75
Employment Date:
Camp Service: Groß-Rosen; NL Parschnitz
Notes:

Kirschke
First Name: Ruth
Birthdate:
Birthplace:
Position: Aufseherin
File Number:
Employment Date:
Camp Service:
Notes:

Kirschkies
First Name: Elfriede
Birthdate:
Birthplace:
Position: Aufseherin
File Number:
Employment Date:
Camp Service:
Notes:

Kirsten
First Name: Käthe
Birthdate: December 11, 1919
Birthplace: Dresden
Position: Aufseherin
File Number: IV 410(F) AR 2629/67
Employment Date: August 16, 1944
Camp Service: Floßenbürg; AL Dresden-Reick
Notes: Permission for service as an "employee of the Reich" granted on November 20, 1944.

Kissel
First Name: Irmgard
Birthdate:
Birthplace:

Position: Aufseherin
File Number:
Employment Date:
Camp Service:
Notes:

Klaas
First Name: Adelheid
Birthdate:
Birthplace:
Position: Aufseherin
File Number:
Employment Date:
Camp Service:
Notes:

Klaembt (born Schoenebeck)
First Name: Elli
Birthdate:
Birthplace:
Position: Aufseherin
File Number:
Employment Date:
Camp Service:
Notes:

Klagge
First Name: Gerda
Birthdate:
Birthplace:
Position: Aufseherin
File Number:
Employment Date:
Camp Service: Ravensbrück
Notes:

Klahre
First Name: Henriette
Birthdate:
Birthplace:
Position: Aufseherin
File Number:
Employment Date:
Camp Service: Neuengamme
Notes:

Klamt
First Name: Gertrud
Birthdate:
Birthplace:
Position: Aufseherin
File Number:
Employment Date:
Camp Service: Groß-Rosen
Notes:

Klare
First Name: Anna
Birthdate:
Birthplace:
Position: Aufseherin
File Number:
Employment Date:
Camp Service: Ravensbrück
Notes:

Klass
First Name: Adelheid
Birthdate:
Birthplace:
Position: Aufseherin
File Number:
Employment Date:
Camp Service: Ravensbrück
Notes:

Klaudat
First Name: Lieselotte
Birthdate: January 20, 1915
Birthplace: Unterföhring
Position: Aufseherin
File Number:
Employment Date: August 28, 1944
Camp Service: Dachau
Notes:

Klaus
First Name: Maria
Birthdate:
Birthplace:
Position: Aufseherin
File Number:
Employment Date:
Camp Service: Ravensbrück
Notes:

Klaus (born Aschbitz)
First Name: Hildegard
Birthdate:
Birthplace:
Position: Aufseherin
File Number:
Employment Date:
Camp Service:
Notes:

Klauß
First Name: Charlotte
Birthdate:
Birthplace:
Position: Aufseherin
File Number: IV 402 AR-Z 37/58
Employment Date:
Camp Service: Auschwitz
Notes:

Klebs
First Name: Lina
Birthdate:
Birthplace:
Position: Aufseherin
File Number:
Employment Date:
Camp Service: Floßenbürg
Notes:

Klee
First Name: Maria
Birthdate:
Birthplace:
Position: Aufseherin

File Number:
Employment Date:
Camp Service:
Notes:

Kleiber
First Name: Käthe
Birthdate:
Birthplace:
Position: Aufseherin
File Number:
Employment Date:
Camp Service:
Notes:

Klein (born Plaubel)
First Name: Anne
Birthdate: June 8, 1887
Birthplace: Gurs
Position: Aufseherin; Chef Oberaufseherin
File Number:
Employment Date: September 14, 1939
Camp Service: Ravensbrück; Sachsenhausen
Notes: One of only two women to ever attain the rank of *Chef Oberaufseherin* (Chief Senior Overseer).

Klein (born Hoffmann)
First Name: Charlotte
Birthdate: June 9, 1923
Birthplace: Stuttgart
Position: Aufseherin
File Number: IV 410 (F) AR 2629/67
Employment Date:
Camp Service: Floßenbürg; AL Hertine; Groß-Rosen; Bergen-Belsen
Notes: Tried by the British for war crimes.

Klein
First Name: Elfriede
Birthdate: April 21, 1922
Birthplace: Waldenburg (Silesia)
Position: Aufseherin
File Number:
Employment Date: September 6, 1944
Camp Service: Ravensbrück; Sachsenhausen
Notes:

Klein
First Name: Johanna
Birthdate:
Birthplace:
Position: Aufseherin
File Number:
Employment Date:
Camp Service:
Notes:

Klein
First Name: Luise
Birthdate:
Birthplace:
Position: Aufseherin
File Number:
Employment Date:

Camp Service:
Notes:

Kleine

First Name: Annemarie
Birthdate: March 8, 1920
Birthplace: Sömmerda
Position: Aufseherin
File Number: IV 429 AR-Z 89/71
Employment Date:
Camp Service: NL Markkleeberg; Sömmerda; NL Lippstadt
Notes:

Kleine

First Name: Lotte
Birthdate:
Birthplace:
Position: Aufseherin
File Number:
Employment Date:
Camp Service:
Notes:

Kleiner

First Name: Margarethe
Birthdate:
Birthplace:
Position: Aufseherin
File Number: IV 409 AR-Z 39/59
Employment Date:
Camp Service: Ravensbrück
Notes:

Kleinert

First Name: Meta
Birthdate:
Birthplace:
Position: Aufseherin
File Number:
Employment Date:
Camp Service:
Notes:

Kleinschmidt (born Peters)

First Name: Charlotte
Birthdate:
Birthplace:
Position: Aufseherin
File Number:
Employment Date:
Camp Service:
Notes:

Kleinschmidt

First Name: Maria
Birthdate:
Birthplace:
Position: Aufseherin
File Number:
Employment Date:
Camp Service: Neuengamme
Notes:

Kleinstüber

First Name: Ruth
Birthdate:
Birthplace:
Position: Aufseherin
File Number:
Employment Date:
Camp Service: Stutthof/Danzig
Notes:

Klembt

First Name: Anna
Birthdate: June 30, 1907
Birthplace: Kutschkau
Position: Aufseherin
File Number:
Employment Date: November 1, 1942
Camp Service: Ravensbrück
Notes:

Klemenz

First Name: Petronella
Birthdate: May 31, 1921
Birthplace: Aulhausen
Position: Aufseherin
File Number:
Employment Date: November 18, 1944
Camp Service: Ravensbrück
Notes:

Klemm

First Name: Charlotte
Birthdate:
Birthplace:
Position: Aufseherin
File Number:
Employment Date:
Camp Service: Floßenbürg
Notes:

Klemm

First Name: Ilse
Birthdate: October 1, 1919
Birthplace: Niederbobritzsch
Position: Aufseherin
File Number: IV 410(F) AR 2629/67
Employment Date: October 13, 1944
Camp Service: Floßenbürg; AL Freiberg
Notes: Permission for service as an "employee of the Reich" granted on December 12, 1944.

Klemm

First Name: Ingeborg
Birthdate: November 10, 1917
Birthplace: Dresden
Position: Aufseherin
File Number:
Employment Date: September 2, 1944
Camp Service: Floßenbürg
Notes:

Klemm

First Name: Vinzenzia
Birthdate:
Birthplace:

Position: Aufseherin
File Number:
Employment Date:
Camp Service: Groß-Rosen
Notes:

Klempat

First Name: Margarete
Birthdate:
Birthplace:
Position: Aufseherin
File Number:
Employment Date:
Camp Service:
Notes:

Klemz (born Richter)

First Name: Ingeborg
Birthdate:
Birthplace:
Position: Aufseherin
File Number:
Employment Date:
Camp Service:
Notes:

Kliehe

First Name: Irmgard
Birthdate:
Birthplace:
Position: Aufseherin
File Number:
Employment Date:
Camp Service:
Notes:

Kliem

First Name: Anni
Birthdate:
Birthplace:
Position: Aufseherin
File Number:
Employment Date:
Camp Service: Ravensbrück
Notes:

Klier

First Name: Gertrud
Birthdate: July 2, 1922
Birthplace: Kronstadt
Position: Aufseherin
File Number: IV 410(F) AR 2629/67
Employment Date: April 1, 1944
Camp Service: Floßenbürg; AL Graslitz
Notes:

Klimpinger

First Name: Berta
Birthdate:
Birthplace:
Position: Aufseherin
File Number:
Employment Date:
Camp Service:
Notes:

Klink

First Name: Gerda
Birthdate:
Birthplace:
Position: Aufseherin
File Number:
Employment Date:
Camp Service:
Notes:

Klink

First Name: Käthe
Birthdate:
Birthplace:
Position: Aufseherin
File Number:
Employment Date:
Camp Service: Neuengamme
Notes:

Klinka

First Name: Käthe
Birthdate: June 6, 1920
Birthplace: Berlin
Position: Aufseherin
File Number:
Employment Date: December 15, 1943
Camp Service: Ravensbrück
Notes:

Klinkenstein

First Name: Elfriede
Birthdate:
Birthplace:
Position: Aufseherin
File Number:
Employment Date:
Camp Service: Neuengamme
Notes:

Klinnert

First Name: Ingeborg
Birthdate: April 11, 1922
Birthplace:
Position: Aufseherin
File Number: IV 429 AR 1941/66(B)
Employment Date:
Camp Service: Ravensbrück; NL Torgau
Notes:

Klofik

First Name: Helena
Birthdate: April 25, 1904
Birthplace:
Position: Aufseherin
File Number: IV 410(F) AR 2629/67
Employment Date: September 8, 1944
Camp Service: Floßenbürg; AL Wilischtal
Notes: Official permission for service as an "employee of the Reich" granted on November 20, 1944.

Klopfer

First Name: Gertrud
Birthdate: September 28, 1921
Birthplace: Leipzig

Position: Aufseherin
File Number: IV 410(F) AR 2629/67
Employment Date: August 16, 1944
Camp Service: Floßenbürg; AL Graslitz
Notes:

Klose

First Name: Ella
Birthdate: July 9, 1914
Birthplace: Nousalz
Position: Aufseherin
File Number:
Employment Date: June 1, 1944
Camp Service: Groß-Rosen
Notes:

Klose

First Name: Erna
Birthdate: February 4, 1921
Birthplace: Peiskersdorf
Position: Aufseherin
File Number:
Employment Date: October, 1944
Camp Service: Groß-Rosen
Notes:

Klose

First Name: Klara
Birthdate: November 12, 1921
Birthplace: Weigenrodau
Position: Aufseherin
File Number:
Employment Date: September 1, 1944
Camp Service: Groß-Rosen
Notes:

Klosendorf

First Name: Olga
Birthdate:
Birthplace:
Position: Aufseherin
File Number:
Employment Date:
Camp Service: Floßenbürg
Notes:

Kloß

First Name: Ruth
Birthdate:
Birthplace:
Position: Aufseherin
File Number:
Employment Date:
Camp Service: Ravensbrück
Notes:

Klotz

First Name: Maria
Birthdate:
Birthplace:
Position: Aufseherin
File Number:
Employment Date:
Camp Service:
Notes:

Klowersa

First Name: Lucie
Birthdate: November 17, 1921
Birthplace: Grenzek
Position: Aufseherin
File Number:
Employment Date: August 1, 1944
Camp Service: Groß-Rosen
Notes:

Klucznick

First Name: Ida
Birthdate:
Birthplace:
Position: Aufseherin
File Number:
Employment Date:
Camp Service:
Notes:

Kluge

First Name: Elisabeth
Birthdate:
Birthplace:
Position: Aufseherin
File Number:
Employment Date:
Camp Service:
Notes:

Kluge

First Name: Margarethe
Birthdate: September 5, 1903
Birthplace: Löderburg (Kalbe)
Position: Aufseherin
File Number:
Employment Date: August 17, 1944
Camp Service: Sachsenhausen
Notes:

Kluger

First Name: Charlotte
Birthdate: January 22, 1909
Birthplace: Grünberg
Position: Aufseherin
File Number:
Employment Date: August 19, 1944
Camp Service: Groß-Rosen
Notes:

Klunker

First Name: Ilse
Birthdate:
Birthplace:
Position: Aufseherin
File Number:
Employment Date:
Camp Service:
Notes:

Klyna

First Name: Elfriede
Birthdate: December 28, 1913
Birthplace: Trautenbach
Position: Aufseherin

File Number:
Employment Date: July 24, 1944
Camp Service: Groß-Rosen
Notes:

Knake (born Ballhouse)
First Name: Annemarie
Birthdate:
Birthplace:
Position: Aufseherin
File Number:
Employment Date:
Camp Service: Neuengamme
Notes:

Knakowski
First Name: Gertrud
Birthdate:
Birthplace:
Position: Aufseherin
File Number:
Employment Date:
Camp Service:
Notes:

Knappe
First Name: Andrea
Birthdate:
Birthplace:
Position: Aufseherin
File Number:
Employment Date:
Camp Service: Ravensbrück
Notes:

Knappe
First Name: Hedwig
Birthdate: March 3, 1920
Birthplace: Altkranz
Position: Aufseherin
File Number:
Employment Date: August 8, 1944
Camp Service: Groß-Rosen
Notes:

Knappe
First Name: Hildegard
Birthdate: April 25, 1920
Birthplace: Marienhof
Position: Aufseherin
File Number:
Employment Date: July 1, 1944
Camp Service: Groß-Rosen
Notes:

Knauer
First Name: Elisabeth
Birthdate: June 2, 1920
Birthplace: Bögendorf (Schweidntz)
Position: Aufseherin
File Number:
Employment Date: March 1, 1944
Camp Service: Groß-Rosen
Notes: Permission for service as an "employee of the Reich" granted on December 22, 1944.

Knauer (born Scholz)
First Name: Hedwig
Birthdate: January 4, 1910
Birthplace: Reichenbach
Position: Aufseherin
File Number:
Employment Date: April 15, 1944
Camp Service: Groß-Rosen
Notes:

Knauf
First Name: Anna
Birthdate:
Birthplace:
Position: Aufseherin
File Number:
Employment Date:
Camp Service: Sachsenhausen
Notes:

Kneitl (or Kneitel; born Wiedemann)
First Name: Maria
Birthdate:
Birthplace:
Position: Aufseherin
File Number:
Employment Date:
Camp Service:
Notes:

Kneryk
First Name: Ludmilla
Birthdate: July 15, 1921
Birthplace: Neurode
Position: Aufseherin
File Number:
Employment Date: October 18, 1944
Camp Service: Groß-Rosen
Notes:

Knickenberg
First Name: Irmgard
Birthdate:
Birthplace:
Position: Aufseherin
File Number:
Employment Date:
Camp Service: Ravensbrück
Notes:

Knittel
First Name: Anna
Birthdate: October 14, 1900
Birthplace: Kamen
Position: Aufseherin
File Number:
Employment Date: July 24, 1944
Camp Service: Groß-Rosen
Notes:

Knittel
First Name: Antonie
Birthdate: September 25, 1918
Birthplace: Bad Reiners
Position: Aufseherin

File Number:
Employment Date: August 1, 1944
Camp Service: Groß-Rosen
Notes:

Knittel
First Name: Helene
Birthdate: August 10, 1920
Birthplace: Lunzenau
Position: Aufseherin
File Number: IV 410(F) AR 2629/67
Employment Date: September 21, 1944
Camp Service: Floßenbürg; AL Plauen; AL Rochlitz
Notes:

Knoblauch
First Name: Elfriede
Birthdate: July 26, 1918
Birthplace: Berlin
Position: Aufseherin
File Number:
Employment Date: August 14, 1944
Camp Service: Groß-Rosen
Notes:

Knoblauch
First Name: Erika
Birthdate: November 15, 1914
Birthplace: Breslau
Position: Aufseherin
File Number:
Employment Date: September 22, 1944
Camp Service: Groß-Rosen
Notes:

Knoblich
First Name: Elisabeth
Birthdate: January 19, 1919
Birthplace: Groß Ilsde
Position: Aufseherin
File Number: 408 AR 2974/65
Employment Date: August 1940
Camp Service: Ravensbrück (August 1940-October 20, 1942); Lublin-Majdanek (October 20, 1942-January 15, 1943)
Notes: According to an investigation, she was so extremely harsh and brutal that even her fellow Aufseherinnen feared her. She was nicknamed *"Halt die Klappe!"* ("Shut up!"); designated as an SS auxiliary.

Knoche
First Name: Helga
Birthdate: July 8, 1923
Birthplace: Lindenthal
Position: Aufseherin
File Number:
Employment Date: August 29, 1944
Camp Service: Ravensbrück
Notes:

Knoeber
First Name: Else
Birthdate:
Birthplace:

Position: Aufseherin
File Number:
Employment Date:
Camp Service:
Notes:

Knoke
First Name: Lieselotte
Birthdate:
Birthplace:
Position: Aufseherin
File Number:
Employment Date:
Camp Service: Ravensbrück
Notes:

Knolleisen
First Name: Hildegard
Birthdate: December 26, 1923
Birthplace: Berlin
Position: Aufseherin
File Number:
Employment Date: July 21, 1944
Camp Service: Groß-Rosen
Notes:

Knop
First Name: Hildegard
Birthdate:
Birthplace:
Position: Aufseherin
File Number:
Employment Date:
Camp Service:
Notes:

Knopfe (born Hoffmann)
First Name: Else
Birthdate: February 29, 1904
Birthplace: Chemnitz
Position: Aufseherin
File Number: IV 410(F) AR 2629/67
Employment Date: August 16, 1944
Camp Service: Floßenbürg; AL Astrawerke; Chemnitz
Notes:

Knospe
First Name: Irmtraut
Birthdate: September 15, 1922
Birthplace: Hartmannsdorf
Position: Aufseherin
File Number:
Employment Date: September 12, 1944
Camp Service: Groß-Rosen
Notes:

Knüpfgans
First Name: Hertha
Birthdate:
Birthplace:
Position: Aufseherin
File Number:
Employment Date:
Camp Service: Groß-Rosen
Notes:

Knüppel

First Name: Maragrete
Birthdate:
Birthplace:
Position: Aufseherin
File Number:
Employment Date:
Camp Service:
Notes:

Knuger

First Name: Irmgard
Birthdate:
Birthplace:
Position: Aufseherin
File Number:
Employment Date:
Camp Service: Groß-Rosen
Notes:

Koberg

First Name: Anna
Birthdate:
Birthplace:
Position: Aufseherin
File Number:
Employment Date:
Camp Service:
Notes:

Koblischek

First Name: Gisela
Birthdate: December 11, 1920
Birthplace: Falkenau
Position: Aufseherin
File Number:
Employment Date: July 21, 1944
Camp Service: Groß-Rosen
Notes:

Koblischke

First Name: Anna
Birthdate: May 16, 1922
Birthplace: Tschenkowitz
Position: Aufseherin
File Number:
Employment Date: July 21, 1944
Camp Service: Groß-Rosen
Notes:

Kobsa

First Name: Klara
Birthdate: December 28, 1922
Birthplace: Grabenau
Position: Aufseherin
File Number:
Employment Date: April 15, 1944
Camp Service: Groß-Rosen
Notes:

Koch

First Name: Elisabeth
Birthdate:
Birthplace:
Position: Aufseherin

File Number:
Employment Date:
Camp Service:
Notes:

Koch

First Name: Else
Birthdate: September 6, 1921
Birthplace:
Position: Aufseherin
File Number:
Employment Date:
Camp Service: Sachsenhausen
Notes:

Koch (born Belling)

First Name: Erika
Birthdate: June 30, 1915
Birthplace: Berlin-Neukölln
Position: Aufseherin
File Number:
Employment Date: April 15, 1944
Camp Service: Sachsenhausen
Notes:

Koch

First Name: Erna
Birthdate: August 2, 1921
Birthplace:
Position: Aufseherin
File Number:
Employment Date:
Camp Service: Sachsenhausen
Notes:

Koch

First Name: Ilse
Birthdate:
Birthplace:
Position: Oberaufseherin and commandant's wife
File Number:
Employment Date:
Camp Service: Ravensbrück; Buchenwald
Notes: Known as the "Bitch of Buchenwald;" tried by the Americans after the war and sentenced to seven years imprisonment; released early, but tried by a German court and again sentenced to prison; committed suicide in 1957 in her prison cell.

Koch

First Name: Marianne
Birthdate: January 24, 1906
Birthplace: Löbau
Position: Aufseherin
File Number: IV 410(F) AR 2629/67
Employment Date: August 23, 1944
Camp Service: Floßenbürg; AL Zwodau
Notes:

Koch

First Name: Walburga
Birthdate: June 21, 1918
Birthplace: Nuremberg
Position: Aufseherin

File Number:
Employment Date: October 24, 1944
Camp Service: Floßenbürg
Notes:

Kochale

First Name: Johanna
Birthdate: June 24, 1922
Birthplace: Zossen
Position: Aufseherin
File Number:
Employment Date: November 25, 1944
Camp Service: Ravensbrück
Notes:

Kochan

First Name: Maria
Birthdate: October 26, 1914
Birthplace: Neu-Driebitz
Position:
File Number:
Employment Date: April 15, 1944
Camp Service: Ravensbrück
Notes:

Kochlausch

First Name: Franziska (Fanny)
Birthdate: April 26, 1907
Birthplace: Pern
Position: Aufseherin
File Number: IV 410(F) AR 2629/67
Employment Date: September 8, 1944
Camp Service: Floßenbürg; AL Hertine
Notes: Permission for service as an "employee of the Reich" granted on November 20, 1944.

Kochnitzki

First Name: Sophie (Sofie)
Birthdate: February 13, 1916
Birthplace: Langensee
Position: Aufseherin
File Number: IV 410(F) AR 2629/67
Employment Date: November 1, 1943
Camp Service: Floßenbürg; AL Zwodau; AL Dresden-Reick
Notes:

Köbele

First Name: Maria
Birthdate:
Birthplace:
Position: Aufseherin
File Number:
Employment Date:
Camp Service:
Notes:

Köhle

First Name: Mathilde
Birthdate: August 13, 1923
Birthplace: Lemberg
Position: Aufseherin
File Number:
Employment Date: August 25, 1944
Camp Service: Ravensbrück; Sachsenhausen
Notes:

Köhler

First Name: Emma
Birthdate: November 2, 1919
Birthplace: Waldenburg
Position: Aufseherin
File Number:
Employment Date: September 2, 1944
Camp Service: Groß-Rosen
Notes:

Köhler

First Name: Margaretha
Birthdate:
Birthplace:
Position: Aufseherin
File Number:
Employment Date:
Camp Service: Groß-Rosen
Notes:

Köhler

First Name: Margarete
Birthdate: July 31, 1922
Birthplace: Petschau
Position: Aufseherin
File Number:
Employment Date: April 1, 1944
Camp Service: Ravensbrück
Notes:

Köhler

First Name: Maria (Marie)
Birthdate: September 3, 1900
Birthplace: Aussig
Position: Aufseherin
File Number: IV 410(F) AR 2629/67
Employment Date: September 8, 1944
Camp Service: Floßenbürg; AL Hertine
Notes:

Köhler

First Name: Therese
Birthdate: October 14, 1902
Birthplace: Syrau
Position: Aufseherin
File Number: IV 410(F) AR 2629/67
Employment Date: September 11, 1944
Camp Service: Floßenbürg; AL Plauen
Notes:

Kölber

First Name: Sofie
Birthdate: July 11, 1921
Birthplace:
Position: Aufseherin
File Number: IV 410(F) AR 2629/67
Employment Date:
Camp Service: Floßenbürg; Holleischen
Notes:

Kölbl

First Name: Anni
Birthdate:
Birthplace:
Position: Aufseherin

File Number:
Employment Date:
Camp Service:
Notes:

König (born Kaaden)

First Name: Elfriede
Birthdate:
Birthplace:
Position: Aufseherin
File Number:
Employment Date:
Camp Service:
Notes:

König

First Name: Lydia
Birthdate: May 12, 1922
Birthplace: Guben
Position:
File Number:
Employment Date: July 30, 1944
Camp Service: Groß-Rosen
Notes:

Köpf

First Name: Margarete
Birthdate:
Birthplace:
Position: Aufseherin
File Number:
Employment Date:
Camp Service:
Notes:

Köpke

First Name: Ursula
Birthdate: September 9, 1921
Birthplace:
Position: Aufseherin
File Number: IV 429 AR 1941/66(B)
Employment Date:
Camp Service: NL Torgau; Ravensbrück
Notes:

Köppchen

First Name: Nelly
Birthdate: May 29, 1921
Birthplace: Delitzsch
Position: Aufseherin
File Number:
Employment Date: June 1, 1943
Camp Service: Ravensbrück
Notes:

Koerber (born Klein)

First Name: Maria
Birthdate:
Birthplace:
Position: Aufseherin
File Number:
Employment Date:
Camp Service:
Notes:

Körner

First Name: Ilse
Birthdate: July 27
Birthplace: Wetterzeube
Position: Aufseherin
File Number:
Employment Date: November 7, 1944
Camp Service: Ravensbrück
Notes:

Körner

First Name: Margot
Birthdate: October 22, 1923
Birthplace: Petersdorf
Position: Aufseherin
File Number:
Employment Date: June 29, 1944
Camp Service: Groß-Rosen
Notes:

Kosling

First Name: Hildegard
Birthdate: June 19, 1921
Birthplace: Berlin-Charlottenburg
Position: Aufseherin
File Number:
Employment Date: September 5, 1944
Camp Service: Sachsenhausen; Ravensbrück
Notes:

Kohl

First Name: Edith
Birthdate: March 1, 1922
Birthplace: Trebnitz
Position: Aufseherin
File Number:
Employment Date: November 29, 1944
Camp Service: Groß-Rosen
Notes:

Kohle

First Name: Dorothea (Thea)
Birthdate: November 8, 1923
Birthplace: Breda
Position:
File Number:
Employment Date: October 15, 1943
Camp Service: Ravensbrück
Notes:

Kohle

First Name: Theodora Kora
Birthdate: February 11, 1922
Birthplace: Breda
Position: Aufseherin
File Number:
Employment Date: August 15, 1944
Camp Service: Ravensbrück
Notes:

Kohler

First Name: Magdalena (Magdalene)
Birthdate: February 21, 1909
Birthplace: Steinach
Position: Aufseherin

File Number: IV 410(F) AR 2629/67
Employment Date: July 10, 1944
Camp Service: Floßenbürg; Kommando Helmbrechts
Notes: A Waffen SS auxiliary since July 10, 1944.

Kohlmann

First Name: Anneliese
Birthdate: March 21, 1921
Birthplace: Hamburg
Position: Aufseherin
File Number:
Employment Date:
Camp Service: Ravensbrück; AL Neugraben; Bergen-Belsen
Notes: Was sentenced to two years imprisonment by the British on May 16, 1946; released immediately for "time served" (pretrial confinement).

Kohnen

First Name: Else
Birthdate: September 15, 1920
Birthplace: Langenbielau
Position: Aufseherin
File Number:
Employment Date: August 1, 1944
Camp Service: Groß-Rosen
Notes:

Koinzer (born Liebelt)

First Name: Lucie
Birthdate: November 19, 1909
Birthplace: Nossdorf
Position: Aufseherin
File Number:
Employment Date: June 15, 1944
Camp Service: Groß-Rosen
Notes:

Kolbe

First Name: Erna
Birthdate: May 20, 1921
Birthplace: Oberaltstadt
Position: Aufseherin
File Number:
Employment Date: September 28, 1944
Camp Service: Groß-Rosen
Notes:

Kolberg

First Name: Gertrud
Birthdate: November 13, 1921
Birthplace: Breslau
Position: Aufseherin
File Number:
Employment Date: September 20, 1944
Camp Service: Groß-Rosen
Notes:

Kolle

First Name: Dora
Birthdate:
Birthplace:
Position: Aufseherin
File Number:
Employment Date:

Camp Service:
Notes:

Koller

First Name: Johanna
Birthdate:
Birthplace:
Position: Aufseherin
File Number:
Employment Date:
Camp Service:
Notes:

Kollhof (married Kraft)

First Name: Martha
Birthdate: September 3, 1912
Birthplace: Berlin
Position: Aufseherin
File Number: IV 410(F) AR 2629/67
Employment Date: September 30, 1944
Camp Service: Floßenbürg
Notes: Permission for service as an "employee of the Reich" granted on November 22, 1944.

Kolling (born Becker)

First Name: Gertrud
Birthdate: June 10, 1918
Birthplace: Tschieser
Position: Aufseherin
File Number:
Employment Date: June 1, 1944
Camp Service: Groß-Rosen
Notes:

Kollwain

First Name: Käthe
Birthdate:
Birthplace:
Position: Aufseherin
File Number:
Employment Date:
Camp Service: Danzig-Stutthof
Notes:

Koloschinski

First Name: Helene
Birthdate:
Birthplace:
Position: Aufseherin
File Number:
Employment Date:
Camp Service:
Notes:

Komma (born Heindl)

First Name: Magdalene
Birthdate:
Birthplace:
Position: Aufseherin
File Number:
Employment Date:
Camp Service:
Notes:

Konrad
First Name: Elisbeth
Birthdate: January 3, 1922
Birthplace: Berlin
Position: Aufseherin
File Number:
Employment Date: July 21, 1944
Camp Service: Groß-Rosen
Notes:

Konrad
First Name: Hildegard
Birthdate: December 4, 1922
Birthplace: Striegau
Position: Aufseherin
File Number:
Employment Date: June 1, 1944
Camp Service: Groß-Rosen
Notes:

Konschak
First Name: Liesbeth
Birthdate: August 6, 1923
Birthplace: Breslau
Position: Aufseherin
File Number:
Employment Date: July 1, 1944
Camp Service: Groß-Rosen
Notes:

Koon (born Wolff)
First Name: Hildegard
Birthdate:
Birthplace:
Position: Aufseherin
File Number:
Employment Date:
Camp Service:
Notes:

Koorn (married Hüse)
First Name: Elisabeth (Gisberta)
Birthdate: April 1, 1923 or April 8, 1923
Birthplace: Rotterdam
Position: Aufseherin
File Number: IV 409 AR 1482/66
Employment Date: 1944
Camp Service: Vught; Ravensbrück, NL Neubrandenburg
Notes: Dutch national; special permission for service as an "employee of the Reich" granted.

Kopecky
First Name: Anna
Birthdate:
Birthplace:
Position: Aufseherin
File Number:
Employment Date:
Camp Service: Ravensbrück
Notes:

Kopischke (or Kopischka; now Eichler)
First Name: Hildegard
Birthdate: August 11, 1923
Birthplace: Berlin

Position: Aufseherin
File Number: IV 410 AR-Z 106/68
Employment Date: September 29, 1944
Camp Service: Floßenbürg; AL Mittweida; AL Holleischen
Notes:

Kopka
First Name: Anna
Birthdate: August 22, 1916
Birthplace: Apolda
Position: Aufseherin
File Number:
Employment Date: March 1, 1943
Camp Service: Ravensbrück
Notes:

Kopp
First Name: Elfriede
Birthdate: July 23, 1920
Birthplace: Wulferstedt
Position: Aufseherin
File Number:
Employment Date: July 11, 1944
Camp Service: Ravensbrück
Notes:

Kopp
First Name: Theresia
Birthdate:
Birthplace:
Position: Aufseherin
File Number:
Employment Date:
Camp Service: Dachau
Notes:

Korallus
First Name: Helene
Birthdate: November 22, 1913
Birthplace: Pellkauen
Position: Aufseherin
File Number:
Employment Date: September 26, 1944
Camp Service: Floßenbürg
Notes: Permission for service as an "employee of the Reich" granted on December 14, 1944

Korde
First Name: Hedwig
Birthdate: December 3, 1922
Birthplace: Niedersteine
Position: Aufseherin
File Number:
Employment Date: August 14, 1944
Camp Service: Groß-Rosen
Notes:

Korfei
First Name: Luise
Birthdate: September 29, 1919
Birthplace:
Position: Aufseherin
File Number: IV 429 AR 1248/68
Employment Date:
Camp Service: Markkleeberg; Ravensbrück
Notes:

Kornblum
First Name: Else
Birthdate: January 6, 1905
Birthplace:
Position: Aufseherin
File Number: IV 429 AR 1941/66(B)
Employment Date:
Camp Service: NL Torgau; Ravensbrück
Notes:

Kornmann
First Name: Sophie
Birthdate: June 8, 1923
Birthplace: Rosenthal
Position: Aufseherin
File Number:
Employment Date: November 3, 1944
Camp Service: Ravensbrück; Sachsenhausen
Notes:

Korsch (born Novak)
First Name: Marianne
Birthdate:
Birthplace:
Position: Aufseherin
File Number:
Employment Date:
Camp Service:
Notes:

Korsig
First Name: Elfriede
Birthdate: December 1, 1913
Birthplace: Rudelsdorf
Position: Aufseherin
File Number:
Employment Date: July 15, 1944
Camp Service: Groß-Rosen
Notes:

Korth
First Name: Ilse
Birthdate:
Birthplace:
Position: Aufseherin
File Number:
Employment Date:
Camp Service:
Notes:

Korthals
First Name: Agnes
Birthdate: November 24, 1911
Birthplace: Riesenburg
Position: Aufseherin
File Number: IV 410(F) AR 2629/67
Employment Date: September 8, 1944
Camp Service: Groß-Rosen; Floßenbürg; Kommando Helmbrechts
Notes: Waffen SS auxiliary since September 6, 1944.

Kosanke (born Rabe)
First Name: Else
Birthdate: January 11, 1912
Birthplace: Pellnow

Position: Aufseherin
File Number: IV 410(F) AR 2629/67
Employment Date: September 1944 (no day provided in her file)
Camp Service: Floßenbürg; AL Mittweida
Notes:

Koschinke
First Name: Klara
Birthdate: August 31, 1921
Birthplace: Stroppen
Position: Aufseherin
File Number:
Employment Date: November 28, 1944
Camp Service: Groß-Rosen
Notes:

Kose
First Name: Alma
Birthdate:
Birthplace:
Position: Aufseherin
File Number:
Employment Date:
Camp Service:
Notes:

Koslowski (born Saßnowski)
First Name: Erna
Birthdate:
Birthplace:
Position: Aufseherin
File Number:
Employment Date:
Camp Service:
Notes:

Koslowsky
First Name: Grete
Birthdate:
Birthplace:
Position: Aufseherin
File Number:
Employment Date:
Camp Service: Ravensbrück
Notes:

Koss
First Name: Fine
Birthdate:
Birthplace:
Position: Aufseherin
File Number:
Employment Date:
Camp Service: Ravensbrück
Notes:

Koszorowski
First Name: Irmgard
Birthdate:
Birthplace:
Position: Aufseherin
File Number:
Employment Date:
Camp Service: Ravensbrück
Notes:

Kotschwar
First Name: Elisabeth
Birthdate:
Birthplace:
Position: Aufseherin
File Number:
Employment Date:
Camp Service: Groß-Rosen
Notes:

Kouba
First Name: Hermine
Birthdate:
Birthplace:
Position: Aufseherin
File Number:
Employment Date:
Camp Service: Ravensbrück
Notes:

Kowa
First Name: Emmy
Birthdate: October 31, 1915
Birthplace: Pforzheim
Position: Aufseherin
File Number:
Employment Date: February 1, 1943
Camp Service: Groß-Rosen
Notes:

Kraatz
First Name: Lucie
Birthdate: August 17, 1916
Birthplace: Mariendorf
Position: Aufseherin
File Number:
Employment Date: September 2, 1944
Camp Service: Floßenbürg
Notes:

Kraatz
First Name: Paula
Birthdate: December 18, 1917
Birthplace: Neubrandenburg
Position: Aufseherin
File Number: IV 410(F) AR 2629/67
Employment Date: May 16, 1943
Camp Service: Floßenbürg; AL Zwodau
Notes:

Krämer
First Name: Ursula
Birthdate: May 9, 1921
Birthplace: Leipzig
Position: Aufseherin
File Number:
Employment Date: December 15, 1943
Camp Service: Ravensbrück
Notes:

Krätke
First Name: Liselotte
Birthdate:
Birthplace:
Position: Aufseherin

File Number:
Employment Date:
Camp Service:
Notes:

Kraft (born Thiel)
First Name: Charlotte
Birthdate: July 18, 1905
Birthplace: Reichenbach
Position: Aufseherin
File Number:
Employment Date: March 1, 1944
Camp Service: Groß-Rosen
Notes:

Kraft (born Müller)
First Name: Frieda
Birthdate:
Birthplace:
Position: Aufseherin
File Number:
Employment Date:
Camp Service: Ravensbrück
Notes:

Kraft (divorced Wette)
First Name: Johanna
Birthdate:
Birthplace:
Position: Aufseherin
File Number:
Employment Date:
Camp Service:
Notes:

Kraft (born Kenning
First Name: Liesbeth
Birthdate:
Birthplace:
Position: Aufseherin
File Number:
Employment Date:
Camp Service: Ravensbrück
Notes:

Krahl
First Name: Margarete
Birthdate: April 12, 1920
Birthplace: Essen
Position: Aufseherin
File Number:
Employment Date: November 2, 1944
Camp Service: Ravensbrück; Sachsenhausen
Notes:

Krahl (born Deutner)
First Name: Ursula
Birthdate:
Birthplace:
Position: Aufseherin
File Number:
Employment Date:
Camp Service:
Notes:

Krambär
First Name: Emmi
Birthdate:
Birthplace:
Position: Aufseherin
File Number:
Employment Date:
Camp Service:
Notes:

Kramer
First Name: Anneliese
Birthdate: August 26, 1921
Birthplace: Berlin
Position: Aufseherin
File Number:
Employment Date: November 24, 1944
Camp Service: Ravensbrück
Notes:

Kramer
First Name: Frieda
Birthdate:
Birthplace:
Position: Aufseherin
File Number:
Employment Date:
Camp Service:
Notes:

Kramer
First Name: Gertrud
Birthdate:
Birthplace:
Position: Aufseherin
File Number:
Employment Date:
Camp Service:
Notes:

Kraus
First Name: Centa
Birthdate:
Birthplace:
Position: Aufseherin
File Number:
Employment Date:
Camp Service:
Notes:

Kraus
First Name: Hildegard
Birthdate: April 20, 1919
Birthplace:
Position: Aufseherin
File Number: IV 410(F) AR 2629/67
Employment Date:
Camp Service: Floßenbürg; AL Plauen
Notes:

Kraus
First Name: Maria
Birthdate:
Birthplace:
Position: Aufseherin

File Number:
Employment Date:
Camp Service: Ravensbrück
Notes:

Krausbeck
First Name: Maria
Birthdate: November 14, 1921
Birthplace: Landsweiler
Position: Aufseherin
File Number:
Employment Date: August 9, 1944
Camp Service: Ravensbrück
Notes:

Krause
First Name: Erna
Birthdate: March 5, 1921
Birthplace: Langenbielau
Position: Aufseherin
File Number:
Employment Date: April 15, 1944
Camp Service: Groß-Rosen
Notes:

Krause
First Name: Hedwig
Birthdate: November 2, 1915
Birthplace: Kunzendorf
Position: Aufseherin
File Number:
Employment Date: September 23, 1944
Camp Service: Groß-Rosen
Notes:

Krause
First Name: Hermine
Birthdate: January 31, 1914
Birthplace: Oberkleinaupa
Position: Aufseherin
File Number:
Employment Date: September 28, 1944
Camp Service: Groß-Rosen
Notes:

Krause
First Name: Herta
Birthdate:
Birthplace:
Position: Aufseherin
File Number:
Employment Date:
Camp Service:
Notes:

Krause
First Name: Hildegard
Birthdate: April 24, 1919
Birthplace: Plauen
Position: Aufseherin
File Number: IV 410 AR 3216/66
Employment Date:
Camp Service: AL Plauen; Neuengamme
Notes:

Krause

First Name: Maria
Birthdate: December 27, 1917
Birthplace: Pilsdorf
Position: Aufseherin
File Number:
Employment Date: July 24, 1944
Camp Service: Groß-Rosen
Notes:

Krause

First Name: Maria
Birthdate: April 25, 1923
Birthplace: Friedrichshain
Position: Aufseherin
File Number:
Employment Date: September 5, 1944
Camp Service: Groß-Rosen
Notes:

Krause

First Name: Vera
Birthdate:
Birthplace:
Position: Aufseherin
File Number:
Employment Date:
Camp Service: Ravensbrück
Notes:

Krauser (married Well)

First Name: Anneliese
Birthdate: August 21, 1920
Birthplace: Frankfurt/Main
Position: Aufseherin
File Number: IV 429 AR-Z 130/70(B)
Employment Date:
Camp Service: Sömmerda; Allendorf; Ravensbrück
Notes:

Krauß

First Name: Walpurga
Birthdate:
Birthplace:
Position: Aufseherin
File Number:
Employment Date:
Camp Service:
Notes:

Krautmacher

First Name: Elfriede
Birthdate:
Birthplace:
Position: Aufseherin
File Number:
Employment Date:
Camp Service:
Notes:

Kreetz (born Hellberg)

First Name: Frieda
Birthdate:
Birthplace:
Position: Aufseherin

File Number:
Employment Date:
Camp Service:
Notes:

Kreger

First Name: Anna
Birthdate: January 19, 1921
Birthplace:
Position: Aufseherin
File Number: IV 410(F) AR 2629/67
Employment Date:
Camp Service: Floßenbürg; AL Holleischen
Notes:

Krehan

First Name: Luise
Birthdate:
Birthplace:
Position: Aufseherin
File Number: IV 409 AR-Z 39/59
Employment Date:
Camp Service: Ravensbrück
Notes:

Kreidenberg

First Name: Käthe
Birthdate:
Birthplace:
Position: Aufseherin
File Number:
Employment Date:
Camp Service:
Notes:

Kreisel

First Name: Erika
Birthdate:
Birthplace:
Position: Aufseherin
File Number:
Employment Date:
Camp Service: Groß-Rosen
Notes:

Kreiser

First Name: Elsbeth
Birthdate:
Birthplace:
Position: Aufseherin
File Number:
Employment Date:
Camp Service:
Notes:

Kreisig

First Name: Herta
Birthdate: February 4, 1921
Birthplace:
Position: Aufseherin
File Number: IV 410(F) AR 2629/67
Employment Date:
Camp Service: Floßenbürg; AL Venusberg
Notes:

Kreitling
First Name: Luise
Birthdate:
Birthplace:
Position: Aufseherin
File Number:
Employment Date:
Camp Service:
Notes:

Kreja
First Name: Irene
Birthdate: February 23, 1914
Birthplace: Berlin
Position: Aufseherin
File Number:
Employment Date: November 9, 1944
Camp Service: Ravensbrück; Floßenbürg
Notes:

Krejci (born Mark)
First Name: Elfriede
Birthdate: September 16, 1919
Birthplace:
Position: Aufseherin
File Number:
Employment Date: March 1, 1944
Camp Service: Floßenbürg
Notes:

Kremtz
First Name: Liddy
Birthdate: February 29, 1904
Birthplace: Siebenlehn (perhaps Siebenleben?)
Position: Aufseherin
File Number: IV 410(F) AR 2629/67
Employment Date: October 1, 1942
Camp Service: Floßenbürg; AL Mehltheuer; AL Zwodau
Notes:

Krennmair
First Name: Maria
Birthdate:
Birthplace:
Position: Aufseherin
File Number:
Employment Date:
Camp Service: Ravensbrück
Notes:

Krenzer
First Name: Hildegard
Birthdate:
Birthplace:
Position: Aufseherin
File Number:
Employment Date:
Camp Service:
Notes:

Kreplin
First Name: Ruth
Birthdate: June 4, 1906
Birthplace: Malchin
Position: Aufseherin

File Number: IV 410(F) AR 2629/67
Employment Date: March 1, 1943
Camp Service: Ravensbrück; Floßenbürg; AL Zwodau
Notes:

Kress
First Name: Agnes
Birthdate:
Birthplace:
Position: Aufseherin
File Number:
Employment Date:
Camp Service:
Notes:

Kretschmar (born Liebers)
First Name: Herta
Birthdate:
Birthplace:
Position: Aufseherin
File Number:
Employment Date:
Camp Service:
Notes:

Kretschmar
First Name: Dora
Birthdate:
Birthplace:
Position: Aufseherin
File Number: IV 410 AR 3016/66
Employment Date:
Camp Service: Floßenbürg; AL Dresden Reick
Notes:

Krüger (born Beyer)
First Name: Margarete
Birthdate:
Birthplace:
Position: Aufseherin
File Number:
Employment Date:
Camp Service:
Notes:

Kretzschmar (or Kretschmar; born Tiebach)
First Name: Herta
Birthdate: April 20, 1922
Birthplace: Berlin
Position: Aufseherin
File Number: IV 410(F) AR 2629/67
Employment Date:
Camp Service: Floßenbürg; AL Hainichen
Notes:

Kretschmar
First Name: Ursula
Birthdate: November 8, 1921
Birthplace: Guben
Position: Aufseherin
File Number:
Employment Date: July 30, 1944
Camp Service: Groß-Rosen
Notes:

Kretschmer (born Schütze)
First Name: Elisabeth
Birthdate:
Birthplace:
Position: Aufseherin
File Number:
Employment Date:
Camp Service: Stutthof/Danzig
Notes:

Kreuzer
First Name: Hildegard
Birthdate: April 18, 1928
Birthplace: Plauen
Position: Aufseherin
File Number: IV 410 AR 3216/66
Employment Date:
Camp Service: Plauen; Ravensbrück
Notes:

Kreuzer
First Name: Renate
Birthdate: February 24, 1923
Birthplace: Pechgrün (Karlsbad)
Position: Aufseherin
File Number:
Employment Date: May 1, 1943
Camp Service: Neuengamme
Notes:

Kricek (or Krizek; married Franz)
First Name: Helene
Birthdate: July 25, 1923
Birthplace: Suchenthal
Position: Aufseherin
File Number: IV 410 AR 3039/66
Employment Date: April 1, 1944
Camp Service: Floßenbürg; NL Holleischen; NL Dresden; NL Mehltheuer
Notes:

Krieghoff
First Name: Magdalene
Birthdate:
Birthplace:
Position: Aufseherin
File Number:
Employment Date:
Camp Service:
Notes:

Kriening
First Name: Emmi (or Emmy)
Birthdate: June 2, 1919
Birthplace:
Position: Aufseherin
File Number: IV 410 (F) AR 2629/67
Employment Date:
Camp Service: Floßenbürg; AL Mittweida; AL Zwodau
Notes:

Krier
First Name: Christine
Birthdate: August 30, 1915
Birthplace: Tscherwenka (Hungary)
Position: Aufseherin
File Number:
Employment Date: September 15, 1944
Camp Service: Neuengamme
Notes: Ethnic German; born and raised in Hungary.

Krinke
First Name: Anna
Birthdate: June 2, 1900
Birthplace: Straßenau
Position: Aufseherin
File Number:
Employment Date: October 1944 (exact date unknown)
Camp Service: Groß-Rosen
Notes:

Krippner
First Name: Else
Birthdate: December 8, 1918
Birthplace: Asch
Position: Aufseherin
File Number:
Employment Date: April 1, 1944
Camp Service: Ravensbrück
Notes:

Krist
First Name: Anna
Birthdate:
Birthplace:
Position: Aufseherin
File Number:
Employment Date:
Camp Service:
Notes:

Krista
First Name: Else
Birthdate: October 13, 1923
Birthplace: Snekisch
Position: Aufseherin
File Number:
Employment Date: October 5, 1944
Camp Service: Groß-Rosen
Notes:

Krönert (born Hänsel)
First Name: Elisabeth
Birthdate:
Birthplace:
Position: Aufseherin
File Number: IV 410 AR 2960/66
Employment Date:
Camp Service: Floßenbürg; Holleischen
Notes: Her training program took place at Holleischen.

Kroha
First Name: Maria
Birthdate: July 21, 1920
Birthplace: Drakowa
Position: Aufseherin
File Number: IV 410(F) AR 2629/67
Employment Date: September 8, 1944
Camp Service: Floßenbürg; AL Hertine
Notes: Permission for service as an "employee of the Reich" granted on November 20, 1944.

Kroll

First Name:	Käthe (Käte)
Birthdate:	October 5, 1918
Birthplace:	Madlow
Position:	Aufseherin
File Number:	IV 410(F) AR 2629/67
Employment Date:	July 30, 1944
Camp Service:	Groß-Rosen; Floßenbürg; AL Hertine
Notes:	

Kronmüller

First Name:	Elfriede
Birthdate:	May 16, 1915
Birthplace:	Falkenau
Position:	Aufseherin
File Number:	IV 410(F) AR 2629/67
Employment Date:	September 8, 1944
Camp Service:	Floßenbürg; AL Oederan
Notes:	Permission for service as an "employee of the Reich" granted on November 20, 1944.

Krosky

First Name:	Ottilie
Birthdate:	October 1, 1910
Birthplace:	Danzig
Position:	Aufseherin
File Number:	IV 410(F) AR 2629/67
Employment Date:	September 9, 1944
Camp Service:	Groß-Rosen; Floßenbürg; Kommando Helmbrechts
Notes:	Service as a Waffen SS auxiliary since September 6, 1944.

Krtitschke

First Name:	Anna
Birthdate:	July 18, 1923
Birthplace:	Merkelsdorf
Position:	Aufseherin
File Number:	
Employment Date:	September 13, 1944
Camp Service:	Groß-Rosen
Notes:	

Krüger

First Name:	Anneliese
Birthdate:	
Birthplace:	
Position:	Aufseherin
File Number:	
Employment Date:	
Camp Service:	Ravensbrück
Notes:	

Krüger

First Name:	Edith
Birthdate:	May 7, 1922
Birthplace:	Oranienburg
Position:	Aufseherin
File Number:	
Employment Date:	October 1, 1942
Camp Service:	Ravensbrück
Notes:	

Krüger

First Name:	Frieda
Birthdate:	
Birthplace:	
Position:	Aufseherin
File Number:	
Employment Date:	
Camp Service:	
Notes:	

Krüger (born Krska)

First Name:	Frieda
Birthdate:	
Birthplace:	
Position:	Aufseherin
File Number:	
Employment Date:	
Camp Service:	
Notes:	

Krüger

First Name:	Hildegard Charlotte
Birthdate:	December 29, 1922
Birthplace:	Berlin
Position:	Aufseherin
File Number:	IV 410(F) AR 2629/67
Employment Date:	August 20, 1944
Camp Service:	Floßenbürg; AL Plauen; AL Osram Berlin
Notes:	Permission for service as an "employee of the Reich" granted on November 22, 1944.

Krüger

First Name:	Ingebourg
Birthdate:	
Birthplace:	
Position:	Aufseherin
File Number:	
Employment Date:	
Camp Service:	
Notes:	

Krüger

First Name:	Margarete
Birthdate:	Unclear: December 15, 1911 (perhaps November 15, 1911)
Birthplace:	Grünberg
Position:	Blockführerin
File Number:	IV 405 AR-Z 191/73
Employment Date:	June 1, 1944
Camp Service:	Groß-Rosen
Notes:	

Krüger (born Krause)

First Name:	Margarete
Birthdate:	
Birthplace:	
Position:	Aufseherin
File Number:	
Employment Date:	
Camp Service:	
Notes:	

Krüger (born Rose)

First Name:	Margarete
Birthdate:	

Birthplace:
Position: Aufseherin
File Number:
Employment Date:
Camp Service:
Notes:

Krüger

First Name: Martha
Birthdate: December 24, 1917
Birthplace: Gardelegen
Position: Aufseherin
File Number:
Employment Date: June 1, 1943
Camp Service: Ravensbrück
Notes: Permission for service as an "employee of the Reich" granted on September 4, 1943.

Krüger

First Name: Ursula
Birthdate:
Birthplace:
Position: Aufseherin
File Number:
Employment Date:
Camp Service:
Notes:

Krüpfganz

First Name: Herta
Birthdate: August 30, 1913
Birthplace: Chemnitz
Position: Aufseherin
File Number:
Employment Date: October 18, 1944
Camp Service: Groß-Rosen
Notes:

Krumm

First Name: Gertrud
Birthdate:
Birthplace:
Position: Aufseherin
File Number:
Employment Date:
Camp Service:
Notes:

Krummen

First Name: Gerda
Birthdate: November 3, 1923
Birthplace: Herzfelde
Position: Aufseherin
File Number:
Employment Date: November 16, 1944
Camp Service: Ravensbrück
Notes:

Krumow

First Name: Erika
Birthdate:
Birthplace:
Position: Aufseherin
File Number:
Employment Date:

Camp Service:
Notes:

Krusch (born Nagel)

First Name: Liesbeth
Birthdate:
Birthplace:
Position: Aufseherin
File Number:
Employment Date:
Camp Service:
Notes:

Krusch

First Name: Lieselotte
Birthdate: October 28, 1902
Birthplace: Grünberg
Position: Aufseherin
File Number:
Employment Date: June 1, 1944
Camp Service: Groß-Rosen
Notes: Permission for service as an "employee of the Reich" granted on December 22, 1944.

Krusch

First Name: Marianne
Birthdate:
Birthplace:
Position: Aufseherin
File Number:
Employment Date:
Camp Service: Groß-Rosen
Notes:

Kruse

First Name: Erna
Birthdate: January 22, 1922
Birthplace: Magdeburg
Position: Aufseherin
File Number: IV 410(F) AR 2629/67
Employment Date: 1944 (no month or day noted in her file)
Camp Service: Floßenbürg; AL Holleischen; AL Astrawerke Chemnitz, Ravensbrück
Notes:

Krutwa

First Name: Marianne
Birthdate: Febraury 11, 1923
Birthplace:
Position: Aufseherin
File Number: IV 410(F) AR 2629/67
Employment Date:
Camp Service: Floßenbürg; AL Holleischen
Notes:

Kryczaniak

First Name: Anna
Birthdate:
Birthplace:
Position: Aufseherin
File Number:
Employment Date:
Camp Service:
Notes:

Krzewitza

First Name: Ottilie
Birthdate:
Birthplace:
Position: Aufseherin
File Number:
Employment Date:
Camp Service:
Notes:

Krzywinski

First Name: Hildegard
Birthdate: June 15, 1921
Birthplace: Niederfeld
Position: Aufseherin
File Number:
Employment Date: June 1, 1944
Camp Service: Groß-Rosen
Notes:

Kubetschek

First Name: Helene
Birthdate: November 12, 1912
Birthplace: Sackisch
Position: Aufseherin
File Number:
Employment Date: August 10, 1944
Camp Service: Groß-Rosen
Notes:

Kubinka

First Name: Dorothea
Birthdate:
Birthplace:
Position: Aufseherin
File Number:
Employment Date:
Camp Service: Sachsenhausen
Notes:

Kubitzky

First Name: Hildegard
Birthdate:
Birthplace:
Position: Aufseherin
File Number:
Employment Date:
Camp Service:
Notes:

Kucharczyk

First Name: Else
Birthdate:
Birthplace:
Position: Aufseherin
File Number:
Employment Date:
Camp Service: Ravensbrück
Notes:

Kühn

First Name: Anna
Birthdate: May 20, 1885
Birthplace: Leipzig
Position: Aufseherin

File Number:
Employment Date: November 1, 1942
Camp Service: Ravensbrück
Notes: Received a special waiver to enlist beyond the maximum age limitation (57 years old at enlistment).

Kügler

First Name: Lina
Birthdate:
Birthplace:
Position: Aufseherin
File Number:
Employment Date:
Camp Service:
Notes:

Kügler

First Name: Martha
Birthdate:
Birthplace:
Position: Aufseherin
File Number:
Employment Date:
Camp Service:
Notes:

Kühn

First Name: Elisabeth
Birthdate: June 30, 1921 (unclear: perhaps June 20, 1921)
Birthplace: Neundorf
Position: Aufseherin
File Number: IV 410(F) AR 2629/67
Employment Date:
Camp Service: Floßenbürg; AL Plauen
Notes:

Kühn

First Name: Franziska
Birthdate: December 3, 1905
Birthplace: Glasendorf
Position: Aufseherin
File Number:
Employment Date: March 1, 1944
Camp Service: Groß-Rosen
Notes: Permission for service as an "employee of the Reich" granted on December 22, 1944.

Kühn

First Name: Hildegard
Birthdate: May 19, 1922
Birthplace: Heinerdorf
Position: Aufseherin
File Number:
Employment Date: June 1, 1944
Camp Service: Groß-Rosen
Notes:

Kühn (born Lenz)

First Name: Ida
Birthdate:
Birthplace:
Position: Aufseherin
File Number:
Employment Date:

Camp Service: Ravensbrück
Notes:

Kühn
First Name: Johanna
Birthdate:
Birthplace:
Position: Aufseherin
File Number:
Employment Date:
Camp Service:
Notes:

Kühn
First Name: Lieselotte
Birthdate:
Birthplace:
Position: Aufseherin
File Number:
Employment Date:
Camp Service: Ravensbrück
Notes:

Kühn
First Name: Lucia (Lucie)
Birthdate: June 21, 1909
Birthplace: Oederau
Position: Aufseherin
File Number: IV 410 (F) AR 2629/67
Employment Date: September 11, 1944
Camp Service: Floßenbürg; AL Oederan, Holleischen
Notes: Permission for service as an "employee of the Reich" granted on November 20, 1944.

Kühn
First Name: Rosamunde
Birthdate: May 3, 1923
Birthplace:
Position: Aufseherin
File Number: IV 406 AR-Z 21/71
Employment Date:
Camp Service: NL Genshagen
Notes:

Kühnast
First Name: Martha
Birthdate: January 21, 1901
Birthplace: Streit
Position: Aufseherin
File Number:
Employment Date: October 10, 1944
Camp Service: Groß-Rosen
Notes:

Kühne
First Name: Hildegard
Birthdate:
Birthplace:
Position: Aufseherin
File Number:
Employment Date:
Camp Service: Ravensbrück
Notes:

Kühne
First Name: Lieselotte
Birthdate: October 29, 1921
Birthplace: Dresden
Position: Aufseherin
File Number: IV 410(F) AR 2629/67
Employment Date:
Camp Service: Floßenbürg; AL Goehle-Werk Dresden
Notes:

Kühnel
First Name: Margarethe
Birthdate: August 16, 1923
Birthplace: Goldbach near Reinerz
Position: Aufseherin
File Number:
Employment Date: March 1, 1944
Camp Service: Groß-Rosen
Notes: Permission for service as an "employee of the Reich" granted on December 22, 1944.

Kühnert
First Name: Marta
Birthdate:
Birthplace:
Position: Aufseherin
File Number:
Employment Date:
Camp Service: Groß-Rosen
Notes:

Kuellmer
First Name: Anna
Birthdate:
Birthplace:
Position: Aufseherin
File Number:
Employment Date:
Camp Service:
Notes:

Kuenstel (or Kunstel; born Strothmann)
First Name: Ella
Birthdate: June 10, 1903
Birthplace: Marten
Position: Aufseherin
File Number:
Employment Date: August 15, 1944
Camp Service: Ravensbrück
Notes:

Kuenzel
First Name: Monika
Birthdate: February 15, 1910
Birthplace: Berlin-Treptow
Position: Aufseherin
File Number:
Employment Date: September 12, 1944
Camp Service: Groß-Rosen
Notes: Permission for service as an "employee of the Reich" granted on September 28, 1944.

Kuenzel
First Name: Ruth
Birthdate: October 30, 1921

Birthplace: Berlin
Position: Aufseherin
File Number:
Employment Date: August 1, 1944
Camp Service: Groß-Rosen
Notes:

Kuenzl

First Name: Maria
Birthdate: August 18, 1904
Birthplace: Schwarau
Position: Aufseherin
File Number:
Employment Date: August 25, 1944
Camp Service: Groß-Rosen
Notes:

Kuenzl

First Name: Rosa
Birthdate: February 9, 1923
Birthplace: Rothau
Position: Aufseherin
File Number: IV 410(F) AR 2629/67
Employment Date:
Camp Service: Floßenbürg; AL Zwodau
Notes:

Küster

First Name: Herta
Birthdate: March 2, 1916
Birthplace: Wittenberge
Position: Aufseherin
File Number:
Employment Date: April 1, 1944
Camp Service: Ravensbrück
Notes:

Kuhle

First Name: Ursula
Birthdate: January 29, 1923
Birthplace: Wittenberg
Position: Aufseherin
File Number: IV 406 AR 1885/68
Employment Date:
Camp Service: Sachsenhausen; NL Berlin-Spandau
Notes:

Kuhn

First Name: Alma
Birthdate: December 1, 1922
Birthplace: Jungbuch
Position: Aufseherin
File Number:
Employment Date: March 1, 1944
Camp Service: Groß-Rosen
Notes: Permission for service as an "employee of the Reich" granted on December 12, 1944.

Kuhn

First Name: Angela
Birthdate: July 18, 1911
Birthplace: Operlipka
Position: Aufseherin
File Number:
Employment Date: March 1, 1944

Kuhn

First Name: Charlotte
Birthdate:
Birthplace:
Position: Aufseherin
File Number:
Employment Date:
Camp Service:
Notes:

Kuhn

First Name: Helene
Birthdate:
Birthplace:
Position: Aufseherin
File Number:
Employment Date:
Camp Service:
Notes:

Kuhn

First Name: Maria
Birthdate: August 4, 1911
Birthplace: Trautenbach
Position: Aufseherin
File Number:
Employment Date: March 1, 1944
Camp Service: Groß-Rosen
Notes:

Kuhnert (born Falkenrich)

First Name: Helene
Birthdate:
Birthplace:
Position: Aufseherin
File Number:
Employment Date:
Camp Service:
Notes:

Kuhnert

First Name: Hildegard
Birthdate: June 4, 1915
Birthplace: Breslau
Position: Aufseherin
File Number:
Employment Date: August 18, 1944
Camp Service: Groß-Rosen
Notes:

Kuhnert

First Name: Klara
Birthdate:
Birthplace:
Position: Aufseherin
File Number:
Employment Date:
Camp Service: Ravensbrück
Notes:

Kuhnt

First Name: Gertrud
Birthdate: May 21, 1922
Birthplace: Wüstegiersdorf
Position: Aufseherin

File Number:
Employment Date: July 28, 1944
Camp Service: Groß-Rosen
Notes:

Kuke

First Name: Erna
Birthdate:
Birthplace:
Position: Aufseherin
File Number:
Employment Date:
Camp Service: Ravensbrück
Notes:

Kulick (born Krastinat)

First Name: Lieselotte
Birthdate:
Birthplace:
Position: Aufseherin
File Number:
Employment Date:
Camp Service: Ravensbrück
Notes:

Kull

First Name: Ilse
Birthdate:
Birthplace:
Position: Aufseherin
File Number:
Employment Date:
Camp Service:
Notes:

Kulms

First Name: Else
Birthdate:
Birthplace:
Position: Aufseherin
File Number:
Employment Date:
Camp Service:
Notes:

Kulow

First Name: Lotte
Birthdate:
Birthplace:
Position: Aufseherin
File Number:
Employment Date:
Camp Service: Ravensbrück
Notes:

Kumetz

First Name: Hedwig
Birthdate:
Birthplace:
Position: Aufseherin
File Number:
Employment Date:
Camp Service:
Notes:

Kummer

First Name: Ilse
Birthdate: March 14, 1909
Birthplace: Plauen
Position: Aufseherin
File Number:
Employment Date: December 15, 1944
Camp Service: Ravensbrück
Notes:

Kummerow

First Name: Ilse
Birthdate:
Birthplace:
Position: Aufseherin
File Number:
Employment Date:
Camp Service:
Notes:

Kummert

First Name: Käthe
Birthdate: October 2, 1912
Birthplace: Schmidtmühlen
Position: Aufseherin
File Number: IV 410(F) AR 2629/67
Employment Date:
Camp Service: Flossenbürg; AL Siemens Nuremberg; AL Holleischen
Notes:

Kunert

First Name: Dora
Birthdate: July 7, 1923
Birthplace: Marklissa
Position: Aufseherin
File Number:
Employment Date: September 26, 1944
Camp Service: Groß-Rosen
Notes:

Kunerth (or Kuhnert)

First Name: Luise
Birthdate: December 1, 1922
Birthplace:
Position: Aufseherin
File Number: IV 410(F) AR 2629/67
Employment Date:
Camp Service: Floßenbürg; AL Holleischen
Notes:

Kunger

First Name: Irmgard
Birthdate: September 14, 1923
Birthplace: Fürstenberg
Position: Aufseherin
File Number:
Employment Date: September 15, 1944
Camp Service: Groß-Rosen
Notes:

Kunienke

First Name: Ilse
Birthdate:
Birthplace:

Position: Aufseherin
File Number:
Employment Date:
Camp Service: Neuengamme
Notes:

Kunig (born Hauguth)
First Name: Ilse
Birthdate:
Birthplace:
Position: Aufseherin
File Number:
Employment Date:
Camp Service: Ravensbrück
Notes:

Kunig
First Name: Klara
Birthdate:
Birthplace:
Position: Aufseherin
File Number: 410 AR 3021/66
Employment Date:
Camp Service: NL Dresden-Universelle; Ravensbrück
Notes: Dismissed from service for being too shy and too polite to the prisoners (delinquent in training); fate unknown since February 13, 1945.

Kunik
First Name: Maria
Birthdate:
Birthplace:
Position: Aufseherin
File Number: IV 419 AR-Z 287/77
Employment Date:
Camp Service: Mauthausen; NL Lenzing
Notes:

Kunik
First Name: Martha
Birthdate:
Birthplace:
Position: Aufseherin
File Number:
Employment Date:
Camp Service:
Notes:

Kunstmann
First Name: Regine
Birthdate: April 22, 1920
Birthplace:
Position: Aufseherin
File Number: IV 410(F) AR 2629/67
Employment Date:
Camp Service: Floßenbürg; AL Holleischen
Notes:

Kunz
First Name: Elisabeth
Birthdate: October 31, 1913
Birthplace: Großdorf
Position: Aufseherin
File Number:

Employment Date: September 13, 1944
Camp Service: Groß-Rosen
Notes:

Kunz (born Piezner)
First Name: Margot
Birthdate: July 19, 1921
Birthplace: Wittenberg
Position: Aufseherin
File Number: 110 AR 918/94
Employment Date:
Camp Service: Wittenberg; Arado-Werke
Notes:

Kunze
First Name: Rosa
Birthdate: January 26, 1907
Birthplace: Chemnitz
Position: Aufseherin
File Number: IV 410(F) AR 2629/67
Employment Date: 1944
Camp Service: Floßenbürg; AL Astrawerke Chemnitz
Notes:

Kunze
First Name: Rosa
Birthdate: March 11, 1916
Birthplace: Oberaltstadt
Position: Aufseherin
File Number:
Employment Date: March 1, 1944
Camp Service: Groß-Rosen
Notes: Official permission for service as an "employee of the Reich" granted on December 22, 1944.

Kuppe
First Name: Gertrud
Birthdate: November 29, 1920
Birthplace: Hermsdorf
Position: Aufseherin
File Number:
Employment Date: July 27, 1944
Camp Service: Groß-Rosen
Notes:

Kurth
First Name: Edith
Birthdate: June 6, 1923
Birthplace: Ollendorf
Position: Aufseherin
File Number:
Employment Date: October 13, 1944
Camp Service: Ravensbrück
Notes:

Kurtzer
First Name: Elfriede
Birthdate: July 14, 1921
Birthplace: Bad Salzbrunn
Position: Aufseherin
File Number:
Employment Date: August 8, 1944
Camp Service: Ravensbrück
Notes:

Kussegg

First Name: Gertrud
Birthdate: April 14, 1914
Birthplace: Braunau
Position: Aufseherin
File Number:
Employment Date: September 13, 1944
Camp Service: Groß-Rosen
Notes:

Kußerow

First Name: Margarete
Birthdate: October 12, 1920
Birthplace: Berlin
Position: Aufseherin
File Number:
Employment Date: July 21, 1944
Camp Service: Groß-Rosen
Notes:

Kussin

First Name: Johanna
Birthdate: September 10, 1923
Birthplace: Altenburg
Position: Aufseherin
File Number: 410 (F) AR 23/68
Employment Date:
Camp Service: Chemnitz
Notes:

Kutta

First Name: Valeria
Birthdate: November 2, 1904
Birthplace: Eichenen/Kattowitz
Position: Aufseherin
File Number:
Employment Date: September 1, 1944
Camp Service: Neuengamme
Notes:

Kuttner

First Name: Hildegard
Birthdate: May 4, 1908
Birthplace: Rengersdorf
Position: Aufseherin
File Number:
Employment Date: August 25, 1944
Camp Service: Groß-Rosen
Notes:

Kwiatkowski

First Name: Margot
Birthdate: September 24, 1923
Birthplace: Wanne-Eikel
Position: Aufseherin
File Number:
Employment Date: October 11, 1944
Camp Service: Neuengamme
Notes:

Kynast

First Name: Martha
Birthdate: September 11, 1921
Birthplace: Sakrau (Sacrau)
Position: Aufseherin

File Number: IV 405 AR- 1651/64
Employment Date: July 1, 1944
Camp Service: Groß-Rosen
Notes: Participated in the Hundsfeld (Groß-Rosen) Death March.

Labude (or Labuda)

First Name: Herta
Birthdate: January 28, 1922
Birthplace: Hundsfeld
Position: Aufseherin
File Number: IV 410 AR-Z 60/67
Employment Date: July 3, 1944
Camp Service: Groß-Rosen; Floßenbürg; AL Zwodau
Notes:

Lächert

First Name: Hildegard
Birthdate: February 19, 1920
Birthplace:
Position: Aufseherin
File Number:
Employment Date:
Camp Service: Ravensbrück; Majdanek; Auschwitz-Brikenau
Notes: Tried by the Poles after the war. Sentenced to prison and released. Retried by a German court for war crimes at Majdanek (June 1975 - November 1981). Sentenced to 10 years imprisonment.

Lachmann (born Reiß)

First Name: Anna
Birthdate: April 28, 1920
Birthplace: Marburg a.d. Lahn
Position: Aufseherin
File Number: IV 429 AR-Z 51/70
Employment Date:
Camp Service: NL Allendorf
Notes:

Lächer (or Lecher, Lechert, Lächert, Läachert, Looecher, Lodscher, or Loscher)

First Name: Hildegard (Hilde)
Birthdate: February 19, 1920
Birthplace:
Position: Aufseherin?
File Number: 110 AR 982/98; 10 AR 465/61
Employment Date:
Camp Service: Bozen? Mauthausen? Auschwitz?
Notes: There seems to be great uncertainty about the identity of this Aufseherin: According to the Jewish Documentation Center in Vienna (Simon Wiesenthal), an Aufseherin Hilde Lecher or Lächer is supposed to have murdered Jewish women in Bozen. After a Frau Lächer spent some time in custody in 1974, the file was officially closed due to Lächer's death in 1995.

Lähn

First Name: Gertrud
Birthdate: September 4, 1906
Birthplace: Neubrandenburg
Position: Aufseherin
File Number:

Employment Date: February 15, 1944
Camp Service: Ravensbrück
Notes:

Lätzsch
First Name: Herta
Birthdate: November 25, 1905
Birthplace: Dresden
Position: Aufseherin
File Number: IV 410 (F) AR 2629/67
Employment Date:
Camp Service: Floßenbürg; AL Goehle-Werk Dresden
Notes:

Lage (born Bergmann)
First Name: Martha
Birthdate: June 24, 1922
Birthplace: Schildberg
Position: Aufseherin
File Number:
Employment Date: November 6, 1944
Camp Service: Groß-Rosen
Notes:

Lahr
First Name: Laura
Birthdate: May 18, 1902
Birthplace: Oberaltstadt
Position: Aufseherin
File Number:
Employment Date: March 1, 1944
Camp Service: Groß-Rosen
Notes:

Lahr
First Name: Theresia
Birthdate: April 17, 1908
Birthplace: Oberaltstadt
Position: Aufseherin
File Number:
Employment Date: March 1, 1944
Camp Service: Groß-Rosen
Notes: Official permission for service as an "employee of the Reich" granted on December 11, 1944.

Lambrecht
First Name: Erna
Birthdate: February 10, 1920
Birthplace: Niederfinow
Position: Aufseherin
File Number:
Employment Date: June 21, 1944
Camp Service: Ravensbrück
Notes:

Lambrecht
First Name: Ina
Birthdate: November 1, 1921
Birthplace: Gotha
Position: Aufseherin
File Number:
Employment Date: August 3, 1944
Camp Service: Ravensbrück
Notes:

Lampe
First Name: Irmgard
Birthdate: May 12, 1922
Birthplace: Aschersleben
Position: Aufseherin
File Number:
Employment Date: September 25, 1944
Camp Service: Ravensbrück
Notes:

Land
First Name: Martha
Birthdate: August 11, 1923
Birthplace:
Position: Aufseherin
File Number:
Employment Date: August 3, 1944
Camp Service: Ravensbrück
Notes:

Lankes
First Name: Emma
Birthdate: October 18, 1911
Birthplace: Unterflossen
Position: Aufseherin
File Number:
Employment Date: July 15, 1942
Camp Service: Ravensbrück
Notes:

Lankl
First Name: Martha
Birthdate: September 17, 1923
Birthplace: Steingrub
Position: Aufseherin
File Number: IV 410(F) AR 2629/67
Employment Date: August 17, 1944
Camp Service: Floßenbürg; AL Zwodau
Notes:

Lang
First Name: Elfriede
Birthdate: October 21, 1922
Birthplace: Oberbahn
Position: Aufsehern: Waffen SS
File Number: IV 410(F) AR 2629/67
Employment Date:
Camp Service: Floßenbürg; Kommando Helmbrechts
Notes: Joined SS-Helferinnen Korps on July 1, 1944; transferred to SS-Aufseherinnen Korps shortly thereafter.

Lang
First Name: Erika
Birthdate: January 15, 1922
Birthplace: Hamburg
Position: Aufseherin
File Number:
Employment Date: August 18, 1944
Camp Service: Groß-Rosen
Notes:

Lang
First Name: Margarete
Birthdate:

Birthplace:
Position: Aufseherin
File Number: 109 AR-Z 257/89
Employment Date:
Camp Service:
Notes:

Lang

First Name: Mathilde
Birthdate: November 7, 1923
Birthplace:
Position: Aufseherin
File Number: IV 410(F) AR 2629/67
Employment Date:
Camp Service: Floßenbürg; AL Holleischen
Notes:

Langbein (born Günther; widowed Langbein; married Paschold)

First Name: Elli
Birthdate: January 16, 1900
Birthplace: Rodach
Position: Aufseherin
File Number: 409 AR-Z 39/59
Employment Date: 1942 (no month/day entry recorded)
Camp Service: Ravensbrück (four week training); Neustadt near Coburg
Notes:

Lange

First Name: Dora
Birthdate: June 8, 1922
Birthplace: Oederan
Position: Oberaufseherin
File Number: IV 410(F) AR 2629/67
Employment Date:
Camp Service: Floßenbürg; AL Holleischen; AL Oederan
Notes:

Lange

First Name: Elfriede
Birthdate:
Birthplace: Eberswalde
Position: Aufseherin
File Number: 10 AR 1750/61
Employment Date:
Camp Service: Helmbrechts
Notes:

Lange

First Name: Elsa
Birthdate:
Birthplace:
Position: Aufseherin
File Number: IIV 409 AR-Z 79/72
Employment Date:
Camp Service: Ravensbrück
Notes:

Lange (born Richter)

First Name: Else
Birthdate: December 9, 1914
Birthplace: Niederau
Position: Aufseherin
File Number:

Employment Date: March 1, 1942
Camp Service: Ravensbrück
Notes:

Lange

First Name: Frieda
Birthdate: January 14, 1918
Birthplace: Löbau (Silesia)
Position: Aufseherin
File Number: IV 410(F) AR 2629/67
Employment Date: October 1, 1944
Camp Service: Ravensbrück; Floßenbürg; AL Holleischen
Notes: Official permission for service as an "employee of the Reich" granted on December 22, 1944.

Lange

First Name: Ilse
Birthdate: December 21, 1918
Birthplace: Dresden
Position: Aufseherin
File Number: IV 410(F) AR 2629/67
Employment Date:
Camp Service: Floßenbürg, AL Zwodau
Notes:

Langefeld

First Name: Johanna
Birthdate: March 5, 1900
Birthplace: Essen-Kupferdreh
Position: Oberaufseherin
File Number:
Employment Date:
Camp Service: Ravensbrück; Auschwitz Birkenau and then back to Ravensbrück
Notes: Praised after the war for the kindness and consideration she extended to inmates; attacked for ineptitude by Auschwitz Commandant Rudolf Höß in his memoirs. Langefeld died on January 26, 1974 in Augsburg.

Langer

First Name: Charlotte
Birthdate: April 4, 1921
Birthplace:
Position: Aufseherin
File Number: IV 410 (F) 2629/67
Employment Date:
Camp Service: Floßenbürg, AL Chemnitz
Notes:

Langer

First Name: Edith
Birthdate: June 29, 1923
Birthplace:
Position: Aufseherin
File Number: IV 410(F) AR 2629/67
Employment Date:
Camp Service: Floßenbürg; AL Plauen
Notes:

Langer

First Name: Erika
Birthdate: June 5, 1920
Birthplace: Berlin
Position: Aufseherin

File Number:
Employment Date: September 16, 1944
Camp Service: Groß-Rosen
Notes:

Langner

First Name: Erika
Birthdate: April 6, 1923
Birthplace: Breslau
Position: Aufseherin
File Number:
Employment Date: June 1, 1944
Camp Service: Groß-Rosen
Notes:

Langner

First Name: Gerda
Birthdate: January 23, 1919
Birthplace: Klein-Dreihof
Position: Aufseherin
File Number:
Employment Date: November 25, 1943
Camp Service: Ravensbrück
Notes:

Langner

First Name: Gerda
Birthdate: June 5, 1923
Birthplace: Berlin
Position: Aufseherin
File Number:
Employment Date: July 25, 1944
Camp Service: Groß-Rosen
Notes:

Larisch

First Name: Maria
Birthdate: January 8, 1914
Birthplace: Oberhohenelbe
Position: Aufseherin
File Number:
Employment Date: August 21, 1944
Camp Service: Groß-Rosen
Notes:

Lattke

First Name: Hildegard
Birthdate: June 30, 1922
Birthplace: Langenbielau
Position: Aufseherin
File Number:
Employment Date: April 15, 1944
Camp Service: Groß-Rosen
Notes: Official permission for service as an "employee of the Reich" granted on December 11, 1944.

Lattwin

First Name: Gerda
Birthdate: October 23, 1922
Birthplace: Sakrau
Position: Aufseherin
File Number:
Employment Date: July 1, 1944
Camp Service: Groß-Rosen
Notes:

Latz (born Wolters)

First Name: Bernhardine
Birthdate: July 26, 1914
Birthplace: Aschersleben
Position: Aufseherin
File Number:
Employment Date: December 19, 1944
Camp Service: Ravensbrück
Notes:

Laubach

First Name: Margarete
Birthdate: December 24, 1916
Birthplace: Göttingen
Position: Aufseherin
File Number:
Employment Date: July 29, 1944
Camp Service: Groß-Rosen
Notes:

Laube

First Name: Erna
Birthdate: September 19, 1922
Birthplace: Modritz
Position: Aufseherin
File Number:
Employment Date: June 1, 1944
Camp Service: Groß-Rosen
Notes:

Launhardt

First Name: Anna
Birthdate: May 31, 1920
Birthplace:
Position: Aufseherin
File Number: IV 410(F) AR 2629/67
Employment Date:
Camp Service: Floßenbürg; AL Hertine
Notes:

Laurer

First Name: Hildegard (Hilde)
Birthdate: Nuremberg
Birthplace: February 12, 1921
Position: Aufseherin
File Number: IV 410(F) AR 2629/67
Employment Date: September 30, 1944
Camp Service: Floßenbürg; AL Holleischen
Notes: Official permission for service as an "employee of the Reich" granted on November 22, 1944.

Laute

First Name: Elisabeth
Birthdate: April 10, 1921
Birthplace: Köthen
Position: Aufseherin
File Number: IV 410(F) AR 2629/67
Employment Date: August 15, 1944
Camp Service: Floßenbürg; AL Wolkenburg
Notes:

Lautenschläger (born Weber)

First Name: Wanda
Birthdate: March 9, 1921
Birthplace: Nöda

Position: Aufseherin
File Number:
Employment Date: September 5, 1944
Camp Service: Floßenbürg; Ravensbrück
Notes:

Lauteritz

First Name: Ruth
Birthdate: October 6, 1919
Birthplace: Chemnitz
Position: Aufseherin
File Number: IV 410(F) AR 2629/67
Employment Date:
Camp Service: Floßenbürg; AL Chemnitz
Notes:

Laux

First Name: Anni
Birthdate: August 6, 1923
Birthplace: Ober-Erlitz
Position: Aufseherin
File Number:
Employment Date: September 13, 1944
Camp Service: Groß-Rosen
Notes:

Lawinsky

First Name: Gerda
Birthdate: August 9, 1920
Birthplace:
Position: Aufseherin
File Number: IV 429 AR-Z 121/71
Employment Date:
Camp Service: Wolfen
Notes:

Lazarowitsch

First Name: Franziska
Birthdate: September 22, 1920
Birthplace: Gora-Humora
Position: Aufseherin
File Number:
Employment Date: September 6, 1944
Camp Service: Ravensbrück
Notes:

Lechner

First Name: Anni
Birthdate: March 28, 1918
Birthplace: Stuttgart
Position: Aufseherin
File Number: IV 410(F) AR 2629/67
Employment Date: January 18, 1944
Camp Service: Floßenbürg; AL Neu Rohlau
Notes:

Lechtenberg (born Block)

First Name: Agnes
Birthdate:
Birthplace:
Position: Aufseherin
File Number: IV 429 AR 1959/66
Employment Date:
Camp Service: NL Essen
Notes:

Lehm

First Name: Margarete
Birthdate: April 30, 1923
Birthplace: Oelsnitz
Position: Aufseherin
File Number:
Employment Date: September 6, 1944
Camp Service: Ravensbrück
Notes:

Lehmann

First Name: Frieda
Birthdate: February 18, 1895
Birthplace: Insorau
Position: Aufseherin
File Number:
Employment Date: May 1, 1943
Camp Service: Ravensbrück
Notes:

Lehmann

First Name: Herta
Birthdate: October 23, 1921
Birthplace: Marsdorf
Position: Aufseherin
File Number:
Employment Date: August 3, 1944
Camp Service: Ravensbrück
Notes:

Lehmann

First Name: Margarete
Birthdate: October 15, 1923
Birthplace: Chemnitz
Position: Aufseherin
File Number: IV 410(F) AR 2629/67
Employment Date: October 1, 1944
Camp Service: Floßenbürg; AL Holleischen
Notes: Official permission for service as an "employee of the Reich" granted on November 22, 1944.

Lehmann

First Name: Martha
Birthdate: June 27, 1905
Birthplace: Folkersdorf
Position: Aufseherin
File Number:
Employment Date: August 16, 1944
Camp Service: Groß-Rosen
Notes:

Leier

First Name: Anna, Elisabeth
Birthdate: August 3, 1919
Birthplace: Altwaßer near Breslau
Position: Aufseherin
File Number:
Employment Date: September 2, 1944
Camp Service: Groß-Rosen
Notes:

Leifheit

First Name: Isolde
Birthdate: 1922 (no month or day noted in her file)
Birthplace:

Position: Aufseherin
File Number:
Employment Date:
Camp Service: Ravensbrück; Mühlhausen
Notes: Originally SS-Kriegshelferin; transferred
                 to camp staff.

Leimböck (born Rödel)

First Name: Rosalie (Rosalia, Rosa); Wilhelmine
Birthdate: April 18, 1911
Birthplace: Augsburg
Position: Aufseherin; Blockleiterin
File Number: 409 AR-Z 39/59; IV 410 (D) AR-Z 147/75
Employment Date: August 1944 (no day noted in file)
Camp Service: Ravensbrück (4 week training); Augsburg-
                 Michelwerke, Dachau
Notes:

Lempke

First Name: Ursula
Birthdate: April 14, 1923
Birthplace: Vorderhagen (Hagenow)
Position: Aufseherin
File Number:
Employment Date: September 24, 1944
Camp Service: Neuengamme
Notes:

Lenk

First Name: Erika
Birthdate: June 1, 1903
Birthplace: Zwickau
Position: Aufseherin
File Number: IV 410 (F) AR 2629/67
Employment Date:
Camp Service: Floßenbürg; AL Dresden; AL Zwodau
Notes:

Lenner

First Name: Gertraud
Birthdate: May 20, 1922
Birthplace: Planitz
Position: Aufseherin
File Number: IV 410(F) AR 2629/67
Employment Date:
Camp Service: Floßenbürg; AL Chemnitz
Notes:

Leonhardt

First Name: Ilse
Birthdate: March 30, 1922
Birthplace: Leipzig
Position: Aufseherin
File Number:
Employment Date: August 9, 1944
Camp Service: Ravensbrück
Notes:

Lepel

First Name: Waltraut
Birthdate: April 10, 1923
Birthplace: Marburg a.d. Lahn
Position: Aufseherin
File Number:
Employment Date: October 6, 1944

Camp Service: Ravensbrück
Notes:

Leuscher

First Name: Martha
Birthdate: February 19, 1921
Birthplace: Häslich
Position: Aufseherin
File Number:
Employment Date: June 1, 1944
Camp Service: Groß-Rosen
Notes:

Leuteritz

First Name: Ruth
Birthdate: October 6, 1919
Birthplace: Chemnitz
Position: Aufseherin
File Number: IV 410(F) AR 2629/67
Employment Date: August 16, 1944
Camp Service: Floßenbürg; AL Chemnitz
Notes:

Leuther

First Name: Elfriede
Birthdate: March 24, 1921
Birthplace: Denitzsch
Position: Aufseherin
File Number:
Employment Date: November 28, 1944
Camp Service: Ravensbrück
Notes:

Leuthold

First Name: Irene
Birthdate: September 19, 1914
Birthplace: Hainischen
Position: Aufseherin
File Number:
Employment Date: September 4, 1944
Camp Service: Floßenbürg; Ravensbrück
Notes:

Lewendowski

First Name: Toni
Birthdate: December 29, 1921
Birthplace: Duisburg
Position: Aufseherin
File Number:
Employment Date: August 22, 1944
Camp Service: Ravensbrück
Notes:

Leykam (born Knöfler)

First Name: Elfriede
Birthdate: August 8, 1913
Birthplace: Zwickau
Position: Aufseherin
File Number:
Employment Date: August 25, 1944
Camp Service: Floßenbürg
Notes:

Lichtenstein

First Name: Anneliese
Birthdate: March 22, 1921
Birthplace: Limbach
Position: Aufseherin
File Number:
Employment Date: August 30, 1944
Camp Service: Floßenbürg
Notes:

Lichter

First Name: Marie
Birthdate: July 14, 1923
Birthplace: Bernsdorf
Position: Aufseherin
File Number:
Employment Date: March 1, 1944
Camp Service: Groß-Rosen
Notes:

Lichter

First Name: Martha
Birthdate: July 29, 1921
Birthplace: Bernsdorf
Position: Aufseherin
File Number:
Employment Date: March 1, 1944
Camp Service: Groß-Rosen
Notes:

Liebau

First Name: Charlotte
Birthdate: August 29, 1923
Birthplace:
Position: Aufseherin
File Number: IV 429 AR 1973/66 (B)
Employment Date:
Camp Service: Sömmerda
Notes:

Liebig

First Name: Anneliese
Birthdate: March 22, 1923
Birthplace: Jordansmühl
Position: Aufseherin
File Number:
Employment Date: August 23, 1944
Camp Service: Groß-Rosen
Notes:

Liebig (born Schwandt)

First Name: Elli
Birthdate: July 14, 1916
Birthplace: Grüneberg
Position: Aufseherin
File Number:
Employment Date: May 15, 1944
Camp Service: Ravensbrück
Notes:

Liebig

First Name: Hedwig
Birthdate: July 9, 1916
Birthplace: Glatz
Position: Aufseherin

File Number:
Employment Date: September 22, 1944
Camp Service: Groß-Rosen
Notes:

Liebsch

First Name: Ilse
Birthdate: August 5, 1922
Birthplace: Bretnik
Position: Aufseherin
File Number:
Employment Date: August 28, 1944
Camp Service: Ravensbrück
Notes:

Liebscher

First Name: Marie (Maria)
Birthdate: September 11, 1912
Birthplace: Risut
Position: Aufseherin
File Number: IV 410(F) AR 2629/67
Employment Date:
Camp Service: Floßebürg; AL Neu Rohlau
Notes:

Lindemann

First Name: Wilma
Birthdate: June 5, 1916
Birthplace: Hamburg
Position: Aufseherin
File Number:
Employment Date: October 20, 1944
Camp Service: Groß-Rosen
Notes:

Lindenau (or Lindelau)

First Name: Ilse
Birthdate: October 30, 1922
Birthplace: Müncheberg
Position: Aufseherin
File Number: IV 410(F) AR 2629/67
Employment Date: September 8, 1944
Camp Service: Groß-Rosen; AL Graslitz
Notes:

Linder

First Name: Wally
Birthdate: February 6, 1919
Birthplace: Chemnitz
Position: Aufseherin
File Number:
Employment Date: August 26, 1944
Camp Service: Floßenbürg
Notes:

Lindner

First Name: Frieda
Birthdate: December 24, 1904
Birthplace: Langenbielau
Position: Aufseherin
File Number:
Employment Date: March 1, 1944
Camp Service: Groß-Rosen
Notes:

Linke

First Name: Gertrud
Birthdate: February 25, 1920
Birthplace:
Position: Aufseherin
File Number:
Employment Date: March 1, 1944
Camp Service: Groß-Rosen
Notes: Official permission for service as an "employee of the Reich" granted on December 11, 1944.

Linke

First Name: Martha
Birthdate: January 27, 1922
Birthplace: Friedeberg
Position: Aufseherin
File Number:
Employment Date: August 16, 1944
Camp Service: Groß-Rosen
Notes:

Linke

First Name: Wanda
Birthdate: March 14, 1923
Birthplace: Wittgenau
Position: Aufseherin
File Number:
Employment Date: June 1, 1944
Camp Service: Groß-Rosen
Notes:

Lipfert

First Name: Lucie
Birthdate: July 4, 1923
Birthplace: Weichmannsdorf
Position: Aufseherin
File Number:
Employment Date: September 5, 1944
Camp Service: Ravensbrück
Notes:

Lippert

First Name: Erna
Birthdate: September 12, 1911
Birthplace: Dresden
Position: Aufseherin
File Number: IV 410(F) AR 2629/67
Employment Date: August 16, 1944
Camp Service: Floßenbürg; AL Goehle-Werk Dresden
Notes: November 20, 1944

Lippmann (born Springer)

First Name: Elli
Birthdate: May 1, 1921
Birthplace: Breslau
Position: Aufseherin
File Number:
Employment Date: April 15, 1944
Camp Service: Groß-Rosen
Notes:

Lippmann

First Name: Hildegard
Birthdate: June 18, 1922
Birthplace: Hainichen

Position: Aufseherin
File Number: IV 410(F) AR 2629/67
Employment Date: August 17, 1944
Camp Service: Floßenbürg; AL Hainichen
Notes:

Liske

First Name: Margarete
Birthdate: November 25, 1923
Birthplace: Bahm
Position: Aufseherin
File Number: IV 410(F) AR 2629/67
Employment Date:
Camp Service: Floßenbürg; AL Graslitz
Notes:

Lisowski

First Name: Hildegard
Birthdate: June 13, 1919
Birthplace: Schwignitz
Position: Aufseherin
File Number:
Employment Date: September 22, 1941
Camp Service: Groß-Rosen
Notes:

Lochte

First Name: Ella
Birthdate: May 31, 1921
Birthplace: Dortmund
Position: Aufseherin
File Number:
Employment Date: August 25, 1944
Camp Service: Ravensbrück
Notes:

Locker

First Name: Philomena
Birthdate: July 6, 1923
Birthplace: Glatz
Position: Aufseherin
File Number:
Employment Date:
Camp Service: Groß-Rosen
Notes:

Löbe

First Name: Gerda
Birthdate: March 9, 1922
Birthplace: Ottendorf
Position: Aufseherin
File Number: IV 410(F) AR 2629/67
Employment Date: August 22, 1944
Camp Service: Floßenbürg; AL Hainichen
Notes:

Löffler (married David)

First Name: Gerda
Birthdate: May 31, 1921
Birthplace: Hannover
Position: Aufseherin
File Number:
Employment Date: June 1, 1944
Camp Service: Ravensbrück
Notes:

Löhner

First Name: Elfriede
Birthdate: April 7, 1922
Birthplace: Kleinwaltersdorf
Position: Aufseherin
File Number: IV 410(F) AR 2629/67
Employment Date: October 13, 1944
Camp Service: Floßenbürg, AL Freiberg
Notes: Official permission for service as an "employee of the Reich" granted on December 12, 1944.

Löpp

First Name: Dora
Birthdate: August 21, 1922
Birthplace: Stocksmühle
Position: Aufseherin
File Number: IV 410(F) AR 2629/67
Employment Date: June 23, 1944
Camp Service: Floßenbürg; AL Zwodau; AL Holleischen
Notes:

Lötsch (or Lötzsch)

First Name: Marianne
Birthdate: March 31, 1915
Birthplace: Chemnitz
Position: Aufseherin
File Number: IV 410(F) AR 2629/67
Employment Date: August 16, 1944
Camp Service: Floßenbürg; AL Astrawerke Chemnitz
Notes:

Löw

First Name: Gisela
Birthdate: February 22, 1921
Birthplace:
Position: Aufseherin
File Number: IV 409 AR-Z 39/59
Employment Date:
Camp Service: Ravensbrück; Meuselwitz
Notes:

Löwe (born Pietzsch)

First Name: Charlotte
Birthdate: September 11, 1914
Birthplace: Torgau
Position: Aufseherin
File Number:
Employment Date: August 18, 1944
Camp Service: Ravensbrück
Notes:

Löwenberg

First Name: Marga
Birthdate: October 25, 1914
Birthplace: Bernsdorf
Position: Aufseherin
File Number:
Employment Date: October 1, 1939
Camp Service: Ravensbrück
Notes:

Loga (born Kickel)

First Name: Martha
Birthdate: December 25, 1919
Birthplace: Redewisch

Position: Aufseherin
File Number:
Employment Date: November 7, 1944
Camp Service: Ravensbrück
Notes:

Lohmann (born Schultze)

First Name: Else
Birthdate: June 15, 1920
Birthplace: Buxtehude
Position: Aufseherin
File Number:
Employment Date: August 24, 1944
Camp Service: Neuengamme
Notes:

Lorenz

First Name: Hildegard
Birthdate: June 10, 1921
Birthplace: Zipsendorf
Position: Aufseherin
File Number:
Employment Date: June 30, 1944
Camp Service: Neuengamme
Notes:

Lorenz

First Name: Ida
Birthdate: April 12, 1909 (possibly April 10, 1909)
Birthplace: Wurzen
Position: Aufseherin
File Number: IV 410(F) AR 2629/67
Employment Date: October 24, 1944
Camp Service: Floßenbürg; AL Venusberg
Notes: Official permission for service as an "employee of the Reich" granted on December 12, 1944.

Lorenz

First Name: Ilse
Birthdate: August 17, 1919
Birthplace: Holzweisig
Position: Aufseherin
File Number:
Employment Date: June 1, 1943
Camp Service: Ravensbrück
Notes:

Lorenzen

First Name: Margarethe (Margarete)
Birthdate: March 19, 1902
Birthplace: Oldensworth
Position: Aufseherin
File Number: IV 410(F) AR 2629/67
Employment Date: July 3, 1944
Camp Service: Floßenbürg; AL Graslitz
Notes:

Lorse

First Name: Melisse
Birthdate: December 16, 1891
Birthplace:
Position: Aufseherin
File Number: IV 429 AR 1964/66
Employment Date:
Camp Service: Dortmund
Notes:

Lorse
First Name: Luise
Birthdate: December 16, 1921
Birthplace: Dortmund
Position: Wächterin
File Number: IV 429 AR 1964/66 B; IV 429 AR-Z 49/71B
Employment Date:
Camp Service: NL Markkleberg; NL Dortmund
Notes:

Loschnat
First Name: Hedwig
Birthdate: September 18, 1922
Birthplace: Sarken
Position: Aufseherin
File Number:
Employment Date: April 1, 1944
Camp Service: Neuengamme
Notes:

Losert
First Name: Hedwig
Birthdate: January 22, 1921
Birthplace: Munich
Position: Aufseherin
File Number:
Employment Date: September 16, 1944
Camp Service: Ravensbrück
Notes:

Ludewig (born Kabis)
First Name: Thora-Hanna (Thoranna)
Birthdate: June 21, 1916
Birthplace: Kempten
Position: Aufseherin
File Number: IV 410(F) AR 2629/67
Employment Date: September 8, 1944
Camp Service: Floßenbürg; Ravensbrück; AL Plauen; AL Chemnitz
Notes: Possibly identical with Thoranna Ludewig (born in 1919).

Ludewig
First Name: Thoranna
Birthdate: June 21, 1919
Birthplace: Erfurt
Position: Aufseherin
File Number: IV 410(F) AR 2629/67
Employment Date:
Camp Service: Floßenbürg; AL Chemnitz; AL Ind.-Werke Plauen; Venuswerke
Notes: Possibly idential with Thora-Hanna Ludewig (born in 1916).

Ludwig
First Name: Gertraud
Birthdate: February 9, 1923
Birthplace: Glauchau
Position: Aufseherin
File Number:
Employment Date: August 25, 1944
Camp Service: Ravensbrück
Notes:

Ludwig
First Name: Gertrud
Birthdate: March 31, 1915
Birthplace:
Position: Aufseherin
File Number:
Employment Date:
Camp Service:
Notes:

Lübbe
First Name: Agnes
Birthdate: June 12, 1920
Birthplace: Hamburg
Position: Aufseherin
File Number:
Employment Date: November 7, 1944
Camp Service: Ravensbrück
Notes:

Lüdcke
First Name: Elfriede
Birthdate: July 2, 1920
Birthplace: Gera
Position: Aufseherin
File Number:
Employment Date: September 5, 1944
Camp Service: Ravensbrück
Notes:

Lungwitz
First Name: Elisabeth
Birthdate: May 29, 1923
Birthplace:
Position: Aufseherin
File Number: IV 410(F) AR 2629/67
Employment Date:
Camp Service: Floßenbürg; AL Graslitz
Notes:

Lungwitz
First Name: Martha
Birthdate: March 18, 1915
Birthplace: Greifendorf
Position: Aufseherin
File Number: IV 410(F) AR 2629/67
Employment Date: August 22, 1944
Camp Service: Floßenbürg
Notes:

Luthe
First Name: Anni (Anna)
Birthdate: March 31, 1922
Birthplace:
Position: Aufseherin
File Number: IV 429 AR 1959/66
Employment Date:
Camp Service: NL Essen
Notes:

Lutz
First Name: Herta
Birthdate: June 13, 1922
Birthplace: Münchhof
Position: Aufseherin

File Number:
Employment Date: May 1, 1943
Camp Service: Ravensbrück
Notes:

Maaken
First Name: Irmgard
Birthdate: June 26, 1924
Birthplace: Hamburg
Position: Aufseherin
File Number:
Employment Date: August 1, 1943
Camp Service: Neuengamme
Notes:

Maas
First Name: Dora
Birthdate: April 23, 1913
Birthplace:
Position: Aufseherin
File Number: IV 410(F) AR 2629/67
Employment Date:
Camp Service: Floßenbürg; AL Zwodau
Notes:

Mach (born Basner)
First Name: Edith
Birthdate:
Birthplace:
Position: Aufseherin
File Number: IV 410 AR 3016/66
Employment Date:
Camp Service: Floßenbürg; AL Dresden-Reick
Notes:

Mach (born Schlenz)
First Name: Emma
Birthdate:
Birthplace:
Position: Aufseherin
File Number: 405 AR 1309/67
Employment Date:
Camp Service: Schatzlar
Notes:

Mach
First Name: Ruth
Birthdate: January 14, 1922
Birthplace: Breslau
Position: Aufseherin
File Number:
Employment Date: September 20, 1944
Camp Service: Groß-Rosen
Notes:

Macherius
First Name: Elfriede
Birthdate: October 11, 1919
Birthplace: Olbernhau
Position: Aufseherin
File Number: IV 410(F) AR 2629/67
Employment Date: August 16, 1944
Camp Service: Floßenbürg; AL Goehle-Werk Dresden
Notes: Official permission for service as an "employee of the Reich" granted on November 20, 1944.

Madaus
First Name: Elisabeth
Birthdate: 1920
Birthplace:
Position: Aufseherin
File Number:
Employment Date:
Camp Service: Ravensbrück; Velten
Notes:

Madel (or Madl; married Tuetsch)
First Name: Elisabeth
Birthdate: September 17, 1920
Birthplace: Hägermühle
Position: Aufseherin
File Number: IV 410 AR-Z 39/59; IV 429 AR-Z 130/70 (B)
Employment Date: Summer 1944 (month and date not in the file).
Camp Service: Ravensbrück; NL Gelsenkirchen; Sömmerda; Berlin, Wolfen; Siemens Work Camp Nuremberg; Buchenwald
Notes:

Mandl (Mandel)
First Name: Maria
Birthdate: 1912 (no month/day noted in her file)
Birthplace: Upper Austria
Position: Oberaufseherin
File Number:
Employment Date:
Camp Service: Ravensbrück; Auschwitz Birkenau
Notes: Tried by the Poles for war crimes and executed on December 2, 1947.

März
First Name: Marie (Maria)
Birthdate: March 16, 1922
Birthplace: Kubin
Position: Aufseherin
File Number: IV 410(F) AR 2629/67
Employment Date: September 30, 1944
Camp Service: Floßenbürg; AL Holleischen
Notes: Official permission for service as an "employee of the Reich" granted on December 12, 1944.

Mäser
First Name: Ingeborg
Birthdate: December 19, 1922
Birthplace: Magdeburg
Position: Aufseherin
File Number:
Employment Date: November 16, 1911
Camp Service: Ravensbrück
Notes:

Mages
First Name: Fanny
Birthdate: February 4, 1921
Birthplace: Mitterteich
Position: Aufseherin
File Number: IV 410(F) AR 2629/67
Employment Date: September 30, 1944
Camp Service: Floßenbürg; AL Holleischen
Notes: Official permission for employment as an "employee of the Reich" granted on December 12, 1944.

Mahler
First Name: Hildegard
Birthdate: January 27, 1922
Birthplace: Borgsdorf
Position: Aufseherin
File Number:
Employment Date: November 1, 1944
Camp Service: Ravensbrück; Sachsenhausen
Notes:

Mains
First Name: Elli
Birthdate: May 15, 1923
Birthplace: Haisbittel
Position: Aufseherin: Waffen SS
File Number: IV 410(F) AR 2629/67
Employment Date:
Camp Service: Floßenbürg; AL Helmbrechts
Notes:

Majewski
First Name: Elisabeth
Birthdate: August 28, 1919
Birthplace: Fraustadt
Position: Aufseherin
File Number:
Employment Date: November 1, 1944
Camp Service: Ravensbrück
Notes:

Malinowski
First Name: Martha
Birthdate: November 4, 1921
Birthplace: Walsum
Position: Aufseherin
File Number:
Employment Date: August 26, 1944
Camp Service: Ravensbrück
Notes:

Manfeld
First Name: Lieselotte
Birthdate: April 6, 1922
Birthplace: Dortmund
Position: Aufseherin
File Number:
Employment Date: September 16, 1944
Camp Service: Ravensbrück
Notes:

Mann
First Name: Herta
Birthdate: September 30, 1923
Birthplace:
Position: Aufseherin
File Number: IV 429 AR 1965/66; IV 429 AR-Z 121/71
Employment Date:
Camp Service: Wolfen
Notes:

Manni (born Bertulies)
First Name: Hildegard
Birthdate: May 20, 1909
Birthplace: Berlin
Position: Aufseherin

File Number:
Employment Date: August 16, 1944
Camp Service: Ravensbrück
Notes:

Marquardt (or Markwart; born Dittmann)
First Name: Erika
Birthdate: September 8, 1921
Birthplace: Wolschow
Position: Aufseherin
File Number:
Employment Date: April 20, 1944
Camp Service: Ravensbrück
Notes:

Marschall
First Name: Alma
Birthdate: August 18, 1919
Birthplace: Rostock
Position: Aufseherin
File Number:
Employment Date: October 18, 1944
Camp Service: Ravensbrück
Notes:

Martin
First Name: Frieda
Birthdate: August 1, 1921
Birthplace: Selb
Position: Aufseherin
File Number: IV 410(F) AR 2629/67
Employment Date: September 30, 1944
Camp Service: Floßenbürg; AL Graslitz; AL Holleischen
Notes: Official permission for employment as an "employee of the Reich" granted on December 12, 1944.

Marx (born Grewe)
First Name: Irmgard
Birthdate: January 9, 1919
Birthplace: Kiel
Position: Aufseherin
File Number:
Employment Date: June 21, 1944
Camp Service: Ravensbrück
Notes:

Marzinak (born Sieg)
First Name: Konstantine
Birthdate: November 10, 1921
Birthplace:
Position: Aufseherin
File Number: IV 406 AR-Z 21/71
Employment Date:
Camp Service: NL Genshagen
Notes:

Mass
First Name: Anneliese
Birthdate: May 4, 1921
Birthplace: Berlin
Position: Aufseherin
File Number:
Employment Date: November 1, 1944
Camp Service: Ravensbrück
Notes:

Massar

First Name: Helene
Birthdate: June 12, 1912
Birthplace: Schafhöfen
Position: Aufseherin
File Number:
Employment Date: February 1, 1939
Camp Service: Ravensbrück
Notes:

Matthei

First Name: Gertrud
Birthdate: January 28, 1918
Birthplace: Zauhiwitz
Position: Aufseherin
File Number:
Employment Date: August 13, 1944
Camp Service: Ravensbrück
Notes:

Mathes (born Brzoska)

First Name: Hilde
Birthdate: March 7, 1909
Birthplace: Erfenschlag
Position: Aufseherin
File Number:
Employment Date: October 1, 1944
Camp Service: Floßenbürg
Notes:

Mau

First Name: Elisabeth
Birthdate: August 24, 1922
Birthplace: Mettmann
Position: Aufseherin
File Number:
Employment Date: October 11, 1944
Camp Service: Ravensbrück
Notes:

Mauersberger

First Name: Gerda
Birthdate: February 20, 1922
Birthplace: Dobraschitz
Position: Aufseherin
File Number: IV 410(F) AR 2629/67
Employment Date: August 2, 1944
Camp Service: Floßenbürg, AL Chemnitz
Notes:

Mauersberger

First Name: Inge
Birthdate: May 24, 1918
Birthplace: Zoeblitz
Position: Aufseherin
File Number:
Employment Date: November 2, 1944
Camp Service: Floßenbürg
Notes:

Max (born Palwitz)

First Name: Elisabeth
Birthdate: December 20, 1909
Birthplace: Dortmund-Hörde
Position: Aufseherin

File Number: IV 429 AR1964/66 B
Employment Date: 1944 (no month or day provided)
Camp Service: Ravensbrück; Buchenwald; NL Dortmund
Notes:

Mayer (born Wöllert)

First Name: Karla
Birthdate: February 7, 1918
Birthplace: Friedland
Position: Leitern eines Sortierkommandos
File Number: II 208 AR-Z 74/60
Employment Date: September 15, 1941
Camp Service: Auschwitz; Lublin-Majdanek
Notes:

Mehnert

First Name: Gerda
Birthdate: December 18, 1920
Birthplace: Niederdorf
Position: Aufseherin
File Number:
Employment Date: September 12, 1944
Camp Service: Floßenbürg; Ravensbrück
Notes:

Meichler

First Name: Elly
Birthdate: September 18, 1921
Birthplace: Klein Berke
Position: Aufseherin
File Number:
Employment Date: June 22, 1944
Camp Service: Ravensbrück
Notes:

Meier

First Name: Agnes
Birthdate: January 20, 1903
Birthplace: Wenig-Walditz
Position:
File Number:
Employment Date: August 12, 1944
Camp Service: Groß-Rosen
Notes:

Meier (born Enscher)

First Name: Elisabeth
Birthdate:
Birthplace:
Position: Aufseherin
File Number: IV 429 AR 89/71
Employment Date:
Camp Service: Markkleeberg
Notes:

Meier (born Mibredt)

First Name: Ellen
Birthdate: March 29, 1916
Birthplace: Berlin
Position: Aufseherin
File Number: IV 410(F) AR 2629/67
Employment Date: September 8, 1944
Camp Service: Floßenbürg; AL Graslitz
Notes: Official permission for service as an "employee of the Reich" granted on November 20, 1944.

Meier

First Name: Ilse
Birthdate: December 1, 1922
Birthplace: Scharfenstein
Position: Aufseherin
File Number: IV 410(F) AR 2629/67
Employment Date: September 8, 1944
Camp Service: Floßenbürg; AL Graslitz
Notes:

Meier

First Name: Marie
Birthdate: March 2, 1921
Birthplace: Schönau near Braunau
Position: Aufseherin
File Number:
Employment Date: September 29, 1944
Camp Service: Groß-Rosen
Notes:

Meier

First Name: Ruth
Birthdate: August 15, 1923
Birthplace: Breslau
Position:
File Number:
Employment Date: August 10, 1944
Camp Service: Groß-Rosen
Notes:

Meierhofer

First Name: Berta (Bertha)
Birthdate: February 3, 1918
Birthplace: Nuremberg
Position: Aufseherin
File Number: IV 410(F) AR 2629/67
Employment Date: September 30, 1944
Camp Service: Floßenbürg; AL Holleischen
Notes:

Meins

First Name: Elli
Birthdate: May 15, 1923
Birthplace: Hoisbüttl
Position: Aufseherin
File Number:
Employment Date: July 3, 1944
Camp Service: Floßenbürg
Notes:

Meisel

First Name: Anni
Birthdate: September 18, 1918
Birthplace: Schmiedeberg
Position: Aufseherin
File Number:
Employment Date: September 29, 1944
Camp Service: Groß-Rosen
Notes:

Meißner

First Name: Margarete
Birthdate: January 1, 1919
Birthplace: Arnstadt
Position: Aufseherin

File Number:
Employment Date: October 10, 1944
Camp Service: Groß-Rosen
Notes:

Melcher

First Name: Elisabeth
Birthdate: March 5, 1921
Birthplace: Altruednitz
Position: Aufseherin
File Number:
Employment Date: December 15, 1943
Camp Service: Ravensbrück
Notes:

Melzer (born Frank)

First Name: Erna
Birthdate: February 4, 1922
Birthplace: Götzen
Position: Aufseherin
File Number: IV 429 AR-Z 51/70
Employment Date:
Camp Service: NL Allendorf
Notes:

Mende

First Name: Erna
Birthdate: March 14, 1903
Birthplace: Kempten
Position: Aufseherin
File Number: IV 410(F) AR 2629/67
Employment Date: October 26, 1944
Camp Service: Ravenbrück; Floßenbürg; AL Freiberg
Notes:

Mende

First Name: Hildegard
Birthdate: November 24, 1922
Birthplace: Jollenbeck
Position: Aufseherin
File Number:
Employment Date: August 16, 1944
Camp Service: Ravensbrück; Terezin
Notes: Served at the "Small Fortress" Ghetto.

Merchel

First Name: Gustel
Birthdate: August 24, 1912
Birthplace: Berlin
Position: Aufseherin
File Number:
Employment Date: December 15, 1944
Camp Service: Ravensbrück
Notes:

Merkle (or Merkele)

First Name: Maria Luise
Birthdate: October 19, 1918
Birthplace: Geislingen
Position: Aufseherin
File Number: 419 AR-Z 173/69
Employment Date:
Camp Service: Natzweiler; NL Geislingen
Notes:

Mertins

First Name: Gertrud
Birthdate: October 31, 1908
Birthplace: Leipzig
Position: Aufseherin
File Number:
Employment Date: October 24, 1944
Camp Service: Floßenbürg; Ravensbrück
Notes:

Mertin

First Name: Käte (Käthe)
Birthdate: February 14, 1901
Birthplace: Magdeburg
Position: Aufseherin
File Number: IV 410(F) AR 2629/67
Employment Date: August 20, 1944
Camp Service: Floßenbürg; AL Osram Berlin; AL Plauen
Notes:

Mewes

First Name: Margarete
Birthdate: February 14, 1914
Birthplace: Fürstenberg
Position: Aufseherin
File Number:
Employment Date: July 1, 1939
Camp Service: Ravensbrück
Notes: Tried by the British for war crimes.

Meyer

First Name: Anni
Birthdate: February 23, 1924
Birthplace: Hüttow
Position: Aufseherin
File Number:
Employment Date: November 8, 1944
Camp Service: Ravensbrück
Notes:

Meyer

First Name: Edith
Birthdate: November 8, 1922
Birthplace:
Position: Aufseherin
File Number: IV 406 AR-Z 21/71
Employment Date:
Camp Service: NL Genshagen
Notes:

Meyer

First Name: Frieda
Birthdate: December 22, 1921
Birthplace: Augsburg
Position: Aufseherin
File Number:
Employment Date: August 21, 1944
Camp Service: Ravensbrück
Notes:

Meyer (born Meute)

First Name: Waltraud
Birthdate: January 31, 1915
Birthplace: Hannover
Position: Aufseherin

File Number:
Employment Date: June 1, 1944
Camp Service: Ravensbrück
Notes:

Michalik (born Weise)

First Name: Hildegard
Birthdate: January 17, 1913
Birthplace: Hainichen
Position: Aufseherin
File Number: IV 410(F) AR 2629/67
Employment Date:
Camp Service: Floßenbürg; AL Hainichen
Notes:

Mielke

First Name: Erna
Birthdate: February 21, 1922
Birthplace: Kamehlen
Position: Aufseherin
File Number:
Employment Date: September 1, 1943
Camp Service: Ravensbrück
Notes: Official permission for service as an "employee of the Reich" granted on December 17, 1943.

Mierzowski

First Name: Emma
Birthdate: November 6, 1915
Birthplace:
Position: Aufseherin
File Number: IV 429 AR 1959/66
Employment Date:
Camp Service: AL Essen
Notes:

Miesl (or Miesel; married Wallner)

First Name: Thea (Therese)
Birthdate: October 15, 1922
Birthplace: Munich-Feldmoching
Position: Aufseherin
File Number: 409 AR-Z 39/59; IV 410 AR 71/73
Employment Date: October 15, 1944
Camp Service: Ravensbrück (four weeks); Dachau; AL Kaufering
Notes:

Minges

First Name: Marianne
Birthdate: July 26, 1923
Birthplace: Flemmlingen
Position: Aufseherin
File Number:
Employment Date: May 1, 1943
Camp Service: Ravensbrück
Notes:

Miklas

First Name: Monika
Birthdate: May 4, 1910
Birthplace: Hindenburg
Position: Aufseherin
File Number:
Employment Date: April 1, 1943
Camp Service: Auschwitz
Notes:

Misch

First Name: Elfriede
Birthdate: March 18, 1920 or March 14, 1920
Birthplace: Stopmünde
Position: Aufseherin
File Number: IV 402 AR-Z 37/58
Employment Date: November 16, 1944
Camp Service: Ravensbrück; Aushwitz
Notes:

Mittag

First Name: Therese
Birthdate: February 14, 1921
Birthplace: Piesteritz
Position: Aufseherin
File Number:
Employment Date: August 16, 1944
Camp Service: Ravensbrück
Notes:

Modes

First Name: Hildegard
Birthdate: September 15, 1921
Birthplace: Grobau
Position: Aufseherin
File Number:
Employment Date: September 6, 1944
Camp Service: Floßenbürg, Ravensbrück
Notes:

Moebius

First Name: Edith
Birthdate: February 17, 1923
Birthplace: Niederlichtenau near Flöha
Position: Aufseherin
File Number: IV 410(F) AR 2629/67
Employment Date: September 8, 1944
Camp Service: Floßenbürg; AL Wilischtal
Notes: Official permission for service as an "employee of the Reich" granted on November 25, 1944. Possibly identical to Gertraud Moebius.

Moebius

First Name: Gertraud
Birthdate: February 17, 1923
Birthplace: Niederlichtenau near Flöha
Position: Aufseherin
File Number: IV 410(F) AR 2629/67
Employment Date: September 8, 1944
Camp Service: Floßenbürg; AL Wilischtal
Notes: Official permission for service as an "employee of the Reich" granted on November 25, 1944. Possibly identical to Edith Moebius.

Möller

First Name: Anni
Birthdate: June 11, 1923
Birthplace: Rostock
Position: Aufseherin
File Number:
Employment Date: November 7, 1944
Camp Service: Ravensbrück
Notes:

Möller

First Name: Erika
Birthdate: April 9, 1923
Birthplace: Dresden
Position: Aufseherin
File Number:
Employment Date: September 8, 1944
Camp Service: Floßenbürg
Notes:

Möller

First Name: Lotte
Birthdate:
Birthplace:
Position: Aufseherin
File Number: IV 409 AR-Z 39/59
Employment Date:
Camp Service: Ravensbrück; Meuselwitz
Notes:

Möller

First Name: Gertrud
Birthdate: 1922
Birthplace:
Position: Aufseherin
File Number:
Employment Date:
Camp Service: Neuengamme; Boizenburg
Notes:

Mohnecke

First Name: Elfriede Hildegard
Birthdate: March 2, 1922
Birthplace: Dorschen
Position: Aufseherin
File Number: JAG 326
Employment Date: October 12, 1944
Camp Service: Ravensbrück; Youth Protective Custody Camp Uckermark
Notes: Sentenced to ten years imprisonment, but was released after five years confinement.

Mol (married Dijs)

First Name: Johanna (Elisabeth)
Birthdate: August 13, 1905
Birthplace: Amsterdam
Position:
File Number: IV 409 AR-Z 39/59
Employment Date:
Camp Service: Ravensbrück
Notes: Dutch national; special permission to become an "employee of the Reich" approved.

Montibeller (married Thieme)

First Name: Irma
Birthdate: August 31, 1921
Birthplace: Telve
Position: Aufseherin
File Number: 409 AR-Z 29/59
Employment Date:
Camp Service: Ravensbrück
Notes:

Moor
First Name: Hildegard
Birthdate: June 22, 1922
Birthplace: Ahlen
Position: Aufseherin
File Number:
Employment Date: September 11, 1944
Camp Service: Neuengamme
Notes:

Motzkuhn (born Kukulies)
First Name: Elfriede
Birthdate: March 23, 1917
Birthplace: Tawe
Position: Aufseherin
File Number: IV 429 AR-Z 51/71 (B)
Employment Date:
Camp Service: Buchenwald, NL Essen
Notes: Service as an SS auxiliary.

Mrosowski
First Name: Helene
Birthdate: April 3, 1922
Birthplace: Mertenau
Position: Aufseherin
File Number:
Employment Date: November 7, 1944
Camp Service: Ravensbrück
Notes:

Mucha
First Name: Agnes
Birthdate: January 5, 1920
Birthplace: Königshütte
Position: Aufseherin
File Number:
Employment Date: November 7, 1944
Camp Service: Ravensbrück
Notes:

Mühlhaus
First Name: Erna
Birthdate: August 25, 1918
Birthplace: Frankfurt/Main
Position: Aufseherin
File Number:
Employment Date: August 25, 1944
Camp Service: Ravensbrück
Notes:

Müller
First Name: Anni
Birthdate: September 23, 1916
Birthplace: Magdeburg
Position: Aufseherin
File Number:
Employment Date: June 24, 1944
Camp Service: Ravensbrück
Notes:

Müller
First Name: Elfriede
Birthdate:
Birthplace:

Position: Aufseherin
File Number: I 110 AR 257/75; IV 409 AR-Z 114/72
Employment Date:
Camp Service: Ravensbrück
Notes: Nicknamed "The Beast of Ravensbrück" by inmates.

Müller (born Kisch)
First Name: Elisabeth
Birthdate: February 15, 1912
Birthplace: "India" in Croatia
Position: Aufseherin
File Number:
Employment Date: August 19, 1944
Camp Service: Ravensbrück
Notes:

Müller
First Name: Elli
Birthdate: December 30, 1919
Birthplace: Neusalz
Position: Aufseherin
File Number:
Employment Date: June 1, 1944
Camp Service: Groß-Rosen
Notes:

Müller
First Name: Else
Birthdate: April 29, 1907
Birthplace: Dresden
Position: Aufseherin
File Number: IV 410(F) AR 2629/67
Employment Date: August 16, 1944
Camp Service: Floßenbürg; AL Goehle-Werk Dresden
Notes: Official permission for service as an "employee of the Reich" granted on November 20, 1944.

Müller
First Name: Else
Birthdate: 1917
Birthplace:
Position: Blockführerin
File Number:
Employment Date:
Camp Service: Göhlewerk Dresden
Notes:

Müller
First Name: Erika
Birthdate: December 26, 1909
Birthplace: Leipzig
Position: Aufseherin
File Number:
Employment Date: November 6, 1944
Camp Service: Floßenbürg
Notes: Permission for service as an "employee of the Reich" granted on December 12, 1944.

Müller
First Name: Gerda
Birthdate: January 27, 1922
Birthplace: Frankenau
Position: Aufseherin
File Number:

Employment Date: September 2, 1944
Camp Service: Floßenbürg
Notes:

Müller

First Name: Herta
Birthdate: December 28, 1921
Birthplace: Dresden
Position: Aufseherin
File Number: IV 410(F) AR 2629/67
Employment Date: August 16, 1944
Camp Service: Floßenbürg; AL Goehle Werk Dresden
Notes:

Müller

First Name: Irma
Birthdate: October 3, 1920
Birthplace: Kaufungen
Position: Aufseherin
File Number:
Employment Date: October 26, 1944
Camp Service: Floßenbürg
Notes:

Müller

First Name: Jutta
Birthdate: April 2, 1921
Birthplace: Groß Poßnack
Position: Aufseherin
File Number:
Employment Date: July 17, 1944
Camp Service: Ravensbrück
Notes:

Müller (born Könen)

First Name: Maria
Birthdate: May 11, 1906
Birthplace: Essen-Rellinghausen
Position: Wächterin
File Number: IV 429 AR-Z 51/71 (Z)
Employment Date:
Camp Service: NL Essen
Notes: Service as an SS auxiliary.

Müller

First Name: Marianne
Birthdate: September 19, 1922
Birthplace: Bad Elster-Reuth
Position: Aufseherin
File Number: IV 410(F) AR 2629/67
Employment Date: September 11, 1944
Camp Service: Floßenbürg; AL Plauen
Notes:

Müller (born Ditmer)

First Name: Marie
Birthdate: June 27, 1922
Birthplace: Nuremberg
Position: Aufseherin
File Number: IV 410(F) AR 2629/67
Employment Date: September 30, 1944
Camp Service: Floßenbürg; AL Holleischen; AL Zwodau
Notes:

Müller

First Name: Martha
Birthdate:
Birthplace:
Position: Aufseherin
File Number: IV 407 AR-Z 174/72
Employment Date:
Camp Service: Stutthof; NL Bruss-Sophienwalde
Notes:

Müller

First Name: Stefanie
Birthdate: March 24, 1921
Birthplace: Bruex
Position: Aufseherin
File Number:
Employment Date: September 25, 1944
Camp Service: Floßenbürg
Notes: Ethnic German; born and raised in Belgium.

Müller

First Name: Wanda
Birthdate: March 20, 1922
Birthplace: Duisburg
Position: Aufseherin
File Number:
Employment Date: July 13, 1944
Camp Service: Ravensbrück
Notes:

Müller-Lentsch

First Name: Emma
Birthdate: December 20, 1906
Birthplace: Weidau
Position: Aufseherin
File Number:
Employment Date: November 15, 1944
Camp Service: Ravensbrück
Notes:

Muenzer

First Name: Gisela
Birthdate: January 27, 1922
Birthplace: Neugranesau
Position: Aufseherin
File Number: IV 410(F) AR 2629/67
Employment Date: April 30, 1944
Camp Service: Floßenbürg; AL Holleischen
Notes:

Mundhenke (born Stiegler)

First Name: Hanna
Birthdate: March 16, 1920
Birthplace: Langenberg
Position: Aufseherin
File Number: IV 410(F) AR 2629/67
Employment Date: August 16, 1944
Camp Service: Floßenbürg; AL Chemnitz
Notes:

Munzel

First Name: Anneliese
Birthdate: April 23, 1916
Birthplace: Strassburg
Position: Aufseherin

File Number:
Employment Date: November 28, 1944
Camp Service: Ravensbrück; Stutthof-Danzig
Notes:

Murowski
First Name: Erika
Birthdate: March 25, 1922
Birthplace: Averlack
Position: Aufseherin
File Number:
Employment Date: November 7, 1944
Camp Service: Ravensbrück
Notes:

Muske
First Name: Wilma
Birthdate: May 21, 1914
Birthplace: Hamburg
Position: Aufseherin
File Number:
Employment Date: September 30, 1944
Camp Service: Neuengamme
Notes:

Nachtwy
First Name: Elsa
Birthdate: September 13, 1923
Birthplace: Hundeshagen
Position: Aufseherin
File Number:
Employment Date: November 3, 1944
Camp Service: Ravensbrück
Notes:

Nadler (or Nadeler; born Bammer)
First Name: Marie
Birthdate: February 25, 1911
Birthplace: Lambrecht
Position: Aufseherin
File Number:
Employment Date: April 20, 1944
Camp Service: Ravensbrück
Notes:

Nagel
First Name: Erika
Birthdate: March 6, 1921
Birthplace: Jungbuch
Position: Aufseherin
File Number:
Employment Date: November 7, 1944
Camp Service: Ravensbrück
Notes:

Nanstadt
First Name: Sophie
Birthdate: September 10, 1922
Birthplace:
Position: Aufseherin
File Number: IV 410(F) AR 2629/67
Employment Date:
Camp Service: Floßenbürg; AL Holleischen
Notes:

Naumann
First Name: Anny
Birthdate: July 4, 1921
Birthplace: Jörnsdorf
Position: Aufseherin
File Number:
Employment Date: November 23, 1944
Camp Service: Ravensbrück
Notes:

Naumannn
First Name: Grete
Birthdate: September 11, 1900
Birthplace:
Position: Aufseherin
File Number: IV 409 AR-Z 78/72
Employment Date:
Camp Service: Youth Protective Custody Camp Uckermark
Notes:

Naumann (divorced Ehlert; born Ließ)
First Name: Hertha
Birthdate: March 26, 1905
Birthplace: Berlin
Position: Aufseherin
File Number: IV 409 AR-Z 77/72
Employment Date: 1939 (no month or date noted in the file).
Camp Service: Ravensbrück; Lublin-Majdanek; Auschwitz; NL Rajsko
Notes:

Naumann
First Name: Katharina
Birthdate: October 29, 1919
Birthplace: Freiberg
Position: Aufseherin
File Number:
Employment Date: October 9, 1944
Camp Service: Ravensbrück
Notes:

Naumann
First Name: Lina
Birthdate: November 13, 1921
Birthplace: Lilienstetten
Position: Aufseherin
File Number:
Employment Date: August 3, 1944
Camp Service: Ravensbrück
Notes:

Naujokat
First Name: Hildegard Therese
Birthdate: February 5, 1920
Birthplace: Dresden
Position: Aufseherin
File Number: IV 410(F) AR 2629/67
Employment Date: September 11, 1944
Camp Service: Floßenbürg; AL Plauen
Notes: Official permission for service as an "employee of the Reich" granted on November 20, 1944.

Nauth
First Name: Louise (Luise)
Birthdate: February 28, 1911

Birthplace: Erfurt
Position: Aufseherin
File Number:
Employment Date: Buchenwald
Camp Service:
Notes:

Neblung (or Nebelung)

First Name: Margarete
Birthdate: August 6, 1923
Birthplace: Magdeburg
Position: Aufseherin
File Number: IV 410(F) AR 2629/67
Employment Date: September 26, 1944
Camp Service: Ravensbrück; Floßenbürg; AL Holleischen
Notes:

Neidel

First Name: Margarethe
Birthdate: August 9, 1920
Birthplace:
Position: Aufseherin
File Number: IV 429 AR 1821/66 (B)
Employment Date:
Camp Service: Ravensbrück; Allendorf
Notes:

Neithold (born Hartmann)

First Name: Elisabeth
Birthdate: February 1, 1914
Birthplace: Leipzig
Position: Aufseherin
File Number:
Employment Date: November 7, 1944
Camp Service: Floßenbürg
Notes: Official permission for service as an "employee of the Reich" granted on December 12, 1944.

Nehm

First Name: Elfriede
Birthdate: August 13, 1922
Birthplace: Oberhausen
Position: Aufseherin
File Number:
Employment Date: August 14, 1944
Camp Service: Ravensbrück
Notes:

Nestler

First Name: Marie (Maja)
Birthdate: August 15, 1922
Birthplace: Bruex
Position: Aufseherin
File Number: IV 410(F) AR 2629/67
Employment Date: September 8, 1944
Camp Service: Floßenbürg; AL Neu Rohlau; AL Hertine
Notes: Ethnic German; born and raised in Belgium. Permission for service as an "employee of the Reich" granted on March 15, 1942.

Neubauer

First Name: Elisabeth
Birthdate: August 28, 1922
Birthplace: Auerbach
Position: Aufseherin

File Number: IV 410(F) AR 2629/67
Employment Date: October 6, 1944
Camp Service: Ravensbrück; Floßenbürg; AL Astrawerke Chemnitz
Notes:

Neudert

First Name: Lydia
Birthdate: July 29, 1919
Birthplace: Niedergründau
Position: Kommandoführerin
File Number: IV 410(F) AR 2629/67
Employment Date: November 25, 1944
Camp Service: AL Hanau
Notes:

Neugebauer

First Name: Dorothea
Birthdate: August 19, 1923
Birthplace: Dresden
Position: Aufseherin
File Number: IV 410(F) AR 2629/67
Employment Date: September 8, 1944
Camp Service: Floßenbürg; AL Dresden Universelle
Notes: Permission for service as an "employee of the Reich" granted on November 20, 1944.

Neugebauer (born Klampfl)

First Name: Resi
Birthdate: February 22, 1921
Birthplace: Landshut (Bavaria)
Position: Aufseherin
File Number:
Employment Date: August 20, 1944
Camp Service: Bergen-Belsen
Notes:

Neumann

First Name: Anneliese
Birthdate: March 30, 1924
Birthplace: Wildau
Position: Aufseherin
File Number:
Employment Date: December 15, 1943
Camp Service: Ravensbrück
Notes: Permission for service as an "employee of the Reich" granted on April 19, 1944.

Neumann

First Name: Hildegard
Birthdate: May 4, 1919
Birthplace: Gabel
Position: Oberaufseherin
File Number:
Employment Date: October 15, 1942
Camp Service: Ravensbrück; Terezin
Notes:

Neumann

First Name: Hildegard
Birthdate: January 30, 1920
Birthplace: Ruden
Position: Aufseherin
File Number:
Employment Date: November 22, 1944

Camp Service: Ravensbrück
Notes:

Neunes (born Lanzendorf)
First Name: Irmgard
Birthdate: December 19, 1921
Birthplace: Gera
Position: Aufseherin
File Number:
Employment Date: September 10, 1944
Camp Service: Ravensbrück
Notes:

Neunuebel
First Name: Marianne
Birthdate: April 14, 1923
Birthplace: Gera
Position: Aufseherin
File Number:
Employment Date: August 15, 1944
Camp Service: Bergen-Belsen
Notes:

Niebuhr
First Name: Elfriede
Birthdate: November 1, 1922
Birthplace: Rostock
Position: Aufseherin
File Number:
Employment Date: November 7, 1944
Camp Service: Ravensbrück
Notes:

Niedner (born Goldmann)
First Name: Edith
Birthdate: February 26, 1922
Birthplace: Freiberg
Position: Aufseherin
File Number: IV 410(F) AR 2629/67
Employment Date: October 13, 1944
Camp Service: Floßenbürg; AL Freiberg
Notes:

Niemand
First Name: Martha
Birthdate: June 3, 1906
Birthplace: Gaßen
Position: Aufseherin
File Number: IV 410(F) AR 2629/67
Employment Date: August 20, 1944
Camp Service: Floßenbürg; Neuengamme; AL Bändorf
Notes:

Niklasch
First Name: Margarethe
Birthdate: March 8, 1923
Birthplace:
Position: Aufseherin
File Number: IV 429 AR 1941/66 (B); IV 421 AR 1941/66 (B)
Employment Date:
Camp Service: Ravensbrück; NL Torgau; Sömmerda
Notes:

Nitzschmann
First Name: Dora
Birthdate: December 23, 1921
Birthplace: Plauen
Position: Aufseherin
File Number:
Employment Date: September 5, 1944
Camp Service: Floßenbürg; Ravensbrück
Notes:

Nitzschner
First Name: Hertha
Birthdate: 1906 (no month or day noted in her file)
Birthplace:
Position: Aufseherin
File Number:
Employment Date:
Camp Service: Dresden
Notes: Sentenced to six years imprisonment by an East German court for maltreatment of prisoners.

Nix
First Name: Maria
Birthdate: March 16, 1922
Birthplace:
Position: Aufseherin
File Number: IV 410(F) AR 2629/67
Employment Date: Floßenbürg; AL Dresden-Reick
Camp Service:
Notes:

Nobis
First Name: Elisabeth
Birthdate: April 28, 1922
Birthplace: Lingen
Position: Aufseherin
File Number:
Employment Date: August 30, 1944
Camp Service: Ravensbrück
Notes:

Noè
First Name: Helga
Birthdate: June 20, 1923
Birthplace: Bremen
Position: Aufseherin
File Number:
Employment Date: August 16, 1944
Camp Service: Ravensbrück
Notes:

Nolte
First Name: Helene
Birthdate: October 29, 1921
Birthplace: Breitenberg
Position: Aufseherin
File Number:
Employment Date: November 8, 1944
Camp Service: Ravensbrück; Sachsenhausen
Notes:

Oehme
First Name: Elise
Birthdate: January 11, 1922
Birthplace: Hennersdorf

Position: Aufseherin
File Number:
Employment Date: October 24, 1944
Camp Service: Floßenbürg; Zschopau
Notes: Permission for service as an "employee of the Reich" granted on December 12, 1944.

Oehme
First Name: Ilse
Birthdate: June 1, 1923
Birthplace: Schlößchen
Position: Aufseherin
File Number:
Employment Date: September 8, 1944
Camp Service: Floßenbürg
Notes:

Oehme (born Forkmann)
First Name: Marga
Birthdate: January 19, 1920
Birthplace: Chemnitz
Position: Aufseherin
File Number: IV 410(F) AR 2629/67
Employment Date: August 16, 1944
Camp Service: Floßenbürg; AL Freiberg; AL Astrawerke Chemnitz
Notes:

Oer
First Name: Maria
Birthdate: August 17, 1920
Birthplace: Freckenhorst
Position: Aufseherin
File Number:
Employment Date: November 2, 1944
Camp Service: Ravensbrück
Notes:

Oertel
First Name: Gerda
Birthdate: October 31, 1914
Birthplace:
Position: Aufseherin
File Number: IV 410(F) AR 2629/67
Employment Date:
Camp Service: Floßenburg; AL Oederan
Notes:

Oertel
First Name: Hedwig
Birthdate: October 31, 1914
Birthplace: Plauen-Bernsdorf
Position: Aufseherin
File Number:
Employment Date: September 8, 1944
Camp Service: Floßenbürg
Notes:

Oertel
First Name: Martha
Birthdate: May 18, 1913
Birthplace: Erdmannsdorf
Position: Aufseherin
File Number:
Employment Date: September 8, 1944

Camp Service: Floßenbürg
Notes: Permission for service as an "employee of the Reich" granted on December 12, 1944.

Oertel
First Name: Martha
Birthdate: November 18, 1922 (or 1921? – unclear)
Birthplace: Auerbach
Position: Aufseherin
File Number: IV 410(F) AR 2629/67
Employment Date: October 1, 1944
Camp Service: Floßenbürg; AL Hollesichen
Notes:

Oettel
First Name: Eva
Birthdate: April 16, 1917
Birthplace: Leipzig
Position: Aufseherin
File Number:
Employment Date: June 15, 1944
Camp Service: Ravensbrück
Notes:

Ogroske
First Name: Erna
Birthdate: May 14, 1918
Birthplace:
Position: Aufseherin
File Number: IV 429 AR 1959/66
Employment Date:
Camp Service: Essen
Notes:

Ohle
First Name: Anna
Birthdate: February 8, 1918
Birthplace: Bresen
Position: Aufseherin
File Number:
Employment Date: November 27, 1944
Camp Service: Ravensbrück
Notes:

Oltersdorf
First Name: Vera
Birthdate: July 25, 1920
Birthplace: Eberswalde
Position: Aufseherin
File Number:
Employment Date: September 17, 1944
Camp Service: Ravensbrück
Notes:

Opelt
First Name: Hilde
Birthdate: April 8, 1921
Birthplace: Auerbach
Position: Aufseherin
File Number:
Employment Date: September 7, 1944
Camp Service: Floßenbürg; Ravensbrück
Notes:

Opitz
First Name: Erna
Birthdate: October 6, 1910
Birthplace: Berlin
Position: Aufseherin
File Number:
Employment Date: October 14, 1942
Camp Service: Ravensbrück
Notes:

Opitz
First Name: Klara
Birthdate: April 16, 1909
Birthplace: Schmhedenberg (Silesia)
Position: Aufseherin
File Number:
Employment Date:
Camp Service: Bergen-Belsen
Notes: Oversaw the garden kommando at Auschwitz Birkenau.

Orlowski (boen Elling)
First Name: Alice, Minna, Elizabeth
Birthdate: September 30, 1903
Birthplace: Berlin
Position: Aufseherin; Komanndoführerin
File Number: IV 407 AR-Z 297/60
Employment Date:
Camp Service: Ravensbrück; Plaszów; Birkenau; Lublin-Majdanek
Notes: Tried by the Poles for war crimes and sentenced to prison; released in 1957; tried by a German court in 1975 for Lublin-Majdanek crimes; died during proceedings

Ossmann
First Name: Wally
Birthdate: February 4, 1919
Birthplace: Nuremberg
Position: (Silesia)
File Number:
Employment Date: September 30, 1944
Camp Service: Floßenbürg
Notes:

Ossyra
First Name: Maria
Birthdate: July 2, 1922
Birthplace: Seben
Position: Aufseherin
File Number:
Employment Date: November 15, 1943
Camp Service: Ravensbrück
Notes:

Ott (born Aufdermauer)
First Name: Anny (Anni or Anna)
Birthdate: October 20, 1920
Birthplace: Essen
Position: Aufseherin
File Number: IV 410(F) AR 2629/67
Employment Date: August 13, 1944
Camp Service: Floßenbürg; AL Zwodau; AL Plauen; AL Graslitz
Notes:

Ottenschläger (married Walter)
First Name: Angela (Angelika)
Birthdate: October 18, 1921
Birthplace: Klein-Gallen
Position: Aufseherin
File Number: IV 410(F) AR 2629/67, IV 410 AR 2960/66
Employment Date: April 15, 1944
Camp Service: Floßenbürg; AL Holleischen
Notes:

Oterdoom
First Name: Johanna
Birthdate: January 10, 1917
Birthplace: Herzogenbusch (Hertogenbosch)
Position: Aufseherin
File Number: IV 409 AR-Z 39/59
Employment Date: April 29, 1944
Camp Service: Ravensbrück; Hetogenbosch
Notes: Dutch national; special permission granted for admission as an "employee of the Reich."

Ouger
First Name: Anneliese
Birthdate:
Birthplace:
Position: Wärterin
File Number: 108 AR 15.048/87
Employment Date:
Camp Service: Floßenbürg
Notes:

Paatzsch
First Name: Brigitte
Birthdate: About 1920 (unclear from file data)
Birthplace:
Position: Aufseherin
File Number: 110/II AR 115/81
Employment Date:
Camp Service:
Notes:

Pacyna
First Name: Olga
Birthdate: February 15, 1921
Birthplace: Jürgenhof
Position: Aufseherin
File Number:
Employment Date: November 7, 1944
Camp Service: Ravensbrück
Notes:

Paesler (married Marotzke)
First Name: Margarete Lucie Klara
Birthdate: January 19, 1916
Birthplace: Berlin
Position: Aufseherin
File Number: IV 406 AR-Z 21/71
Employment Date:
Camp Service: NL Genshagen
Notes:

Pagel (or Pagl)
First Name: Marianne
Birthdate: April 30, 1923
Birthplace: Kirchberg

Position: Aufseherin
File Number:
Employment Date: November 4, 1944
Camp Service: Mauthausen
Notes:

Pajonk

First Name: Sophie
Birthdate: August 6, 1921
Birthplace: Lugersta
Position: Aufseherin
File Number:
Employment Date: August 2, 1944
Camp Service: Groß-Rosen
Notes: Czech national; special permission granted for service as an "employee of the Reich."

Pallaoro (born Hunner)

First Name: Albine
Birthdate: December 4, 1916
Birthplace: Linz a.d. Donau (Linz on the Danube)
Position: Aufseherin
File Number:
Employment Date: September 15, 1944
Camp Service: Mauthausen; Ravensbrück
Notes:

Pallaske

First Name: Martha
Birthdate: August 31, 1913
Birthplace: Neusalz
Position: Aufseherin
File Number:
Employment Date: July 8, 1944
Camp Service: Groß-Rosen
Notes:

Pallwitz

First Name: Elisabeth
Birthdate: December 2, 1909
Birthplace:
Position: Aufseherin
File Number: IV 429 AR 1964/66
Employment Date:
Camp Service: Dortmund
Notes:

Panitz

First Name: Susanne
Birthdate: April 6, 1923
Birthplace: Mischwitz
Position: Aufseherin
File Number: IV 410 AR 3291/66
Employment Date:
Camp Service: Floßenbürg; NL Willischthal
Notes:

Panizza

First Name: Gertrud
Birthdate: July 21, 1914
Birthplace: Berlin
Position: Aufseherin
File Number:
Employment Date: November 2, 1944
Camp Service: Ravensbrück; Sachsenhausen
Notes:

Paraknewitz

First Name: Marianne
Birthdate: September 19, 1914
Birthplace: Tabaningen
Position: Aufseherin
File Number:
Employment Date: September 15, 1944
Camp Service: Ravensbrück
Notes:

Paschta

First Name: Emma
Birthdate: January 21, 1918
Birthplace: Altrognitz
Position: Aufseherin
File Number:
Employment Date: September 28, 1944
Camp Service: Groß-Rosen
Notes:

Pasler

First Name: Hildegard
Birthdate: May 10, 1925
Birthplace:
Position: Erstaufseherin of a *Strafkommando* (first overseer of a punishment detail)
File Number: IV 410(F) AR 2629/67
Employment Date:
Camp Service: Floßenbürg
Notes:

Passehl

First Name: Gerda
Birthdate: May 15, 1919
Birthplace: Berlin
Position: Aufseherin
File Number: IV 410(F) AR 2629/67
Employment Date: March 1, 1943
Camp Service: Ravensbrück; Floßenbürg; AL Neu Rohlau
Notes:

Patzelt

First Name: Elfriede
Birthdate: May 9, 1921
Birthplace: Beutengrund
Position: Aufseherin
File Number:
Employment Date: July 27, 1944
Camp Service: Groß-Rosen
Notes:

Patzer

First Name: Anneliese
Birthdate: January 4, 1920
Birthplace: Leipzig
Position: Aufseherin
File Number: IV 410(F) AR 2629/67
Employment Date:
Camp Service: Floßenbürg; AL J. Werke Plauen
Notes:

Paul

First Name: Elfriede
Birthdate: September 18, 1916
Birthplace: Cainsdorf
Position: Rapportführerin

File Number: IV 410(F) AR 2629/67
Employment Date: August 16, 1944
Camp Service: Floßenbürg; AL Goehle-Werk Dresden
Notes: Permission for service as an "employee of the Reich" granted on November 20, 1944.

Pauli

First Name: Margot
Birthdate: March 23, 1923
Birthplace: Chemnitz
Position: Aufseherin
File Number:
Employment Date: August 26, 1944
Camp Service: Floßenbürg
Notes:

Pawletzki

First Name: Helene
Birthdate: January 10, 1921
Birthplace:
Position: Aufseherin
File Number: IV 406 AR-Z 21/71
Employment Date:
Camp Service: NL Genshagen
Notes:

Payrleitner

First Name: Amalie
Birthdate: June 16, 1922
Birthplace: Vienna
Position: Aufseherin
File Number:
Employment Date: October 1, 1944
Camp Service: Mauthausen; Ravensbrück
Notes:

Peege

First Name: Johanna
Birthdate: June 21, 1921
Birthplace: Leipzig
Position: Aufseherin
File Number:
Employment Date: December 15, 1943
Camp Service: Ravensbrück
Notes: Permission for service as an "employee of the Reich" granted on April 19, 1944.

Pertuch

First Name: Leone
Birthdate: January 18, 1923
Birthplace: Göppersdorf
Position: Aufseherin
File Number: IV 410(F) AR 2629/67
Employment Date: August 1, 1944
Camp Service: Floßenbürg; AL Graslitz
Notes:

Peschke (born Fruen)

First Name: Elisabeth
Birthdate: September 24, 1922
Birthplace: Rheydt
Position: Aufseherin
File Number:
Employment Date:
Camp Service: Natzweiler
Notes:

Pessiner

First Name: Ella
Birthdate: 1895 (no month or day noted in her file)
Birthplace:
Position: Aufseherin
File Number:
Employment Date:
Camp Service: Auschwitz; Ravensbrück
Notes:

Petermann

First Name: Erna
Birthdate:
Birthplace:
Position: Lagerführerin
File Number: 9 AR-Z 85/60
Employment Date:
Camp Service: Groß-Werther; Dora-Nordhausen
Notes:

Petersen

First Name: Christiane
Birthdate: October 28, 1899
Birthplace: Flensburg
Position: Aufseherin
File Number:
Employment Date: September 2, 1944
Camp Service: Floßenbürg
Notes:

Petersohn

First Name: Elfriede
Birthdate: August 28, 1920
Birthplace:
Position: Aufseherin
File Number: IV 406 AR-Z 21/71
Employment Date:
Camp Service: NL Genshagen
Notes:

Pethke

First Name: Dora
Birthdate: February 4, 1922
Birthplace: Berlin
Position: Aufseherin
File Number:
Employment Date: August 31, 1944
Camp Service: Groß-Rosen
Notes:

Petyrek

First Name: Ursula
Birthdate: October 8, 1921
Birthplace: Priepert
Position: Aufseherin
File Number: IV 410(F) AR 2629/67
Employment Date:
Camp Service: Floßenbürg; AL Holleischen
Notes:

Petzak

First Name: Anna
Birthdate: July 26, 1917
Birthplace: Oberaltstadt
Position: Aufseherin
File Number:

Employment Date: March 1, 1944
Camp Service: Groß-Rosen
Notes:

Petzold
First Name: Anni
Birthdate: December 14, 1919
Birthplace: Steinpleis
Position: Aufseherin
File Number:
Employment Date: September 1, 1943
Camp Service: Ravensbrück
Notes: Permission for service as an "employee of the Reich" granted on December 17, 1943.

Petzoldt
First Name: Johanna
Birthdate: January 4, 1915
Birthplace:
Position: Aufseherin
File Number: IV 410(F) AR 2629/67
Employment Date:
Camp Service: Floßenbürg; AL Plauen
Notes:

Pfeiffer
First Name: Elfriede
Birthdate: January 22, 1917
Birthplace: Breslau
Position: Aufseherin
File Number:
Employment Date: September 20, 1944
Camp Service: Groß-Rosen
Notes:

Pfeifer (born Hofmann)
First Name: Lilly
Birthdate: April 24, 1922
Birthplace: Zwickau
Position: Aufseherin: Waffen SS
File Number: IV 410(F) AR 2629/67
Employment Date: August 26, 1944
Camp Service: Floßenbürg; AL Mittweida
Notes: Service as a Waffen SS auxiliary.

Pfeiffer
First Name: Wally
Birthdate: June 16, 1923
Birthplace:
Position: Aufseherin
File Number: IV 410(F) AR 2629/67
Employment Date:
Camp Service: Floßenbürg; AL Holleischen
Notes:

Pflock (born Göring)
First Name: Maria
Birthdate:
Birthplace:
Position: Aufseherin
File Number: IV 409 AR-Z 39/59
Employment Date:
Camp Service: Ravensbrück; Meuselwitz
Notes:

Pfohl (born Gall)
First Name: Emma
Birthdate: March 22, 1904
Birthplace: Niederlangenau
Position: Aufseherin
File Number:
Employment Date: March 1, 1943
Camp Service: Groß-Rosen
Notes: Permission for as an "employee of the Reich" employment granted on June 26, 1944.

Pfrötzschner (or Pfrötschner)
First Name: Elfriede
Birthdate: November 12, 1922
Birthplace: Theuma
Position: Aufseherin
File Number: IV 410(F) AR 2629/67
Employment Date: September 6, 1944
Camp Service: Ravensbrück; Floßenbürg; AL Chemnitz
Notes:

Pfuhl
First Name: Elisabeth
Birthdate: May 19, 1920
Birthplace: Teplitz-Schönau
Position: Aufseherin
File Number: IV 410(F) AR 2629/67
Employment Date: September 18, 1944
Camp Service: Floßenbürg; AL Hertine
Notes: Permission for service as an "employee of the Reich" granted on November 20, 1944.

Pichler (born Stumme)
First Name: Therese
Birthdate: June 15, 1911
Birthplace: Salzthal
Position: Aufseherin
File Number:
Employment Date: September 15, 1944
Camp Service: Mauthausen
Notes:

Pickelmann
First Name: Lilo
Birthdate: January 9, 1925
Birthplace:
Position: Blockleiterin
File Number: IV 410(F) AR 2629/67
Employment Date:
Camp Service: Floßenbürg
Notes:

Piekut
First Name: Margarete
Birthdate: December 12, 1921
Birthplace: Marienwerder
Position: Aufseherin
File Number: IV 410(F) AR 2629/67
Employment Date:
Camp Service: Floßenbürg; AL Holleischen
Notes:

Pielsen
First Name: Wilhelmine
Birthdate: July 12, 1908

Birthplace: Dülken
Position: Aufseherin
File Number:
Employment Date: October 15, 1942
Camp Service: Ravensbrück
Notes:

Pietsch

First Name: Elisabeth
Birthdate: November 22, 1912
Birthplace: Weigelsdorf
Position: Aufseherin
File Number:
Employment Date: August 1, 1944
Camp Service: Groß-Rosen
Notes:

Pietsch

First Name: Ella
Birthdate: September 21, 1897
Birthplace: Berlin
Position: Aufseherin
File Number:
Employment Date: December 1, 1937
Camp Service: Ravensbrück
Notes:

Pietsch

First Name: Klara
Birthdate: July 12, 1922
Birthplace: Langenbielau
Position: Aufseherin
File Number:
Employment Date: October 30, 1944
Camp Service: Groß-Rosen
Notes: Permission for service as an "employee of the Reich" granted on December 11, 1944.

Pietzschmann

First Name: Erika
Birthdate: Apri 9, 1923
Birthplace:
Position: Aufseherin
File Number: IV 410(F) AR 2629/67
Employment Date:
Camp Service: Floßenbürg; AL Dresden
Notes:

Pilling

First Name: Johanna
Birthdate: February 6, 1921
Birthplace: Reichenbach/Eule
Position: Aufseherin
File Number:
Employment Date: April 15, 1944
Camp Service: Sachsenhausen; Groß-Rosen
Notes:

Pilz

First Name: Lisa
Birthdate: March 12, 1923
Birthplace: Niederdodeln
Position: Aufseherin
File Number:

Employment Date: September 25, 1944
Camp Service: Ravensbrück
Notes:

Pilz

First Name: Rosa
Birthdate: August 19, 1920
Birthplace: Schönborg
Position: Aufseherin
File Number:
Employment Date: August 11, 1944
Camp Service: Groß-Rosen
Notes:

Pimpl (or Pimpel)

First Name: Anni
Birthdate: February 2, 1921
Birthplace: Lauterbach-Stadt
Position: Aufseherin
File Number: IV 410(F) AR 2629/67
Employment Date: September 25, 1944
Camp Service: Floßenbürg; AL Holleischen
Notes: Permission for service as an "employee of the Reich" granted on November 22, 1944.

Pinske

First Name: Frieda
Birthdate: 1916 (no month or day noted in her file)
Birthplace:
Position: Aufseherin
File Number:
Employment Date:
Camp Service: Arado-Werke Wittenberg
Notes:

Pischel

First Name: Hedwig
Birthdate: December 13, 1922
Birthplace: Dittersbach
Position: Aufseherin
File Number:
Employment Date: July 22, 1944
Camp Service: Groß-Rosen
Notes:

Pischel

First Name: Martha
Birthdate: November 28, 1913
Birthplace: Engelsberg
Position: Aufseherin
File Number:
Employment Date: August 25, 1944
Camp Service: Groß-Rosen
Notes:

Pladek (or Pladeck; married Heer)

First Name: Edith
Birthdate: January 10, 1912
Birthplace: Berlin
Position: Aufseherin
File Number: 410 AR 2531/66
Employment Date: September 8, 1944
Camp Service: Floßenbürg; AL Graslitz
Notes:

Plescher
First Name: Caecilie
Birthdate: May 7, 1899
Birthplace:
Position: Aufseherin
File Number: IV 410(F) AR 2629/67
Employment Date:
Camp Service: Floßenbürg; AL Hertine
Notes:

Plessing
First Name: Elfriede
Birthdate: August 10, 1923
Birthplace: Leipzig
Position: Aufseherin
File Number:
Employment Date: November 2, 1944
Camp Service: Floßenbürg
Notes:

Plichtil
First Name: Maria
Birthdate: November 5, 1906
Birthplace: Bensdorf
Position: Aufseherin
File Number:
Employment Date: October 10, 1944
Camp Service: Groß-Rosen
Notes:

Plonski
First Name: Gertrud
Birthdate: August 2, 1904
Birthplace: Magdeburg
Position: Aufseherin
File Number:
Employment Date: June 30, 1944
Camp Service: Ravensbrück
Notes:

Plusczik
First Name: Ursula
Birthdate: May 10, 1922
Birthplace: Lahgwitz (or Berlin)
Position: Aufseherin
File Number: IV 410(F) AR 2629/67
Employment Date: August 20, 1944
Camp Service: Floßenbürg; AL Holleischen; AL Osram Berlin; AL Plauen
Notes: Permission for service as an "employee of the Reich" granted on November 20, 1944.

Pölsleitner
First Name: Eleonore
Birthdate: October 2, 1920
Birthplace: Unterach
Position: Aufseherin
File Number:
Employment Date: November 1, 1944
Camp Service: Mauthausen
Notes:

Pöschel
First Name: Helene
Birthdate: July 12, 1921

Birthplace: Gautzsch
Position: Aufseherin
File Number: IV 429 AR 1248/68
Employment Date:
Camp Service: Ravensbrück; Neubrandenburg; Markkleeberg
Notes:

Pötzsch (born Meitner)
First Name: Rosa
Birthdate: June 30, 1912
Birthplace: Kunnersdorf
Position: Aufseherin
File Number:
Employment Date: September 8, 1944
Camp Service: Floßenbürg, Ravensbrück
Notes:

Pohl (born Riedel)
First Name: Ida
Birthdate: December 26, 1908
Birthplace: Langenöle
Position: Aufseherin
File Number:
Employment Date: July 1, 1944
Camp Service: Groß-Rosen
Notes:

Pohl
First Name: Lina
Birthdate: July 1, 1922
Birthplace: Laubnitz
Position: Aufseherin
File Number:
Employment Date: June 15, 1944
Camp Service: Groß-Rosen
Notes:

Pollak
First Name: Gertrud
Birthdate:
Birthplace:
Position: Aufseherin
File Number: IV 410 AR 3016/66
Employment Date:
Camp Service: Floßenbürg; AL Dresden Reick
Notes:

Pollmann (married Schaefer
First Name: Eva
Birthdate: Januuary 29, 1922
Birthplace: Militisch (Hungary)
Position: Aufseherin
File Number: IV 429 AR-Z 130/70 (B)
Employment Date:
Camp Service: Ravensbrück; Meuselwitz
Notes: Ethnic German; born and raised in Hungary.

Ponikau
First Name: Elfriede
Birthdate: November 8, 1921
Birthplace: Prößdorf
Position: Aufseherin
File Number:
Employment Date: November 20, 1944

Camp Service: Ravensbrück
Notes:

Porstein (born Gläser)
First Name: Marianne
Birthdate: January 26, 1921
Birthplace: Chemnitz
Position: Aufseherin
File Number: IV 410(F) AR 2629/67
Employment Date: August 16, 1944
Camp Service: Floßenbürg; AL Astrawerke Chemnitz
Notes:

Pracht
First Name: Helene
Birthdate: August 11, 1921
Birthplace: Oberhausen
Position: Aufseherin
File Number:
Employment Date: October 26, 1944
Camp Service: Ravensbrück
Notes:

Prade
First Name: Else
Birthdate: March 19, 1907
Birthplace: Görsdorf
Position: Aufseherin
File Number:
Employment Date: September 14, 1944
Camp Service: Groß-Rosen
Notes:

Prebeck
First Name: Erna
Birthdate: September 4, 1923
Birthplace: Quierschied
Position: Aufseherin
File Number:
Employment Date: December 18, 1944
Camp Service: Ravensbrück
Notes:

Preibisch (born Rex)
First Name: Luise
Birthdate: January 8, 1921
Birthplace: Geschingen
Position: Aufseherin
File Number:
Employment Date: December 16, 1944
Camp Service: Ravensbrück
Notes:

Preiß
First Name: Erna (Anna)
Birthdate: July 4, 1913
Birthplace: Groß Peterwitz
Position: Aufseherin
File Number:
Employment Date: September 1, 1944
Camp Service: Groß-Rosen
Notes: Permission for service as an "employee of the Reich" granted on November 25, 1944.

Pretzsch
First Name: Gertrud
Birthdate: September 17, 1905
Birthplace: Freiberg
Position: Aufseherin
File Number: IV 410(F) AR 2629/67
Employment Date: October 25, 1944
Camp Service: Floßenbürg; AL Freiberg
Notes:

Pritzkoleit (born Becker)
First Name: Dorothea
Birthdate: October 10, 1912 or November 10, 1912
Birthplace: Saarbrücken
Position: Aufseherin
File Number: IV 402 AR-Z 37/58
Employment Date: 1943 (no month or day noted in her file)
Camp Service: Auschwitz Birkenau
Notes:

Prüflinger
First Name: Hildegard (Hilde)
Birthdate: December 30, 1919
Birthplace: Nuremberg
Position: Aufseherin
File Number: IV 410(F) AR 2629/67
Employment Date: September 30, 1944
Camp Service: Floßenbürg; AL Holleischen
Notes:

Pühra
First Name: Herta
Birthdate: September 9, 1922
Birthplace: Trossau
Position: Aufseherin
File Number:
Employment Date: August 22, 1944
Camp Service: Ravensbrück
Notes:

Puls
First Name: Lieselotte
Birthdate: July 21, 1922
Birthplace: Waschow near Wittenberg
Position: Aufseherin
File Number:
Employment Date: September 11, 1944
Camp Service: Neuengamme
Notes:

Purschke (born Montag)
First Name: Barbara
Birthdate: April 7, 1919
Birthplace: Jägerhof
Position: Aufseherin
File Number:
Employment Date: November 27, 1944
Camp Service: Ravensbrück
Notes:

Purucker
First Name: Else
Birthdate:
Birthplace:
Position: Aufsehein

File Number: IV 429 AR 1981/66
Employment Date:
Camp Service: Buchenwald; NL Taucha
Notes:

Pusch
First Name: Gertrud
Birthdate: September 25, 1921
Birthplace: Falkenau
Position: Aufseherin
File Number: IV 410(F) AR 2629/67
Employment Date: April 1, 1944
Camp Service: Floßenbürg; AL Zwodau
Notes:

Quaas
First Name: Ilse
Birthdate: October 7, 1920
Birthplace: Schnauderhainichen
Position: Aufseherin
File Number:
Employment Date: November 20, 1944
Camp Service: Ravensbrück
Notes:

Quast
First Name: Marianne
Birthdate: October 4, 1920
Birthplace: Duisburg
Position: Aufseherin
File Number:
Employment Date: November 8, 1944
Camp Service: Floßenbürg; Ravensbrück
Notes:

Raab
First Name: Marianne
Birthdate: December 9, 1915
Birthplace: Reichenberg
Position: Aufseherin
File Number:
Employment Date: October 8, 1942
Camp Service: Ravensbrück
Notes:

Raabe
First Name: Emma
Birthdate: September 3, 1892
Birthplace: Langenburg
Position: Aufseherin
File Number:
Employment Date: October 1, 1942
Camp Service: Ravensbrück
Notes:

Raack
First Name: Hildegard
Birthdate: June 2, 1923
Birthplace:
Position: Aufseherin
File Number: IV 410(F) AR 2629/67
Employment Date:
Camp Service: Floßenbürg; AL Dresden-Reick
Notes:

Rabe
First Name: Margarete
Birthdate: October 2, 1923
Birthplace: Neustadt-Clewe
Position: Aufseherin
File Number: IV 409 AR-Z 78/72; 40-2/3; JAG 326
Employment Date: November 7, 1944
Camp Service: Ravensbrück; Youth Protective Custody Camp Uckermark
Notes: Tried April 14–26, 1948 by a British court in Hamburg and sentenced to life imprisonment for selecting 3000 females to be murdered in Uckermark; the sentence was reduced to 21 years, but she was set free on February 26, 1954 (after five years and ten months of confinement).

Rabestein
First Name: Gertrud
Birthdate: January 5, 1903
Birthplace: Naumburg
Position: Aufseherin; Oberwachtmeisterin
File Number: 3-6/313
Employment Date:
Camp Service: Ravensbrück; Lichtenburg; Naumburg Prison
Notes: Sentenced to life imprisonment by an East German court.

Rabowski
First Name: Wera (Vera)
Birthdate: April 16, 1913
Birthplace: Hamburg
Position: Aufseherin
File Number:
Employment Date: October 7, 1944
Camp Service: Neuengamme
Notes:

Racek
First Name: Margaretha (Margaret[h?]e; Grete)
Birthdate: March 24, 1923
Birthplace: Teplitz-Schönau
Position: Aufseherin
File Number: IV 410(F) AR 2629/67
Employment Date: September 8, 1944
Camp Service: Floßenbürg; AL Hertine
Notes: Permission for service as an "employee of the Reich" granted on November 20, 1944.

Rachbauer
First Name: Antonia
Birthdate: April 12, 1904
Birthplace: Neukirchen
Position: Aufseherin
File Number:
Employment Date: November 1, 1944
Camp Service: Mauthausen
Notes:

Raddatz
First Name: Dorothea
Birthdate: December 5, 1922
Birthplace: Hannover
Position: Aufseherin
File Number:

Employment Date: April 20, 1944
Camp Service: Ravensbrück
Notes:

Radtke (born Ostermann)

First Name: Lotte Johanna
Birthdate: August 8, 1923
Birthplace: Hamburg
Position: Aufseherin
File Number: IV 404 AR-Z 70/74
Employment Date:
Camp Service: Neuengamme; NL Beendorf; Helmstedt
Notes: Nicknamed „*Die Deutsche*" (The German) by inmates.

Rätsch

First Name: Anna (Anny)
Birthdate: January 23, 1908
Birthplace:
Position: Aufseherin
File Number: IV 429 AR 1248/68; IV 429 AR 1941/66(B)
Employment Date:
Camp Service: NL Torgau; Markkleeburg
Notes:

Rätsch

First Name: Margarethe
Birthdate: November 24, 1922
Birthplace: Freiberg
Position: Aufseherin
File Number: IV 410(F) AR 2629/67
Employment Date: October 26, 1944
Camp Service: Floßenbürg; AL Freiberg
Notes: Permission for service as an "employee of the Reich"granted on December 12, 1944.

Rafoth (born Lange)

First Name: Charlotte
Birthdate: June 1, 1919
Birthplace: Neuenkirchen
Position: Aufseherin
File Number: IV 429 AR-Z 50/71 (B)
Employment Date:
Camp Service: Buchenwald; NL Gelsenkirchen; KL Sömmerda
Notes:

Rainer

First Name: Maria
Birthdate: February 11, 1915
Birthplace: Munich
Position: Aufseherin
File Number:
Employment Date: September 16, 1944
Camp Service: Ravensbrück
Notes:

Ramdohr

First Name: Gertraud
Birthdate: May 9, 1922
Birthplace: Heiligenthal
Position: Aufseherin
File Number:
Employment Date: August 28, 1944
Camp Service: Ravensbrück
Notes:

Randig

First Name: Wally
Birthdate: March 20, 1920
Birthplace: Neustadt
Position: Aufseherin
File Number: IV 410(F) AR 2629/67
Employment Date: August 26, 1944
Camp Service: Floßenbürg; Kommando Helmbrechts
Notes:

Randow

First Name: Erika
Birthdate: July 17, 1919
Birthplace: Neustrehlitz
Position: Aufseherin
File Number:
Employment Date: October 12, 1944
Camp Service: Ravensbrück
Notes:

Rascher

First Name: Elsa
Birthdate: November 8, 1915
Birthplace: Kirchberg
Position: Aufseherin
File Number: I-110 AR 93/71
Employment Date:
Camp Service: Mauthausen; NL Markkleeberg
Notes:

Rau

First Name: Käthe
Birthdate: July 1, 1920
Birthplace: Forst
Position: Aufseherin
File Number:
Employment Date: July 1, 1943
Camp Service: Ravensbrück
Notes:

Rauer

First Name: Frieda
Birthdate: 1914 (no month or day noted in her file)
Birthplace: Berlin
Position: Aufseherin
File Number: 409 AR 2488/66
Employment Date:
Camp Service: NL Schönefeld
Notes:

Raulf

First Name: Gerda
Birthdate:
Birthplace:
Position: Aufseherin
File Number: IV 421 AR 1941/66 (B)
Employment Date:
Camp Service: Ravensbrück; NL Torgau
Notes:

Rauner

First Name: Anna
Birthdate: June 25, 1923
Birthplace: Littitz (Sudetenland)
Position: Aufseherin
File Number: IV 410(F) AR 2629/67

Employment Date: March 30, 1944
Camp Service: Floßenbürg; AL Zwodau; AL Holleischen
Notes: Ethnic German; born and raised in the Sudetenland.

Rauschenbach

First Name: Berta; Anny; Walli
Birthdate: September 16, 1922
Birthplace: Kreibitsch
Position: Aufseherin
File Number: IV 409 AR-Z 39/59; IV 409 AR-Z 78/72
Employment Date: July 18, 1944
Camp Service: Ravensbrück
Notes:

Rauscher

First Name: Irma
Birthdate: October 14, 1918
Birthplace: Tischau near Teplitz
Position: Aufseherin
File Number: IV 410 (F) AR 2629/67
Employment Date: September 8, 1944
Camp Service: Floßenbürg; AL Hertine
Notes: Permission for service as an "employee of the Reich" granted on November 20, 1944.

Rech (married Laskowski)

First Name: Lieschen (Liesl) Anna Luise
Birthdate: January 10, 1923
Birthplace: Oranienburg
Position: Aufseherin
File Number: IV 410(F) AR 2629/67; 3-6/313
Employment Date:
Camp Service: Floßenbürg; AL Mittweida; Rüstungsbetrieb Auer Oranienburg; Ravensbrück; NL Gelsenkirchen; Buchenwald; Benefeld
Notes:

Rech

First Name: Maria
Birthdate: May 3, 1921
Birthplace: Oranienburg
Position: Aufseherin
File Number: IV 410(F) AR 2629/67
Employment Date: June 22, 1944
Camp Service: Floßenbürg; Sachsenhausen
Notes:

Reggenthin

First Name: Grete
Birthdate: December 15, 1921
Birthplace: Schwenthin
Position: Aufseherin
File Number:
Employment Date: October 12, 1944
Camp Service: Ravensbrück
Notes:

Rehfeld

First Name: Frieda
Birthdate: November 11, 1919
Birthplace: Rheidt
Position: Aufseherin
File Number:
Employment Date: October 17, 1944

Camp Service: Neuengamme
Notes:

Rehm

First Name: Elfriede
Birthdate: August 14, 1918
Birthplace: Langenbach
Position: Blockleiterin
File Number:
Employment Date: October 1, 1944
Camp Service: Floßenbürg
Notes: Permission for service as an "employee of the Reich" granted on December 12, 1944.

Reich

First Name: Gertrud
Birthdate: September 4, 1920
Birthplace:
Position: Aufsehrin
File Number: IV 410(F) AR 2629/67
Employment Date:
Camp Service: Floßenbürg; AL Neu Rohlau
Notes:

Reiche

First Name: Gertrud
Birthdate:
Birthplace:
Position: Aufseherin
File Number: IV 409 AR-Z 39/59
Employment Date:
Camp Service: Ravensbrück; Meuselwitz
Notes:

Reichel

First Name: Editha
Birthdate: November 24, 1916
Birthplace: Berlin
Position: Aufseherin
File Number:
Employment Date: October 15, 1944
Camp Service: Ravensbrück
Notes:

Reichert

First Name: Klara
Birthdate:
Birthplace:
Position: Aufseherin
File Number: IV 407 AR-Z 73/72; IV 407AR-Z 45/72
Employment Date:
Camp Service: Stutthof, NL Rußenschin
Notes:

Reichert

First Name: Lore
Birthdate: October 3, 1923
Birthplace: Ludweiler
Position: Aufseherin
File Number: 403 AR-Z 56/67
Employment Date:
Camp Service: Herzogenbosch
Notes:

Reichwald

First Name: Gerda
Birthdate: May 19, 1921
Birthplace: Berlin
Position: Aufseherin
File Number:
Employment Date: December 1, 1943
Camp Service: Ravensbrück
Notes: Permission for service as an "employee of the Reich" granted on June 21, 1944.

Reiher

First Name: Ruth Gertrud
Birthdate: January 10, 1892
Birthplace: Oelsnitz
Position: Aufseherin
File Number: IV 429 AR-Z 130/70 (B)
Employment Date:
Camp Service: Sömmerda
Notes:

Reimann (born Reichelt)

First Name: Katharina
Birthdate: November 29, 1908
Birthplace: Striegau
Position: Aufseherin
File Number:
Employment Date: June 1, 1944
Camp Service: Groß-Rosen
Notes:

Reinhold

First Name: Anneliese
Birthdate: March 9, 1923
Birthplace: Grünow
Position: Aufseherin
File Number:
Employment Date: October 12, 1944
Camp Service: Ravensbrück
Notes:

Reinhold

First Name: Elfriede
Birthdate: August 9, 1921
Birthplace: Erlkenschwick
Position: Aufseherin
File Number: IV 410(F) AR 2629/67
Employment Date: August 21, 1944
Camp Service: Floßenbürg; AL Rochlitz; AL Graslitz
Notes:

Reinsch

First Name: Toni
Birthdate: February 13, 1922
Birthplace: Neuköln (Berlin)
Position: Aufseherin
File Number:
Employment Date: April 1, 1944
Camp Service: Ravensbrück
Notes:

Reischer

First Name: Anna
Birthdate: March 3, 1921
Birthplace: Enzesfeld

Position: Aufseherin
File Number:
Employment Date: September 1, 1944
Camp Service: Mauthausen
Notes:

Reischick (or Reischik) (born Padua)

First Name: Berta
Birthdate: July 9, 1921
Birthplace: Karlsbad
Position: Aufseherin
File Number: IV 410(F) AR 2629/67
Employment Date: April 1, 1944
Camp Service: Floßenbürg; AL Holleischen
Notes:

Reischl

First Name: Rosa
Birthdate: September 16, 1920
Birthplace: Gensewies
Position: Aufseherin
File Number:
Employment Date: November 1, 1942
Camp Service: Auschwitz
Notes:

Reisner

First Name: Irmgard
Birthdate: December 31, 1903
Birthplace: Falkenberg
Position: Aufseherin
File Number:
Employment Date: March 1, 1944
Camp Service: Ravensbrück
Notes:

Reiterer

First Name: Hildegard
Birthdate: October 10, 1922
Birthplace: Dunkelstein
Position: Aufseherin
File Number:
Employment Date: September 1, 1944
Camp Service: Mauthausen
Notes:

Repschläger

First Name: Gretchen
Birthdate: October 1, 1922
Birthplace: Lunow
Position: Aufseherin
File Number:
Employment Date: August 16, 1944
Camp Service: Floßenbürg; Stutthof; Danzig
Notes:

Ressel (or Rössl)

First Name: Charlotte
Birthdate:
Birthplace:
Position: Second Lagerführerin
File Number: 405 AR 1745/68
Employment Date: 1941 (no month or day noted)
Camp Service: Gabersdorf
Notes:

Ressler
First Name: Anna
Birthdate: October 27, 1920
Birthplace: Alt-Hutta
Position: Aufseherin
File Number:
Employment Date: April 15, 1944
Camp Service: Groß-Rosen
Notes:

Reuther
First Name: Dora
Birthdate: January 25, 1912
Birthplace: Hohenstein-Ernst.
Position: Aufseherin
File Number: IV 410(F) AR 2629/67
Employment Date:
Camp Service: Floßenbürg; AL Goehle-Werk Dresden
Notes:

Reuther
First Name: Frieda
Birthdate:
Birthplace:
Position: Aufseherin
File Number: IV 409 AR-Z 39/59
Employment Date:
Camp Service: Ravensbrück
Notes:

Richter
First Name: Alice
Birthdate: June 20, 1912
Birthplace: Niedersedlitz
Position: Aufseherin
File Number:
Employment Date: October 24, 1944
Camp Service: Floßenbürg
Notes:

Richter
First Name: Elfriede
Birthdate: September 4, 1906
Birthplace: Breslau
Position: Aufseherin
File Number:
Employment Date: June 3, 1944
Camp Service: Groß-Rosen
Notes:

Richter
First Name: Gerda
Birthdate: May 4, 1923
Birthplace: Torgau
Position: Aufseherin
File Number:
Employment Date: November 1, 1944
Camp Service: Ravensbrück
Notes:

Richter
First Name: Hanni
Birthdate: February 16, 1923
Birthplace: Friedrichsgrün
Position: Aufseherin

File Number: IV 410(F) AR 2629/67
Employment Date: August 26, 1944
Camp Service: Floßenbürg; AL Chemnitz
Notes:

Richter (perhaps married as „Junghaus?")
First Name: Hilde
Birthdate: October 15, 1923
Birthplace: Großolbersdorf
Position: Aufseherin
File Number: IV 410(F) AR 2629/67
Employment Date: October 1, 1944
Camp Service: Floßenbürg; AL Holleischen
Notes: Permission for service as an "employee of the Reich" granted on December 12, 1944.

Richter
First Name: Margarete
Birthdate: March 18, 1910
Birthplace: Zichtow
Position: Aufseherin
File Number:
Employment Date: August 12, 1944
Camp Service: Groß-Rosen
Notes:

Rieche (born Opitz)
First Name: Ilse (Maria Minna)
Birthdate: July 23, 1921
Birthplace: Leipzig
Position: Aufseherin
File Number: IV 409 AR-Z 39/59; IV 429 AR-Z 22/74
Employment Date: August 8, 1944
Camp Service: Hasag Werke NL Leipzig; Schönau
Notes:

Riechers
First Name: Helga
Birthdate: June 14, 1922
Birthplace: Friedrichskoog
Position: Aufseherin
File Number:
Employment Date: November 7, 1944
Camp Service: Ravensbrück
Notes:

Riedel
First Name: Asta
Birthdate: April 7, 1922
Birthplace:
Position: Aufseherin
File Number: IV 410(F) AR 2629/67
Employment Date:
Camp Service: Floßenbürg; AL Plauen
Notes:

Riedel
First Name: Irmentraut
Birthdate: June 7, 1914
Birthplace:
Position: Aufseherin
File Number:
Employment Date:
Camp Service: Neuengamme
Notes:

Rieke

First Name: Bernhardine
Birthdate: December 20, 1919
Birthplace: Hameln
Position: Aufseherin
File Number:
Employment Date: July 1, 1944
Camp Service: Ravensbrück
Notes:

Riemer

First Name: Käthe
Birthdate: May 24, 1922
Birthplace: Hamburg
Position: Aufseherin
File Number:
Employment Date: August 25, 1944
Camp Service: Ravensbrück
Notes:

Rieper

First Name: Ingeborg
Birthdate: November 20, 1905
Birthplace: Altona (Hamburg)
Position: Aufseherin
File Number:
Employment Date: September 20, 1944
Camp Service: Neuengamme
Notes:

Rietschel

First Name: Ella
Birthdate: May 21, 1905
Birthplace: Schönwalde
Position: Aufseherin
File Number:
Employment Date: June 15, 1944
Camp Service: Groß-Rosen
Notes:

Rinke

First Name: Erna
Birthdate: October 27, 1922
Birthplace: Landeshut
Position: Aufseherin
File Number:
Employment Date: July 3, 1944
Camp Service: Groß-Rosen
Notes:

Rinke

First Name: Gertrud
Birthdate: November 22, 1921
Birthplace: Friedland
Position: Aufseherin
File Number:
Employment Date: September 1, 1944
Camp Service: Groß-Rosen
Notes:

Rinne

First Name: Elli
Birthdate: June 3, 1923
Birthplace: Sprickens near Brennerförde
Position: Aufseherin

File Number:
Employment Date: August 19, 1944
Camp Service: Bergen-Belsen
Notes:

Rizzl (born Richter)

First Name: Isolde
Birthdate: July 4, 1923
Birthplace:
Position: Aufseherin
File Number: IV 410(F) AR 2629/67
Employment Date:
Camp Service: Floßenbürg; AL Freiberg

Rißmann

First Name: Hildegard
Birthdate: June 26, 1922
Birthplace:
Position: Aufseherin
File Number: IV 406 AR-Z 21/71
Employment Date:
Camp Service: NL Genshagen
Notes:

Ritschel

First Name: Vera
Birthdate: July 21, 1923
Birthplace:
Position: Aufseherin
File Number:
Employment Date: IV 410(F) AR 2629/67
Camp Service: Floßenbürg; AL Hertine
Notes:

Ritter

First Name: Anni
Birthdate:
Birthplace:
Position: Aufseherin
File Number: IV 429 AR 1941/66 (B)
Employment Date:
Camp Service: NL Torgau
Notes:

Robel

First Name: Anna
Birthdate: May 11, 1921
Birthplace:
Position: Aufseherin
File Number: IV 410(F) AR 2629/67; 410 AR 3021/66
Employment Date:
Camp Service: Floßenbürg; NL Dresden Universelle
Notes:

Roblik

First Name: Erna
Birthdate: February 11, 1923
Birthplace: Sommerfeld
Position: Aufseherin
File Number:
Employment Date: June 15, 1944
Camp Service: Groß-Rosen
Notes:

Rodenhausen

First Name: Helene
Birthdate: November 4, 1914
Birthplace: Bürgeln
Position: Aufseherin
File Number: IV 429 AR-Z 51/70
Employment Date:
Camp Service: NL Allendorf
Notes:

Röhl

First Name: Käthe
Birthdate: September 9, 1919
Birthplace:
Position: Aufseherin
File Number: IV 410 (F) AR 2629/67
Employment Date: 1944 (no month or day noted in her file)
Camp Service: Floßenbürg; AL Zwodau; Ravensbrück
Notes:

Römer

First Name: Ida
Birthdate: June 14, 1914
Birthplace: Hamburg
Position: Aufseherin
File Number:
Employment Date: September 14, 1944
Camp Service: Neuengamme
Notes:

Römer

First Name: Ingeborg
Birthdate: May 18, 1923
Birthplace: Dresden
Position:
File Number: IV 410(F) AR 2629/67
Employment Date: September 8, 1944
Camp Service: Floßenbuerg; AL Dresden Universelle
Notes: Permission for service as an "employee of the Reich" not granted (*Einstellung nicht genehmigt: Verfg.SS-WVHA-GO-Dr.Sch./Kl./To.v.31.10.1944*).

Rönne

First Name: Margarete
Birthdate: March 1, 1900
Birthplace: Hamburg
Position: Aufseherin
File Number:
Employment Date: July 21, 1944
Camp Service: Groß-Rosen
Notes:

Rösch

First Name: Ingeborg
Birthdate: December 24, 1923
Birthplace: Großolbersdorf
Position: Aufseherin
File Number:
Employment Date: September 8, 1944
Camp Service: Floßenbürg
Notes:

Rösel (born Reihorn)

First Name: Irma
Birthdate: November 25, 1921
Birthplace: Bernsdorf
Position: Aufseherin
File Number:
Employment Date: March 1, 1944
Camp Service: Bernsdorf
Notes:

Rösler

First Name: Hilde
Birthdate: August 8, 1921
Birthplace: Langenbielau
Position: Aufseherin
File Number:
Employment Date: August 2, 1944
Camp Service: Groß-Rosen
Notes:

Rösner

First Name: Gertraud
Birthdate: November 25, 1921
Birthplace: Rothenbach
Position: Aufseherin
File Number:
Employment Date: September 2, 1944
Camp Service: Groß-Rosen
Notes:

Rößler (born Franz)

First Name: Margarete
Birthdate: June 16, 1913
Birthplace: Lobenstein
Position: Aufseherin
File Number: IV 429 AR-Z 89/71; IV 409 AR-Z 39/59
Employment Date: August 17, 1944
Camp Service: Ravensbrück; Hasag Werke Leipzig; Markkleeberg
Notes:

Rogel

First Name: Else
Birthdate: November 9, 1922
Birthplace: Langenbielau
Position: Aufseherin
File Number:
Employment Date: March 1, 1944
Camp Service: Groß-Rosen
Notes:

Rohde

First Name: Hilde
Birthdate: May 25, 1922
Birthplace: Dellstadt
Position: Aufseherin
File Number:
Employment Date: November 16, 1944
Camp Service: Ravensbrück
Notes:

Rohe

First Name: Frieda
Birthdate:
Birthplace:

Position: Aufseherin
File Number: IV 409 AR-Z 39/59
Employment Date:
Camp Service: Ravensbrück
Notes:

Rohland
First Name: Klara
Birthdate: June 29, 1919
Birthplace: Gieboldehausen
Position: Aufseherin
File Number: 110 AR 48/93
Employment Date:
Camp Service: Buchenwald; Duderstadt
Notes:

Rohland
First Name: Magdalene
Birthdate: April 24, 1923
Birthplace: Gieboldehausen
Position: Aufseherin
File Number: 110 AR 48/93
Employment Date:
Camp Service: Buchenwald; Duderstadt
Notes:

Rohrbach
First Name: Martha
Birthdate: May 26, 1913
Birthplace: Neurohrbach
Position: Aufseherin
File Number:
Employment Date: September 1, 1944
Camp Service: Groß-Rosen
Notes:

Rosalie (or Rosiwal)
First Name: Maria
Birthdate: 1913
Birthplace:
Position: Aufseherin
File Number: 109 AR-Z 257/89
Employment Date:
Camp Service: Ravensbrück
Notes:

Rose
First Name: Charlotte
Birthdate:
Birthplace:
Position: Aufseherin
File Number: IV 407 AR-Z 174/72
Employment Date:
Camp Service: Stutthof, Bruß-Sophienwalde
Notes:

Rose (born Hermann)
First Name: Erna
Birthdate: Februay 20, 1908
Birthplace: Ibenbueren
Position: Oberaufseherin
File Number: IV 409 AR-Z 39/59
Employment Date:
Camp Service: Ravensbrück
Notes:

Rosenberger
First Name: Marga
Birthdate: June 23, 1923
Birthplace: Plauen
Position: Aufseherin
File Number: IV 410(F) AR 2629/67
Employment Date: September 6, 1944
Camp Service: Ravensbrück, AL Chemnitz
Notes:

Rosenthal
First Name: Erna
Birthdate: October 9, 1921
Birthplace: Steinbeck
Position: Aufseherin
File Number:
Employment Date: July 1, 1944
Camp Service: Groß-Rosen
Notes:

Rotermund
First Name: Elfriede
Birthdate: December 3, 1921
Birthplace: Darmstadt
Position: Aufseherin
File Number:
Employment Date: August 18, 1944
Camp Service: Groß-Rosen
Notes:

Rothe (born Wagenknecht)
First Name: Erna
Birthdate: May 16, 1910
Birthplace: Wolfersdorf
Position: Aufseherin
File Number:
Employment Date: June 1, 1944
Camp Service: Groß-Rosen
Notes:

Rother (born Hellmann)
First Name: Herta
Birthdate: November 24, 1911
Birthplace: Bädnitz
Position: Aufseherin
File Number:
Employment Date: June 1, 1944
Camp Service: Groß-Rosen
Notes:

Rott
First Name: Rosa
Birthdate: February 27, 1923
Birthplace: Platthitz
Position: Aufseherin
File Number: IV 410(F) AR 2629/67
Employment Date: April 1, 1944
Camp Service: Floßenbürg; AL Holleischen
Notes:

Rudelt
First Name: Elfriede
Birthdate: April 26, 1923
Birthplace: Ottendorf
Position: Aufseherin

File Number: IV 410(F) AR 2629/67
Employment Date: September 17, 1944
Camp Service: Floßenbürg; AL Hainichen
Notes:

Rudisch
First Name: Anna
Birthdate: June 8, 1912
Birthplace: Dülken
Position: Aufseherin
File Number:
Employment Date: July 25, 1944
Camp Service: Groß-Rosen
Notes:

Rudisch
First Name: Rosa
Birthdate: June 4, 1914
Birthplace: Mannheim
Position: Aufseherin
File Number:
Employment Date: March 1, 1944
Camp Service: Groß-Rosen
Notes:

Rudlof
First Name: Marin
Birthdate: March 20, 1905
Birthplace: Parschnitz
Position:
File Number:
Employment Date: July 24, 1944
Camp Service: Groß-Rosen
Notes:

Rudolph
First Name: Elfriede
Birthdate: August 31, 1921
Birthplace: Frankenberg
Position: Aufseherin
File Number:
Employment Date: September 8, 1944
Camp Service: Floßenbürg
Notes:

Rudolph
First Name: Gerda
Birthdate: June 30, 1919
Birthplace: Falkenau
Position: Aufseherin
File Number: IV 410(F) AR 2629/67
Employment Date: September 8, 1944
Camp Service: Floßenbürg; AL Oederan
Notes:

Rudolph
First Name: Lieselotte
Birthdate: March 23, 1922
Birthplace: Falkenau
Position: Aufseherin
File Number: IV 410(F) AR 2629/67
Employment Date: August 16, 1944
Camp Service: Floßenbürg; Al Oederan
Notes: Permission for service as an "employee of the Reich" granted on November 21, 1944.

Rück
First Name: Else
Birthdate: April 21, 1904
Birthplace: Heidenheim
Position: Aufseherin
File Number:
Employment Date:
Camp Service: Natzweiler
Notes:

Rüger
First Name: Hildegard
Birthdate: November 21, 1922
Birthplace: Hainichen
Position: Aufseherin
File Number: IV 410(F) AR 2629/67
Employment Date:
Camp Service: Floßenbürg; AL Hainichen
Notes:

Rüger
First Name: Lisa
Birthdate: December 18, 1919
Birthplace: Benisch
Position: Aufseherin
File Number: IV 410(F) AR 2629/67
Employment Date: August 21, 1944
Camp Service: Floßenbürg; AL Plauen; AL Rochlitz
Notes:

Ruf (born Förg)
First Name: Kreszenzia (or Kreszenz)
Birthdate: April 15, 1919
Birthplace: Günzburg
Position: Aufseherin
File Number: 419 AR-Z 173/69
Employment Date:
Camp Service: Natzweiler; Geislingen
Notes:

Ruhmann
First Name: Paula
Birthdate: September 11, 1922
Birthplace: Nuremberg
Position: Aufseherin
File Number: IV 410(F) AR 2629/67
Employment Date: September 30, 1944
Camp Service: Floßenbürg; AL Holleischen
Notes: November 22, 1944

Runge (married Vollrath)
First Name: Elfriede (Else)
Birthdate: January 17, 1920
Birthplace: Fürstenberg
Position: Aufseherin
File Number: IV 402 AR-Z 37/58
Employment Date:
Camp Service: Auschwitz
Notes:

Rupert (or Rupp, Ruppert, Rupperts, or Ruperts)
First Name: Elisabeth (or Käthe)
Birthdate: About 1915 (no month or date noted in her file)
Birthplace:
Position: Aufseherin; Rapportführerin

File Number: 108 AR-Z 458/88
Employment Date:
Camp Service: Auschwitz Birkenau
Notes:

Ruschel
First Name: Maria
Birthdate:
Birthplace:
Position: Aufseherin
File Number: 410 AR 3017/66
Employment Date: March 12, 1945
Camp Service: Floßenbürg; Dresden-Zeiß-Ikon-Goehle-Werk
Notes:

Rust (born Schulz)
First Name: Luise
Birthdate: January 14, 1915
Birthplace: Varel
Position: Aufseherin
File Number: IV 402 AR-Z 37/58
Employment Date:
Camp Service: Auschwitz
Notes:

Ryan (born Braunsteiner)
First Name: Hermine
Birthdate: July 16, 1919
Birthplace: Vienna
Position: Aufseherin
File Number:
Employment Date:
Camp Service: Ravensbrück; Lublin-Majdanek
Notes: Fled poastwar Europe on false D.P. papers and came to the United States. Married an American contractor. West German authorities tracked her down in the early 1970s. Tried in Düsseldorf from 1975-1981 in the Majdanek Trial and sentenced to life imprisonment. Awarded "Kriegsverdienstkreuz II Klassen" in 1943.

Sachse
First Name: Erika
Birthdate: June 10, 1923
Birthplace:
Position: Aufseherin
File Number: IV 410(F) AR 2629/67
Employment Date:
Camp Service: Floßenbürg; AL Chemnitz
Notes:

Sachse
First Name: Gertrud
Birthdate: May 15, 1921
Birthplace: Reichenbach
Position: Aufseherin
File Number: IV 410(F) AR 2629/67
Employment Date: September 9, 1944
Camp Service: Floßenbürg; AL Plauen; AL Chemnitz
Notes:

Sackretz
First Name: Frieda
Birthdate: December 21, 1923
Birthplace: Sergen

Position: Aufseherin
File Number:
Employment Date: November 1, 1942
Camp Service: Ravensbrück
Notes:

Sader
First Name: Elfriede
Birthdate: June 5, 1923
Birthplace: Frankfurt a.d. Oder
Position: Aufseherin
File Number:
Employment Date: August 6, 1944
Camp Service: Groß-Rosen
Notes:

Sadrinna
First Name: Wilhelmina
Birthdate: April 30, 1905
Birthplace: Dortmund
Position: Aufseherin
File Number: IV 429 AR 1964/66 (B)
Employment Date:
Camp Service: Buchenwald; Dortmund
Notes:

Sahm
First Name: Lotte
Birthdate:
Birthplace: Zschopau
Position: Aufseherin
File Number:
Employment Date: September 8, 1944
Camp Service: Floßenbürg
Notes:

Salewski
First Name: Helene
Birthdate: October 10, 1919
Birthplace: Neuteich
Position: Aufseherin
File Number:
Employment Date: June 26, 1944
Camp Service: Ravensbrück
Notes:

Salzinger
First Name: Centa
Birthdate: June 4, 1922
Birthplace: Gangkofen
Position: Aufseherin
File Number: IV 410(F) AR 2629/67
Employment Date:
Camp Service: Floßenbürg; AL Graslitz
Notes:

Salweel
First Name: Anneliese
Birthdate: January 12, 1923
Birthplace: Keller
Position: Aufseherin
File Number: IV 410(F) AR 2629/67
Employment Date:
Camp Service: Floßenbürg; AL Zwodau; AL Holleischen
Notes:

The Camp Women

Sandner

First Name: Käthe
Birthdate: January 6, 1924
Birthplace: Schönbach
Position: Aufseherin
File Number: IV 410(F) AR 2629/67
Employment Date:
Camp Service: Floßenbürg; AL Graslitz
Notes:

Sarisch (born Leder)

First Name: Adelheid
Birthdate: May 8, 1923
Birthplace: Trautenau
Position: Aufseherin
File Number:
Employment Date: April 15, 1944
Camp Service: Groß-Rosen
Notes:

Saroch

First Name: Ingeborg
Birthdate:
Birthplace:
Position: Aufseherin
File Number: IV 410 (F) AR 2629/67
Employment Date:
Camp Service: Floßenbürg; Al Chemnitz
Notes:

Sassnick

First Name: Elfriede
Birthdate: October 12, 1921
Birthplace: Berlin
Position: Aufseherin
File Number:
Employment Date: October 15, 1942
Camp Service: Ravensbrück
Notes:

Sauer

First Name: Irmgard
Birthdate: October 27, 1921
Birthplace: Dresden
Position: Aufseherin
File Number:
Employment Date: October 24, 1944
Camp Service: Floßenbürg
Notes:

Saumann

First Name: Elfriede
Birthdate: August 5, 1921
Birthplace: Dortmund
Position: Aufseherin
File Number:
Employment Date: September 18, 1944
Camp Service: Ravensbrück
Notes:

Saupe

First Name: Margarete
Birthdate: August 13, 1912
Birthplace: Leipzig
Position: Aufseherin

File Number:
Employment Date: July 15, 1944
Camp Service: Ravensbrück
Notes:

Schaal (born Weist)

First Name: Berta
Birthdate: April 18, 1914
Birthplace: Trautenau
Position: Aufseherin
File Number:
Employment Date: March 1, 1944
Camp Service: Groß-Rosen
Notes:

Schachtner (married Glücksmann)

First Name: Hermine
Birthdate: June 19, 1926
Birthplace: Wettzell
Position: Aufseherin; Blockleiterin
File Number: IV 402 AR-Z 37/58
Employment Date:
Camp Service: Auschwitz
Notes:

Schacke

First Name: Rosa
Birthdate: October 3, 1914
Birthplace: Dresden
Position: Aufseherin
File Number:
Employment Date: September 4, 1944
Camp Service: Neuengamme
Notes:

Schadde

First Name: Josepha
Birthdate:
Birthplace:
Position: Aufseherin
File Number:
Employment Date:
Camp Service: Augsburg
Notes:

Schade (born Zeidler)

First Name: Klara
Birthdate: March 3, 1904
Birthplace: Sagan
Position: Aufseherin
File Number:
Employment Date: June 1, 1944
Camp Service: Groß-Rosen
Notes:

Schade

First Name: Margot
Birthdate:
Birthplace:
Position: Aufseherin
File Number: 410 AR 3017/66; 410 AR 3016/66
Employment Date:
Camp Service: Floßenbürg; Zeiß-Ikon-Goehle-Werke-Dresden
Notes:

Schadowski

First Name: Margarete
Birthdate: October 11, 1921
Birthplace: Landeshut
Position: Aufseherin
File Number:
Employment Date: October 3, 1944
Camp Service: Groß-Rosen
Notes:

Schaefer

First Name: Edeltraud
Birthdate: February 20, 1921
Birthplace: Teplitz-Schönau
Position: Aufseherin
File Number:
Employment Date: Septmeber 8, 1944
Camp Service: Floßenbürg
Notes:

Schaefer

First Name: Lutgard
Birthdate: November 20, 1916
Birthplace:
Position: Dienstführerin
File Number: 9 AR 1378/61
Employment Date:
Camp Service: Youth Protective Custody Camp Uckermark
Notes:

Schaefer

First Name: Margarethe
Birthdate: May 2, 1920
Birthplace: Dreihausen
Position: Aufseherin
File Number: IV 429 AR 1821/66 (B)
Employment Date:
Camp Service: Mühlhausen
Notes:

Schaefer

First Name: Martha
Birthdate: July 26, 1909
Birthplace:
Position: Aufseherin
File Number: IV 410 (F) AR 2629/67
Employment Date:
Camp Service: Floßenbürg; Buchenwald
Notes:

Schaeffer

First Name: Ingeborg
Birthdate: December 12, 1921
Birthplace: Berlin
Position: Aufseherin
File Number:
Employment Date: July 22, 1944
Camp Service: Groß-Rosen
Notes:

Schäning

First Name: Ursula
Birthdate: January 28, 1923
Birthplace: Poppendorf
Position: Aufseherin

File Number:
Employment Date: September 10, 1944
Camp Service: Neuengamme
Notes:

Schaps (born Diekow)

First Name: Margarete
Birthdate: July 6, 1905
Birthplace: Swinemünde
Position: Aufseherin
File Number:
Employment Date: August 31, 1944
Camp Service: Ravensbrück
Notes:

Scharf

First Name: Gertrud
Birthdate: September 27, 1923
Birthplace: Liebau
Position: Aufseherin
File Number:
Employment Date: September 29, 1944
Camp Service: Groß-Rosen
Notes:

Scharf

First Name: Marianne
Birthdate:
Birthplace:
Position: Aufseherin
File Number: IV 409 AR-Z 39/59
Employment Date:
Camp Service: Ravensbrück
Notes:

Scharf

First Name: Sophie
Birthdate: January 28, 1923
Birthplace: Erzweiler (Saar)
Position: Aufseherin
File Number:
Employment Date: September 1, 1944
Camp Service:
Notes:

Schart (born Uhla)

First Name: Vincencia
Birthdate: December 11, 1923
Birthplace: Pilnikau
Position: Aufseherin
File Number:
Employment Date: April 15, 1944
Camp Service: Groß-Rosen
Notes:

Schatz

First Name: Hildegard
Birthdate: March 26, 1920
Birthplace: Bromberg
Position: Aufseherin
File Number: IV 410 AR-Z 174/76; IV 410(F) AR 2629/67
Employment Date: November 3, 1943
Camp Service: Floßenbürg; AL Neu Rohlau
Notes:

Schauder

First Name: Magdalene
Birthdate: October 1, 1923
Birthplace: Mersdorf
Position: Aufseherin
File Number:
Employment Date: August 18, 1944
Camp Service: Groß-Rosen
Notes:

Schbesta

First Name: Anna
Birthdate: July 17, 1907
Birthplace: Vienna
Position: Aufseherin
File Number:
Employment Date: October 14, 1944
Camp Service: Ravensbrück; Mauthausen
Notes:

Scheddin

First Name: Gerda
Birthdate: August 12, 1918
Birthplace: Neuehutten
Position: Aufseherin
File Number:
Employment Date: September 1, 1944
Camp Service: Ravensbrück
Notes:

Scheer

First Name: Edda
Birthdate: September 25, 1900
Birthplace: Graz
Position: Aufseherin
File Number:
Employment Date: October 14, 1944
Camp Service: Ravensbrück; Mauthausen
Notes:

Scheffler

First Name: Margarete
Birthdate: April 24, 1920
Birthplace: Weißwasser 0/L
Position: Aufseherin
File Number:
Employment Date: August 18, 1944
Camp Service: Groß-Rosen
Notes:

Schehak

First Name: Hedwig
Birthdate: August 10, 1902
Birthplace: Trautenau
Position: Aufseherin
File Number:
Employment Date: March 1, 1944
Camp Service: Groß-Rosen
Notes:

Scheiblich

First Name: Hildegard
Birthdate: March 26, 1906
Birthplace: Lappine
Position: Aufseherin

File Number:
Employment Date: March 16, 1943
Camp Service: Ravensbrück
Notes:

Scheit

First Name: Elsiabeth
Birthdate: January 7, 1922
Birthplace: Fürth
Position: Aufseherin
File Number:
Employment Date: September 8, 1944
Camp Service: Floßenbürg
Notes:

Schekolin

First Name: Aloisia
Birthdate: May 2, 1922
Birthplace: Mötschendorf
Position: Aufseherin
File Number:
Employment Date: October 14, 1944
Camp Service: Ravenbrück; Mauthausen
Notes:

Schelm (born Garges)

First Name: Rosemarie
Birthdate: April 26, 1921
Birthplace: Hannover
Position: Aufseherin
File Number:
Employment Date: April 15. 1944
Camp Service: Ravensbrück
Notes:

Schenke

First Name: Irene
Birthdate: August 5, 1921
Birthplace: Weißenborn
Position: Aufseherin
File Number:
Employment Date: October 12, 1944
Camp Service: Floßenbürg
Notes:

Scheuerman (born Schmidt)

First Name: Ottilie
Birthdate: September 30, 1913
Birthplace: Mainz
Position: Aufseherin
File Number:
Employment Date: August 30, 1944
Camp Service: Ravensbrück
Notes:

Schettler

First Name: Elli
Birthdate: June 12, 1920
Birthplace: Jabel
Position: Aufseherin
File Number:
Employment Date: November 7, 1944
Camp Service: Ravensbrück
Notes:

Schettler

First Name: Hella
Birthdate: December 8, 1923
Birthplace: Jabel
Position: Aufseherin
File Number:
Employment Date: November 7, 1944
Camp Service: Ravensbrück
Notes: Sister or twins perhaps (two distinct files)?

Schiefersmüller

First Name: Julie
Birthdate: December 14, 1912
Birthplace: Perg O.D.
Position: Aufseherin
File Number:
Employment Date: November 1, 1944
Camp Service: Neuengamme
Notes:

Schiller

First Name: Anneliese
Birthdate:
Birthplace:
Position: Aufseherin
File Number: 409 AR 1482/66
Employment Date:
Camp Service: Neubrandenburg
Notes:

Schimmeier (born Duczuk)

First Name: Anna
Birthdate: April 16, 1911
Birthplace: Flatow
Position: Aufseherin
File Number:
Employment Date: August 25, 1944
Camp Service: Sachsenhausen
Notes:

Schirmbeck

First Name: Johanna
Birthdate: January 20, 1919
Birthplace: Dortmund
Position: Aufseherin
File Number: IV 429 AR-Z 22/74; IV 429 AR-Z 39/59
Employment Date: August 1944
Camp Service: Ravensbrück; Dortmund; Bergen-Belsen
Notes:

Schirmbeck

First Name: Sophie
Birthdate:
Birthplace:
Position: Aufseherin
File Number: IV 410 AR 2960/66
Employment Date:
Camp Service: Floßenbürg; NL Holleischen
Notes:

Schirmer

First Name: Waltraud
Birthdate:
Birthplace:
Position: Aufseherin

File Number: 410 AR 1750/61
Employment Date:
Camp Service: Grünberg
Notes:

Schirmer (married Isner)

First Name: Waltraud
Birthdate: September 21, 1927
Birthplace: Berlin
Position: Wächterin
File Number: 108 AR-Z 550/88
Employment Date:
Camp Service: Floßenbürg
Notes:

Schirrwagen (born Szirnike)

First Name: Ella
Birthdate: December 8, 1916
Birthplace: Usglöcknen (Heidekrug)
Position: Aufseherin
File Number:
Employment Date: September 15, 1944
Camp Service: Ravensbrück; Sachsenhausen
Notes:

Schleipfer

First Name: Gertrud
Birthdate: September 27, 1914
Birthplace: Munich
Position: Aufseherin
File Number:
Employment Date: February 5, 1941
Camp Service: Ravensbrück
Notes:

Schleizer

First Name: Herta
Birthdate: September 12, 1920
Birthplace: Hamburg
Position: Aufseherin
File Number:
Employment Date: September 19, 1944
Camp Service: Groß-Rosen
Notes:

Schlichtherle (born Lutz)

First Name: Kreszenz
Birthdate:
Birthplace:
Position: Aufseherin
File Number: IV 409 AR-Z 78/72
Employment Date:
Camp Service: Ravensbrück
Notes:

Schlichtherrle

First Name: Zenta
Birthdate: August 3, 1918
Birthplace: Augsburg
Position: Aufseherin
File Number:
Employment Date: August 21, 1944
Camp Service: Ravensbrück
Notes:

Schlicke
First Name: Herta
Birthdate: April 6, 1922
Birthplace:
Position: Aufseherin
File Number: IV 410 (F) AR 2629/67
Employment Date:
Camp Service: Floßenbürg; NL Holleischen; AL Freiberg
Notes:

Schlinke
First Name: Erna
Birthdate: September 20, 1923
Birthplace: Duberow or Belgrade
Position: Aufseherin
File Number:
Employment Date:
Camp Service: Ravensbrück; Sachsenhausen
Notes: Ethnic German; born and raised in Slovakia.

Schleunner
First Name: Gerda
Birthdate: January 4, 1916
Birthplace: Grimmitschau (Saxony)
Position: Aufseherin
File Number:
Employment Date:
Camp Service: Sachsenhausen
Notes:

Schlittmeyer
First Name: Therese
Birthdate: April 18, 1915
Birthplace: Bottrop
Position: Aufseherin
File Number:
Employment Date: April 1, 1940
Camp Service: Ravensbrück
Notes:

Schamlisch
First Name: Helene
Birthdate: September 8, 1914
Birthplace: Breslau
Position: Aufseherin
File Number:
Employment Date: August 14, 1944
Camp Service: Groß-Rosen
Notes:

Schmähl
First Name: Meta
Birthdate: January 3, 1922
Birthplace: Buselwitz
Position: Aufseherin
File Number:
Employment Date: December 18, 1944
Camp Service: Ravenbrück
Notes:

Schmeel
First Name: Emma
Birthdate: April 12, 1920
Birthplace: Eberswalde
Position: Aufseherin

File Number:
Employment Date: August 30, 1944
Camp Service: Ravensbrück
Notes:

Schmehl
First Name: Gertrud
Birthdate: April 16, 1918
Birthplace: Lomeitz
Position: Aufseherin
File Number:
Employment Date: June 29, 1944
Camp Service: Groß-Rosen
Notes:

Schmeier
First Name: Helga
Birthdate: January 17, 1922
Birthplace: Berlin
Position: Blockleiterin
File Number:
Employment Date: November 13, 1944
Camp Service: Sachsenhausen
Notes:

Schmeißer
First Name: Else
Birthdate: August 18, 1916
Birthplace: Wolfenbüttel
Position: Aufseherin
File Number: 409 AR 2488/66
Employment Date:
Camp Service: Sachsenhausen
Notes:

Schmelter
First Name: Edith
Birthdate: December 12, 1922
Birthplace:
Position: Aufseherin
File Number: IV 429 AR 1957/66 (B)
Employment Date:
Camp Service: Ravensbrück; Sömmerda
Notes:

Schmette
First Name: Gertrud
Birthdate: March 5, 1923
Birthplace: Dittersbach
Position: Aufseherin
File Number:
Employment Date: September 2, 1944
Camp Service: Groß-Rosen
Notes:

Schmidt
First Name: Anna
Birthdate: November 20, 1921
Birthplace: Dürnberg
Position: Aufseherin; Erstaufseherin
File Number: IV 410(F) AR 2629/67
Employment Date:
Camp Service: Floßenbürg, AL Holleischen, AL Graslitz
Notes:

Schmidt

First Name: Brungard
Birthdate: July 7, 1923
Birthplace: Michalssakuten
Position: Aufseherin
File Number:
Employment Date: July 10, 1944
Camp Service: Ravensbrück
Notes:

Schmidt (born Koblitz)

First Name: Elfriede
Birthdate: 1924 (no month or day noted)
Birthplace:
Position: Aufseherin
File Number: IV 405 AR-Z 223/74
Employment Date:
Camp Service: Groß-Rosen; NL Sackisch
Notes:

Schmidt (born Waschwill)

First Name: Else (Maria)
Birthdate: February 4, 1923
Birthplace: Essen-Borbeck
Position: Aufseherin
File Number: IV 429 AR 1973/66 (B)
Employment Date:
Camp Service: Ravensbrück; NL Sömmerda;
NL Gelsenkirchhen; Buchenwald
Notes:

Schmidt

First Name: Erna
Birthdate: June 3, 1922
Birthplace: Nuremberg
Position: Aufseherin
File Number: IV 410(F) AR 2629/67; IV 409 AR-Z 39/59
Employment Date:
Camp Service: Floßenbürg; Kommando Helmbrechts
Notes: File notes that she was an "employee of the Reich" since July 10, 1944; served as a Waffen-SS auxiliary.

Schmidt

First Name: Frieda
Birthdate: November 2, 1922
Birthplace: Peterswaldau
Position: Aufseherin
File Number:
Employment Date: March 1, 1944
Camp Service: Groß-Rosen
Notes:

Schmidt

First Name: Hedwig
Birthdate: October 15, 1908
Birthplace: Oppeln
Position: Aufseherin
File Number:
Employment Date: August 18, 1944
Camp Service: Groß-Rosen
Notes:

Schmidt

First Name: Herta
Birthdate: June 23, 1914
Birthplace: Markersdorf
Position: Aufseherin
File Number:
Employment Date: November 2, 1944
Camp Service: Groß-Rosen
Notes:

Schmidt

First Name: Hildegard
Birthdate: March 30, 1921
Birthplace: Breslau
Position: Aufseherin
File Number:
Employment Date: June 1, 1944
Camp Service: Ravensbrück
Notes:

Schmidt (married Broders)

First Name: Ilse
Birthdate: May 22, 1923
Birthplace: Heide
Position: Aufseherin
File Number: IV 410(F) AR 2629/67
Employment Date:
Camp Service: Floßenbürg; AL Wolkenburg; NL Zwodau
Notes:

Schmidt

First Name: Irmgard
Birthdate: March 13, 1918
Birthplace: Leipzig
Position: Aufseherin
File Number:
Employment Date: July 2, 1944
Camp Service: Ravensbrück
Notes:

Schmidt

First Name: Johanna
Birthdate: September 18, 1921
Birthplace: Friedland
Position: Aufseherin
File Number:
Employment Date: September 1, 1944
Camp Service: Groß-Rosen
Notes:

Schmidt

First Name: Lieselotte
Birthdate:
Birthplace:
Position: Aufseherin
File Number: IV 429 AR 1821/66 (B)
Employment Date:
Camp Service: Ravensbrück
Notes:

Schmidt

First Name: Margarete
Birthdate: December 2, 1914
Birthplace: Zilnisdorf
Position: Aufseherin

File Number:
Employment Date:　October 12, 1944
Camp Service:　Groß-Rosen
Notes:

Schmidt (born Seidl or Seidel)
First Name:　Margarete
Birthdate:　May 5, 1922
Birthplace:　Hapersbirk-Falkenau
Position:　Aufseherin
File Number:　410 AR 2960/66
Employment Date:　1940 (no day and month not noted in her file).
Camp Service:　Floßenbürg; Holleischen
Notes:

Schmidt
First Name:　Maria
Birthdate:　March 14, 1918
Birthplace:　Freudenstein
Position:　Aufseherin
File Number:
Employment Date:　September 1, 1944
Camp Service:　Sachsenhausen
Notes:

Schmidt
First Name:　Marianne
Birthdate:　February 6, 1922
Birthplace:
Position:　Aufseherin
File Number:　IV 410 (F) AR 2629/67
Employment Date:
Camp Service:　Floßenbürg; Holleischen
Notes:

Schmidt
First Name:　Marta
Birthdate:
Birthplace:
Position:　Aufseherin
File Number:　IV 429 AR 1821/66 (B)
Employment Date:
Camp Service:　Ravensbrück
Notes:

Schmidt
First Name:　Marta
Birthdate:　January 31, 1917
Birthplace:　Camin
Position:　Aufseherin
File Number:
Employment Date:　August 31, 1944
Camp Service:　Groß-Rosen
Notes:

Schmidt
First Name:　Martha
Birthdate:　June 18, 1923
Birthplace:　Kreblitz
Position:　Aufseherin
File Number:
Employment Date:　October 12, 1944
Camp Service:　Ravensbrück; Sachsenhausen
Notes:

Schmidt
First Name:　Renate
Birthdate:　October 28, 1923
Birthplace:　Olila
Position:　Aufseherin
File Number:
Employment Date:　September 8, 1944
Camp Service:　Ravensbrück
Notes:

Schmidt
First Name:　Rosa
Birthdate:　October 15, 1900
Birthplace:　Trautenau
Position:　Aufseherin: Waffen SS
File Number:
Employment Date:　March 1, 1944
Camp Service:　Groß-Rosen
Notes:

Schmidt
First Name:　Rosa
Birthdate:　August 30, 1913
Birthplace:　Nuremberg
Position:　Aufseherin
File Number:　IV 409 AR-Z 39/59
Employment Date:
Camp Service:　Floßenbürg; Kommando Helmbrechts; Ravensbrück
Notes:　File notes that she was a member of the *Totenkopfverbände* (Death Head units) since July 10, 1944.

Schmidtke
First Name:　Hildegard
Birthdate:　May 7, 1917
Birthplace:　Gorz
Position:　Aufseherin
File Number:
Employment Date:　August 1, 1944
Camp Service:　Groß-Rosen
Notes:

Schmied
First Name:　Hermine
Birthdate:　July 23, 1920
Birthplace:　Freistadt
Position:　Aufseherin
File Number:
Employment Date:　September 15, 1944
Camp Service:　Ravensbrück; Mauthausen
Notes:

Schmiedel (born Sturbert)
First Name:　Charlotte
Birthdate:　May 16, 1904
Birthplace:　Leipzig
Position:　Aufseherin
File Number:
Employment Date:　August 14, 1944
Camp Service:　Ravensbrück
Notes:

Schmogro

First Name: Frieda
Birthdate: May 12, 1913
Birthplace: Wernersdorf
Position: Aufseherin
File Number:
Employment Date: October 3, 1944
Camp Service: Groß-Rosen
Notes:

Schmolawe

First Name: Hella
Birthdate: April 28, 1907
Birthplace: Groß Schmograu
Position: Aufseherin
File Number:
Employment Date: September 3, 1944
Camp Service: Groß-Rosen
Notes:

Schneemann

First Name: Anneliese
Birthdate: April 8, 1920
Birthplace: Theisen
Position: Aufseherin
File Number:
Employment Date: November 29, 1944
Camp Service: Ravensbrück
Notes:

Schneider

First Name: Berta
Birthdate: October 26, 1898
Birthplace: Rudelstadt
Position: Aufseherin
File Number:
Employment Date: July 27, 1944
Camp Service: Groß-Rosen
Notes:

Schneider

First Name: Erna
Birthdate: April 10, 1916
Birthplace: Waldenburg
Position: Aufseherin
File Number:
Employment Date: August 8, 1944
Camp Service: Groß-Rosen
Notes:

Schneider (born Fuhrmann)

First Name: Friederike (Friedel)
Birthdate: September 30, 1911
Birthplace: Vienna
Position: Aufseherin; Blockführerin
File Number: IV 402 AR-Z 37/58; STA Wien 15 St 12.079/
64; 9-4/61
Employment Date:
Camp Service: Auschwitz; NL Babice (Babitz); Auschwitz-
Birkenau; Ravensbrück; Holleischen
Notes:

Schneider

First Name: Hedwig
Birthdate: May 19, 1923
Birthplace: Kamenz
Position: Aufseherin
File Number:
Employment Date: September 7, 1944
Camp Service: Groß-Rosen
Notes:

Schneider

First Name: Irmgard
Birthdate: October 23, 1923
Birthplace: Eberswalde
Position: Aufseherin
File Number:
Employment Date: November 10, 1944
Camp Service: Ravensbrück
Notes:

Schneider

First Name: Margarete
Birthdate: November 16, 1915
Birthplace: Langenbielau
Position: Aufseherin
File Number:
Employment Date: April 15, 1944
Camp Service: Groß-Rosen
Notes:

Schneider

First Name: Maria
Birthdate: December 13, 1921
Birthplace: Düren
Position: Aufseherin
File Number:
Employment Date: August 8, 1944
Camp Service: Sachsenhausen
Notes:

Schneider (married Schotte)

First Name: Marianne
Birthdate: July 10, 1917
Birthplace: Dresden
Position: Aufseherin
File Number: IV 410(F) AR 2629/67
Employment Date:
Camp Service: Floßenbürg; AL Dresden; Zeiß-Ikon-Werk
Dresden; Holleischen
Notes:

Schneider

First Name: Marianne
Birthdate: July 19, 1919
Birthplace: Dresden
Position: Aufseherin
File Number: IV 410 AR- 3016/66
Employment Date:
Camp Service: AL Dresden Reick
Notes:

Schneider

First Name: Ursula
Birthdate: December 14, 1922
Birthplace: Berlin

Position: Aufseherin
File Number:
Employment Date: September 8, 1944
Camp Service: Ravensbrück; Sachsenhausen
Notes:

Schöber
First Name: Gertrud
Birthdate: May 1, 1916
Birthplace: Leipzig
Position: Aufseherin
File Number:
Employment Date: December 1, 1942
Camp Service: Ravensbrück
Notes:

Schöler
First Name: Herta
Birthdate: January 9, 1921
Birthplace: Westwalde
Position: Aufseherin
File Number:
Employment Date: September 5, 1944
Camp Service: Groß-Rosen
Notes:

Schöler
First Name: Marie
Birthdate: November 26, 1905
Birthplace: Tettendorf
Position: Aufseherin
File Number:
Employment Date: August 25, 1944
Camp Service: Groß-Rosen
Notes:

Schön
First Name: Dora
Birthdate:
Birthplace: Grüneberg
Position: Kommandoführerin
File Number: 10 AR 1750/61
Employment Date:
Camp Service: Helmbrechts; Kommando Helmbrechts
Notes:

Schön
First Name: Maria
Birthdate:
Birthplace:
Position: Aufseherin
File Number: IV 409 AR-Z 39/59
Employment Date:
Camp Service: Ravensbrück
Notes:

Schönebeck
First Name: Ella
Birthdate: July 12, 1912
Birthplace: Geestgottberg
Position: Aufseherin
File Number:
Employment Date: April 1, 1944
Camp Service: Ravensbrück
Notes:

Schöps (born Grüning)
First Name: Käthe
Birthdate: November 5, 1914
Birthplace: Rosenheim
Position: Aufseherin
File Number:
Employment Date: September 11, 1944
Camp Service: Ravensbrück
Notes:

Schollmeyer
First Name: Anni
Birthdate: April 2, 1923
Birthplace: Dortmund
Position: Aufseherin
File Number:
Employment Date: September 18, 1944
Camp Service: Ravensbrück
Notes:

Scholz
First Name: Ida
Birthdate:
Birthplace:
Position: Aufseherin
File Number: IV 405 AR 2796/67
Employment Date:
Camp Service: NL Gräben
Notes:

Scholze
First Name: Maria
Birthdate: October 11, 1911
Birthplace:
Position: Aufseherin
File Number: IV 410(F) AR 2629/67
Employment Date:
Camp Service: Floßenbürg; AL Hertine
Notes:

Schot
First Name: Catharina
Birthdate: March 15, 1925
Birthplace: Amsterdam
Position: Aufseherin
File Number:
Employment Date: May 17, 1944
Camp Service: Ravensbrück
Notes: Dutch national; granted special permission to serve as an "employee of the Reich."

Schott
First Name: Elfriede
Birthdate: March 9, 1922
Birthplace: Wetter
Position: Aufseherin
File Number: IV 429 AR 1821/66 (B)
Employment Date:
Camp Service: Ravensbrück; Allendorf; Behring-Werke Marburg
Notes:

Schrank
First Name: Anna
Birthdate: September 28, 1921

Birthplace: Schönau
Position: Aufseherin
File Number:
Employment Date: November 1, 1943
Camp Service: Ravensbrück
Notes:

Schrank

First Name: Frieda
Birthdate: March 10, 1911
Birthplace: Berlin
Position: Aufseherin
File Number:
Employment Date: August 1, 1944
Camp Service: Ravensbrück
Notes:

Schreiber

First Name: Maria
Birthdate: January 9, 1921
Birthplace: Lichtewerden
Position: Aufseherin
File Number:
Employment Date:
Camp Service: Auschwitz III (Buna Monowitz)
Notes:

Schreiber

First Name: Marta
Birthdate: April 12, 1905
Birthplace: Wils
Position: Aufseherin
File Number:
Employment Date: June 15, 1940
Camp Service: Ravensbrück
Notes:

Schreiter (born Kaufmann?)

First Name: Gertrud
Birthdate: December 27, 1912
Birthplace: Berlin
Position: Aufseherin
File Number:
Employment Date:
Camp Service: Ravensbrück
Notes: Tried and executed by the British on September 28, 1948.

Schrenk

First Name: Hermine
Birthdate: May 11, 1924
Birthplace: Heufurt
Position: Aufseherin
File Number:
Employment Date: July 6, 1943
Camp Service: Ravensbrück
Notes:

Schreyer

First Name: Marie
Birthdate: July 24, 1920
Birthplace: Horn
Position: Aufseherin
File Number:

Employment Date: June 23, 1944
Camp Service: Ravenbrück
Notes:

Schröder

First Name: Emmi
Birthdate: January 14, 1923
Birthplace: Streelitz-Alt
Position: Aufseherin
File Number:
Employment Date: October 12, 1944
Camp Service: Ravensbrück
Notes:

Schröder

First Name: Klara
Birthdate: November 18, 1899
Birthplace: Heuhof (Mecklenburg)
Position: Aufseherin
File Number: IV 410(F) AR 2629/67
Employment Date: 1944 (no month and day noted in her file).
Camp Service: Floßenbürg; AL Plauen; AL Zwodau
Notes:

Schröder (born Falk)

First Name: Margarete
Birthdate: May 2, 1923
Birthplace: Magdeburg
Position: Aufseherin
File Number:
Employment Date: September 14, 1944
Camp Service: Ravensbrück
Notes:

Schröers

First Name: Irmgard
Birthdate: May 31, 1883
Birthplace: Kochem
Position: Aufseherin
File Number:
Employment Date: January 1, 1938
Camp Service: Ravensbrück
Notes:

Schröter

First Name: Helene
Birthdate:
Birthplace:
Position: Aufseherin
File Number: IV 409 AR-Z 39/59
Employment Date:
Camp Service: Ravensbrück
Notes:

Schubert

First Name: Gisela
Birthdate: May 3, 1909
Birthplace:
Position: Aufseherin
File Number: IV 410(F) AR 2629/67
Employment Date:
Camp Service: Floßenbürg; AL Zwodau; Groß-Rosen
Notes:

Schubert

First Name: Liesbeth
Birthdate: March 28, 1909
Birthplace: Plauen
Position: Aufseherin
File Number: IV 410(F) AR 2629/67
Employment Date:
Camp Service: Floßenbürg; AL Chemnitz; NL Mehltheuer
Notes:

Schubert

First Name: Ruth
Birthdate: February 23, 1903
Birthplace: Leuchten
Position: Aufseherin
File Number:
Employment Date: August 4, 1944
Camp Service: Groß-Rosen
Notes: Captured by Soviet forces and ostensibly taken to a *gulag*; fate unknown.

Schüller

First Name: Gertrud
Birthdate:
Birthplace:
Position: Aufseherin
File Number: IV 409 AR-Z 39/59
Employment Date:
Camp Service: Ravensbrück; Meuselwitz
Notes:

Schueoer

First Name: Frieda
Birthdate: May 2, 1912
Birthplace: Berlin
Position: Aufseherin
File Number:
Employment Date: September 1, 1944
Camp Service: Ravensbrück; Sachsenhausen
Notes:

Schümann (married Ungewiß)

First Name: Ruth
Birthdate: October 12, 1920
Birthplace: Berlin
Position: Aufseherin
File Number: IV 409 AR-Z 39/59; IV 409 AR 1483/66
Employment Date:
Camp Service: Ravensbrück; NL Malchow
Notes: Allegedly had been sentenced to death in 1949 by a French court in Rastatt, but in 1969 she was also brought before a Polish proceeding for war crimes. It is likely that her French sentence was commuted and she was eventually released.

Schüneke

First Name: Elfriede
Birthdate: August 24, 1919
Birthplace: Paray
Position: Aufseherin
File Number:
Employment Date: October 17, 1944
Camp Service: Ravensbrück
Notes:

Schüßler

First Name: Hilde
Birthdate: Sometime in 1910
Birthplace: Probably Glöven; questioned in personnel file.
Position: Is alleged to have been an Oberaufseherin of a Sachsenhausen subcamp.
File Number: IV 406 AR 745/67
Employment Date:
Camp Service: Sachsenhausen
Notes:

Schütt

First Name: Anneliese
Birthdate: November 21, 1921
Birthplace: Rostock
Position: Aufseherin
File Number:
Employment Date: June 1, 1943
Camp Service: Ravensbrück
Notes:

Schultheis

First Name: Margarete
Birthdate: June 27, 1922
Birthplace: Gimbweiler (Birkenfeld)
Position: Aufseherin
File Number:
Employment Date: July 3, 1944
Camp Service: Sachsenhausen
Notes:

Schult

First Name: Maria
Birthdate: March 10, 1920
Birthplace: Admannshagen
Position: Aufseherin
File Number:
Employment Date: November 1, 1944
Camp Service: Ravensbrück
Notes:

Schultz

First Name: Elfriede
Birthdate: October 7, 1922
Birthplace: Hamburg
Position: Aufseherin
File Number:
Employment Date: July 13, 1944
Camp Service: Ravensbrück
Notes:

Schulz

First Name: Elfriede
Birthdate: December 23, 1921
Birthplace: Mönchsdorf
Position: Aufseherin
File Number: IV 410(F) AR 2629/67
Employment Date:
Camp Service: Floßenbürg; AL Plauen
Notes:

Schulz

First Name: Elisabeth
Birthdate: April 19, 1923
Birthplace: Schwerin

Position: Aufseherin
File Number:
Employment Date: September 16, 1944
Camp Service: Ravensbrück; Sachsenhausen
Notes:

Schulz
First Name: Ella
Birthdate: August 27, 1901
Birthplace: Hamburg
Position: Aufseherin
File Number: 40-2/3; JAG 276
Employment Date:
Camp Service: Fuhlsbüttel; Hamburg
Notes: Worked for the Gestapo since 1935; was sentenced to seven years imprisonment by the British on November 3, 1947 for maltreatment of prisoners, but was released after only four years.

Schulz
First Name: Gerda
Birthdate: February 5, 1920
Birthplace: Berlin
Position: Aufseherin
File Number:
Employment Date: November 13, 1944
Camp Service: Sachsenhausen
Notes:

Schulz
First Name: Margarete
Birthdate: March 19, 1918
Birthplace:
Position: Aufseherin
File Number:
Employment Date:
Camp Service:
Notes:

Schulze
First Name: Elisabeth
Birthdate: April 29, 1921
Birthplace: Wittstock a.d. Doße
Position: Aufseherin
File Number:
Employment Date: September 1, 1944
Camp Service: Sachsenhausen
Notes:

Schulze
First Name: Ilse
Birthdate: December 8, 1921
Birthplace: Zinnberg
Position: Aufseherin
File Number: IV 410 (F) AR 2629/67
Employment Date:
Camp Service: Floßenbürg; AL Rochlitz
Notes:

Schulze
First Name: Maria
Birthdate: June 19, 1922
Birthplace: Sangerhausen
Position: Aufseherin

File Number: IV 410(F) AR 2629/67
Employment Date:
Camp Service: Floßenbürg; AL Wolkenburg
Notes:

Schumacher (born Kubatha)
First Name: Annemarie
Birthdate: May 24, 1912
Birthplace: Pleß
Position: Aufseherin
File Number:
Employment Date: June 15, 1944
Camp Service: Ravensbrück
Notes:

Schumacher
First Name: Erika
Birthdate: March 1, 1922
Birthplace: Hohenlychen
Position: Aufseherin
File Number:
Employment Date: November 20, 1944
Camp Service: Ravensbrück
Notes:

Schumann
First Name: Elli
Birthdate:
Birthplace:
Position: Aufseherin
File Number: 409 AR 1482/66
Employment Date:
Camp Service:
Notes:

Schupan
First Name: Margarete
Birthdate: January 11, 1923
Birthplace: Ellingen
Position: Aufseherin
File Number:
Employment Date: August 28, 1944
Camp Service: Ravensbrück
Notes:

Schurr
First Name: Bertha
Birthdate:
Birthplace:
Position: Aufseherin
File Number: IV 402 AR-Z 37/58
Employment Date:
Camp Service: Auschwitz
Notes: Accused of beating inmates while they were eating.

Schuster
First Name: Anna
Birthdate:
Birthplace:
Position: Aufseherin
File Number: IV 414 AR-Z 3/65
Employment Date: November 1941 (day not noted in her file)
Camp Service: Ravensbrück; Auschwitz
Notes:

Schuster

First Name:	Hildegard
Birthdate:	November 14, 1912
Birthplace:	Berlin
Position:	Aufseherin
File Number:	
Employment Date:	September 1, 1939
Camp Service:	Ravensbrück
Notes:	

Schuster

First Name:	Johanna
Birthdate:	May 26, 1920
Birthplace:	Wintersdorf
Position:	Aufseherin
File Number:	
Employment Date:	August 15, 1944
Camp Service:	Sachsenhausen
Notes:	

Schuster (born Dillinger)

First Name:	Josefa
Birthdate:	September 20, 1921
Birthplace:	Augsburg
Position:	Aufseherin
File Number:	
Employment Date:	March 1942
Camp Service:	Ravensbrück; NL Feldenmark; NL Grüneberg-Nordbahn
Notes:	

Schwab

First Name:	Rosa
Birthdate:	
Birthplace:	
Position:	Aufseherin
File Number:	IV 409 AR-Z 39/59
Employment Date:	
Camp Service:	Ravensbrück
Notes:	

Schwabe

First Name:	Hildegard
Birthdate:	September 24, 1922
Birthplace:	Oranienburg
Position:	Aufseherin
File Number:	
Employment Date:	June 23, 1944
Camp Service:	
Notes:	

Schwalm

First Name:	Ruth
Birthdate:	September 27, 1921
Birthplace:	Schwerte
Position:	Aufseherin
File Number:	
Employment Date:	September 18, 1944
Camp Service:	Ravensbrück
Notes:	

Schwartz

First Name:	Erika
Birthdate:	June 19, 1919
Birthplace:	Heilugenhaus
Position:	Aufseherin
File Number:	
Employment Date:	November 14, 1944
Camp Service:	Ravensbrück
Notes:	

Schwartze (married Kettner)

First Name:	Hedwig
Birthdate:	May 13, 1920
Birthplace:	Sömmerda
Position:	Aufseherin
File Number:	IV 429 AR-Z 51/70
Employment Date:	
Camp Service:	NL Allendorf
Notes:	

Schwarz (born Latusch)

First Name:	Meta
Birthdate:	April 19, 1920
Birthplace:	Kloßow
Position:	Aufseherin
File Number:	
Employment Date:	August 15, 1944
Camp Service:	Ravensbrück
Notes:	

Schwarzkopf

First Name:	Ida
Birthdate:	August 30, 1913
Birthplace:	Giebersleben
Position:	Aufseherin
File Number:	
Employment Date:	October 1, 1942
Camp Service:	Ravensbrück
Notes:	

Schwidder

First Name:	Charlotte
Birthdate:	September 2, 1922
Birthplace:	Ottsch-Heide
Position:	Aufseherin
File Number:	
Employment Date:	September 16, 1944
Camp Service:	Ravensbrück
Notes:	

Scxesny (or Sczesny)

First Name:	Vera
Birthdate:	July 16, 1920
Birthplace:	Berlin
Position:	Aufseherin
File Number:	IV 410(F) AR 2629/67
Employment Date:	
Camp Service:	Floßenbürg; AL Graslitz
Notes:	

Sebastian

First Name:	Margarete
Birthdate:	April 26, 1909
Birthplace:	Guben
Position:	Aufseherin
File Number:	
Employment Date:	July 21, 1944
Camp Service:	Groß-Rosen
Notes:	

Sedlacek
First Name: Editha
Birthdate: December 28, 1909
Birthplace: Rosenthal
Position: Aufseherin
File Number:
Employment Date: August 30, 1944
Camp Service: Ravensbrück
Notes:

Seeman
First Name: Gertrud
Birthdate: July 19, 1918
Birthplace: Wittenberg
Position: Aufseherin
File Number:
Employment Date: April 1, 1944
Camp Service: Ravensbrück
Notes:

Seibt
First Name: Gerda
Birthdate: April 29, 1913
Birthplace: Berlin
Position: Aufseherin
File Number:
Employment Date: November 20, 1944
Camp Service: Ravenbrück
Notes:

Seidl (or Seidel)
First Name: Paula
Birthdate: June 1, 1923
Birthplace: Bleistadt
Position: Aufseherin
File Number: IV 410 (F) AR 2629/67
Employment Date:
Camp Service: Floßenbürg; AL Zwodau
Notes:

Seidel
First Name: Elfriede
Birthdate: April 24, 1921
Birthplace: Lichtewerden
Position: Aufseherin
File Number:
Employment Date:
Camp Service: Auschwitz III (Buna Monowitz)
Notes:

Seidel
First Name: Ella
Birthdate: October 3, 1909
Birthplace: Rebesgruen
Position: Aufseherin
File Number:
Employment Date: September 7, 1944
Camp Service: Floßenbürg
Notes:

Seidel (born Ohlig)
First Name: Frieda
Birthdate: June 3, 1902
Birthplace: Standorf
Position: Aufseherin

File Number:
Employment Date: June 1, 1944
Camp Service: Groß-Rosen
Notes:

Seidel
First Name: Helga
Birthdate: August 1, 1922
Birthplace: Mähr. Rothwasser
Position: Aufseherin
File Number:
Employment Date: November 5, 1944
Camp Service: Groß-Rosen
Notes:

Seidel
First Name: Margarethe
Birthdate: May 5, 1922
Birthplace: Härspirk
Position: Aufseherin
File Number:
Employment Date: April 1, 1944
Camp Service: Floßenbürg
Notes:

Seifert
First Name: Else
Birthdate: May 8, 1913
Birthplace: Linda
Position: Aufseherin
File Number: IV 410 (F) AR 2629/67
Employment Date:
Camp Service: Floßenbürg; AL Holleischen; AL Oederan
Notes:

Seifert
First Name: Ilse
Birthdate:
Birthplace:
Position: Aufseherin
File Number: IV 429 AR 1973/66 (B)
Employment Date:
Camp Service: Lippstadt
Notes:

Seifert
First Name: Linda
Birthdate: January 29, 1908
Birthplace: Dorfstadt
Position: Aufseherin
File Number:
Employment Date: September 7, 1944
Camp Service: Ravenbrück
Notes:

Seinwill
First Name: Grete
Birthdate: February 17, 1921
Birthplace: Tubschen
Position: Aufseherin
File Number:
Employment Date: November 23, 1944
Camp Service: Ravensbrück
Notes: Possibly the same as Lotte Seinwill.

Seinwill

First Name: Lotte
Birthdate: February 17, 1921
Birthplace: Tubschen
Position: Aufseherin
File Number:
Employment Date: November 23, 1944
Camp Service: Ravensbrück
Notes: Possibly the same as Grete Seinwill.

Seiß (married Tilp)

First Name: Johanna
Birthdate: July 26, 1920
Birthplace: Bad Köstritz
Position: Lageraufseherin
File Number: 110 AR 1350/93
Employment Date: 1944 (month and day not noted in her file)
Camp Service: Allendorf; Luderstadt; Siemens-Werk Gera
Notes:

Seliger

First Name: Johanna
Birthdate: October 6, 1922
Birthplace: Breslau
Position: Aufseherin
File Number:
Employment Date: September 20, 1944
Camp Service: Groß-Rosen
Notes:

Sell (married Marbach)

First Name: Irmtraut
Birthdate: May 20, 1923
Birthplace: Kyritz
Position: Aufseherin
File Number: IV 429 AR 1821/66 (B)
Employment Date:
Camp Service: Buchenwald; Allendorf
Notes: According to her file, she had been a member of the *Totenkopfverbände* (Death Head's units) since September 1944.

Seltmann

First Name: Ursula
Birthdate: April 30, 1918
Birthplace: Lucka
Position: Aufseherin
File Number:
Employment Date: September 5, 1944
Camp Service: Ravenbrück
Notes:

Semmler

First Name: Hertha
Birthdate:
Birthplace:
Position: Aufseherin
File Number: IV 409 AR-Z 39/59
Employment Date:
Camp Service: Ravensbrück
Notes:

Semper

First Name: Helene
Birthdate: September 14, 1920

Birthplace: Friedrichshain
Position: Aufseherin
File Number:
Employment Date: October 30, 1944
Camp Service: Groß-Rosen
Notes:

Senftleben

First Name: Erna
Birthdate: February 14, 1920
Birthplace: Lippen
Position: Aufseherin
File Number:
Employment Date: June 1, 1944
Camp Service: Groß-Rosen
Notes:

Seuß (born Baptist)

First Name: Gunda
Birthdate: November 13, 1921
Birthplace:
Position: Aufseherin
File Number: IV 406 AR-Z 21/71
Employment Date:
Camp Service: NL Genshagen
Notes:

Seyringer

First Name: Rosa
Birthdate: July 10, 1922
Birthplace: Schwertberg
Position: Aufseherin
File Number:
Employment Date: November 1, 1944
Camp Service: Mauthausen
Notes:

Sgoll

First Name: Hildegard
Birthdate: September 10, 1921
Birthplace: Berlin
Position: Aufseherin
File Number:
Employment Date: October 5, 1944
Camp Service: Groß-Rosen
Notes:

Sichhardt

First Name: Inge
Birthdate: May 6, 1922
Birthplace: Berlin
Position: Aufseherin
File Number:
Employment Date: March 1, 1942
Camp Service: Ravensbrück
Notes:

Sickroth

First Name: Gertrud
Birthdate: December 2, 1921
Birthplace: Erfurt
Position: Aufseherin
File Number:
Employment Date: January 21, 1944
Camp Service: Ravensbrück
Notes:

Sieber

First Name:	Gertrud
Birthdate:	March 31, 1929
Birthplace:	Bobernick
Position:	Aufseherin
File Number:	
Employment Date:	May 2, 1944
Camp Service:	Groß-Rosen
Notes:	Youngest female to serve as an Aufseherin (15 years old at induction). Gertrud and Margarete Sieber are sisters.

Sieber

First Name:	Helga
Birthdate:	December 8, 1919
Birthplace:	Grünberg
Position:	Aufseherin
File Number:	
Employment Date:	June 1944
Camp Service:	Groß-Rosen
Notes:	

Sieber

First Name:	Margarete
Birthdate:	June 28, 1922
Birthplace:	Bobernick
Position:	Aufseherin
File Number:	
Employment Date:	June 1, 1944
Camp Service:	Groß-Rosen
Notes:	

Siefert

First Name:	Irmgard
Birthdate:	September 18, 1923
Birthplace:	Eisenach
Position:	Aufseherin
File Number:	
Employment Date:	January 28, 1944
Camp Service:	Ravensbrück
Notes:	

Sieger

First Name:	Rosa
Birthdate:	August 30, 1910
Birthplace:	Königshau
Position:	Aufseherin
File Number:	
Employment Date:	March 1, 1944
Camp Service:	Groß-Rosen
Notes:	

Siegert (born Diflo)

First Name:	Eleonore
Birthdate:	November 18, 1913
Birthplace:	Mainz
Position:	Aufseherin
File Number:	
Employment Date:	August 31, 1944
Camp Service:	Ravensbrück
Notes:	

Siegert

First Name:	Maria
Birthdate:	May 29, 1921
Birthplace:	Neustadt
Position:	Aufseherin
File Number:	IV 410 (F) AR 2629/67
Employment Date:	October 1, 1942
Camp Service:	Floßenbürg; AL Zwodau
Notes:	

Siegler

First Name:	Johanna
Birthdate:	May 11, 1923
Birthplace:	Eisendorf
Position:	Aufseherin
File Number:	IV 410(F) AR 2629/67
Employment Date:	1944
Camp Service:	Floßenbürg; AL Holleischen
Notes:	

Sieler

First Name:	Hanna
Birthdate:	March 16, 1920
Birthplace:	
Position:	Aufseherin
File Number:	IV 410(F) AR 2629/67
Employment Date:	
Camp Service:	Floßenbürg; AL Chemnitz
Notes:	

Sieler

First Name:	Anneliese
Birthdate:	October 20, 1923
Birthplace:	Chemnitz
Position:	Aufseherin
File Number:	IV 410 (F) AR 2629/67
Employment Date:	1944
Camp Service:	Floßenbürg; AL Astrawerke Chemnitz
Notes:	

Siepmann

First Name:	Therese
Birthdate:	October 14, 1919
Birthplace:	Bochum
Position:	Aufseherin
File Number:	IV 409 AR-Z 78/72
Employment Date:	August 22, 1944
Camp Service:	Ravensbrück
Notes:	

Sievers

First Name:	Hildegard
Birthdate:	February 20, 1912
Birthplace:	Halstenbeck
Position:	Aufseherin
File Number:	
Employment Date:	July 17, 1944
Camp Service:	Ravensbrück
Notes:	

Simon

First Name:	Paula
Birthdate:	
Birthplace:	
Position:	Aufseherin
File Number:	IV 410 AR 3039/66
Employment Date:	
Camp Service:	NL Mehltheuer; NL Venusberg
Notes:	

Simon (married Walz)

First Name: Paula
Birthdate: January 30, 1921
Birthplace: Hamburg or Homburg
Position: Aufseherin
File Number: IV 410(F) AR 2629/67
Employment Date: 1944
Camp Service: Floßenbürg; AL Zwodau
Notes:

Skarbath

First Name: Rosa
Birthdate: July 12, 1914
Birthplace:
Position: Aufseherin
File Number: IV 429 AR 1964/66
Employment Date:
Camp Service: Dortmund
Notes:

Snurova (or Snurawa)

First Name: Hanne (or Johanna)
Birthdate:
Birthplace:
Position: Aufseherin
File Number: IV 402 AR-Z 37/58
Employment Date:
Camp Service: Auschwitz
Notes: Polish national; granted special permission to serve as an "employee of the Reich."

Sobisch

First Name: Waltraut
Birthdate: December 14, 1920
Birthplace: Hannover
Position: Aufseherin
File Number:
Employment Date: October 9, 1944
Camp Service: Neunengamme
Notes:

Sötbeer

First Name: Ilse
Birthdate: January 2, 1922
Birthplace: Hamburg
Position: Aufseherin
File Number:
Employment Date: September 14, 1944
Camp Service: Neuengamme
Notes:

Sollich (or Sollisch; born Niksch)

First Name: Else ("Miksch")
Birthdate:
Birthplace:
Position: Aufseherin
File Number: 108 AR-Z 458/88; IV 402 AR-Z 37/58
Employment Date:
Camp Service: Auschwitz Birkenau
Notes: Polish national; special permission granted to serve as an "employee of the Reich."

Sommer (born Bösenmüller)

First Name: Berta
Birthdate: February 21, 1911

Birthplace: Neundorf
Position: Aufseherin
File Number: IV 405 AR 1635/68
Employment Date:
Camp Service: Groß-Rosen, NL Kratzau II
Notes:

Sommer (born Klein)

First Name: Gertrud
Birthdate: January 28, 1915
Birthplace: Frankendorf
Position: Aufseherin
File Number:
Employment Date: September 11, 1944
Camp Service: Ravensbrück
Notes:

Sosana

First Name: Luise
Birthdate: June 17, 1917
Birthplace: Gelsenkirchen
Position: Aufseherin
File Number:
Employment Date: November 7, 1944
Camp Service: Ravensbrück
Notes:

Sperlich

First Name: Gertrud
Birthdate: April 27, 1915
Birthplace:
Position: Aufseherin
File Number: IV 406 AR-Z 21/71; IV 406 2476/66
Employment Date:
Camp Service: Ravensbrück; NL Genshagen
Notes:

Spahn

First Name: Juliana
Birthdate: November 15, 1921
Birthplace: Aachen
Position: Aufseherin
File Number:
Employment Date: August 19, 1944
Camp Service: Ravensbrück
Notes:

Spindler

First Name: Martha
Birthdate: February 8, 1908
Birthplace: Neustadt
Position: Aufseherin
File Number: IV 409 AR-Z 39/59
Employment Date:
Camp Service: Neustadt-Coburg; Ravensbrück
Notes:

Spitzner

First Name: Elsa
Birthdate: August 16, 1904
Birthplace:
Position: Aufseherin
File Number: IV 410 AR(F) 2629/67
Employment Date:
Camp Service: Floßenbürg; AL Chemnitz
Notes:

Sporleder

First Name: Anni (Anna)
Birthdate:
Birthplace:
Position: Aufseherin
File Number: 409 AR-Z 39/59
Employment Date:
Camp Service: Ravensbrück
Notes: According to the affidavit of Erna Mühlhaus (sworn on November 5, 1968), there was an "Anni Sporleder" who came from the region around Marburg and who was trained at Ravensbrück to be an Aufseherin. The name "Anna" Sporleder appears on the Ravensbrück bank (pay) manifest.

Sporn

First Name: Ursula
Birthdate: August 9, 1919
Birthplace: Berlin
Position: Aufseherin
File Number:
Employment Date: August 15, 1944
Camp Service: Bergen-Belsen
Notes:

Spranger

First Name: Ruth
Birthdate: December 20, 1920
Birthplace: Oelsnitz i. V.
Position: Aufseherin
File Number:
Employment Date: September 11, 1944
Camp Service: Floßenbürg
Notes:

Sprindt (or Sprind)

First Name: Gretl (or Margarete)
Birthdate: Unclear: sometime in 1915 (no month or day noted in her file)
Birthplace: Rheinland
Position: Aufseherin
File Number: IV 406 Ar 278/68
Employment Date:
Camp Service: NL Auer
Notes:

Stabler

First Name: Erika
Birthdate:
Birthplace:
Position: Aufseherin
File Number: IV 409 AR-Z 39/59
Employment Date:
Camp Service: Ravensbrück
Notes:

Stäcker

First Name: Elisabeth
Birthdate:
Birthplace:
Position: Aufseherin
File Number: IV 409 AR-Z 39/59
Employment Date:
Camp Service: Ravensbrück; Meuselwitz
Notes:

Staeger

First Name: Gertrud
Birthdate: May 10, 1905
Birthplace: Berlin
Position: Aufseherin
File Number: IV 410(F) AR 2629/67; IV 410 AR 3016/66
Employment Date: 1944
Camp Service: Floßenbürg; AL Plauen; Zeiß-Ikon Werk; Dresden-Reick; AL Zwodau, AL Fa.Osram Berlin
Notes:

Stahl

First Name: Erna
Birthdate: January 20, 1907
Birthplace: Alfelde
Position: Aufseherin
File Number: IV 410 AR 3016/66
Employment Date:
Camp Service: Floßenbürg; AL Zwodau; AL Plauen, Osram Werke Berlin; AL Drseden
Notes:

Stalzer

First Name: Josefa
Birthdate: January 5, 1894
Birthplace: Vienna
Position: Aufseherin
File Number:
Employment Date: November 1, 1943
Camp Service: Ravensbrück
Notes:

Stapel

First Name: Paula
Birthdate: September 10, 1918
Birthplace: Kantnitz
Position: Aufseherin
File Number:
Employment Date: October 12, 1944
Camp Service: Ravensbrück
Notes:

Starmann

First Name: Elisabeth
Birthdate: February 20, 1923
Birthplace:
Position: Aufseherin
File Number: IV 410(F) AR 2629/67
Employment Date:
Camp Service: Floßenbürg; AL Holleischen
Notes:

Staude

First Name: Elfriede
Birthdate: November 1, 1903
Birthplace: Sackisch
Position: Aufseherin
File Number: IV 429 AR-Z 1965/66, IV 429 AR-Z 121/71
Employment Date:
Camp Service: Ravensbrück; Wolfen
Notes:

Staude

First Name: Elfriede
Birthdate: May 16, 1920

Birthplace:
Position: Aufseherin
File Number: IV 410(F) AR 2629/67
Employment Date:
Camp Service: Floßenbürg; AL Graslitz
Notes:

Steinbeck (born Wöstenfeld)

First Name: Emmy
Birthdate: April 21, 1911
Birthplace: Sieker
Position: Aufseherin
File Number:
Employment Date: October 22, 1944
Camp Service: Ravensbrück
Notes:

Steinert

First Name: Fanny
Birthdate:
Birthplace:
Position: Aufseherin
File Number: IV 409 AR-Z 39/59
Employment Date:
Camp Service: Ravensbrück; Meuselwitz
Notes:

Steigüber

First Name: Margarete
Birthdate: June 7, 1922
Birthplace: Witzenhausen
Position: Blockleiterin
File Number:
Employment Date: November 4, 1944
Camp Service: Ravensbrück
Notes:

Steinsiek

First Name: Anna
Birthdate: November 25, 1922
Birthplace: Sorgwitten
Position: Aufseherin
File Number:
Employment Date: August 30, 1944
Camp Service: Ravensbrück
Notes:

Stellmann (married Putzke)

First Name: Ilse
Birthdate: November 27, 1923
Birthplace: Misburg
Position: Aufseherin
File Number: IV 406 AR-Z 21/71
Employment Date:
Camp Service: NL Genshagen
Notes:

Stern

First Name: Irmgard
Birthdate: March 31, 1922
Birthplace: Berlin
Position: Aufseherin
File Number: 409 AR-Z 39/59
Employment Date: Autumn 1944 (September 15, 1944-
December 31, 1944)

Camp Service: Ravensbrück; Agfa-Camera Werk Munich.
Notes: Was repeatedly ill and was allowed to leave service as Aufseherin upon her own, as well as her mother's, request.

Stetekorn

First Name: Marianne
Birthdate: June 11, 1920
Birthplace: Chemnitz
Position: Aufseherin
File Number: IV 410(F) AR 2629/67
Employment Date:
Camp Service: Floßenbürg; AL Astrawerke Chemnitz
Notes:

Steuwe

First Name: Lieselotte
Birthdate: May 3, 1913
Birthplace: Bielefeld
Position: Aufseherin
File Number:
Employment Date: August 30, 1944
Camp Service: Ravensbrück
Notes:

Sticht

First Name: Irmgard
Birthdate:
Birthplace:
Position: Aufseherin
File Number: IV 429 AR 1959/66
Employment Date:
Camp Service: Ravensbrück
Notes:

Stöcke

First Name: Gertrud
Birthdate: December 29, 1920
Birthplace: Pleetz
Position: Aufseherin
File Number:
Employment Date: November 7, 1944
Camp Service: Ravensbrück
Notes:

Stöcker

First Name: Hilda
Birthdate: May 28, 1923
Birthplace:
Position: Aufseherin
File Number: IV 410(F) AR 2629/67
Employment Date:
Camp Service: Floßenbürg, Holleischen, AL Nuremberg; AL Zwodau
Notes:

Stöhr

First Name: Elfriede
Birthdate: July 22, 1923
Birthplace: Ellbogen
Position: Aufseherin
File Number: IV 410 (F) AR 2629/67
Employment Date:
Camp Service: Floßenbürg; AL Holleischen; AL Freiberg
Notes:

Stojkow

First Name: Maria
Birthdate: April 21, 1925
Birthplace: Gumbosch
Position:
File Number:
Employment Date: June 1, 1943
Camp Service: Ravensbrück
Notes:

Stolp

First Name: Emmi
Birthdate: May 22, 1923
Birthplace: Warbende
Position: Aufseherin
File Number:
Employment Date: October 11, 1944
Camp Service: Ravensbrück
Notes:

Stolper

First Name: Maria
Birthdate:
Birthplace:
Position: Aufseherin
File Number: IV 409 AR-Z 39/59
Employment Date:
Camp Service: Ravensbrück
Notes:

Stork

First Name: Ruth
Birthdate: January 7, 1918
Birthplace: Köln
Position: Aufseherin
File Number:
Employment Date: June 30, 1944
Camp Service: Ravensbrück
Notes:

Strak

First Name: Theresia
Birthdate:
Birthplace:
Position: Aufseherin
File Number: IV 409 AR-Z 39/59
Employment Date:
Camp Service: Ravensbrück
Notes:

Stramm

First Name: Paula
Birthdate: October 18, 1921
Birthplace: Neubuckow
Position: Aufseherin
File Number:
Employment Date: November 7, 1944
Camp Service: Ravensbrück
Notes:

Strauß

First Name: Edith
Birthdate: March 5, 1923
Birthplace:
Position: Aufseherin

File Number: IV 410(F) AR 2629/67
Employment Date:
Camp Service: Floßenbürg; AL Holleischen
Notes:

Strayle

First Name: Rosa
Birthdate: April 15, 1921
Birthplace: Wittlingen
Position: Aufseherin
File Number:
Employment Date: November 7, 1944
Camp Service: Ravensbrück
Notes:

Streher (or Ströher)

First Name: Irmgard
Birthdate:
Birthplace: Chodau
Position: Aufseherin
File Number: IV 406 AR-Z 52/72
Employment Date:
Camp Service: NL Klein-Malchow; Sachsenhausen
Notes:

Ströher

First Name: Margareta
Birthdate: January 14, 1923
Birthplace: Kodau
Position: Aufseherin
File Number: IV 410(F) AR 2629/67
Employment Date:
Camp Service: Floßenbürg; AL Holleischen
Notes:

Stützer

First Name: Maria
Birthdate: May 15, 1923
Birthplace: Heyerode
Position: Aufseherin
File Number:
Employment Date: August 25, 1944
Camp Service: Ravensbrück
Notes:

Stummer

First Name: Charlotte
Birthdate: Unclear; about 1920
Birthplace: Jessnitz
Position: Aufseherin
File Number: IV 409 AR-Z 57/70
Employment Date:
Camp Service: Neubrandenburg; AL Magdeburg; Nuremberg;
Kommando Helmbrechts
Notes:

Sturm

First Name: Lieselotte
Birthdate: October 26, 1921
Birthplace: Breslau
Position: Aufseherin
File Number: IV 405 1651/64
Employment Date: April 8, 1944
Camp Service: AL Hundsfeld; Ravensbrück; NL Zittau;
Groß-Rosen
Notes:

Sudhaus
First Name: Hildegard
Birthdate: January 24, 1918
Birthplace: Dortmund
Position: Aufseherin
File Number:
Employment Date: August 25, 1944
Camp Service: Floßenbürg
Notes:

Süß (born Reischl)
First Name: Rosa
Birthdate: September 16, 1920
Birthplace: Gänswies
Position: Aufseherin
File Number: IV 407 AR-Z 297/60
Employment Date:
Camp Service: Lublin-Majdanek; Auschwitz
Notes:

Syfuß
First Name: Helene
Birthdate: March 25, 1917
Birthplace: Berlin
Position: Aufseherin
File Number: IV 410(F) AR 2629/67
Employment Date: 1944
Camp Service: Floßenbürg; AL Plauen; AL Zwodau
Notes:

Szaroletta
First Name: Maria
Birthdate: October 3, 1914
Birthplace: Dresden
Position: Aufseherin
File Number:
Employment Date: September 14, 1944
Camp Service: Neuengamme
Notes:

Tautz
First Name: Elfriede
Birthdate: May 2, 1923
Birthplace: Kötteritsch
Position: Aufseherin
File Number:
Employment Date: September 11, 1944
Camp Service: Ravensbrück
Notes:

Tazia
First Name: Käte
Birthdate: Unclear: sometime between 1914 and 1916
Birthplace:
Position: Aufseherin
File Number: 109 AR-Z 273/89
Employment Date:
Camp Service: Hamburg-Sasel
Notes:

Theis
First Name: Maria Regine
Birthdate: September 17 (or 27), 1923
Birthplace: Thiergarten
Position: Aufseherin

File Number: IV 429 AR-Z 130/70 (B)
Employment Date:
Camp Service: Sömmerda
Notes:

Theissen (born Ostrowski)
First Name: Emma
Birthdate:
Birthplace:
Position: Aufseherin
File Number: IV 429 AR-Z 51/71 B
Employment Date:
Camp Service: Buchenwald; NL Essen
Notes:

Thiel
First Name: Marianne
Birthdate:
Birthplace: Hamburg
Position: Aufseherin
File Number: IV 402 AR-Z 37/58
Employment Date:
Camp Service: Auschwitz
Notes:

Thoenissen (born Martin)
First Name: Anna Klara
Birthdate: February 14, 1901
Birthplace: Neustadt near Coburg
Position: Aufseherin
File Number: 409 AR-Z 39/59
Employment Date: Unclear: sometime between 1942 and 1944
Camp Service: Ravensbrück; Neustadt
Notes:

Thormann
First Name: Gerda
Birthdate: September 8, 1920
Birthplace: Niederfinow
Position: Aufseherin
File Number:
Employment Date: November 10, 1944
Camp Service: Ravensbrück
Notes:

Thomas
First Name: Irene
Birthdate: January 24, 1920
Birthplace: Kasslin
Position: Aufseherin
File Number:
Employment Date: April 1, 1944
Camp Service: Ravensbrück
Notes:

Tiedemann
First Name: Eva
Birthdate: January 6, 1921
Birthplace: Stralsund
Position: Aufseherin
File Number:
Employment Date: September 11, 1944
Camp Service: Ravensbrück
Notes:

Tietje
First Name: Erna
Birthdate: October 21, 1897
Birthplace: Althagen
Position: Aufseherin
File Number: IV 402 AR-Z 37/58
Employment Date:
Camp Service: Auschwitz
Notes:

Tilse
First Name: Helga
Birthdate: November 13, 1920
Birthplace: Wittenberge
Position: Aufseherin
File Number:
Employment Date: April 1, 1944
Camp Service: Ravensbrück
Notes:

Toboreck
First Name: Elisabeth
Birthdate: July 5, 1923
Birthplace: Laband
Position: Aufseherin
File Number:
Employment Date: November 28, 1944
Camp Service: Ravensbrück
Notes:

Tölle
First Name: Charlotte
Birthdate:
Birthplace:
Position: Aufseherin
File Number: IV 409 AR-Z 39/59
Employment Date:
Camp Service: Ravensbrück
Notes:

Tönges (widowed Lippold; born Elmshaeuser)
First Name: Elisabeth
Birthdate: June 18, 1923
Birthplace: Marburg a.d. Lahn
Position: Aufseherin
File Number: IV 429 AR-Z 51/70
Employment Date:
Camp Service: NL Allendorf
Notes:

Tolle
First Name: Martha
Birthdate: May 10, 1921
Birthplace: Duderstadt
Position: Aufseherin
File Number:
Employment Date: November 3, 1944
Camp Service: Ravensbrück; Sachsenhausen
Notes:

Tomalski
First Name: Martha
Birthdate: December 12, 1905
Birthplace: Strehlen
Position: Aufseherin

File Number:
Employment Date: June 1, 1944
Camp Service: Ravensbrück
Notes:

Tomaske
First Name: Anni
Birthdate: March 29, 1923
Birthplace: Sattow
Position: Aufseherin
File Number:
Employment Date: November 7, 1944
Camp Service: Ravensbrück
Notes:

Tomaske
First Name: Else Ida (Frieda)
Birthdate: November 27, 1910
Birthplace: Kalzig
Position: Aufseherin
File Number: IV 410(F) AR 2629/67; IV 410 AR 3216/66
Employment Date:
Camp Service: Floßenbürg; NL Plauen; Osram Werke Berlin
Notes:

Tornow
First Name: Christa
Birthdate: September 16, 1923
Birthplace: Brodowin
Position: Aufseherin
File Number:
Employment Date: September 11, 1944
Camp Service: Ravensbrück
Notes:

Trabitz
First Name: Frieda
Birthdate: October 18, 1923
Birthplace: Staßfurt
Position: Aufseherin
File Number: IV 410(F) AR 2629/67
Employment Date:
Camp Service: Floßenbürg; AL Zwodau; Ravensbrück
Notes:

Traebert (born Schmidt)
First Name: Frieda
Birthdate: September 14, 1907
Birthplace: Nauen
Position: Aufseherin
File Number:
Employment Date: February 1, 1944
Camp Service: Ravensbrück
Notes:

Tragel
First Name: Sophie
Birthdate: November 15, 1921
Birthplace: Waldsassen
Position: Aufseherin
File Number:
Employment Date: November 7, 1944
Camp Service: Ravensbrück
Notes:

Trampnau (born Brödel)

First Name: Margarete
Birthdate: March 8, 1905
Birthplace: Berlin
Position: Aufseherin
File Number:
Employment Date: August 17, 1944
Camp Service: Sachsenhausen
Notes:

Trebbin

First Name: Ruth
Birthdate: August 13, 1923
Birthplace: Berlin
Position: Aufseherin
File Number:
Employment Date: October 5, 1944
Camp Service: Ravensbrück
Notes:

Treffer

First Name: Otilie
Birthdate:
Birthplace:
Position: Aufseherin
File Number: IV 409 AR-Z 39/59
Employment Date:
Camp Service: Ravensbrück
Notes:

Trocha (born Linde)

First Name: Hilda
Birthdate: May 31, 1919
Birthplace: Wanzow
Position: Aufseherin
File Number:
Employment Date: August 15, 1944
Camp Service: Ravensbrück
Notes:

Tuchardt

First Name: Gerda
Birthdate: April 24, 1923
Birthplace: Rostock
Position: Aufseherin
File Number:
Employment Date: November 7, 1944
Camp Service: Ravensbrück
Notes:

Türk

First Name: Irmgard
Birthdate: March 22, 1922
Birthplace: Senftenhütte
Position: Aufseherin
File Number:
Employment Date: August 30, 1944
Camp Service: Ravensbrück
Notes:

Uhlig

First Name: Elfriede
Birthdate: May 9, 1921
Birthplace:
Position: Aufseherin

File Number: IV 410(F) AR 2629/67; IV 410 AR 2960/66
Employment Date: Probably November 27, 1944
Camp Service: Floßenbürg; AL Freiberg; NL Holleischen
Notes:

Uhlig

First Name: Ingeborg
Birthdate: June 9, 1920
Birthplace: Chemnitz
Position: Aufseherin
File Number: IV 410(F) AR 2629/67
Employment Date: Probably August 25, 1944
Camp Service: Floßenbürg; AL Astrawerke Chemnitz
Notes:

Uhlig

First Name: Käthe
Birthdate: October 28, 1915
Birthplace: Chemnitz
Position: Aufseherin
File Number: IV 410(F) 2629/67
Employment Date: Probably November 2, 1944
Camp Service: Floßenbürg; AL Hainichen
Notes:

Ulischberger

First Name: Gertrud
Birthdate: March 20, 1921
Birthplace: Grun
Position: Aufseherin
File Number:
Employment Date: October 11, 1944
Camp Service: Ravensbrück
Notes:

Ullrich (born Bauch)

First Name: Hedwig
Birthdate: January 31, 1902
Birthplace: Weißstein (Silesia)
Position: Lagerleiterin
File Number: 409 AR 1494/66; 9 AR 1225/1960
Employment Date:
Camp Service: NL Belzig
Notes:

Ulm (now Walden)

First Name: Luise (Maria)
Birthdate: November 11, 1922
Birthplace: Butzbach
Position: Aufseherin
File Number: IV 429 AR 1821/66 (B); IV 429 AR-Z 51/70
Employment Date:
Camp Service: Ravensbrück; Allendorf
Notes:

Ulrich

First Name: Marianne
Birthdate:
Birthplace:
Position: Aufseherin
File Number: 410 AR 3021/66
Employment Date:
Camp Service: NL Dresden-Universelle
Notes:

Unger (born Bernhardt)
First Name: Dora
Birthdate: March 17, 1914
Birthplace: Berbersdorf
Position: Aufseherin
File Number: IV 410(F) AR 2629/67; IV 410 AR-Z 60/67
Employment Date:
Camp Service: Floßenbürg; AL Hainichen; AL Zwodau
Notes:

Unger
First Name: Trude
Birthdate: June 24, 1923
Birthplace: Wilkau
Position: Aufseherin
File Number: IV 410(F) AR 2629/67
Employment Date:
Camp Service: Floßenbürg; AL Chemnitz
Notes:

Urbat
First Name: Maria
Birthdate: July 3, 1905
Birthplace: Niedergorke
Position: Aufseherin
File Number:
Employment Date: March 1, 1943
Camp Service: Ravensbrück
Notes:

Vaessen
First Name: Elisabeth (Wilhelmine, Gerda, Maria)
Birthdate: February 19, 1923
Birthplace: Vught (Holland)
Position: Aufseherin
File Number: IV 409 AR-Z 39/59
Employment Date:
Camp Service: Ravensbrück
Notes:

Valentin
First Name: Margarethe
Birthdate: June 15, 1916
Birthplace: Plauen
Position: Aufseherin
File Number: IV 410(F) AR 2629/67; IV 410 AR 3216/66
Employment Date:
Camp Service: Floßenbürg; AL Chemnitz; AL Plauen
Notes:

Veit
First Name: Ursula
Birthdate: March 22, 1922
Birthplace: Bolley
Position: Aufseherin
File Number:
Employment Date: August 15, 1944
Camp Service: Ravensbrück
Notes:

Veltenaar
First Name: Maria
Birthdate: September 2, 1923
Birthplace: Rotterdam
Position: Aufseherin
File Number:
Employment Date: September 26, 1944
Camp Service: Ravensbrück
Notes: Dutch national; special permission granted to serve as an "employee of the Reich."

Verstegen
First Name: Gertrud
Birthdate: April 10, 1918
Birthplace: Elten
Position: Aufseherin
File Number:
Employment Date: September 1, 1944
Camp Service: Neuengamme
Notes:

Vettermann
First Name: Ilse
Birthdate: March 3, 1913
Birthplace: Berlin
Position: Aufseherin
File Number:
Employment Date: September 13, 1944
Camp Service: Ravensbrück
Notes:

Vogel
First Name: Emma
Birthdate: June 11, 1921
Birthplace: Rüßdorf
Position: Aufseherin
File Number:
Employment Date: October 1, 1942
Camp Service: Ravensbrück
Notes:

Voges
First Name: Marianne
Birthdate: August 25, 1922
Birthplace: Plauen
Position: Aufseherin
File Number: IV 410 AR 3216/66
Employment Date:
Camp Service: AL Plauen
Notes:

Vogt
First Name: Edith
Birthdate: June 29, 1923
Birthplace: Waldenburg (Silesia)
Position: Aufseherin
File Number: IV 410(F) AR 2629/67
Employment Date: Probably October 5, 1944
Camp Service: Floßenbürg; AL Plauen
Notes:

Vogt
First Name: Gerda
Birthdate: January 6, 1923
Birthplace: Kreuzburg
Position: Aufseherin
File Number:
Employment Date: September 1, 1944
Camp Service: Ravensbrück
Notes:

Voigt

First Name: Frieda
Birthdate: October 12, 1918
Birthplace: Schönhagen
Position: Aufseherin
File Number:
Employment Date: June 21, 1944
Camp Service: Ravensbrück
Notes:

Volkenrath

First Name: Elisabeth
Birthdate: Schönau
Birthplace: September 5, 1919
Position: Aufseherin; Rapportführerin; Oberaufseherin
File Number: IV 409 AR-Z 39/59
Employment Date:
Camp Service: Ravensbrück; Auschwitz Birkenau; Bergen-Belsen
Notes: Tried and convicted of war crimes by the British and executed on December 13, 1945.

von der Hülst

First Name: Annemie (Anni)
Birthdate:
Birthplace:
Position: Oberaufseherin
File Number: IV 404 AR 607/67
Employment Date:
Camp Service: Neuengamme; NL Hamburg-Wandsbek
Notes:

von der Wielen

First Name: Euphemia
Birthdate: April 9,1915
Birthplace:
Position: Aufseherin
File Number: IV 406 AR-Z 21/71; IV 406 AR 2476/66
Employment Date:
Camp Service: Ravensbrück; NL Genshagen
Notes:

von Kettler (born Freifrau)

First Name: Ellen
Birthdate:
Birthplace:
Position: Aufseherin
File Number: IV 409 AR-Z 39/59
Employment Date:
Camp Service: Ravensbrück
Notes:

von Lonski

First Name: Gertrud
Birthdate: January 20, 1921
Birthplace: Harburg-Wilhelmsburg
Position: Aufseherin
File Number:
Employment Date: September 8, 1944
Camp Service: Neuengamme
Notes:

Vootz

First Name: Hedwig
Birthdate: February 25, 1915

Birthplace: Dükken
Position: Aufseherin
File Number:
Employment Date: November 1, 1942
Camp Service: Ravensbrück
Notes:

Wagener

First Name: Emmi
Birthdate: March 3, 1922
Birthplace: Brüchehof
Position: Aufseherin
File Number:
Employment Date: September 18, 1944
Camp Service: Ravensbrück
Notes:

Wagner

First Name: Anna
Birthdate: August 7, 1923
Birthplace: Marpingen
Position: Aufseherin
File Number:
Employment Date: October 17, 1944
Camp Service: Neuengamme
Notes:

Wagner

First Name: Anemarie
Birthdate: May 5, 1893
Birthplace: Rommersdorf
Position: Aufseherin
File Number: IV 429 AR-Z 130/70 (B)
Employment Date:
Camp Service: Sömmerda
Notes:

Wagner

First Name: Annemarie
Birthdate: August 29, 1921
Birthplace:
Position: Aufseherin
File Number:
Employment Date:
Camp Service: Neuengamme
Notes:

Wagner

First Name: Marianne
Birthdate: December 8, 1919
Birthplace: Wolkenburg
Position: Aufseherin
File Number: IV 410(F) AR 2629/67; 410 AR 2531/66
Employment Date:
Camp Service: Floßenbürg; NL Graslitz; AL Plauen; AL Rochlitz
Notes:

Wagner

First Name: Martha
Birthdate: December 11, 1921
Birthplace: Frose
Position: Aufseherin
File Number: IV 406 AR-Z 21/71
Employment Date:

Camp Service: NL Genshagen
Notes:

Wagner

First Name: Olga
Birthdate: November 5, 1921
Birthplace: Unterradling
Position: Aufseherin
File Number:
Employment Date: June 16, 1944
Camp Service: Ravensbrück
Notes:

Wagner

First Name: Ruth
Birthdate: October 29, 1920
Birthplace: Gaulsheim
Position: Aufseherin
File Number: IV 404 AR-Z 235/73
Employment Date:
Camp Service: Neuengamme; NL Lübberstedt
Notes: Since Ruth Wagner was a very common name, the two "Ruth Wagners" are not necessarily identical.

Wagner

First Name: Ruth
Birthdate:
Birthplace:
Position: Aufseherin
File Number: IV 429 AR 1941/66(B)
Employment Date:
Camp Service: NL Torgau
Notes: Since Ruth Wagner was a very common name, the two "Ruth Wagners" are not necessarily identical.

Walla

First Name: Gertrud
Birthdate: March 19, 1922
Birthplace: Festenberg
Position: Aufseherin
File Number:
Employment Date: June 1, 1944
Camp Service: Ravensbrück
Notes:

Walter

First Name: Frieda
Birthdate:
Birthplace:
Position: Aufseherin
File Number: IV 409 AR-Z 39/59
Employment Date:
Camp Service: Ravensbrück; Bergen-Belsen
Notes:

Walzcak

First Name: Wanda
Birthdate: August 11, 1923
Birthplace: Pottrop (Bottrop)
Position: Aufseherin
File Number:
Employment Date: November 8, 1944
Camp Service: Ravensbrück
Notes:

Wappler

First Name: Lotte
Birthdate: December 22, 1921
Birthplace: Plauen
Position: Aufseherin
File Number: IV 410 (F) AR 2629/67; IV 410 AR 3216/66; IV 410 AR 3039/66
Employment Date:
Camp Service: Floßenbürg; AL Plauen; NL Mehtheuer
Notes:

Wasilow

First Name: Annemarie
Birthdate: December 10, 1921
Birthplace: Warxbüttel
Position: Aufseherin
File Number:
Employment Date: September 30, 1944
Camp Service: Neuengamme
Notes:

Wassmuth (born im Ort)

First Name: Elfriede
Birthdate: April 10, 1912
Birthplace: Dortmund
Position: Aufseherin
File Number: IV 409 AR-Z 39/59; IV 429 AR 1964/66
Employment Date:
Camp Service: Ravensbrück; NL Dortmund
Notes:

Wastat

First Name: Sophie
Birthdate: September 10, 1922
Birthplace: Ublick (East Prussia)
Position: Aufseherin
File Number: IV 410 (F) AR 2629/67
Employment Date:
Camp Service: Floßenbürg; Wolkenburg
Notes:

Waurr

First Name: Sophie
Birthdate: March 26, 1920
Birthplace: Dulsig/Warthegau
Position: Aufseherin
File Number:
Employment Date: September 9, 1944
Camp Service: Neuengamme
Notes:

Weber (born Lämmerhirt)

First Name: Charlotte
Birthdate: May 14, 1923
Birthplace: Großolbersdorf
Position: Aufseherin
File Number:
Employment Date: October 1, 1944
Camp Service: Floßenbürg
Notes:

Weber

First Name: Else
Birthdate:
Birthplace:

Position: Oberaufseherin
File Number: 8 AR-Z 268/59
Employment Date:
Camp Service: Lublin-Majdanek
Notes:

Weber

First Name: Inge Marga Marggot
Birthdate: 1920 (no month or day noted in her file)
Birthplace:
Position: Aufseherin; Kommandoführerin
File Number: IV 404 AR 1405/67
Employment Date:
Camp Service: Neuengamme; NL Lübberstadt
Notes:

Weber

First Name: Ingeborg
Birthdate: January 1, 1921
Birthplace:
Position: Aufseherin
File Number:
Employment Date: August 2, 1944
Camp Service:
Notes:

Weberschock

First Name: Erika
Birthdate: March 4, 1922
Birthplace:
Position: Aufseherin
File Number: IV 410(F) AR 2629/67
Employment Date:
Camp Service: Floßenbürg; AL Dresden Reick
Notes:

Wegner (born Röger)

First Name: Hildegard
Birthdate: January 21, 1923
Birthplace: Hainichen
Position: Aufseherin
File Number: IV 410(F) AR 2629/67
Employment Date: Probably November 2, 1944
Camp Service: Floßenbürg; AL Hainichen
Notes:

Weichert

First Name: Frieda
Birthdate:
Birthplace:
Position: Aufseherin
File Number: IV 410 AR 3016/66
Employment Date:
Camp Service: Floßenbürg; Zeiß-Ikon-Werk Dresden-Reick
Notes:

Weidemann

First Name: Gerda
Birthdate: December 12, 1922
Birthplace: Torgau
Position: Aufseherin
File Number:
Employment Date: July 15, 1944
Camp Service: Ravensbrück
Notes:

Weidl (or Weidel)

First Name: Gertrud
Birthdate: April 30, 1914
Birthplace:
Position: Aufseherin
File Number: IV 410(F) AR 2629/67
Employment Date:
Camp Service: Floßenbürg; AL Plauen
Notes:

Weiner

First Name: Adelheid
Birthdate: July 15, 1920
Birthplace: Alt-Rothwasser
Position: Aufseherin
File Number:
Employment Date: June 22, 1944
Camp Service: Ravensbrück
Notes:

Weinreich

First Name: Irma
Birthdate: October 29, 1921
Birthplace: Chemnitz
Position: Aufseherin
File Number:
Employment Date: August 26, 1944
Camp Service: Floßenbürg
Notes:

Weiß

First Name: Ingelene
Birthdate: June 11, 1922
Birthplace: Berlin-Lichterfelde
Position: Aufseherin
File Number: IV 410(F) AR 2629/67; IV 410 AR 3016/66
Employment Date:
Camp Service: Floßenbürg; Zeiß-Ikon Werk Dresden Reick; AL Osram Berlin, Plauen,
Notes:

Weißflog

First Name: Maria
Birthdate: May 23, 1915
Birthplace:
Position: Aufseherin
File Number: IV 410(F) AR 2629/67
Employment Date:
Camp Service: Floßenbürg; AL Oederen
Notes:

Werner (born Bindig; married Fuß)

First Name: Edith
Birthdate: April 10, 1923
Birthplace: Oederan
Position: Aufseherin
File Number: IV 4110(F) AR 2629/67
Employment Date: Probably September 27, 1944
Camp Service: Floßenbürg; AL Oederan
Notes:

Weniger (or Winniger; born Mühlan or Myland) – hand-written in *Fraktur* script

First Name: Gertrud (Gertrude)
Birthdate: December 29, 1920

Birthplace: Schönau (Schlesien)
Position: Aufseherin; Oberaufseherin; Rapportführerin
File Number: IV 402 AR-Z 37/58; IV 410 (F) AR 2629/67
Employment Date:
Camp Service: AL Oederan; Floßenbürg; Auschwitz
Notes:

Werner

First Name: Elsa
Birthdate: December 3, 1912
Birthplace: Penig
Position: Aufseherin
File Number: IV 410((F) AR 2629/67
Employment Date:
Camp Service: Floßenbürg; AL Wolkenburg
Notes:

Werner

First Name: Frieda
Birthdate: March 22, 1921
Birthplace: Wittenberg
Position: Aufseherin
File Number: VI 117 AR 1579/65
Employment Date:
Camp Service: NL Belzig-Treuenbrietzen
Notes:

Werner

First Name: Gertraud
Birthdate: June 17, 1921
Birthplace: Leipzig
Position: Aufseherin
File Number:
Employment Date: August 15, 1944
Camp Service: Ravensbrück
Notes:

Werner (born Sage)

First Name: Hilda
Birthdate: September 11, 1910
Birthplace:
Position: Aufseherin
File Number: IV 410 (F) AR 2629/67
Employment Date:
Camp Service: Floßenbürg; AL Wolkenburg; AL Zwodau
Notes:

Werner

First Name: Marianne
Birthdate: February, 7 1918
Birthplace:
Position: Aufseherin
File Number: IV 410(F) AR 2629/67
Employment Date:
Camp Service: Floßenbürg AL C.Lorenz Mittweida
Notes:

Werner

First Name: Marianne
Birthdate: October 9, 1922
Birthplace: Chemnitz
Position: Aufseherin
File Number: IV 410 (F) AR 2629/67
Employment Date: February 6, 1943
Camp Service: Floßenbürg; AL Chemnitz
Notes:

Wessel (born Danke)

First Name: Elisabeth
Birthdate: December 14, 1909
Birthplace:
Position: Aufseherin
File Number: IV 406 AR 2476/66
Employment Date:
Camp Service: Ravensbrück
Notes:

Wessel (born Bücker)

First Name: Hedwig
Birthdate: July 6, 1917
Birthplace: Mellingen
Position: Aufseherin
File Number:
Employment Date: August 30, 1944
Camp Service: Ravensbrück
Notes:

Westfeld

First Name: Erika
Birthdate: May 16, 1923
Birthplace: Bahrdorf
Position: Aufseherin
File Number:
Employment Date: June 1, 1942
Camp Service: Ravensbrück
Notes:

Westphal

First Name: Frieda
Birthdate: October 22, 1918
Birthplace: Hamburg
Position: Aufseherin
File Number:
Employment Date: September 30, 1944
Camp Service: Neuengamme
Notes:

Wetzel

First Name: Vera
Birthdate: December 7, 1923
Birthplace: Oranienburg
Position: Aufseherin
File Number: IV 410(F) AR 2629/67
Employment Date: 1943 (no month day noted in her file)
Camp Service: Floßenbürg; AL Neu Rohlau
Notes:

Weyndels

First Name: Hansi
Birthdate: June 10, 1923
Birthplace: Breda (Holland)
Position: Aufseherin
File Number:
Employment Date: August 8, 1944
Camp Service: Ravensbrück
Notes: Ethnic German; born and raised in the Netherlands.

Wiechert

First Name: Emmi
Birthdate: April 6, 1923
Birthplace: Duisburg
Position: Aufseherin

File Number:
Employment Date: September 25, 1944
Camp Service: Neuengamme
Notes:

Wiemeler
First Name: Johanna
Birthdate: April 17, 1917
Birthplace: Borchorst
Position: Aufseherin
File Number: IV 410(F) AR 2629/667
Employment Date: 1944
Camp Service: Floßenbürg, AL Graslitz
Notes:

Wienäber
First Name: Herta
Birthdate: October 12, 1919
Birthplace: Querenhorst
Position: Aufseherin
File Number:
Employment Date: August 19, 1944
Camp Service: Ravensbrück
Notes:

Wiese
First Name: Martha
Birthdate: September 16, 1921
Birthplace: Dortmund
Position: Aufseherin
File Number:
Employment Date: November 7, 1944
Camp Service: Ravensbrück
Notes:

Wieser
First Name: Josefine
Birthdate: June 7, 1923
Birthplace:
Position: Aufseherin
File Number: IV 410(F) AR 2629/67
Employment Date:
Camp Service: Floßenbürg; Sachsenhausen; AL Mittweida
Notes:

Wilde (or Vilde; born Jung)
First Name: Amalie
Birthdate: May 12, 1924 or June 2, 1922
Birthplace: Holzheim or Munich
Position: Aufseherin
File Number: 9-16/359
Employment Date: September 1941 (no day noted in her file)
Camp Service: Buchenwald
Notes: Possibly these are two different women?

Wilke
First Name: Elly
Birthdate: December 1, 1921
Birthplace: Domnitz
Position: Aufseherin
File Number: IV 410(F) AR 2629/67
Employment Date:
Camp Service: Floßenbürg; AL Rochlitz
Notes:

Wilke
First Name: Ilse
Birthdate: February 18, 1923
Birthplace: Domnitz
Position: Aufseherin
File Number: IV 410(F) AR 2629/67
Employment Date: 1944
Camp Service: Floßenbürg; AL Rochlitz
Notes:

Wilke (born Herpich)
First Name: Liska-Alice
Birthdate: March 29, 1907
Birthplace: Hohendorf
Position: Aufseherin
File Number: IV 410(F) AR 2629/67
Employment Date:
Camp Service: Floßenbürg; AL Chemnitz; AL Plauen
Notes:

Wilksch
First Name: Gusti (Auguste)
Birthdate: October 1, 1914
Birthplace: Emden
Position: Aufseherin
File Number: IV 410(F) AR 2629/67
Employment Date: April 10, 1944
Camp Service: Floßenbürg; AL Chemnitz
Notes:

Willach
First Name: Rosa
Birthdate: December 22, 1906
Birthplace: Weiden
Position: Aufseherin
File Number:
Employment Date: November 11, 1944
Camp Service: Ravensbrück
Notes:

Windler
First Name: Anneliese
Birthdate: January 6, 1924
Birthplace: Greifswald
Position: Aufseherin
File Number:
Employment Date: November 8, 1944
Camp Service: Ravensbrück
Notes:

Winkler
First Name: Erna
Birthdate: June 13, 1900
Birthplace: Wechselburg
Position: Aufseherin
File Number: IV 410(F) AR 2629/67
Employment Date: 1944 (no month or day noted in her file)
Camp Service: Floßenbürg; AL Rochlitz
Notes:

Winkler
First Name: Thea
Birthdate: 1922 (no month or day noted in her file)
Birthplace:
Position: Aufseherin

File Number:
Employment Date:
Camp Service: Groß-Rosen
Notes:

Winster

First Name: Else
Birthdate: September 2, 1922
Birthplace:
Position: Aufseherin
File Number: IV 409 AR-Z 39/59
Employment Date:
Camp Service: Ravensbrück
Notes:

Winter

First Name: Betti
Birthdate: May 8, 1922
Birthplace:
Position: Aufseherin
File Number: IV 410(F) AR 2629/67
Employment Date:
Camp Service: Floßenbürg; Luftfahrtgerätewerk Zwodau
Notes:

Wisotzki

First Name: Johanna
Birthdate: August 26, 1919
Birthplace:
Position: Aufseherin; Oberaufseherin of NL Bromberg
File Number: IV 407 AR-Z 170/72
Employment Date:
Camp Service: Stutthof; Bromberg-Ost
Notes:

Wöllert

First Name: Elsbeth
Birthdate: July 26, 1921
Birthplace: Bergfeld
Position: Aufseherin
File Number:
Employment Date: October 13, 1944
Camp Service: Ravensbrück
Notes:

Wötzel (born Drehmann)

First Name: Frieda
Birthdate: January 27, 1907
Birthplace: Zehlenrode
Position: Aufseherin; Blockführerin
File Number: 3-6/313, 409 AR 89/93
Employment Date: August 30, 1944
Camp Service: Ravensbrück; Barth
Notes: Sentenced to life imprisonment by an East German court on August 8, 1966.

Wohlers

First Name: Gertrud
Birthdate: November 16, 1913
Birthplace:
Position: Aufseherin
File Number: IV 406 AR 645/69
Employment Date:
Camp Service: Ravensbrück
Notes:

Wolf

First Name: Anna
Birthdate: July 9, 1920
Birthplace: Eisendorf
Position: Aufseherin
File Number: IV 410 (F) AR 2629/67
Employment Date: 1944
Camp Service: Floßenbürg; AL Holleischhenn
Notes:

Wolf (married Studer)

First Name: Anna
Birthdate:
Birthplace:
Position: Aufseherin
File Number: IV 402 AR 290/75
Employment Date:
Camp Service: Auschwitz; Floßenbürg
Notes:

Wolf

First Name: Ernestine
Birthdate: October 14, 1920
Birthplace: Gieshübel
Position: Aufseherin
File Number:
Employment Date: November 8, 1944
Camp Service: Ravensbrück
Notes:

Wolf

First Name: Lotte
Birthdate: January 2, 1923
Birthplace: Kukan orGablenz
Position: Aufseherin
File Number:
Employment Date: April 20, 1944
Camp Service: Sachsenhausen
Notes:

Wüstenbecker (born Isemann)

First Name: Auguste
Birthdate: March 16, 1917
Birthplace: Lemgow
Position: Aufseherin
File Number:
Employment Date: June 5, 1944
Camp Service:
Notes:

Wunder

First Name: Gertraude
Birthdate:
Birthplace:
Position: Aufseherin
File Number: IV 429 AR 1248/68
Employment Date:
Camp Service: Ravensbrück; NL Markkleeberg
Notes:

Wyndelts

First Name: Hanna
Birthdate: June 10, 1923
Birthplace: Breda (Holland)
Position: Aufseherin

File Number:
Employment Date:
Camp Service: Ravensbrück
Notes: Born in the Netherlands; no employment date provided – only "Employment granted on November 20, 1944" (file doesn't state whether she was an Ethnic German or not).

Zaha
First Name: Elfriede (Frieda)
Birthdate: March 28, 1923
Birthplace: Wostrowo
Position: Aufseherin
File Number: IV 410(F) AR 2629/67
Employment Date: June 13,1944
Camp Service: Floßenbürg; Al Freiberg; AL Holleischen
Notes:

Zahren
First Name: Christine
Birthdate: January 19, 1907
Birthplace: Viersgen
Position: Aufseherin
File Number: IV 409 AR-Z 78/72
Employment Date: June 15, 1944
Camp Service: Ravensbrück; Sachsenhausen; Wittenberg-Lutterstadt
Notes:

Zaradnick
First Name: Liesel
Birthdate: April 10, 1916
Birthplace: Fischern
Position: Aufseherin
File Number:
Employment Date: April 1, 1944
Camp Service: Ravensbrück
Notes:

Zech
First Name: Katharina
Birthdate: October 31, 1922
Birthplace: Neu-Palanzka
Position: Aufseherin
File Number:
Employment Date: August 2, 1944
Camp Service: Ravensbrück
Notes:

Zeh (married Burkert)
First Name: Dora
Birthdate: September 7, 1905
Birthplace: Plauen
Position: Aufseherin
File Number: IV 410 (F) AR 2629/67
Employment Date: September 5, 1944
Camp Service: Holleischen; Floßenbürg; AL Plauen
Notes:

Zeh
First Name: Maria
Birthdate:
Birthplace:
Position: Aufseherin
File Number: IV 410 AR 3039/66

Employment Date:
Camp Service: NL Mehltheuer
Notes:

Zeidler
First Name: Eleonore
Birthdate: April 9, 1913
Birthplace: Uterrich
Position: Aufseherin
File Number:
Employment Date: April 1, 1944
Camp Service: Ravensbrück
Notes:

Zengerle (born Mailänder)
First Name: Anna
Birthdate: April 26, 1903
Birthplace: Heidenheim
Position: Aufseherin
File Number:
Employment Date:
Camp Service: Ravensbrück; Natzweiler
Notes:

Zerm
First Name: Anni
Birthdate:
Birthplace:
Position: Rapportführerin
File Number: 112 AR 12.014/88
Employment Date:
Camp Service: Geisenheim
Notes:

Zeuge (born Rothe)
First Name: Hertha
Birthdate: November 27, 1909
Birthplace:
Position: Aufseherin
File Number: IV 410 AR-Z 106/68
Employment Date:
Camp Service: NL Mittweida
Notes:

Zickert
First Name: Margarete
Birthdate: August 30, 1914
Birthplace: Bad Freienwalde
Position: Aufseherin
File Number:
Employment Date: November 30, 1944
Camp Service: Ravensbrück
Notes:

Ziegelmeyer
First Name: Rosa
Birthdate: May 20, 1919
Birthplace: Lorch
Position: Aufseherin
File Number: IV 419 AR-Z 172/69
Employment Date:
Camp Service: NL Geisenheim, Maschinen-Fabrik Johannisberg
Notes:

Zieger (born Hirsch)
First Name: Gerda
Birthdate: July 24, 1922
Birthplace:
Position: Aufseherin
File Number: IV 410(F) AR 2629/67
Employment Date:
Camp Service: Floßenbürg; AL Freiberg
Notes:

Ziegler
First Name: Maria
Birthdate:
Birthplace:
Position: Aufseherin
File Number: IV 409 AR-Z 39/59
Employment Date:
Camp Service: Ravensbrück
Notes:

Ziegler
First Name: Theresia
Birthdate: November 9, 1906
Birthplace: Grünberg
Position:
File Number:
Employment Date:
Camp Service:
Notes: Employment not granted (*Voffg. SS-WVHA-GO-DF.Sch/Kl.To. v. 31.10.1944*).

Zielonka
First Name: Susanne
Birthdate: April 6, 1921
Birthplace: Hohndorf
Position: Aufseherin
File Number:
Employment Date: August 28, 1944
Camp Service: Bergen-Belsen
Notes:

Zietmann
First Name: Liesbeth
Birthdate: June 7, 1922
Birthplace:
Position: Aufseherin
File Number: IV 429 AR-Z 1965/66; IV 4299 AR-Z 121/71
Employment Date:
Camp Service: Ravensbrück; Wolfen
Notes:

Zietelmann (born Hentschel)
First Name: Erna
Birthdate: April 26, 1917
Birthplace: Chemnitz
Position: Aufseherin
File Number:
Employment Date: August 15, 1944
Camp Service: Bergen-Belsen
Notes:

Zimmer (born Mezel)
First Name: Emma
Birthdate: August 14, 1888
Birthplace: Schlüchtern
Position: Aufseherin
File Number:
Employment Date: June 1, 1943
Camp Service: Ravensbrück
Notes: Dismissed from service near the end of the war either due to advanced age or chronic alcoholism; executed for war crimes by the British on September 20, 1948.

Zimmer
First Name: Elfriede, Edith
Birthdate: May 9, 1922
Birthplace: Hohenbach (Poland)
Position: Aufseherin
File Number: 109 AR-Z 33/89
Employment Date:
Camp Service: Ravensbrück; Auschwitz Birkenau
Notes: Ethnic German; born and raised in Poland.

Zimmermann
First Name: Emma (Emmi)
Birthdate: February 20, 1922
Birthplace: Duernberg
Position: Aufseherin
File Number: IV 410(F) AR 2629/67
Employment Date:
Camp Service: Floßenbürg; Holleischen
Notes:

Zimmermann (born Zinke)
First Name: Johanna
Birthdate:
Birthplace:
Position: Aufseherin
File Number: IV 429 AR 1973/66 (B)
Employment Date:
Camp Service: Ravensbrück; Soemmerda; Meuselwitz
Notes:

Zimmermann
First Name: Wilma
Birthdate: March 3, 1923
Birthplace: Cramon
Position: Aufseherin
File Number:
Employment Date: November 7, 1944
Camp Service: Ravensbrück
Notes:

Zitzke
First Name: Margarete
Birthdate:
Birthplace:
Position: Aufseherin
File Number: IV 409 AR-Z 39/59
Employment Date:
Camp Service: Ravensbrück
Notes:

Zlotos
First Name: Gertrud
Birthdate:
Birthplace:
Position: Aufseherin
File Number: IV 402 AR-Z 37/58

Employment Date:
Camp Service: Auschwitz
Notes:

Zockoll (born Stiller)

First Name: Meta
Birthdate: September 16, 1907
Birthplace: Breslau
Position: Aufseherin
File Number: IV 405 AR-1651/64
Employment Date: 1944 (no month or day noted in her file)
Camp Service: Hundsfeld; Kratzau
Notes: Participated in the Hundsfeld Death March (Groß-Rosen), but stated to a denazification proceeding that the Aufseherinnen were not armed.

Zöllner

First Name: Hertha
Birthdate:
Birthplace:
Position: Aufseherin
File Number: IV 409 AR-Z 39/59

Employment Date:
Camp Service: Ravensbrück; Meuselwitz
Notes:

Zoll

First Name: Margarete
Birthdate: April 5, 1917
Birthplace: Frankfurt/Main
Position: Aufseherin
File Number: 409 AR-Z 39/59
Employment Date: October 15, 1943
Camp Service: Ravensbrück; Büro-Opitz
Notes:

Zühlke

First Name: Ruth
Birthdate: December 26, 1917
Birthplace:
Position: Aufseherin
File Number: IV 406 AR 2576/66
Employment Date:
Camp Service: Ravensbrück
Notes:

3

THE CAMP WOMEN:
Assignments, Ranks, and Assorted Pertinent Data

"All cruelty needs is a lack of a sense of morality and brutalization by daily routines. The guards flogged, tormented, and killed prisoners – not because they had to, but because they were allowed to, no holds barred."

- Wolfgang Sofsky, *The Order of Terror*

ENTRANCE

Until the Third Reich was on the verge of collapse, procedures were maintained for training and integrating new Aufseherinnen into guard units within the camps. Whether the women were enlistees, conscripts, or mandated quota inductees from German factories, all had to be screened and evaluated. As noted in Chapter 1, this included a medical examination, a police background check, and an analysis of the candidate's general knowledge. The questions from one such test (*"Prüfangsfragen für SS-Helferinnen"*) are translated below, with the original document appearing after the translation:

Examination Questions for SS-Assistants

1. When did the Russian campaign begin?
2. When did the first German train line begin operation and on what stretch did it connect?
3. What are the names of the peninsulas in the south of Europe?
4. What is the name of the island on which Napoleon was exiled to the second time?
5. What is the meaning of the abbreviation SS?
6. 1/2 divided by 1/4 =
7. When and where was the Führer born?
8. What is the purpose of the sterilization law?
9. Which hereditary diseases do you know?
10. How heavy is a kilogram of iron?
11. Which states have a border to the Mediterranean Sea?
12. What was the darkest day of the movement?
13. Who discovered printing?
14. What is race?
15. 46,131 –13,794 divided by 9 X 2_ + (3/4 + 0.10) divided by (3/9 divided by 1/27) –999.15 =
16. Where did Adolf Hitler write the book *Mein Kampf*?
17. Where does the Danube (Donau) begin and end?
18. Who is the military commander of the Native German Army?
19. Which seas does the Suez Canal connect to?
20. What does *Weltanschauung* mean?

While I don't want to belabor the issue, I must reiterate something I stated at the outset of my examination of the *SS-Aufseherinnen*: the women's files, by-and-large, rank far below the enlisted men's files with regard to completeness and accuracy. Moreover, if we observe further that the enlisted men's personal files are not nearly as complete as that of their commanding officers, just how limited is the data for the women?

All this notwithstanding, there are some data that merit analysis. The initial area of the card file that we can and should consider is the women's place of birth.

Prüfungsfragen für SS-Helferinnen

1. Wann begann der Rußlandfeldzug ? *am 22.6.41*

2. Wann wurde die erste deutsche Eisenbahn in Betrieb genommen und auf welcher Strecke verkehrte sie ? *1835 von Nürnberg nach Fürth*

3. Wie heißen die drei Halbinseln im Süden Europas ? *Balkanhalbinsel, Appenninenhalbinsel, Pyrenäenhalbinsel*

4. Wie heißt die Insel, auf die Napoleon zum zweiten Male verbannt wurde ? *St. Helena*

5. Was bedeutet die Abkürzung SS ? *Saal-Schutz*

6. 1/2 : 1/4 = *2*

7. Wann und wo wurde der Führer geboren ? *am 20.4.89 in Braunau am Inn*

8. Was will das Sterilisationsgesetz ? *Die Erhaltung der gesunden Erbmasse durch die Verhinderung des schlechten Nachwuchses*

9. Welche Erbkrankheiten kennen Sie ? *Schwachsinn, Epylepsie, Hüftlahmheit*

10. Wie schwer ist 1 kg Eisen ? *1 kg*

11. Welche Staaten grenzen an das Mittelmeer ? *Griechenland, Albanien, Serbien, Kroatien, Italien, Frankreich, Spanien, Marokko, Lybien, Ägypten*

12. Welches war der schwärzeste Tag der Bewegung ? *9. Nov. 1923*

13. Wer ist der Erfinder der Buchdruckerkunst ? *Gutenberg*

14. Was ist Rasse ? *Rasse ist Zugehörigkeit zu einem Volksstamm, dessen Eigenheiten durch die Lebensforderungen bestimmt sind.*

15. 46 131 - 13 794 : 9 . 2 1/2 + (3/4 + 0,10) : (3/9 : 1/27) - 999,15

(handwritten calculations)

Opposite and above: Examination Questions for SS-Auxiliaries (BDC-National Archives II)

BIRTHPLACE

Hitler and Himmler had elevated the "Germanic workers of the soil" (*"Völkischer Bauerschaft"*) to a sacred place in the Nazi vision of a better future. With the exaltation of rural Germany a key element of the Nazi program, it is not surprising that farming communities reciprocated by ultimately providing the majority of the rank-and-file concentration camp guards.[1] As previously noted (see Chapter 1, endnote number 11), three of the most notorious overseers came from the rural area surrounding Ravensbrück itself. While more women came from rural than urban areas, the following list reflects the cities with the highest number of *Aufseherinnen* born in them:

Category 1

Berlin 93
Dresden 32
Chemnitz 29
Leipzig 28
Hamburg 26
Breslau 25
Grünberg 21
Nuremberg 19
Dortmund 17
Plauen 16
Augsburg 14
Langenbielau 12
Magdeburg 11
Hainichen 11
Wittenberg 9

Reichenbach 8
Essen 8
Neusalz 8
Neustadt 7
Vienna 7
Waldenburg 7
Trautenau 7
Duisburg 7
Munich 6
Falkenau 6
Oranienburg 6
Oberaltstadt 6
Bernsdorf 5
Freiberg 5
Guben 5
Neurode 5
Hannover 5
Hermsdorf 5
Peterswaldau 5
Rostock 5
Auerbach (Erzgebirge) 5
Breda 5
Eberswalde 5
Erfurt 4
Gladbeck 4
Halley 4
Hindenberg 4
Landeshut (Bavaria) 4
Schönau 4
Standorf 4

Teplitz-Schönau 4
Torgau 4
Zwickau 4
*Number of cities contributing
fewer than four women* 945

AGE

From its inception, Nazism was to be a youth movement. In Hitler's own words, the young were *"der Baustein unseres Reiches"* ("the foundation stone of our empire").[2] However, as a result of the sharp downturn in Germany's fortunes during the war, most women only had the opportunity to assume positions of responsibility late in Nazism's existence. Since it was crucial for the Nazi system to operate as smoothly and efficiently as possible during these desperate times, there was a tendency to fill the leadership ranks of the female guard force with women who had proven themselves. As a result, more experienced women generally moved into the higher echelons of the overseer corps. There were exceptions, however. Irma Grese oversaw 18,000 Central European women in Birkenau's "C" Camp at the age of nineteen.[3] Nevertheless, the *Chef Oberaufseherinnen* (only two women ever achieved this status) were middle aged during their terms of service.

By late 1944, of course, the 17-45 (21-45 prior to 1943) age limitations were lifted and virtually anyone able to move was sought for service. The youngest and oldest overseers are shown below in Category 2 as well as the year of birth and age of employment averages:

Category 2

The oldest person to serve: Anna Kühn, born on May 20, 1885 in Leipzig, was 57 years old when she was employed as an Aufseherin in Ravensbrück. She entered service on special waiver in November 1942.

The youngest person to serve: Gertrud Sieber, born on March 31, 1929 in Bobernick was 15 years old when she was employed as an Aufseherin in Groß-Rosen on May 2, 1944.

The average year of birth: 1917

The average age of employment: 26

ASSIGNMENTS

Prior to the advent of World War II, a woman entering service as an overseer was considered an "employee of the Reich" and was then assigned to FKL-Ravensbrück for her three week training course. After the war broke out, the new recruits and conscripts were placed under the supervision of the *Waffen-SS* and trained at Groß-Rosen and Floßenbürg. As previously noted, German corporations which used the abundant slave labor pool occasionally had their own guards. However, when Propaganda Minister Josef Goebbels called for Germany to attain *"totaler Kriegseinsatz"* (mobilization for total war) on August 24, 1944, Himmler mandated that the factory guards be fully conscripted directly into the *Waffen-SS,* and, in turn, German Big Business found its own trained guards being commandeered by the Nazi regime.

The significance of all of these training developments was that women who entered the guard force did not receive a uniform standard of training or assignment. In turn, women had vastly different experiences, and by perusing the personnel files one can readily see the myriad of situations and permanent duty assignments that the majority of the women experienced. Some overseers were fortunate and had only one, stable assignment throughout their tenure in the guard staff. Others, owing largely to the military debacle the nation was experiencing, were moved frequently from one bad situation to another – ultimately culminating in supervising a death march and being taken by Soviet forces – never to be seen alive again.

The following is a breakdown of Aufseherinnen by camp assignments. Note that subcamp (*Außenlager*) or adjacent camp (*Nebenlager*) designations have been omitted. In addition, only a very large work detail that eventually turned into a death march (*Kommando Heimbrechts*) has been included. Multiple service assignments by many overseers have been tabulated into the table as well.

Category 3

Ravensbrück 958
Floßenbürg 561
Groß-Rosen 541
Neuengamme 158
Sachsenhausen 89
Auschwitz (Birkenau and Buna Monowitz included) . 56
Stutthof (sometimes combined with Danzig) 31
Buchenwald 24
Kommando Heimbrechts 22
Danzig (sometimes combined with Stutthof) 20

```
Wache                                    Außenkommando
              Frauen-Konzentrationslager Ravensbrück
          A r b e i t s e i n t e i l u n g  für den 24.Aug.42  7 Uhr
```

Kommando	Aufseherinnen	Zahl Aufs.	Zahl Hftl.
Amt W V Gut:			
1. Kellerbruch	Wedde, Pucia	2	35 gem.
2. Hühnerfarm			8 IBV
3. Gutshof	Mewes, Ritschel	2	35 gem.
Rüstungsbetriebe:			
4. Marine-Hauptw.Lager	Ehlert	1	30 gem.
5. Sass-Fabrik	Riedl II	1	15 gem.
6. Wäscherei Huve	Lorenz I	1	15 gem.
7. Lufthauptmunitionsamt	Witthuhn	1	30 gem.
8. Fa. Siemens	Scheuerer	1	90 gem.
Privatbetriebe:			
9. Gut Hindenburg	Dittmann, Bartel	2	30 gem.
10. Gut Osterne	Meinel, Gallinat	2	40 gem.
11. Fa. Uppenthal	Gräfe II	1	14 gem.
12. Gut Ribbeck	Tack, Jäcker	2	30 gem.
13. Obstgut Metzenthin	Kassen	1	20 gem.
14. Faserstoff-Gärtn.	Fischer	1	10 gem.
15. Gärtn.Mehlhase Zehdenik	Kopp	1	10 gem.
16. Gärtn. Opitz	Schreiter, Burg	2	20 gem.
17. Gut Wentow	Frick, Hernges	2	30 gem.
18. Forstamt Menz	Pfannstiel, Sacher	2	25 gem.
19. Gut Godendorf	Erdmann, Kraus	2	30 gem.
20. Sanat. Hohenlychen	Teetz, Grese	2	40 gem.
21. Sägewerk Barnewitz	Mortka, Strojny	2	25 gem.
Gut Harzwalde			(10 IBV)
Amtsgr. C Bauleitung			
22. Bauleitg. Büro			5 BV
23. Arbeiterkantine	Borchardt	1	10 IBV
24. Straße pflastern	Handke	1	20 gem.
25. Steine laden alte Abl.	Helbig	1	30 Jud.
26. Straßenbau Strafbl.	Laschke, Tribus	2	50 gem.
27. Humus auswerfen)	Maßmann, Huber	4	100 gem.
" z.d.Führergs.) Strfbl.	Saretzki, Seltmann		
28. Humus planieren	Weber	1	10 gem.
29. Kanalbau Bl. 17	Arneth	1	
Amt W V Bauleitg. Gut			
30. Straßenbau neues Gut	Lächert, Schneider	2	25 gem.
Amt W VI Bekleidungswerke:			
31. Bekl.Werke Büro	Nickel	1	7 gem.
32. Angorazucht	Krüger I, Scheffler	2	35 gem.
33. Rohrmattenweberei	Liehr,Leopold,Wöllert	3	70 gem.
Lager:			
34. Polit. Abt.	Buha 25	2	20 Pol.
35. Erkenn. Dst.	Bauer I	1	2 Pol.
36. Hausgarten, Reimann, Renner		4.5	6 IBV
37. Haus Götzinger	Tschenisch		4 IBV
38. Ladekommando	Kramer Boeddeker	1 10 24 gem.	
39. Lagergärtnerei	Plathe	1	8 gem.
40. Gartenanlagen	Krüger III	1	18 gem.
41. Kartoffelkeller	Immerheiser, Herm	2	60 gem.
42. Reinigungskommando			9 IBV
43. Ställe	Biehl II, Langegger	2	18 gem.
44. Holzhacken	Helbig	(1)	36 Jud.
45. Beerenpflücken	Schuster	1	10 IBV
46. Müllkolonne	Teetz Becker Kramer	1	15 gem.
47. Haferfeld	Lorenz II	1	10 gem.
48. Weg z. See bauen Strfbl.	Borrmann II,	1	40 gem.
49. Kommandantur Reing.	Arneth	1	20 gem.

```
    Post.Leu. 18       Technische Abt. 5
Tor, Kläranl.: Tschenisch,   Fürsorge: Schröers,   Effekten: Pusch,
Mauthausen: Boeddeker, Fraede.                      Gethlich,
    Ablösun 20
```

Sömmerda 19
Mauthausen 19
Dachau 19
Bergen-Belsen 14
Majdanek-Lublin 11

Once the women were sent to the camp, prison, youth protective custody camp, subcamp, adjacent camp, or external detail, the next pressing issue was what sort of daily assignment they would receive. These assignments could be extended – perhaps even made permanent – or they could last for as little as a half a day or night, or an entire night. Page 239 shows the FKL-Ravensbrück duty assignment roster for August 24, 1942.

RANKS/POSITIONS

In her short overview of the history of the female guard force, Irmtraud Heike has correctly noted that unlike their male counterparts, " ... the *Aufseherinnen differentiated themselves from each other less through the different ranks but more through different 'Aufgabenbereiche'* ("areas of responsibilities").[4] Ranks always mattered, especially in a system like the one the Nazis had generated. Nevertheless, the opportunity for women in key positions to assign individuals through the network of upper echelon command leaders had a tremendous impact on the lives of the average guards. Critical to getting things done in the camps were the aides to the Oberaufseherin – the *Rapportführereinnen* and the *Blockführereinnen*. The *Rapportführerinnen* were the "reporting leaders," and they functioned as a link between the senior overseers and the various female blocks (barracks). Just below the *Rapportführerinnen* were the *Blockführerinnen* (Barracks leaders) and they oversaw an entire housing unit of women prisoners. These female guards determined the daily routine for the women under their supervision and utilized other *Aufseherinnen, Hilfsaufseherinnen*, and supervisory prisoners (*Blockälteste* [Block elder] and *Stubenälteste* [Barrack's Room senior]) to accomplish the *Blockführerin*'s "missions." It was through collusion with these individuals that the camp structure was organized and efficiently run.

As noted in Chapter 1, once a *Hilfsaufseherin* (assistant overseer) had become a full-fledged Aufseherin, permanent duty stations were assigned. Those rare Aufseherinnen who had leadership potential, special skills in completing their assignments, simply were favorites of an *Oberaufseherin*, or were particularly pitiless in disciplining prisoners, could be promoted to *Erstaufseherin* ("first guard"). The result of such a promotion was immediate: more power, more clout in the women's portion of a camp or protective custody facility, and higher wages. The next plateau was the very powerful and influential *Oberaufseherin* ("senior overseer"). The senior overseer was roughly the equivalent of a male officer (although she could never order a male to do anything). In addition, the *Oberaufseherin* was a member of the command staff of the camp. Her powers over all the women guards beneath her were close to absolute, and subordinate female guards had to insure that they did not do anything that would anger her. She had the right to assign Aufseherinnen to various posts and details. A breach of some camp regulation could result in an overseer being assigned to long periods of an external detail in inclement weather. Additionally, the offending guard might be put on a double assignment (work detail by day – block leader by night). Finally, the worst situation of all, the disciplined Aufseherin could be assigned to a *Strafkommando* (punishment detail) or receive the same "twenty-five lashes to the derrier" punishment that a prisoner had to endure. Rarely did this occur, but when it did, an added humiliation was decreed – fellow Aufseherinnen would participate in administering the whipping. Of the thousands of Aufseherinnen who served in the camps, subcamps, adjacent camps, work details, and youth protective custody camps, only two women ever were to achieve the highest rank of *Chef Oberaufseherin* – Anne Klein-Plaubel and Luise Brunner. Ironically, very little is known or documented about either woman.

The following is a list of the ranks of the female guard force:

Category 4

SS Aufseherinnen 3230
SS Chef Oberaufseherinnen 3
SS Oberaufseherin 17
Second SS Oberaufseherinnen 1
SS Wächterinnen (Sicherheitsdienst Gefängnis [SD prison]) 7
SS members (technically assigned to the SS) 16
Waffen-SS members (under the jurisdiction of the Waffen-SS) 15
SS Helferinnenen 16
Kommando Führerinnen 4
Lagerleiterinnen/-führerinnen 5
Stellv. Lagerleiterinnen/-führerinnen 4
Funktionerin 1

Rapportführerinnen 5

Blockführerinnen/-leiterinnen 8

Scharführerinnen 2

Chef Oberaufseherinnen:
Brunner, Luise
Klein, born Plaubel, Anne

Oberaufseherinnen:
Becher, born Stark, Gertrud
Bernigau, Jane (Gerda)
Binz, Dorathea (*stellvertretende* [Replacement])
Oberaufseherin)
de Hüber, Margarethe
Dell'Antonia, Martha
Essmann, Marianne
Freinberger, Margarete
Grabner, Else
Grese, Irma
Hempel, born Herdlitschke, Anna
Lange, Dora
Langefeld, Johanna
Rose, born Hermann, Erna
von der Hülst, Annemarie (Anni)
Weber, Else
Weninger/Winniger, born Mühlau/Myland, Gertrud(e)
Wisotzki, Johanna

SS Members (technically "assigned" to the Waffen-SS):
Bässler, Elisabeth
Balkenhol, Maria
Börstler, Frieda
Burkhardt, Elfrieda
Dreschler, Ruth
Geulin, Karoline
Gutzeit, Loni
Hille, Susanne
Hönigsberg, Franziska
Hühnerbeing, Ruth
Isert, Maria
Kässner, Margarete
Knoblich, Elisabeth
Motzkuhn, Elfriede
Müller, Maria
Pinske, Frieda

Under the jurisdiction of the Waffen-SS:
Achterberg, Erna

Becker, Erika Ruth
Dell'Antonia, Martha
Garbisch, Maria
Grebs, Herta
Haupt, Erika
Haase, Herta
Kohler, Magdalena
Korthals, Agnes
Krosky, Ottille
Lang, Elfriede
Mains, Elli
Pfeiffer, Lilly
Schmidt, Erna
Schmidt, Rosa

MARITAL STATUS

Heinrich Himmler had encouraged male members of the SS to marry, and single German women had been encouraged to bear as many children as they could through state sponsored *Lebensborn* ("Foundation of Life") homes.[5] Great care was taken to prove a so-called racially pure lineage, and since the Third Reich was mortally challenged from subhuman nations, the SS – the purest of the pure – had to become the racial shock troops as well as the racial reproducers.

As with every other facet of Nazi society, the emphasis was always on the importance of the males. Because of the necessities of waging a two front international conflict, many of the old adages about the German women remaining at home were ignored and mass conscription now put these previous "defenders of home and hearth" in the camps. Nevertheless, many did marry – frequently SS men.

According to their files, only a little over fourteen percent (253 of the 3,622 Aufseherinnen) were married. One might reasonably suggest that with the encouragement of *Lebensborn* as well as the more immediate concerns of defending the Reich, marriage would have been difficult at best. Despite the pressures and tensions of Germany's rapid deterioration, only four files note a formal divorce. Also, one should bear in mind that the overseers who came from southern Germany would most likely be Roman Catholic and a formal divorce would be out of the question for the most of these women. Naturally, in many cases, the war itself may have very well contributed to an informal estrangement. Nevertheless, at least on paper, the overseers had an amazingly low rate.

Equally amazing was the fact that only three female guards lost their husbands during the conflict. One could expect three wives to lose their husbands to natural causes during peacetime. Since the women were not allowed to fight armed external enemies (unarmed, defenseless enemies within the barbed wire were "fair game" of course), their husbands would be even less likely to be widowers.

As was noted in Chapter 1, the single women had numerous opportunities for sexual liaisons with male guards. While it was strictly forbidden for any sort of relationship with inmates, some overseers secretly violated the formal prohibition known as "The Race and Resettlement Act." In the perverted world of the camps, truly anything was possible.

AWARDS AND DECORATIONS

Unlike the case of male guards, the opportunity for special commendation was apparently limited for the women. Despite the fact that over thirty-six hundred women served at one time or another as overseers, only the following women received official recognition via awards, commendations, and/or decorations:

NAME: AWARD/DECORATION

Bernigau, Jane: *"Kriegsverdienstkreuz II. Klasse ohne Schwerter"* (War Service Cross – 2nd Class without Swords)
Danz, Luise: *"Kriegsverdienstkreuz II. Klasse ohne Schwerter"* (War Service Cross – 2nd Class without Swords)
Ryan, Hermine (Braunsteiner): *"Kriegsverdienstkreuz II. Klasse* (awarded 1943)

Recommended for the same medal:
John, Anna
Hofman, Irmgard

NOBILITY

Although service in the Aufseherinnenkorps was open to all ethnic Germans in good health and with no criminal backgrounds, as we have previously seen, the vast majority of overseers came from lower class families. However, the following female guards could claim aristocratic backgrounds:

von der Hülst, Annemie (Anni)
von der Wielen, Euphemia
von Kettler (Freifrau), Ellen

NON-GERMAN AND NON-AUSTRIAN OVERSEERS

It was possible for non-ethnic German women to serve as auxiliaries in the SS. However, special permission had to be obtained from the SS inspector-general's office in Oranienburg. Of course, toward the end of the war, frequently "field" decisions were taken that occasionally elevated non-German females and even Kapos to supervisory positions over prisoners. When the initial death marches began in January 1945, housewives and single women with no formal training whatsoever were hauled out to drive the near dead inmates further into the oblivion on these aimless forced marches. From this time until the Third Reich fell in early May, more and more women, many who had been considered *Tiermenschen* (subhumans) themselves, were thrust into semi-overseer roles. Below are the non-German women who were officially admitted to the cadre of female guards:

Category 5

NAME	NATIONALITY
Alfering (born Voorkman), Helene (Hillena)	Dutch
Bendnorz (born Tyalik), Anna	Croat
Belza, Stanislawa	Pole
Blaschka, Ida	Slav
Ciarzinski, Apolinia	Pole
Danneboom, Christa	Dutch
Dominik (born Labjon), Henriette	French
Gombert, Marcella	Italian
Grabowski, Martha	Pole
Gryska, Elfriede	Czech
Heikens, Hilliena-Grietje	Dutch
Heinen, Aracelli	French
Heykop, Cenntije Jacoba	Slav
Hrdy, Anna	(possibly) Hungarian
Koorn, Gisberta	Dutch
Mol (born Dije), Johanna	Dutch
Oterdoom, Johanna	Dutch
Pajonk, Sophie	Czech
Pollmann, Eva	Hungarian
Schot, Catharina	Dutch
Snurova (or Snurawa), Hanne	Pole
Sollich (or Sollisch; born Niksch), Else ("Misch")	Croat
Wyndelts, Hanna	(possibly) Dutch

MEDICAL MATTERS

One of the primary concerns for all SS personnel was the real potential for contracting a fatal illness. The overcrowded conditions of the camps, the terrible sanitary conditions that led thousands of inmates to waste away and die, and the daily stress and frequent bad weather, all created a dangerous environment for the SS overseers. Periodically massive epidemics broke out in most of the major camps and generally the precautions taken were simply to seal off the camp and allow the disease to run its course with the inmates. In this brutal world that the Nazis had created, the attitude was: let's kill off as many as possible via disease, but let's not endanger ourselves in the process!

After all the file searching, I have not found one documented case of an SS woman succumbing to disease. Naturally, this does not mean that it did not occur; however, I simply did not find a single case. A fellow camp guard and boy-friend of one of the women did die shortly prior to the end of the war from typhus he had contracted at Bergen-Belsen.

One of the perks for "employees of the Reich" was access to medical care free of charge. As I noted in the Introduction, occasionally documents can be used to place particular SS women at particular places at particular times. This is true with regard to the Auschwitz SS military hospital document below.

The medical examination record card above was retrieved from the records of the hospital after the Soviet forces liberated Auschwitz in January 1945. This demonstrates that Aufseherin Grese had been concerned enough about the possibility of having contracted syphilis that she had herself checked via the Wasserman test. Grese had led a promiscuous lifestyle at Birkenau and had had many lovers – both male and female. Although her test for syphilis was negative, she later would become pregnant and would have an abortion illegally performed on her by a Jewish inmate-doctor. This is an interesting document and evidence that the debauchery ultimately did catch up with many Nazis.

Medical Analysis for Syphilis (Wasserman Test) –Irma Grese (APMO Hyg. Inst. No. 10690)

CAMP ADMINISTRATION

A point that has been made clear throughout this analysis of the SS women is that they were "schooled" in the finer points of terror training. In this topsy-turvy world, one way an overseer could get in trouble was to be too "nice." A case in point is the Aufseherin Klara Kunig who was ousted for that very "offense." On the other hand, one individual existed who was so offensive that the nickname fellow overseers had for her was "Shut Your Mouth!" (see Knoblich, Elisabeth).

All this notwithstanding, it would be a distortion to say that mundane matters did not filter into the daily routine of the camp staff. While the *Lagerordnung* (the basic regulations that pertained to all camps) was the essential guideline for all SS women, each camp would be administered by a commandant who set the tone and pace of the institution. On pages 245-246 is Auschwitz Standing Order No. 27/[19]44.

POSTWAR JUSTICE AND PUNISHMENT

Retribution frequently preceded formal judgment in the case of the concentration/death camp guards. Even today, well over fifty five years after the camps were liberated, one only has to see the films made of the mounds of dead, emaciated, and rotting bodies piled about these death factories, to understand why the SS guards – women and men alike – would in many cases be quickly murdered by inmates and liberators alike. As noted earlier, this would be particularly true in the areas liberated by Soviet forces.

While the Soviets held the initial war crimes trial in July 1943, the Poles, British, French, Dutch, Norwegians, and Americans quickly followed suit. The male SS were tried, convicted, and executed in far greater numbers than the women. There are many reasons for this – the most obvious being that the men outnumbered the women by almost five to one.[6] In addition, western cultures have generally been reluctant to execute the bearers of life. Although there have been women who have proven themselves more than deserving of the ultimate punishment, there has been a real hesitancy to eliminate even the most cold-blooded, diabolical murderess. Even when the American and French courts invoked the death penalty for German murderesses (and in the American case the death penalty was passed against two euthanasia attendants – not SS women), the sentences were ultimately overturned.

The verdicts of the various western courts are relatively easy to access, but little is known about the fates of those camp guards apprehended by the Yugoslavs, Romanians, and Albanians. Thanks to Frau Riße and Simon Weber, we have some data on some Aufseherinnen taken by the former East German courts. Below are the judgments of the proceedings against overseers:

Category 6
Aufseherinnen Sentenced To Death

NAME	DATE EXECUTED	RESPONSIBLE NATION
Bayer, Sydonia	Unknown	Poland
Binz, Dorothea	May 2, 1947	Great Britain
Bormann, Juana	December 13, 1945	Great Britain
Bösel, Grete	May 2, 1947	Great Britain
Brand[e]l, Therese	December 2, 1947	Poland
Closius, Ruth	July 29, 1948	Great Britain
Grese, Irma	December 13, 1945	Great Britain
Hildner, Ruth	May 2, 1947	Czechoslovakia
Jankowsky, Christel	Unknown; sentenced – fate unknown	East Germany
Mand[e]l, Maria	December 2, 1947	Poland
Schreiter, Gertrud	September 20, 1948	Great Britain
Volkenrath, Elisabeth	December 13, 1945	Great Britain
Zimmer, Emma	September 20, 1947	Great Britain

Of the thirteen known overseers who were executed, all but Sydonia Bayer were trained at FKL-Ravensbrück. Dorothea Binz had served as the chief trainer and overseer there. Juana Bormann, Irma Grese, and Elisabeth Volkenrath were condemned to death for their roles at Auschwitz and Bergen-Belsen. Dorothea Binz, Grete Bösel, Gertrud Schreiter, and Emma Zimmer were condemned to death for their roles at the Ravensbrück. Maria Mandel and Therese Brandel were given the ultimate punishment for their involvement at Auschwitz-Birkenau, and, likewise, Ruth Closius was sentenced to death for her role in the Uckermark Youth Protective Custody Camp (Block 27 at Ravensbrück).

The case against Ruth Hildner was focused on her role as the chief overseer of the Helmbrechts Death March. Sydonia Bayer was convicted for her participation in mass murder as the senior Aufseherin at Litzmannstadt (the Lodz Ghetto). Many more Auseherinnen were likely executed without trial in the east.

PAŃSTWOWE MUZEUM
Auschwitz-Birkenau w Oświęcimiu
Dział Dokumentacji Archiwalnej

O d p i s .

Der Standortälteste der Waffen-SS. Auschwitz,den 1.November

Standortbefehl Nr. 27/44.

1. **Bestrafung.**
   Ich habe einen Kommandanturangehörigen mit Arrest bestraft,weil
   er ein dringendes dienstliches Schreiben nicht sofort weitergab.

2. **Vergütung bei Verlust von Eigentum durch Feindeinwirkung.**
   Es wird darauf hingewiesen , dass bei Verlust selbstbeschafftere
   Gegenstände nur Vergütungen stattfinden können , wenn diese un -
   bedingt zur Ausübung des Dienstes erforderlich waren.
   Verlust an Geld darf nur bis zur Höhe eines Monatsbetrages des
   Wehrsoldes erstattet werden.
   Die Mitführung wertvoller und überflüssiger Stücke geschieht
   während des Krieges auf eigene Gefahr.

3. **Annahme von Umzugsgut und leeren Möbelwagen.**
   Die weitere Verschlechterung der Wagenlage und die erhöhten An-
   forderungen an den Laderaum der Reichsbahn für die Bedürfnissen
   der Wehrmacht und die Abfuhr rüstungs- und ernährungswichtigen
   Güter zwingen dazu , den Versand von Umzugsgut und leeren Möbelwagen weiter einzuschränken.
   Die Aufgabe
   a) leerer und beladener Möbelwagen,
   b) von Umzugs-und Evakuierungsgut als Wagenladung und
      Frachtstückgut sowie Beförderung neuer Mobel von Pri-
      vatpersonen, z.B. Bombengeschädigter, nach deren neuem
      Wohnort ist nur zulässig, wenn eine schriftliche Umzugs-
      genehmigung des für den Versandort zuständigen Nahe
      bevollmächtigten erteilt wird.
      Die Genehmigung hierfür erteilt nur das Landratsamt
      Bielitz. Die genauen Bestimmungen über den Versand von
      Umzugsgut usw. können gegebenenfalls bei der Abteilung
      Unterkunft eingesehen werden.

4. **Dienstreisen.**
   Unter Bezug auf die neue Kriegsreiseverordnung haben alle Wehr-
   machtsangehörigen bei Dienstreisen amtliche Unterkunft , Unter-
   offiziere und Mannschaften auch amtliche Verpflegung in An -
   •/

Pages 245-246: Standing Order Nr. 27/44 –Auschwitz, November 1,1943 (APMO Dpr. No. Lod/396)

PAŃSTWOWE MUZEUM
Auschwitz-Birkenau w Oświęcimiu
Dział Dokumentacji Archiwalnej   - 5 -

diese gemeinen Fahrradmarder zu überführen .

Die jetzt entwendeten Fahrräder haben folgende Kennzeichen :

   Diensträder :Nr. 82,83, ZB 57,"Presto" Rahmen-Nr 1352982
                  239,Fabr.-Nr. 639146,

   Privaträder : "Olympia" , Fahrgestell Nr.189918 , Rahmen
             schwarz lackiert, Lenker verchromt, gelber
             Ledersattel, Dynamo-Lichtanlage (Lampe und
             Dynamo verchromt) ,
             "Apollo" Nr. 4043150 ohne Lampe, schwarz
             lackiert, graue Holzgriffe.

Zweckdienliche Angaben sind an den Gerichts-SS-Führer zu

richten .

14.Verloren -gefunden.

   Am 26.10.44 ist auf der Strasse Auschwitz -Raisko eine braune

Aktentasche mit Inhalt (Handtasche ,Brieftasche mit verschie-

denen Papieren und Geldbetrag , 1 Buch " Die Borgia " u.a.

verloren gegangen .

   Als gefunden wurden abgegeben :
      1 Erkennungsmarke LW.BK. 47/XI Nr. 9
      1 Erkennungsmarke "SS-Geb.Jgr.E.Batl.Nord Nr.78 "
      1 silb. Infanterie-Sturmabzeichen
      1 Schlüsselbund in Ledertasche.

Die verlorenen bezw. gefundenen Gegenstände sind auf der

Dienststelle des SS- Standortältesten , Zimmer 24, abzugeben

bezw. gegen Nachweis abzuholen .

15.Ungültige Ausweise.

   Folgende Ausweise bezw. Armbinden gingen verloren und werden

für ungültig erklärt : vor Missbrauch wird gewarnt :

Standortausweis Aufseherin Hildegard Lachert,geb.19. 2.20
              Kommandantur K.L.Auschwitz II

Nr.2142 Stanislaus Paszek,geb. 1.4.22 besch.b.Fa Falk

Nr.1629 Alexander Jarosch, " 17.7.84 " " " Huta.

              gez. B a e r
            SS-Sturmbannführer.

Aufseherinnen Sentenced to Prison

NAME	SENTENCE	RESPONSIBLE NATION
Arps, Charlotte	1-3 years imprisonment	East Germany
Bergmann, Erika	Life imprisonment	East Germany
Bisäke, Margarete	1 year imprisonment	East Germany
Bothe, Herta	10 years imprisonment (released on 12-22-51)	Great Britain
Danz, Luise	Life imprisonment (released Poland in 1957; later retried for murder at NL Malchow in 1996)	Germany
Fabritzek, Agnes	5 years imprisonment	East Germany
Gebhardt, Luise	5 years imprisonment	East Germany
Göritz, Ilse	Life imprisonment	East Germany
Hartmann, Elly	Prosecuted but findings absent from *Zentralestelle* (Ludwigsburg) files.	East Germany
Heise, Gertrud	7 years imprisonment (released after serving 6)	Great Britain
Heise, Gertrud	7 years imprisonment	Great Britain
Hempel, Anna	10 years imprisonment (released on 12-22-51)	Great Britain
Hörn, Käthe	7 years imprisonment	United States
Jürss, Ulla	Life imprisonment	East Germany
Kilkowski, Wally	9 months imprisonment	East Germany
Koch, Ilse	4 years imprisonment and later (released and retrie Germany for murder; sentenced to life imprisonment; committed suicide in prison in 1957)	United States
Kohlmann, Anneliese	2 years (released for pretrial confinement [timed served])	United States
Lächert, Hildegard	Life imprisonment (released Poland and later in 1957; retried for Majdanek crimes and imprisoned again)	Germany
Monnecke, Elfriede	10 years imprisonment (released after 5 years)	Great Britain
Nitzschmer, Hertha	6 years imprisonment	East Germany
Orlowski, Alice	Life imprisonment (released after ten years)	Poland
Rabe, Margarethe	Life imprisonment (sentenced reduced on appeal to 21 years; released on 2-26-54 after serving 5 years/10 months)	Great Britain
Rabestein, Gertrud	Life imprisonment	East Germany
Ryan (born Braunsteiner) Hermine	Life imprisonment (tried for Majdanek crimes)	Germany
Schulz, Ella	7 years imprisonment (released after 4 years)	Great Britain
Wötzel, Frieda	Life imprisonment	East Germany

CONCLUSIONS

The antifeminist policy of the Third Reich limited the role of the Aufseherinnen. They came late to service and they came late to the war, but it was usually not a matter of their collective choice. Primarily because the German fortunes were diminishing from late 1941-early 1942, the Nazi leadership begrudgingly had to call up women for guard duty. Partly because of the original policy of keeping women in domestic situations, most women remained reluctant to join the ranks of the female guard corps. In addition, the majority of Germans knew very well that the camps were places of humiliation, degradation, and punishment. Primarily for these reasons, the overseers played their parts late in the history of the Third Reich, and for the majority, only after being conscripted. Nazi racist policy certainly encouraged the overseers to be as cruel as they pleased to the prisoners under their control. Nevertheless, it is important to point out that there were a few, generally at great personal risk, who acted decently throughout their service. Most of the women came from rural areas of Germany. The majority were from lower socio-economic backgrounds and had limited formal education. They were usually given an accelerated training program at Ravensbrück and then were dispersed to various camps. Very few ever rose above the rank of Aufseherin. The largest contingent of Aufseherinnen served without distinction or much notice and slipped into obscurity after the war. Those who were not in the camps as the war ended and who were not immediately apprehended by liberating forces could easily blend into the masses of displaced persons ("D.P.s") milling about a ravaged Europe. Also, unlike their male counterparts, the female guards did not have to worry about the blood type tattoos to identify them. Unfortunately, owing to the absence of a central database, thorough research on the female perpetrators has been absent.

Notes:

[1] While many rural youth undoubtedly were impressed with Hitler and Himmler's view of a "New Order" built on a peasant aristocracy, a secondary motivation also existed: many rural youth saw no future "down on the farm" and, in turn, they sought adventure in a new setting – the SS – "the elite guard!" Cf. Höhne, *Death's Head*, p. 136.

[2] *Völkischer Beobachter*, May 2, 1938, p. 2.

[3] Phillips (ed.), *Belsen Trial*, xii.

[4] Heike, "... da es sich ja lediglich um die Bewachung der Häftlinge handelt," p. 226.

[5] Unwed mothers who bore children for the Third Reich were lauded by Himmler, yet this state sponsored encouragement flew in the face of older values, and, indeed, of many of the early Nazi expressions of "family values." Since Nazi Germany had to generate thousands of new Aryan men in short order, the program never came close to bridging the replacement gap. Indeed, it was the obsession that Hitler and Himmler possessed concerning the great racial war Germany was waging that led to this ill-fated program. For a more complete analysis of the *Lebensborn* program, see Koonz, *Mothers in the Fatherland*, pp. 398-402.

[6] As of July 6, 1944, there were approximately 24,000 members of the *"Totenkopfverbände"* (the "Death's Head" units, the concentration camp guards) according to the SS statistics division in Oranienburg. Höhne, *Death's Head* xii.

SOURCES

Published Sources

Astor, Gerald. *The "Last" Nazi: The Life and Times of Dr. Joseph [sic] Mengele*. New York: Donald I. Fine, 1983.

Bauer, Yehuda. "The Death Marches, January-May, 1945." *Modern Judaism*. Vol. 3, No. 1, 1-21.

Baumeister, Roy F. *Evil: Inside Human Violence and Cruelty*. New York: W.H. Freeman, 1996.

Baynes, Norman H., ed. *The Speeches of Adolf Hitler: April 1922-August 1939*. London: Oxford University Press, 1942, Vol. I.

Bezwinska, Jadwiga and Danuta Czech, eds. *KL Auschwitz Seen by the SS: Höß, Broad,* [and] *Kremer.* Trans. Constantine Fitzgibbon. Oswiecim: Panstwowe Muzeum, 1978.

Blackburn, Gilmer W. *Education in the Third Reich: Race and History in Nazi Textbooks*. Albany: State University of New York, 1985.

Blanford, Edmund. *Under Hitler's Banner: Serving The Third Reich*. Shrewsbury, UK: Airlife Publishing, 1996.

Brown, Daniel Patrick. *The Beautiful Beast: The Life & Crimes of SS-Aufseherin Irma Grese*. Ventura, CA: Golden West Historical Publications, 1996.

Browning, Christopher R. *Ordinary Men: Reserve Police Battalion 101 and the Final Solution in Poland*. New York: Harper, 1992.

Dawidowicz, Lucy S. *The War Against the Jews, 1933-1945*. New York: Holt, Rinehart, and Winston, 1773.

Domarus, Max, ed. *Hitler: Reden und Proklamationen, 1931-1945*. Volume I. Würzburg: Verlags-Drückerei Schmidt, 1962.

Eicke, Theodor. *Disziplinar- und Strafforderung für das Gefängenenlager. Trials of the Major Criminals Before the International Military Tribunal* (42 Volumes, Nuremberg 1945-1949). Volume XXVI, PS 778, October 1, 1933.

Feig, Konnilyn. *Hitler's Death Camps: The Sanity of Madness*. New York: Holmes & Meier, 1981.

Fenelon, Fania with Marcelle Routier. *Playing for Time*. Translated Judith Landry. New York: Antheneum, 1977.

Finkelstein, Norman and Ruth Birn. *A Nation on Trial: The Goldhagen Thesis and Historical Truth*. New York: Owl Books, 1998.

Fischer, Klaus P. *The History of an Obsession: German Judeophobia and the Holocaust*. New York: Continuum, 1998.

Frankfurter Zeitung. September 15, 1935. P. 1.

Franz-Willing, Georg. *Der Hitlerbewegung: Der Ursprung*. Berlin-Hamburg: Preussich Oldendorf, 1962.

Fritsche, Peter. *Germans into Nazis*. Cambridge, MA: Harvard University Press, 1998.

Goldhagen, Daniel Jonah. *Hitler's Willing Executioners: Ordinary Germans and the Holocaust*. New York: *Knopf, 1996*.

Hart, Kitty. *Return to Auschwitz*. New York: Atheneum, 1982.

Heike, Irmtraud. *"da es sich ja lediglich die Bewachung der Häftlinge handelt ..."* in *Frauen in Konzentrationslagern:*

Bergen-Belsen [und] *Ravensbrück.* eds. Claus Füllberg-Stolberg et al. Bremen: Edition Temmen, 1994. 221-239.

Hepp, Michael. *"Vorhof zur Hölle: Mädchen in Jugendschutzlager Uckermark"* in *Opfer und Täterinnen.* ed. Angelika Ebbinghaus. Frankfurt/Main: Fischer Taschenbuch Verlag, 1987. 239-270.

Hilberg, Raul. *The Destruction of the European Jews.* Chicago: Quadrangle, 1967.

Höhne, Heinz. *The Order of the Death's Head: The Story of Hitler's SS.* Trans. Richard Berry. New York: Coward-McCann, 1969.

Höß, Rudolf. *Kommandant in Auschwitz: Autobiographische Aufzeichnungen. Stuttgart:* Walter Verlag, 1958. Appendix No. 8.

"Inferno on Trial," *Time.* October 8, 1945, p. 36.

James, Clive. "Blaming the Germans." *New Yorker.* April 22, 1996, 44-50.

Joffe, Josef. "Review: Goldhagen's *Willing Executioners." New York Review Review of Books.* November 28, 1996. 18-21.

Joffe, Josef. "Letters to the Editor." *New York Review of Books.* February 6, 1997. 40.

Kershaw, Ian. *Hitler.* Essex, UK: Pearson, 1991.

Kleine Wiener Kriegszeitung ["Abbreviated Vienna War Newspaper"]. January 20, 1945. p. 6.

Koch, H. W. *The Hitler Youth: Origins and Development 1922-45.* New York: Stein and Day, 1975.

Kolb, Eberhard. *Bergen-Belsen, Geschichte des "Aufenhaltslagers."* Hannover: Verlag für Literatur und Zeitgeschelen, 1962.

Koonz, Claudia. *Mothers in the Fatherland: Women, the Family, and Nazi Politics.* New York: St. Martin's, 1987.

Kraus, Ota and Erich Kulka. *The Death Factory: Documents on Auschwitz.* Trans. Stephen Jolly. Oxford: Pergamon House, 1968.

Krausnick, Helmut and Hans-Heinrich Wilhelm. *Die Truppe des Weltanschauungskrieges.* Stuttgart: Deutsche Verlags-Anstalt, 1981.

Krausnick, Helmut, Hans Buchheim, Martin Broszat, and Hans-Adolf Jacobsen. *Anatomy of the SS-State.* Trans. Richard Barry. New York: Walker, 1968.

Langbein, Hermann. *Menschen in Auschwitz. Vienna: Europaverlag, 1972.*

Laska, Vera. *Women in the Resistance and in the Holocaust: The Voices of Eyewitnesses.* Westport, CT: Greenwood, 1983.

Levin, Nora. *The Holocaust: The Destruction of European Jewry, 1933-1945.* New York: Crowell, 1968.

Lengyel, Olga. *Five Chimneys: The Story of Auschwitz.* Trans. Paul B. Weiss. Chicago: Ziff-Davis, 1947.

Levy-Hass, Hanna. *Inside Belsen.* Trans. Ronald Taylor. Totowa, NJ: Barnes & Noble, 1982.

Lipstadt, Deborah. *Denying the Holocaust: The Growing Assault on Truth and Memory.* New York: Free Press, 1993.

Littel, Franklin. *Hyping the Holocaust: Scholars Answer Goldhagen.* New York: Marion Westfield, 1997.

Lustgarten, Edgar. *The Business of Murder. New York: Charles Scribner's Sons, 1968.*

MacLean, French. *The Camp Men: The SS Officers Who Ran the Nazi Concentration Camp System.* Atglen, PA: Schiffer, 1999.

Mann, Erika. *Zehn Millionen Kinder: Die Erziehung der Jugend in Dritten Reich.* Amsterdam: Uerido Verlag, 1938.

Milton, Sybil. "The Victims of Violence: German and German-Jewish Women." in *Different Voices* eds. Carol Rittner and John K. Roth. New York: Paragon, 1991. 220-228.

Morrison, Jack W. *Ravensbrück: Everyday Life in a Woman's Concentration Camp 1939-45.* Princeton, NJ: Markus Wiener, 2000.

Nietzsche, Friedrich. *Jenseits von Gut und Böse: Vorspiel einer Philosophie der Zukunft.* Stuttgart: Philip Reclam, 1993 [1886]. No. 146.

Organisationsbuch der NSDAP. Munich 1943 [original publication 1935]. *Trials of the Major War Criminals Before the International Military Tribunal.* (42 Volumes, Nuremberg, 1945-1949).1922 Series. A-PS and 2640-PS.

Owings, Alison. *Frauen: German Women Recall the Third Reich.* New Brunswick, NJ: Rutgers University Press, 1995.

Pauwels, Jacques. *Women, Nazis, and Universities: Female University Students in the Third Reich, 1933-1945.* Westport, CT: Greenwood, 1984.

Perl, Gisella. *I Was a Doctor in Auschwitz.* New York: International Universities Press, 1948.

Phillips, Raymond, ed. *The Trial of Josef Kramer and Forty-Four Others (The Belsen Trial).* London: William Hodge, 1949.

Playfair, Giles and Derrick Sington. *The Offenders: Society and the Atrocious Crime.* London: Secker and Warsburg, 1957.

Posner, Gerald and John Ware. *Mengele: The Complete Story.* New York: McGraw-Hill, 1986.

Rabinowitz, Dorothy. *New Lives.* New York: Knopf, 1976.

Rauschning, Hermann. *Gespräche mit Hilter.* New York: Europa Verlag, 1940.

Reichsführer-SS Befehl von 14.8.43.

Reider, Frederic. *The Order of the SS: How Did it Happen.* London: W. Foulsham, 1981.

Reitlinger, Gerald. *The SS: Alibi of a Nation.* London: Heinemann, 1956.

Report of the Deputy Judge Advocate for War Crimes – European Command. June-1944-July 1948.

Rittner, Carol and John K. Roth, eds. *Different Voices: Women and the Holocaust.* New York: Paragon, 1991.

Rückerl, Adalbert. *The Investigation of Nazi Crimes, 1945-1978: A Documentation.* Trans. Derrick Rutter. New York: Archon, 1980.

Russell of Liverpool, Lord. *The Scourage of the Swastika: A Short History of Nazi Crimes.* London: Cassell, 1954.

Schmidt, Matthias. *Albert Speer: Das Ende eines Mythos – Speers wahre Rolle im Dritten Reich.* Munich: Scherz Verlag, 1982.

Schnabel, Reimund, ed. *Macht ohne Moral: Eine Dokumentation ueber die SS.* Frankfurt/Main: Röderbergerverlag, 1967.

Schoenbaum, David. *Hitler's Social Revolution: Class and Status in Nazi Germany, 1933-39.* New York: W.W. Norton, 1980.

Segev, Tom. *Soldiers of Evil: The Commandants of the Nazi Concentration Camps.* Trans. Haim Watzman. New York: McGraw-Hill, 1987.

Shermer, Michael and Alex Grobman. *Denying History: Who Say the Holocaust Never Happened and Why Do They Say It?* Berleley, CA: University of California Press, 2000.

Smith, Bradley F. *Heinrich Himmler: A Nazi in the Making, 1900-1926.* Palo Alto, CA: Hoover Institution Press/Stanford University Press, 1971.

Sofsky, Wolfgang. *The Order of Terror: The Concentration Camp.* Trans. William Templer. Princeton, NJ: Princeton University Press, 1997.

Stein, George H. *The Waffen SS: Hitler's Elite Guard at War, 1939-1945.* Ithaca, NY: Cornell University Press, 1966.

Storr, Anthony. *Human Aggression.* London: Penguin, 1968.

Suhren, Fritz. Affidavit. *Trials of the Major War Criminals Before the International Military Tribunal* (42 Volumes, Nuremberg 1945-1949). Nuremberg Documents No. D-746a (March 8, 1946) and No. D-746b (March 19, 1946).

Taake, Claudia. *Angeklagt: SS-Frauen vor Gericht.* Oldenburg: Universitaet Oldenburg, 2000.

Tillon, Germaine. *Ravensbrück.* Trans. Gerald Satterwaite. Garden City, NJ: Doubleday, 1975.

Van der Vat, Dan. *The Good Nazi: The Life & Lies of Albert Speer.* New York: Houghton Mifflin, 1997.

"verurteilt, vergessen und wieder angeklagt – das Leben der SS-Frau D." ("denounced, forgotten, and accused again – the life of SS Woman D."). *Frankfurter Rundschau,* March 27, 1996, p. 6.

Völkischer Beobachter, May 2, 1938, p. 2.

Unpublished Sources

Firestone, Renee (nee Weinfeld). Interviewed by the author in conjunction with Lilika Salzar. August 6, 1992. Beverly Hills, California.

Generalstaatsanwalt der Demokratischen Republik. Letter from Deputy Attorney-General Wieland. June 1, 1987.

Glowna Komisja Ladania Zbrodni Hitlerowskich w Polsce – Institut Pamieci Narodowej. Letter to the author. March 15, 1990.

Letters to the British Government. FO 371/50997, Nos. 5, 6, and 7. T. No. 15172. Kew Gardens, London. Various dates in November 1945.

Log, SS-Lager-Lazarett, Panstwowe Muzeum Auschwitz-Birkenau w Oswiecimiu.

National Archives [II] of the United States, College Park, Maryland. *Microfilm Publication A3343 – Series SF, Records of SS Female Functionaries (non-Aufseherinnen) from* the Berlin Document Center.

SS-Hyg. Inst/5 segr. 3, p. 33 (No. 10690), Panstwowe Muzeum Auschwitz-Birkenau w Oswiecimiu.

Tichauer, Helen (*"Zippi aus der Schreibstube"*). Interviewed by the author. July 29, 2000. New York City.

Films (documentaries)

Deutsche am Galgen. *"Teil 3: Britische Kriegsverbrecher Prozeße 1945-1949."* Prod. und Dir. Bengt von zur Mühlen. CHRONOS-Film GmbH, 1999.

MAPS

Overview Map Detailing All of the Concentration Camps, Prisons, and Work Houses of Germany—roughly 10,000! (BAK 183/L40618)

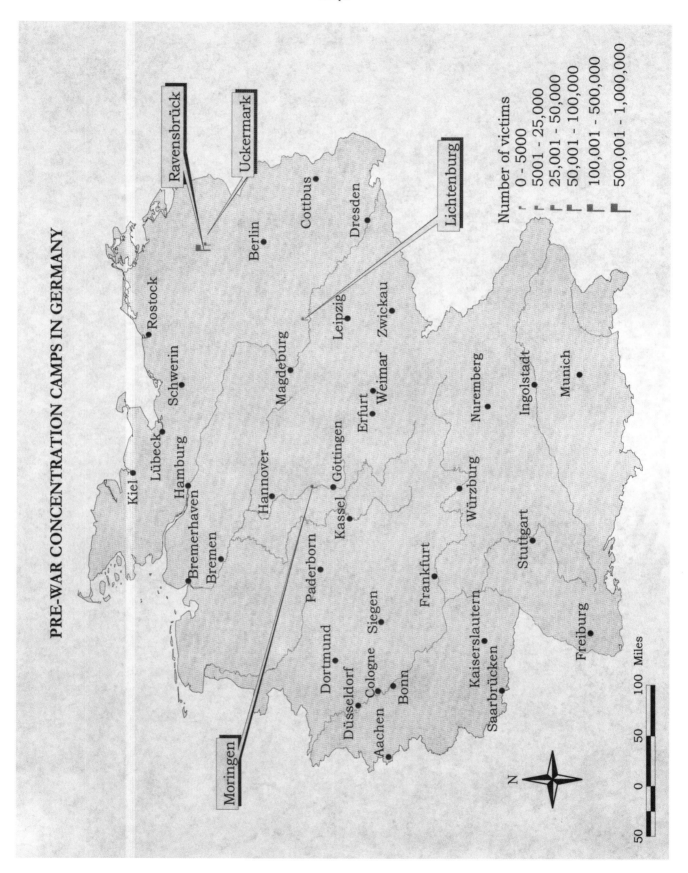

PRE-WAR CONCENTRATION CAMPS IN GERMANY

Ravensbrück

Uckermark

Lichtenburg

Moringen

Number of victims
0 - 5000
5001 - 25,000
25,001 - 50,000
50,001 - 100,000
100,001 - 500,000
500,001 - 1,000,000

Kiel
Lübeck
Rostock
Schwerin
Hamburg
Bremerhaven
Bremen
Berlin
Cottbus
Dresden
Hannover
Magdeburg
Leipzig
Zwickau
Paderborn
Kassel
Göttingen
Erfurt
Weimar
Dortmund
Düsseldorf
Cologne
Siegen
Aachen
Bonn
Frankfurt
Würzburg
Nuremberg
Kaiserslautern
Saarbrücken
Stuttgart
Ingolstadt
Munich
Freiburg

N

0   50   100   Miles
50

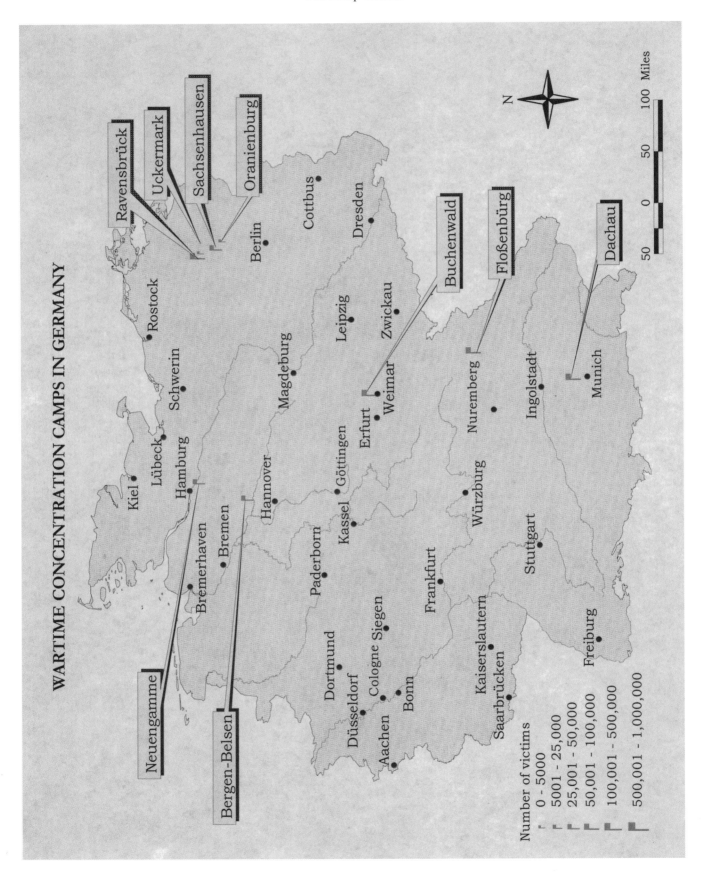

WARTIME CONCENTRATION CAMPS IN GERMANY

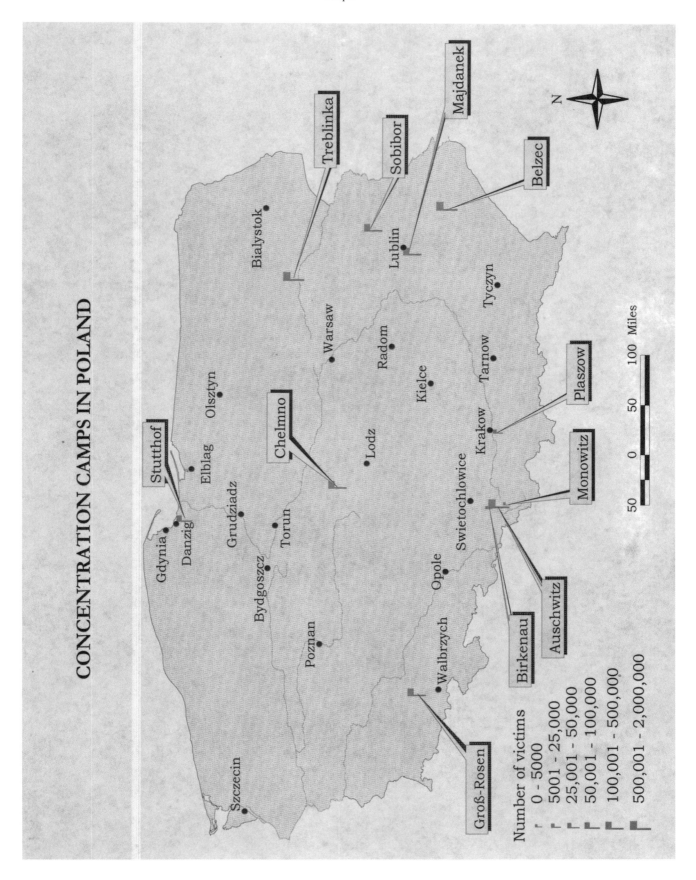

CONCENTRATION CAMPS IN POLAND

Number of victims
- 0 - 5000
- 5001 - 25,000
- 25,001 - 50,000
- 50,001 - 100,000
- 100,001 - 500,000
- 500,001 - 2,000,000

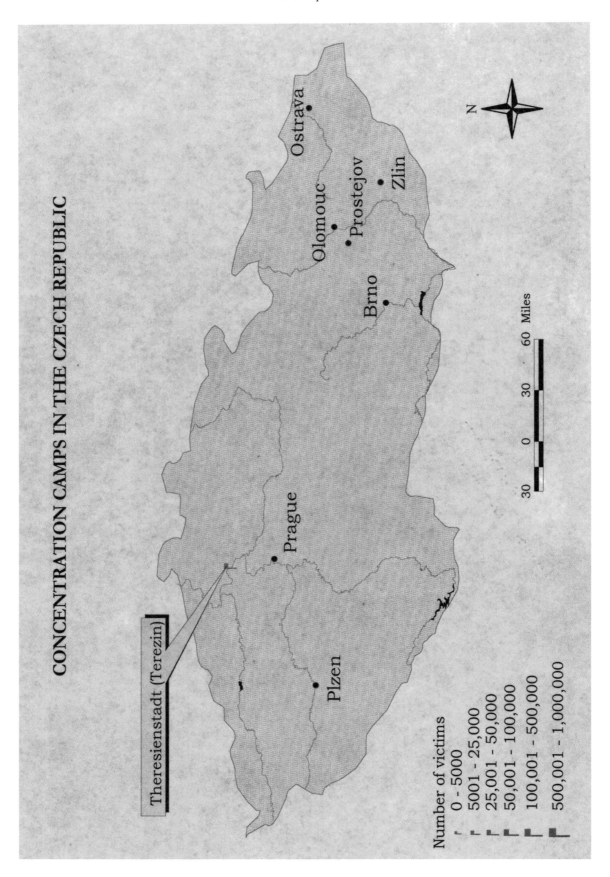

CONCENTRATION CAMPS IN THE CZECH REPUBLIC

Theresienstadt (Terezin)

Ostrava

Olomouc
Prostejov
Zlin

Brno

Prague

Plzen

Number of victims
0 - 5000
5001 - 25,000
25,001 - 50,000
50,001 - 100,000
100,001 - 500,000
500,001 - 1,000,000

N

30   0   30   60 Miles

PHOTOGRAPH SECTION

KL-Sachsenhausen: Forbidden Zone – Entrance Forbidden You Will Be Shot! (BAK 146/83/100/35A)

KL-Dachau: February 11, 1936 – A BdM Leader Visits a Concentration Camp (BAK 152/A6/7/13A)

KL-Dachau: May 1936 – BdM Leaders Visit a Concentration Camp (BAK152/M/30)

Promotional Photo for SS Aufseherinnen Recruitment (The Edmund L. Blanford Collection)

"Raise the Banner" – an SS Auferherin Performing Flag Raising Ceremonies (Deutsche am Galgen, Teil 3: Britische Kriegsverbrecher Prozeße 1945-1949)

Right: SS Aufseherin Hildegard Mende, Small Fortress Terezin Ghetto (TMM, courtesy of USHMM)

SS Oberaufseherin Hildegard Neumann, Ghetto Chief Overseer, Terezin Ghetto (TMM, courtesy of USHMM)

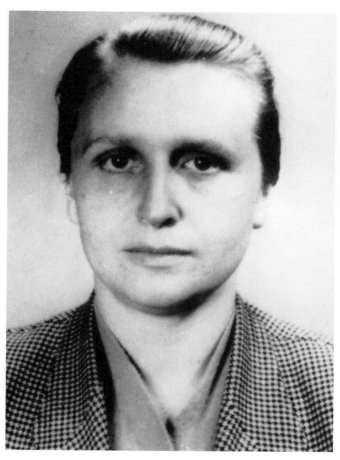

Ingebourg Krueger Prior to Enlistment as an SS Aufseherin (YV 1584/89)

Irma Grese Prior to Enlistment as an SS Aufseherin (The Peter Wiebke collection)

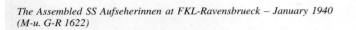

*The Assembled SS Aufseherinnen at FKL-Ravensbrueck – January 1940
(M-u. G-R 1622)*

Reichsfuehrer SS Himmler's Inspection of the SS Aufseherinnen (M-u. G-R 1624)

KL-Buchenwald: SS Aufseherinnen "at ease" (BArch-ZwArch D.–H.:2M 1630 A.1T2, Bildtafel 9, Teil 1/Frauen, Bl. 29)

SS Aufseherinnen Enjoying Free Time (BArch-ZwArch D.–H.:2M 1630 A.1T2, Bildtafel 9, Teil 1/Frauen, Bl. 24)

SS Oberaufseherin Johanna Langefeld Negotiating Prisoner Releases with Red Cross Chief Count Folke Bernadotte – FKL-Ravensbruek, Spring 1945 (YV Photo Archive, courtesy of USHMM)

SS women forced out of their quarters at Bergen-Belsen. (Deutsche am Galgen, Teil 3: Britische Kriegsverbrecher Prozeße 1945-1949)

American Army officer directing former SS women at a detention camp. (National Archives, Records Administration, Washington, D.C.)

SS women shortly after arrest at Bergen-Belsen, April 1945. (Deutsche am Galgen, Teil 3: Britische Kriegsverbrecher Prozeße 1945-1949)

SS women being escorted by British troops after capture. (Deutsche am Galgen, Teil 3: Britische Kriegsverbrecher Prozeße 1945-1949)

OPPOSITE:
Top: "Raise the Banner" – Morning Flag Raising Ceremonies. (Deutsche am Galgen, Teil 3: Britische Kriegsverbrecher Prozeße 1945-1949)
Bottom: "Party Time" – SS Aufseherinnen Socializng After Hours. (Deutsche am Galgen, Teil 3: Britische Kriegsverbrecher Prozeße 1945-1949)

A Female Arbeitskommando ("work detail") Outside Birkenau – note the Funktionshaeftlingen (Kapos) Keeping the Lines Formed. (Wanda Jakubowska's "The Last Stage")

Auschwitz Liberation: January 1945 (APMO, courtesy of USHMM)

U.S. Army troops examining Waffen-SS prisoners of war for identifying tattoos. (Russell & Marilyn Moll, courtesy of USHMM 18710)

SS Aufseherinnen Forced to Bury the Corpses at KL-Bergen-Belsen – April 1945 (BAK 183/A0706/18/8)

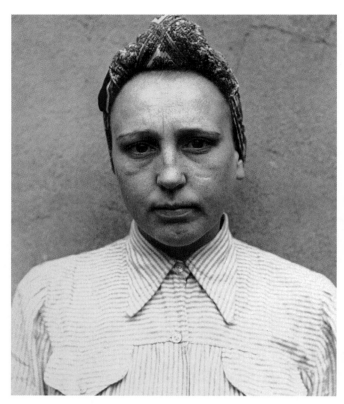

Bergen-Belsen trial Defendant Frieda Walter (IWM [BU9695], courtesy of USHMM)

Bergen-Belsen Trial Defendant Klara Opitz (IWM [BU9705], courtesy of USHMM)

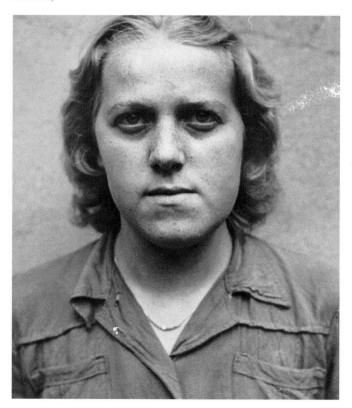

Bergen-Belsen Trial Defendant Herta Bothe (IWM [BU9691], courtesy of USHMM)

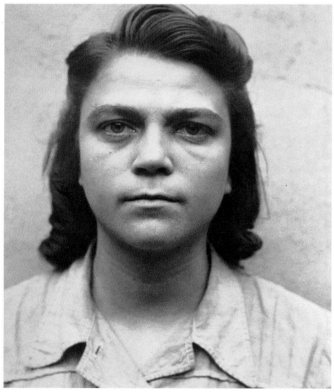

Bergen-Belsen Trial Defendant Charlotte Klein (IWM [BU9698], courtesy of USHMM)

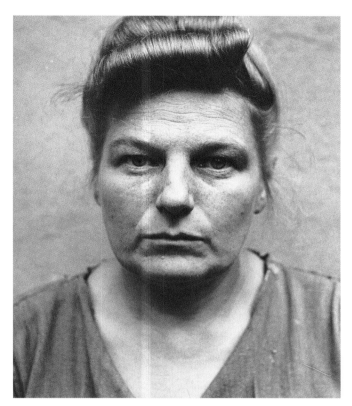

Bergen-Belsen Trial Defendant Herta Ehlert (IWM [BU9690], courtesy of USHMM)

Bergen-Belsen Trial Defendant Magdalene Kessel (WW)

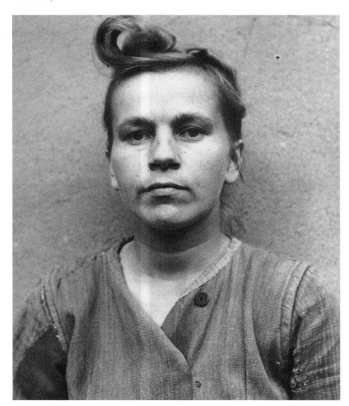

Bergen-Belsen Trial Defendant Elisabeth Volkenrath (IWM [BU9689], courtesy of USHMM)

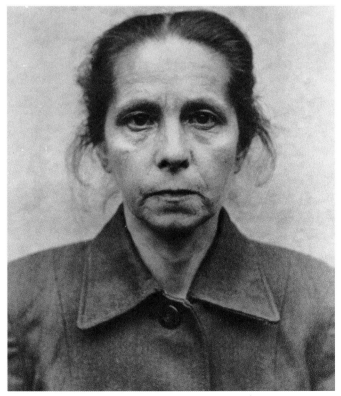

Bergen-Belsen Trial Defendant Juana Bormann (IWM [BU9682], courtesy of USHMM)

Bergen-Belsen Trial Defendant Hildegard Hehnal (IWM [BU9688], courtesy of USHMM)

Bergen-Belsen Trial Defendant Irma Grese (IWM BU9700)

Bergen-Belsen Trial Defendant Irma Grese (full profile) (IWM BU9701)

"The Bitch of Buchenwald" – Ilse Koch at her Trial (YV 4613/1037)

The Trial of the Bergen-Belsen Guards – Lüneburg, September 17 - November 17, 1945 (USHMM 12775)

The First Auschwitz Trial – Female Defendants (Left to Right: Therese Brand[e]l, Alice Orlowski, Luise Danz, and Hildegard Lächert) (APMO, courtesy of USHMM 21258/73)

The First Auschwitz Trial Female Defendants (Left to Right: Luise Danz and Hildegard Lächert) (APMO, courtesy of USHMM 21258/71)

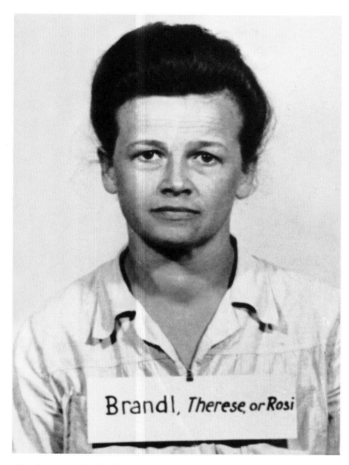
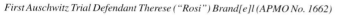

First Auschwitz Trial Defendant Therese ("Rosi") Brand[e]l (APMO No. 1662)

First Auschwitz Trial Defendant Maria Mand[e]l (APMO No. 1882)

PHOTOGRAPH CREDITS

(Abbreviations)

APMO	Archives-Panstwowe Museum, Oswiecim (Auschwitz)
BAK	Bundesarchiv-Koblenz
BArch-ZwArch D.H.	Bundesarchiv-Zwischenarchiv Dahlwitz-Hoppengarten
IWM	Imperial War Museum
M-u.G-R	Mahn-und Gedenkstätte-Ravensbrück
TMM	Terezin Memorial Museum
USHMM	U.S. Holocaust Memorial Museum
WW	Wide World
YV	Yad Vashem, Jerusalem

INDEX

Allied Control Council, 22

Ancient Rome (examples for BdM girls), 15

Arbeitskommando ("work detail"), 9, 10, 19

Armbruster, Margarete, 9

Außenlager (subcamp), 17, 25, 238

Auschwitz Concentration/Death Camp Complex, 9, 10, 18, 19, 22, 243; external work detail photo; 268-269; liberation photo, 270-271

Außenkommando (external detail), 19, 20

Baumeister, Roy F., 10

Bayer (German pharmaceutical company), 16

Belsen Trial, 17, 21; photo, 278-279

Bergen-Belsen Concentration Camp, 20

Bernadotte, Count Folke (Swedish Red Cross Coordinator), 265

Bernigau, Jane, 19, 242

Bimko, Ada, 21

Binz, Dorothera, 19, 23n

Blockälteste (chief functionary), 21, 240

Blockleiterin (female block leader), 19

Bolshevism, 21

Bothe, Herta; photo, 274

Blut und Boden ("blood and soil"), 15

Bormann, Juana; photo, 275

Brach, Joanna, 17

Brand[e]l; photo, 281

"Brigitte" (last name unknown), 18

Brunner, Luise, 11n, 240

Buchenwald Concentration Camp, 21; off-duty SS Aufseherinnen photo, 264

Buchenwald Trial, 21

Bund deutscher Mädel (BdM), 15; Dachau visitation photos, 259

Bundesarchiv-Berlin, 10

Burkner, Trude, 15

Case No. 12-1497, 22

Cernyak-Spatz, Susan, 8, 9

Corpus delicti (absence of …) , 20

Cranfield, British Major L.S.W., 9

Dachau Concentration Camp, 18; BdM leaders visitation photos, 259

Danz, Luise, 22, 242; photos, 280

Darré, Walter, Nazi Agricultural Minister, 23n

David, Anna, 16

Death Marches, 8, 9, 14, 21

Dienstkunde (knowledge of service), 17

Dokumentationsarchiv des Österreichischen Widerstandes, 11n

Drechsel, Margot, 20, 25-26

Ehlert, Herta, 17, 19; photo, 275

Eicke, Theodor, Dachau Commandant, 19

Einsatzgruppen ("mobile killing units"), 9, 10

Entnazifierzierung (denazification), 22

Erstaufseherin ("first guard"); 19, 240

"Fliegendes Standgericht" (flying court martial), 21

Frühappell" ("daily early roll call"), 19

Funktionshäftlinge (prisoner functionaries or "Kapos"), 15-16

General Assembly (Nazi Party), 8

Gleichschaltung ("coordination"), 15

Glücks, *Obergruppenführer* Richard, 24n

Goebbels, Josef, 21, 238

Goldhagen, Daniel Jonah (Goldhagen Thesis), 8

Grese, Irma, 12n, 17, 19-21, 238, 243, 244; syphilis test document, 243; photos, 261, 276

Häftlingsblock (prisoner's block), 19

Häftlingsselbstverwaltung (self-government of prisoners), 15-16

Hauptlager (main [concentration] camp), 17

Hehnal, Hildegard; photo, 276

Heinkel (German aircraft company), 16

Hempel, Anna, 17

Hempel, Christa, 22

Himmler, Heinrich, Reichsführer-SS, original idea for female guards, 9, 14; strong support after January 1940 tour of Ravensbrück, 16; use of dogs, 20;

obsession with *Lebensborn movement,* *23n*, 237, 241, 248n

Hitler Jugend (Hitler Youth), 15

Hitler, Adolf, antifeminist attitude, 14; obsession with *Lebensborn* movement, 248n

Höhn, Elisabeth, 22

Höß, Rudolf (Auschwitz Commandant), 19, 20

Hundführerinnen (female dog leaders), 20

I.G. Farben (German industrial company), 16

Irving, David, Holocaust denier, 14

"Judenrein" (clean of Jews), 21

Kapo – see *Funktionshäftlinge*

Kessel, Magdalene; photo, 275

Klein, Charlotte; photo, 274

Klein-Plaubel, Ann, 11n, 240

Koch, Ilse, 21; photo, 277

Kögel, Max, 19

Kommando (detail), 9

Kopper, Helen (the Polish "Doctor of Music"), 24n

Kramer, Josef (Birkenau and later Bergen-Belsen Camp Commandant), 20

Krasnodar, USSR, 21

"Krieg der Vernichtung" (war of annihiliation), 21

Krueger, Ingebourg; photo, 261

Küche, Kleider, Kinder, und Kirche, 15

Lächert, Hildegard, 11, 22; photos, 280

Lagerordnung (basic camp regulations), 18, 244

Langefeld, Johanna, 18, 19; photo with Count Bernadotte, 265

Lichtenberg (near Torgau) Women's Concentration Camp, 15

Lohbauer, Hildegard, 25

Luukonen, Mrs. Fanny, 14

Mahn- und Gedenkstätte-Ravensbrück, 9, 25

Majdanek Concentration Camp, 21

Majdanek Trial (initial), 21

Majdanek Trial (Düsseldorf), 22

Malchow, Ravensbrück subcamp, 22

Mand[e]l, Maria, 17; photo, 281

Mende, Hildegard; photo, 260

Mengele, Dr. Josef, 12n

Mewes, Margarete, 23n

Moringen (bei Göttingen) Workhause, 15

National Archives II (College Park, MD), 10

National Socialist Frauenschaft (Nazi Women's Group), 15

Nazi Party (NSDAP), antifeminist attitude, 8

*Nebenslager (*adjacent camp to a concentration camp), 17, 25, 238

Neumann, Hildegard, 261

Nietzsche, Friedrich, 11

Nuremberg Trial, 22

Oberaufseherin (senior supervisor), 18, 19

Opitz, Klara; photo, 274

Orlowski, Alice; photo, 280

Overseers (*SS-Aufseherinnen*): role in the death marches, 8; subservient role in SS, 8; sensationalist interest, 10-11; Himmler's creation, 14; Finnish model, 14; BdM recruitment, 15; original guards drawn from *NS-Frauenschaft, 15;* enticement for simply watching prisoners in physically effortless work," 16; compulsory service call-up, 16-17; war industries' connection, 17; training, 16-17; induced brutality, 17; humane overseers, 16-17; debauchery, 17; free rein to inflict pain in camps, 17-18; assignments, 10, 18; camp commandants disdain for overseers, 19-20; use of "accessories" (whips, pistols, and dogs), 20; nicknames, 20; postwar advantages to avoid accountability,20, 22; postwar judgments, 22, 244-248; ongoing investigations, 22

Pánstwowe Muzeum w Oswiecimiu (Auschwitz), 10

Plaszów Work Camp, 22

Pohl, Oswald, 16

Polizeigefängnisaufsichtsdienst (Police Protective Service), 17

Ravensbrück Women's Concentration Camp, 8, 9, 10, 16-18, 20, 22, 238, 240, 244, 248

Reichsangestellte ("employees of the Reich"), 8, 25

Reichsarbeitsdienst (German Labor Service), 16

Reinhardt, Käthe, 22

Roth, Jolana, 9

Rupp, Käthe, 23n

Ryan, Hermine (born Braunsteiner), 22

Sachsenhausen Concentration Camp, warning photo, 258

Schadenfreude ("malicious pleasure"), 19

Schubert, Ruth, 22

Sicherheitsdienst (Security Service of the SS), 17

Siemens (German industrial company), 16

Sorge, (first name unknown), 22

Speer, Albert, 15

"Sportmachen" ("to make sport"), 19

SS-Aufseherinnen (sing. *Aufseherin*), see Overseers

SS-Gefolge (SS followers), 8

SS-Helferinnen (SS-auxiliaries), 14, 235

SS-Hilfsaufseherinnen (assitant overseer), 240

SS-Kriegshelferinnenkorps (the corps of SS-assistants), 17

SS-Wirtschafts und Verwaltungshauptamt (WVHA), 16

Staatsfeinde ("enemies of the state"), 15

Strafkommando (punishment detail), 19, 240

Suhren, Fritz, 12n

Tichauer, Helen (*"Zippi aus der Schreibstube"),* 20, 23n

Tiermenschen (Nazi view of subhumans), 17, 242

Tillon, Germaine, 17-18

Totenkopfverbände ("Death's Head units"), 15, 248n

Verteidigerin der Heimat ("defender of the homeland"), 15

Volkenrath, Elisabeth; photo, 275

Völkerischer Bauerschaft ("German workers of the soil"), 15, 237

Volksgemeinschaft (racial community), 16

Waffen-SS, 11n, 12n, 16, 25, 238

Walter, Frieda; photo, 274

Wannsee Conference, 23n

Wehrmachtshelferinnenkorps, 12n

"Weltmacht oder Niedergang" (world domination or ruin), 21

Witzler, Margarete, 22

Yad Vashem (Jerusalem), 10

Zentralestelle der Landesjustizverwalt-ungen-Ludwigsburg, 10, 22, 25